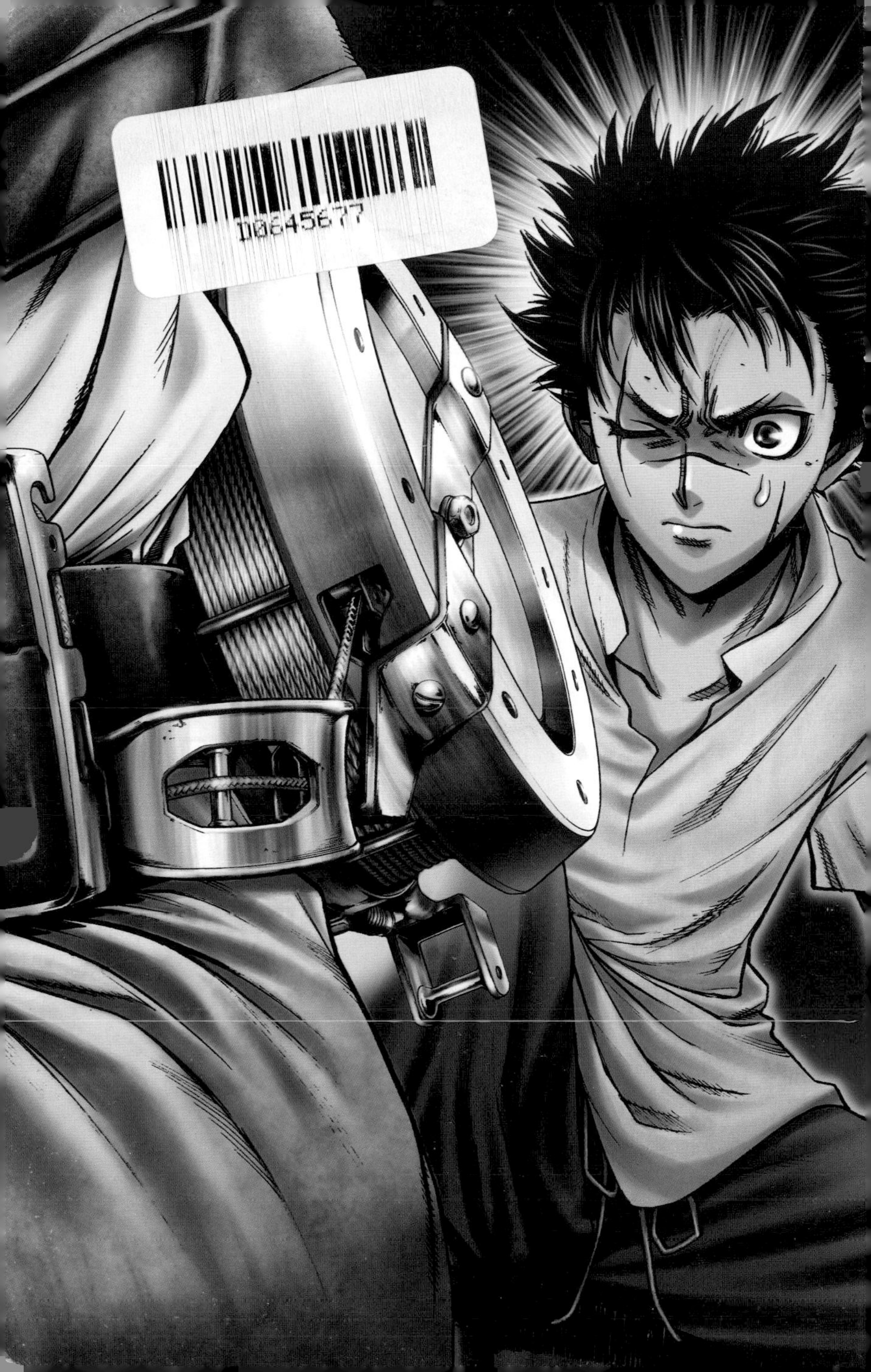

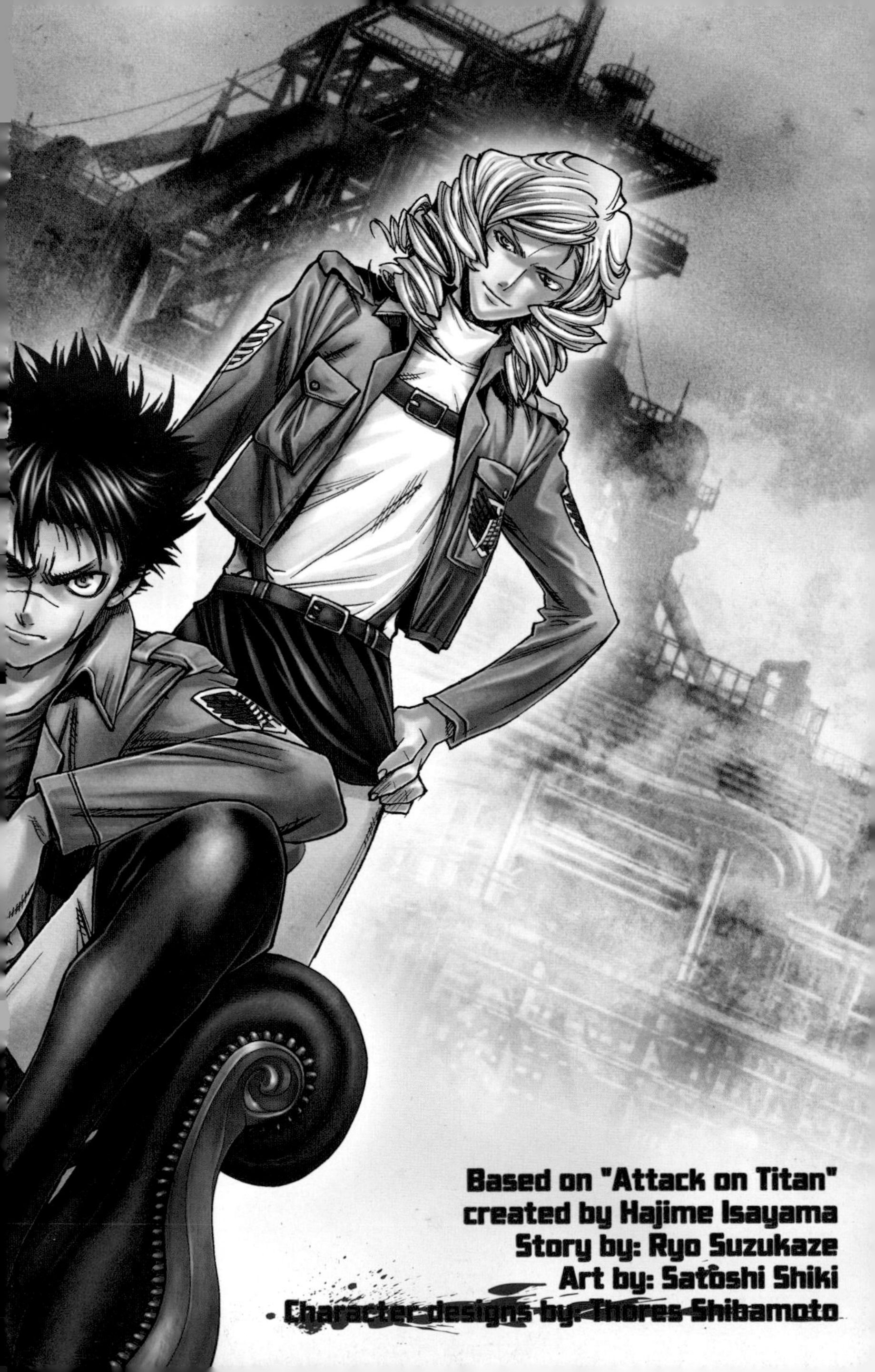

Based on "Attack on Titan"
created by Hajime Isayama
Story by: Ryo Suzukaze
Art by: Satoshi Shiki
Character designs by: Thores Shibamoto

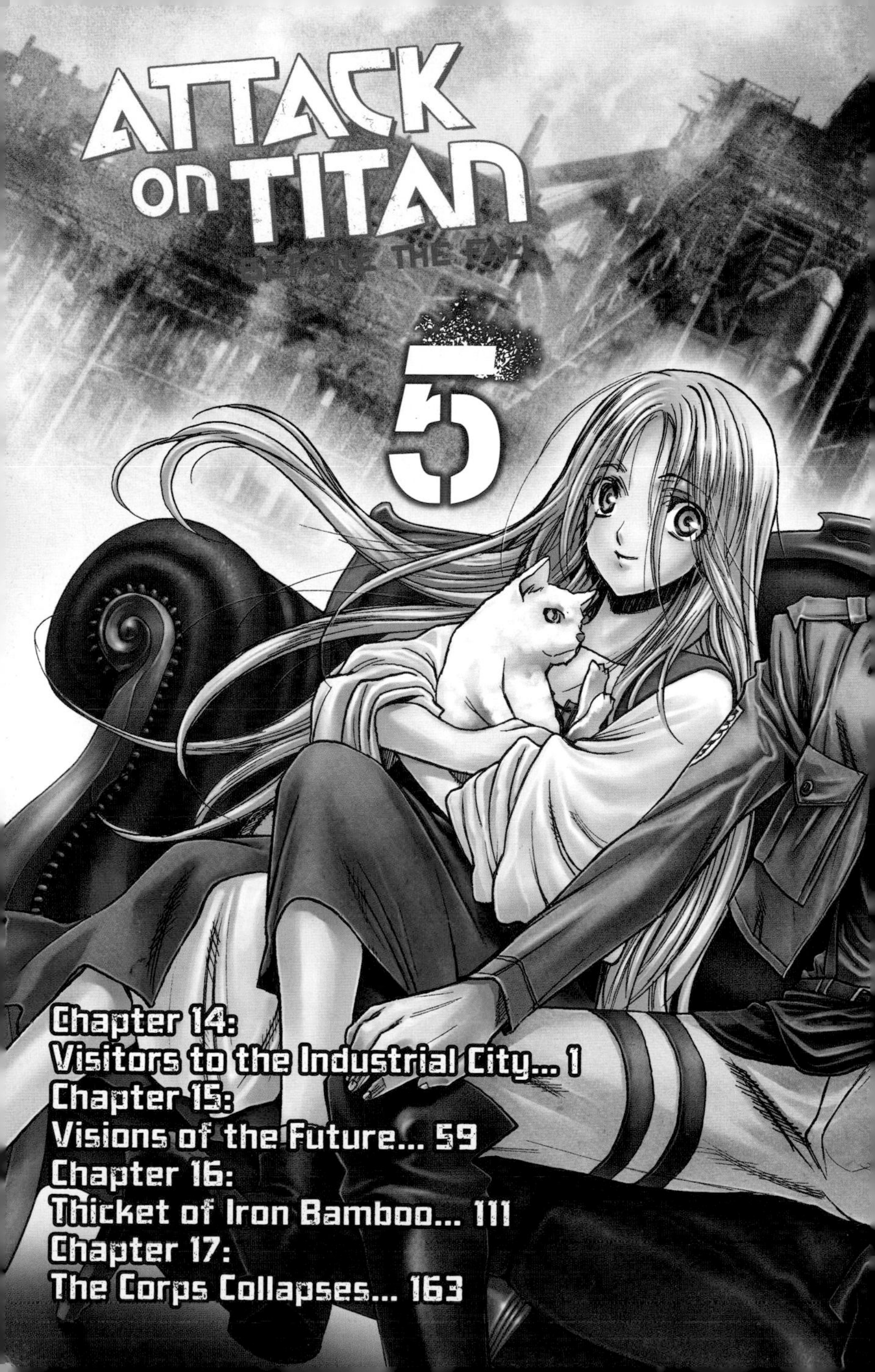

Attack on Titan

Before the Fall

5

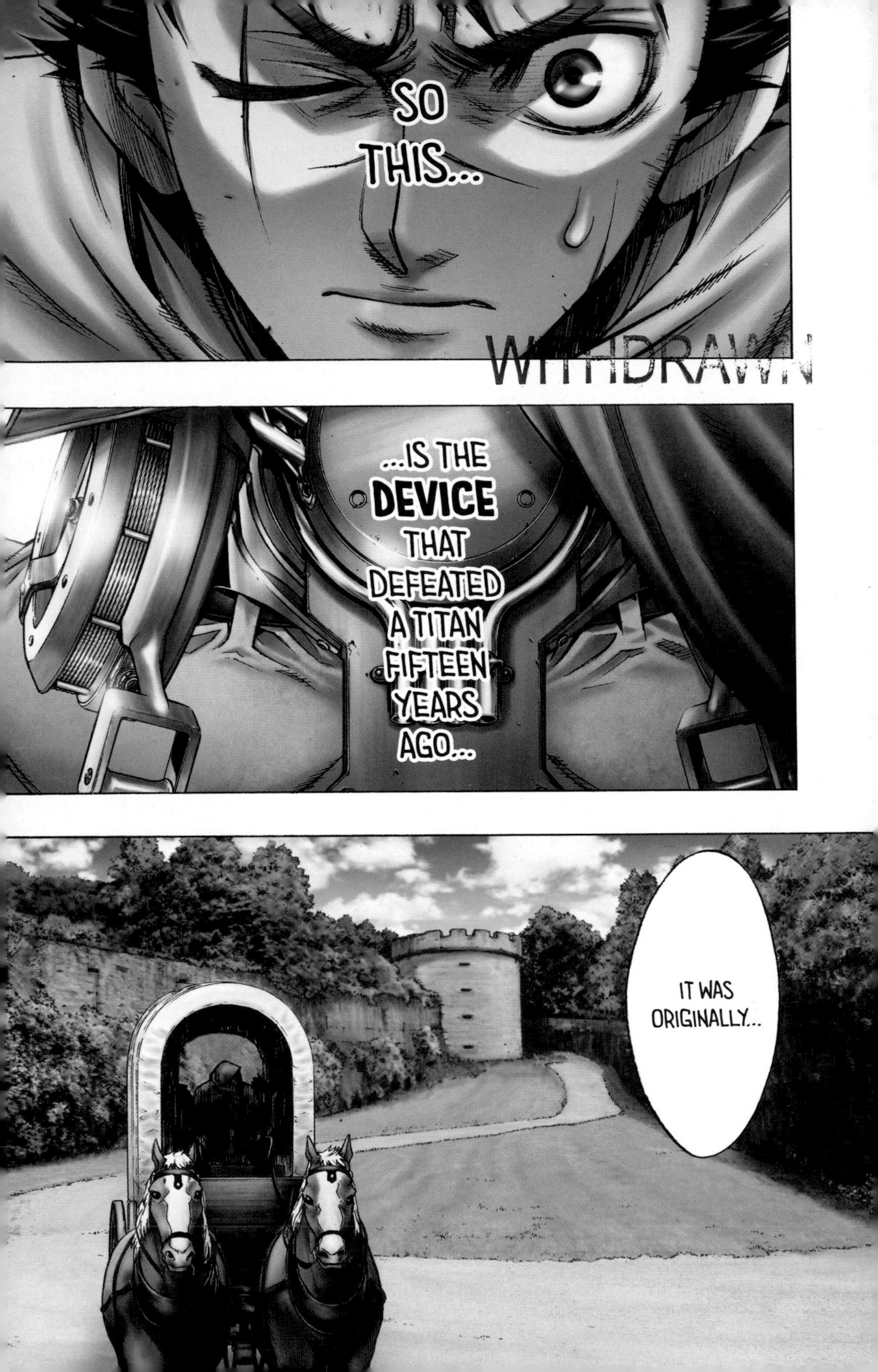
SO THIS...
...IS THE **DEVICE** THAT DEFEATED A TITAN FIFTEEN YEARS AGO...
IT WAS ORIGINALLY...

Character Profiles

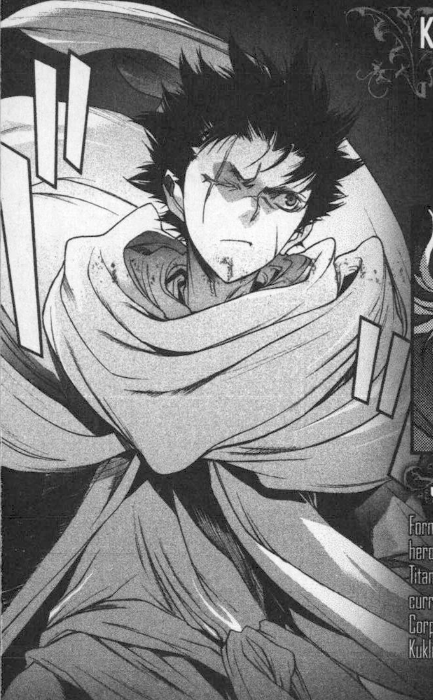

Kuklo

A boy born from a dead body packed into the vomit of a Titan, which earned him the moniker, "Son of a Titan." His father was Heath Mansel, squad leader in the Survey Corps, and his mother was Elena, who helped bring the Titans inside the Wall. He escaped the Inocencio mansion with Sharle when it was attacked by Titan-worshipers. After that, he was arrested by the MPs for a crime he did not commit, and sentenced to exile. Currently 15 years old.

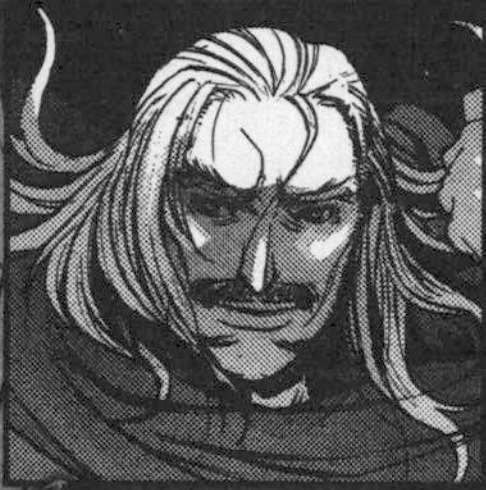

Jorge Pikale

Former captain of the Survey Corps, a hero who was the first human to defeat a Titan in battle, and father to Carlo. He is currently an instructor for the Training Corps. At Carlo's request, he saved Kuklo's life.

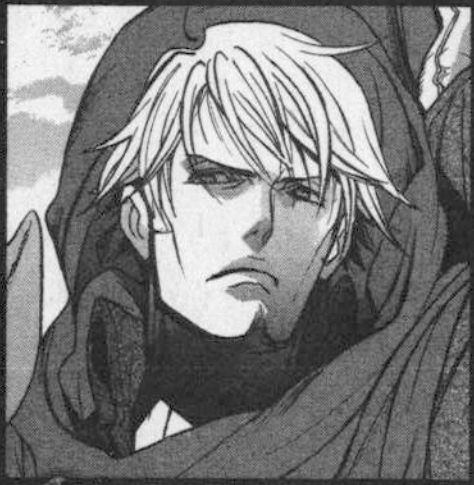

Carlo Pikale

Survey Corps captain. He joined the same time as Heath, Kuklo's father. As a simple soldier at age 18, he discovered Elena's remains in the Titan's vomit, and witnessed Kuklo's birth. Now the captain of the newly-reformed Survey Corps, he is 33 years old.

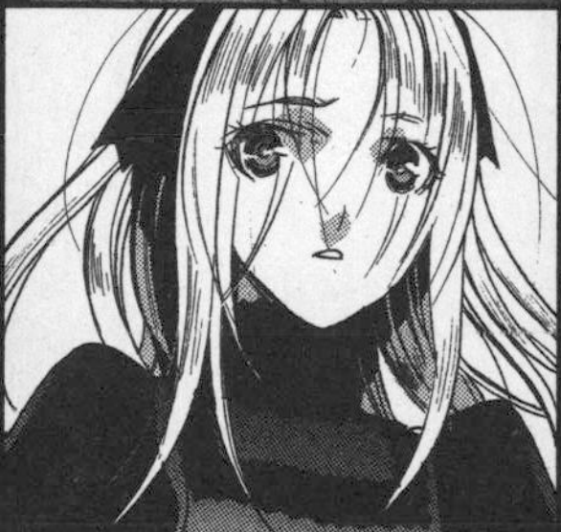

Sharle Inocencio

First daughter of the Inocencio family. She attempted to kill Kuklo after he was brought to the mansion, but became his only friend and taught him language when she realized that he was human, not a monster. When Titan-worshipers invaded her home, she left with Kuklo and had a falling out with her brother Xavi. Since Kuklo's capture by the MPs, she's been hiding out in the industrial city. Currently 15 years old.

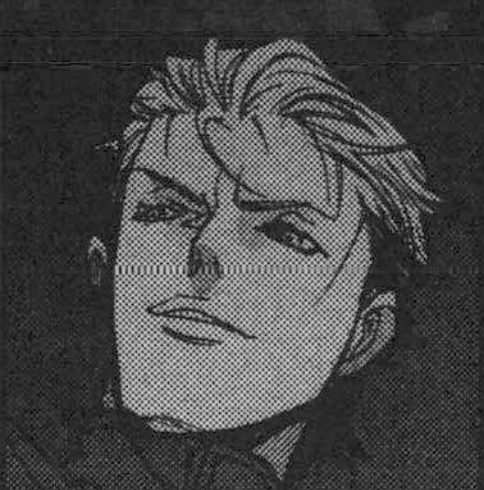

Xavi Inocencio

Sharle's brother, firstborn of the Inocencio children. His father Dario raised him to lead the Corps. He believes that Kuklo brought the Titan-worshipers into his home, and took the boy's right eye with his blade. As a member of the Training Corps, he exhibits his superiority in every facet.

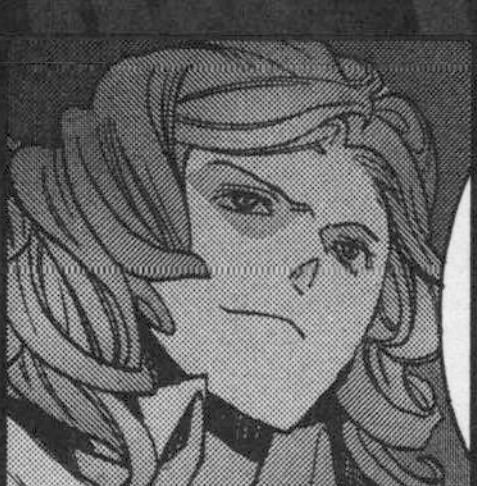

Cardina Baumeister

Son of the Baumeister family, one of the most prominent conservatives. He was thrown into prison as a result of his father's political schemes, but was rescued along with Kuklo by Jorge. Formerly Sharle's betrothed.

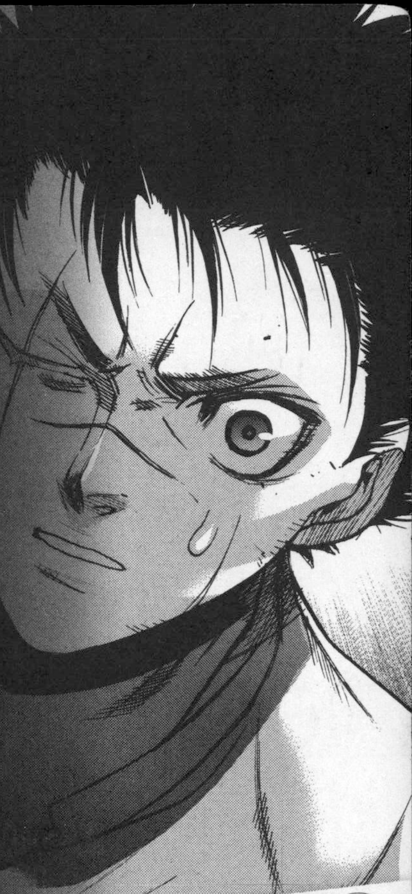

The Story So Far

When a Titan terrorized Shiganshina District and left behind a pile of vomit, a baby boy was miraculously born of a pregnant corpse. This boy was named Kuklo, the "Son of a Titan," and treated as a sideshow freak. Eventually the wealthy merchant Dario Inocencio bought Kuklo to serve as a punching bag for his son, Xavi. On the other hand, Xavi's sister Sharle decided to teach him the words and knowledge of humanity instead.

Kuklo put together an escape plan over two long years, but on the day of the escape, tragedy struck the Inocencio mansion. A group of Titan-worshipers invaded, seeking to take back the Titan's Son. They murdered Dario and many of the mansion servants. Kuklo narrowly managed to save Sharle and Xavi from harm, but Xavi accused him of being in league with the attackers, and took out his right eye. Kuklo took Sharle and escaped from Wall Sheena into Shiganshina.

In Shiganshina District, the Survey Corps was back in action, preparing for its first expedition outside of the wall in fifteen years. Kuklo wanted to see a Titan to confirm that he was indeed a human being. He left Sharle behind and snuck into the expedition's cargo wagon. As he hoped, the Survey Corps ran across a Titan, but it was far worse of a monster than he expected. The group suffered grievous losses, but thanks to Captain Carlo and Kuklo's idea, they eventually retreated safely behind Wall Maria.

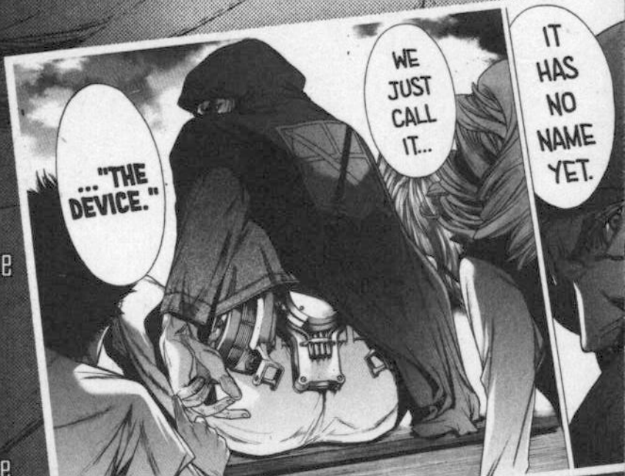
IT HAS NO NAME YET.
WE JUST CALL IT...
..."THE DEVICE."

Kuklo helped the Survey Corps survive, but inside the walls he was greeted by the Military Police, who wanted the "Titan's Son" on charges of murdering Dario. In prison, he met Cardina, a charming young man put in prison over political squabbles. They hoped to escape to safety when exiled beyond the Wall, but found themselves surrounded by a pack of Titans. It was through the help of Jorge, former Survey Corps Captain and first human to defeat a Titan, that the two boys escaped with their lives. The equipment that Jorge used was the very "device" that was the key to defeating the Titan those fifteen years ago.

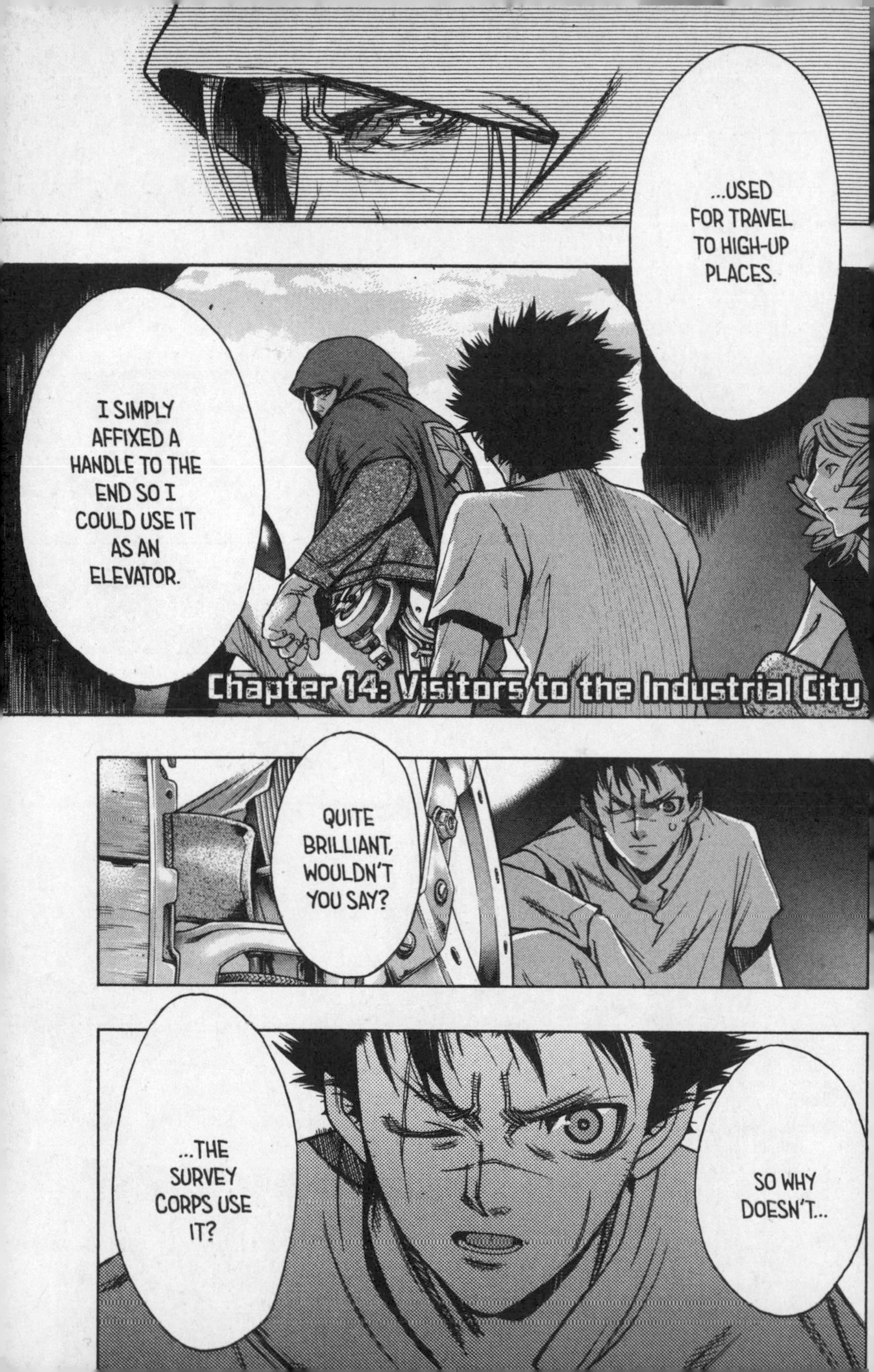
...USED FOR TRAVEL TO HIGH-UP PLACES.
I SIMPLY AFFIXED A HANDLE TO THE END SO I COULD USE IT AS AN ELEVATOR.
Chapter 14: Visitors to the Industrial City
QUITE BRILLIANT, WOULDN'T YOU SAY?
SO WHY DOESN'T...
...THE SURVEY CORPS USE IT?

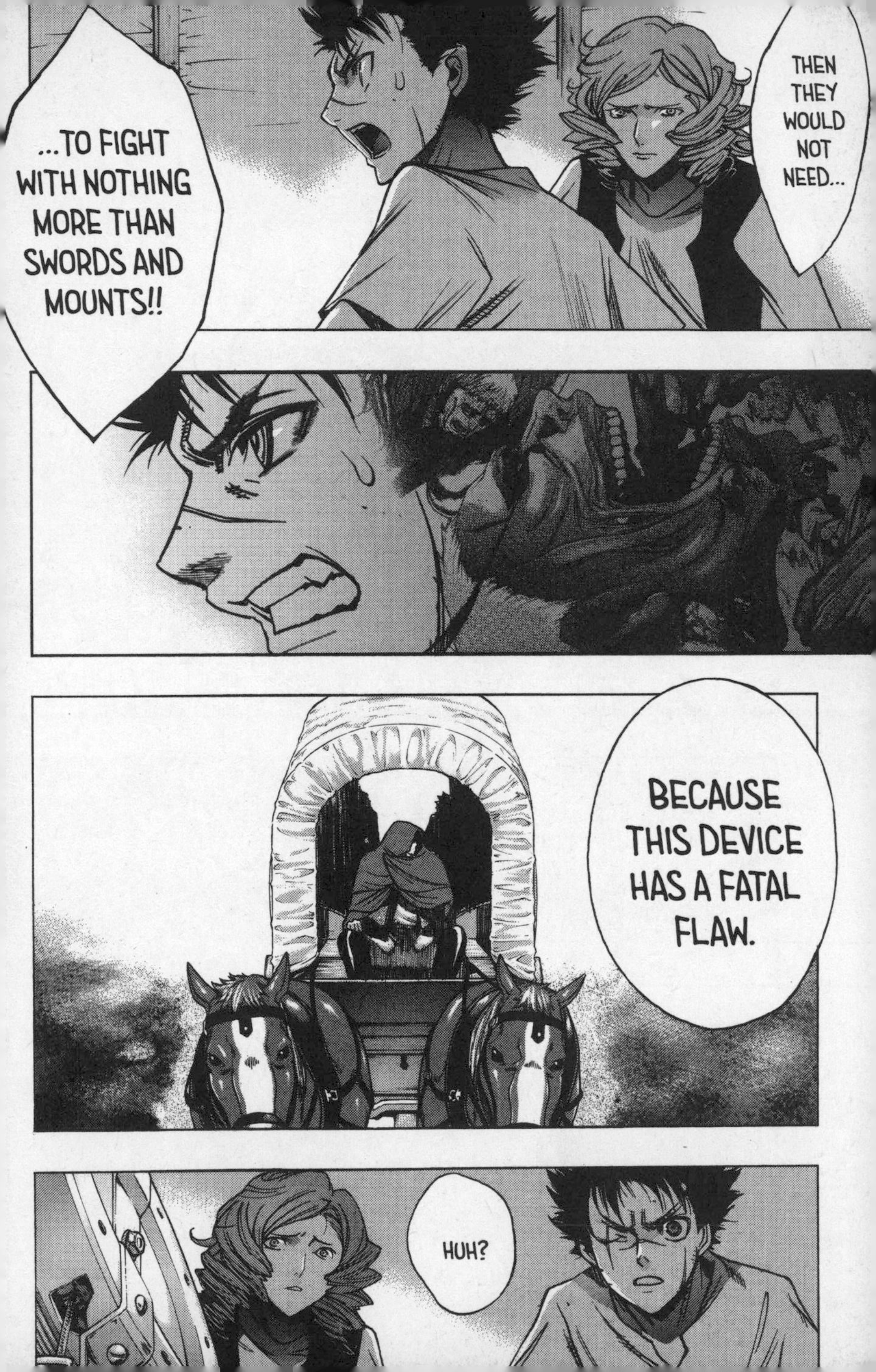
THEN THEY WOULD NOT NEED...
...TO FIGHT WITH NOTHING MORE THAN SWORDS AND MOUNTS!!
BECAUSE THIS DEVICE HAS A FATAL FLAW.
HUH?

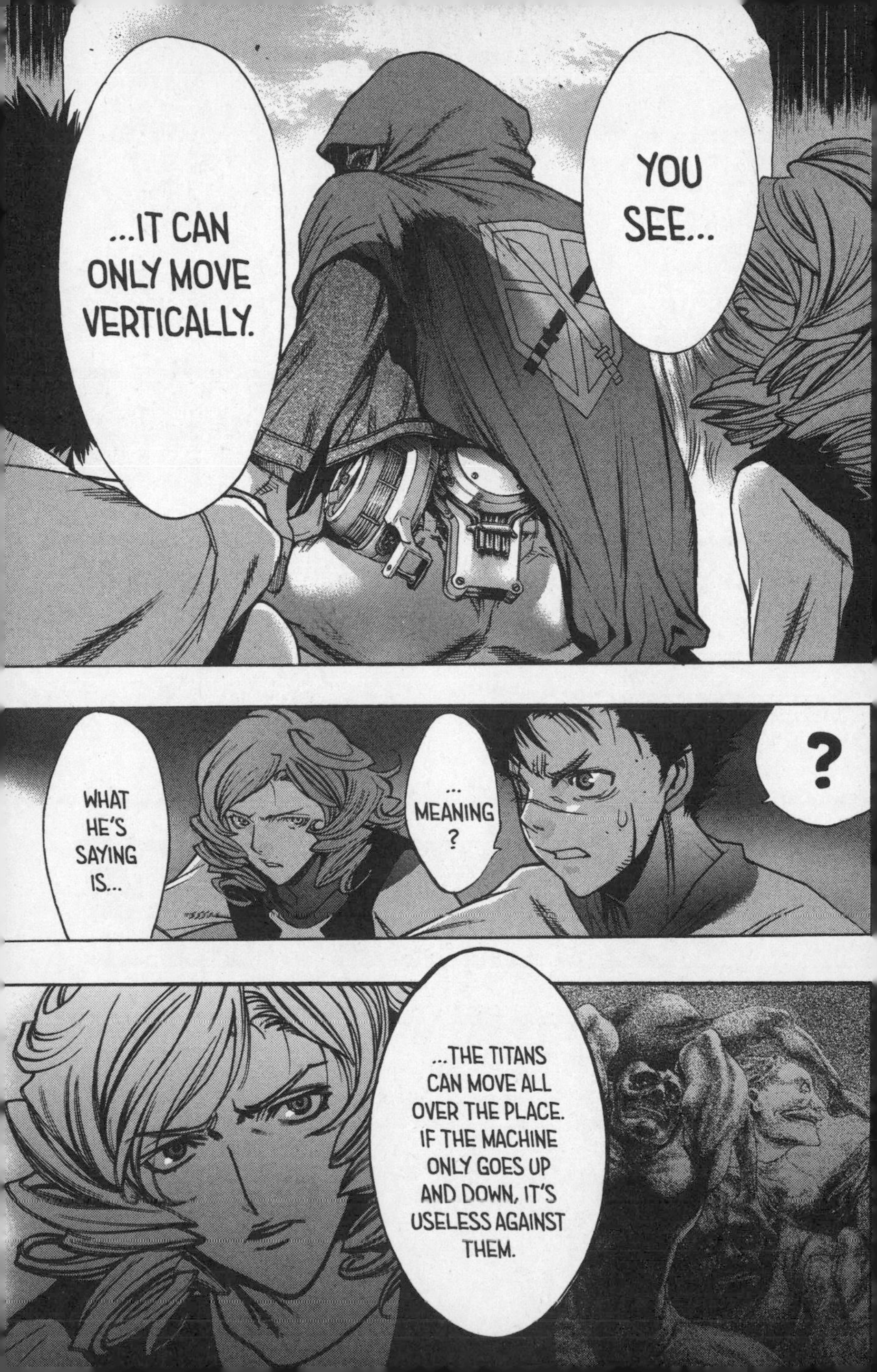
YOU SEE...
...IT CAN ONLY MOVE VERTICALLY.
?
... MEANING ?
WHAT HE'S SAYING IS...
...THE TITANS CAN MOVE ALL OVER THE PLACE. IF THE MACHINE ONLY GOES UP AND DOWN, IT'S USELESS AGAINST THEM.

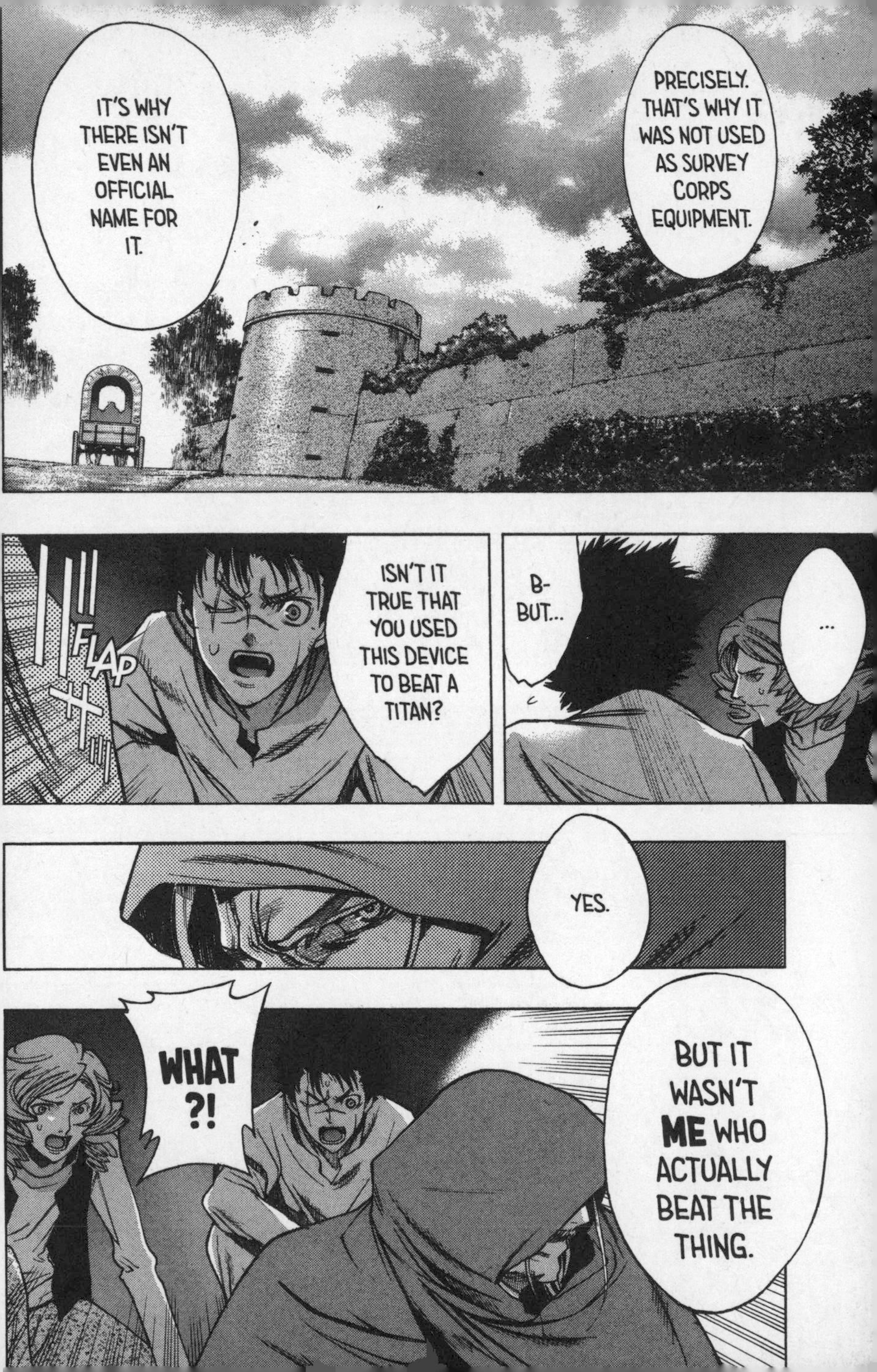
PRECISELY. THAT'S WHY IT WAS NOT USED AS SURVEY CORPS EQUIPMENT.
IT'S WHY THERE ISN'T EVEN AN OFFICIAL NAME FOR IT.
...
B-BUT...
ISN'T IT TRUE THAT YOU USED THIS DEVICE TO BEAT A TITAN?
FLAP
YES.
BUT IT WASN'T **ME** WHO ACTUALLY BEAT THE THING.
WHAT?!

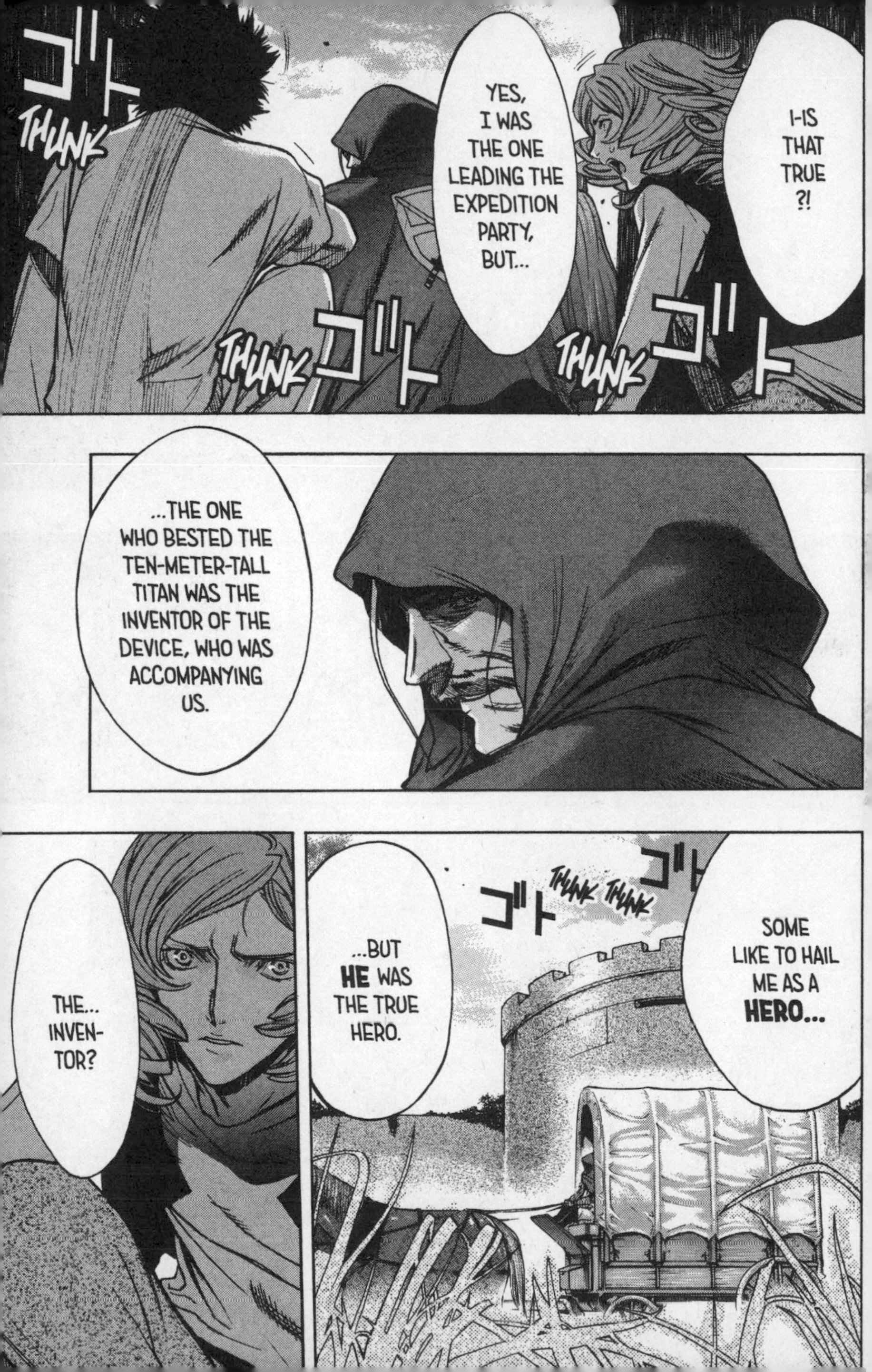

I-IS THAT TRUE?!
YES, I WAS THE ONE LEADING THE EXPEDITION PARTY, BUT...
ゴト THUNK
ゴト THUNK
ゴト THUNK
...THE ONE WHO BESTED THE TEN-METER-TALL TITAN WAS THE INVENTOR OF THE DEVICE, WHO WAS ACCOMPANYING US.
SOME LIKE TO HAIL ME AS A **HERO...**
ゴト THUNK
ゴト THUNK
...BUT **HE** WAS THE TRUE HERO.
THE... INVEN-TOR?

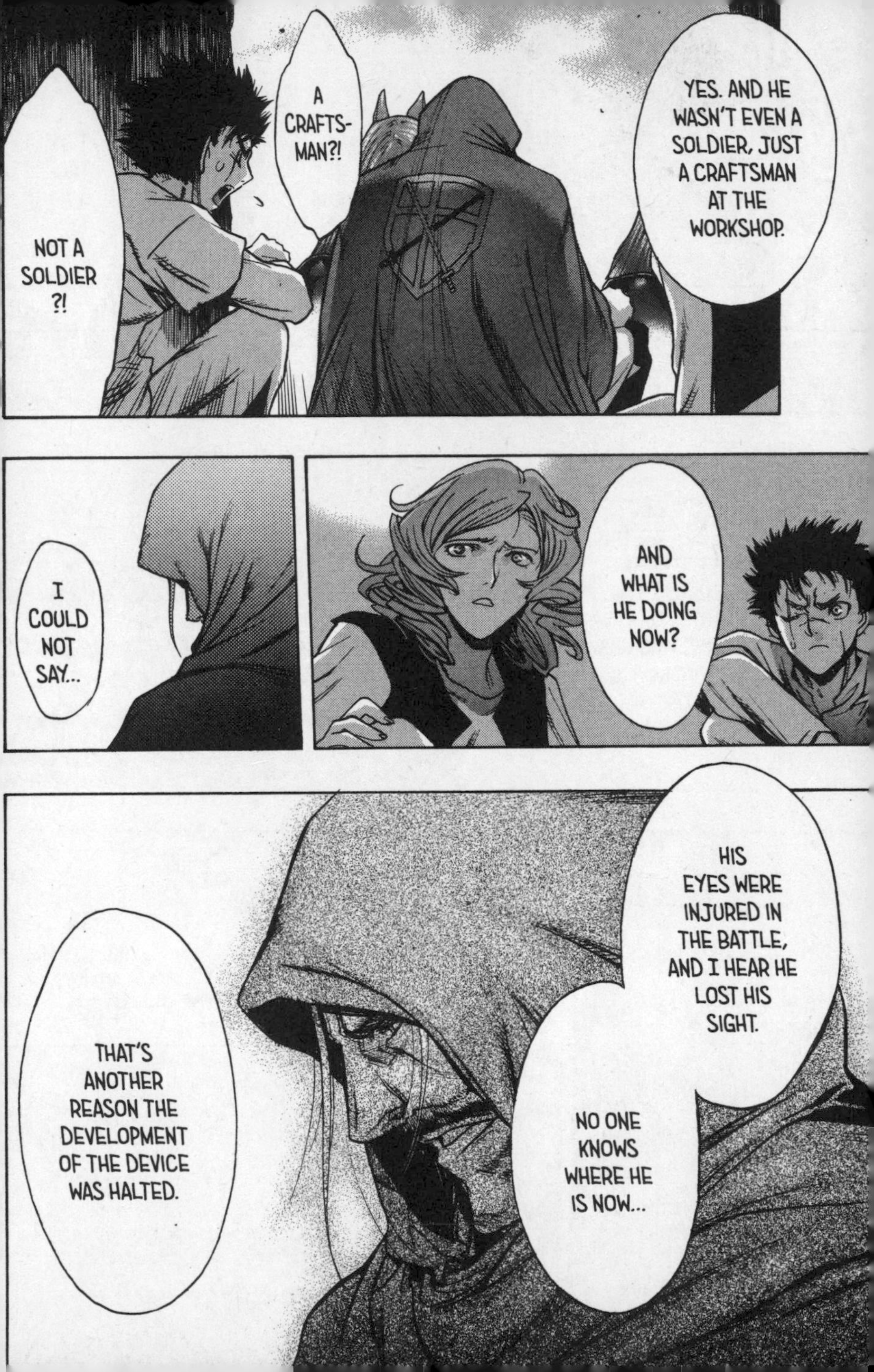
YES. AND HE WASN'T EVEN A SOLDIER, JUST A CRAFTSMAN AT THE WORKSHOP.
A CRAFTS-MAN?!
NOT A SOLDIER ?!
AND WHAT IS HE DOING NOW?
I COULD NOT SAY...
HIS EYES WERE INJURED IN THE BATTLE, AND I HEAR HE LOST HIS SIGHT.
NO ONE KNOWS WHERE HE IS NOW...
THAT'S ANOTHER REASON THE DEVELOPMENT OF THE DEVICE WAS HALTED.

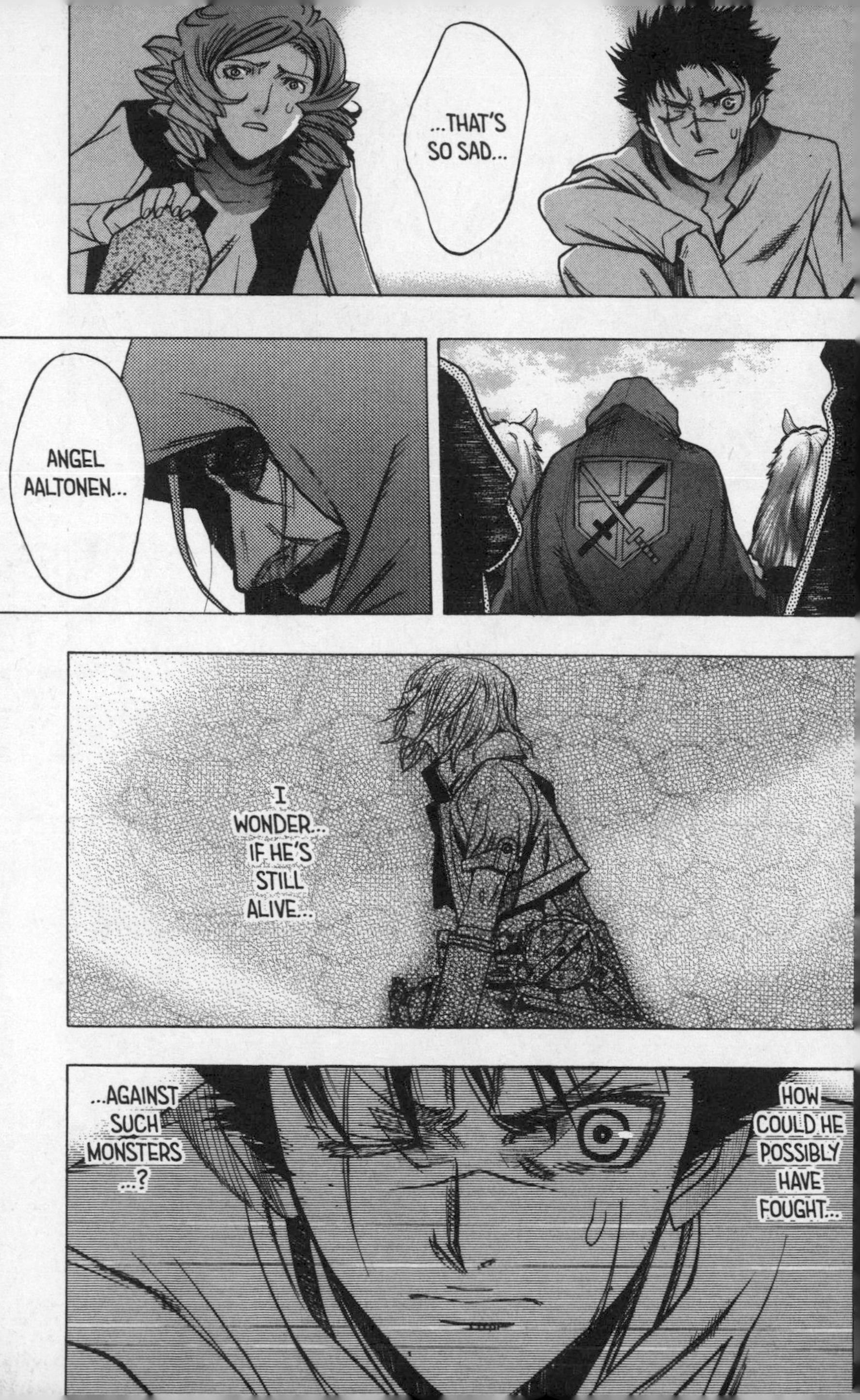
...THAT'S SO SAD...
ANGEL AALTONEN...
I WONDER... IF HE'S STILL ALIVE...
HOW COULD HE POSSIBLY HAVE FOUGHT...
...AGAINST SUCH MONSTERS ...?

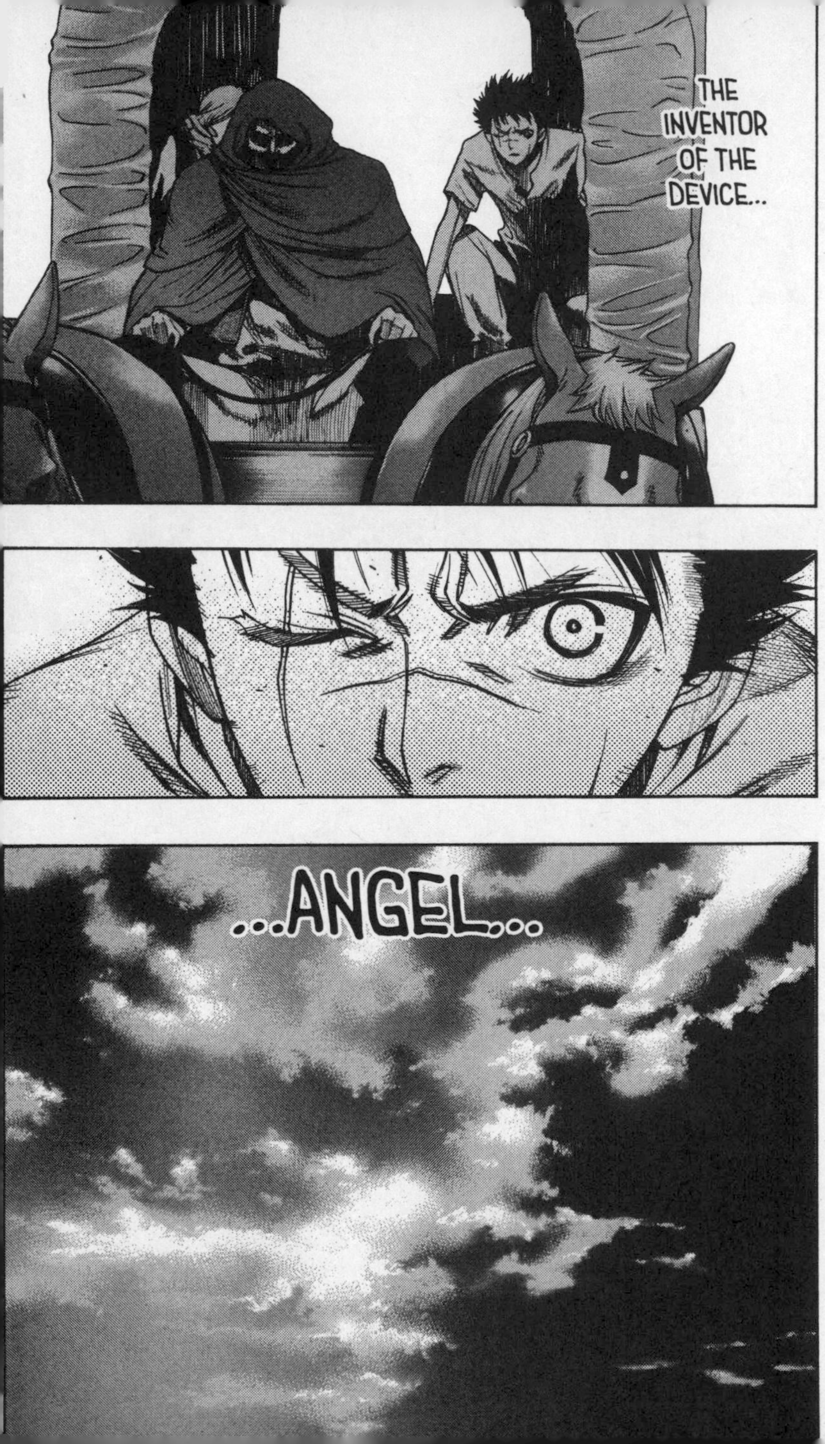
THE INVENTOR OF THE DEVICE...
...ANGEL...

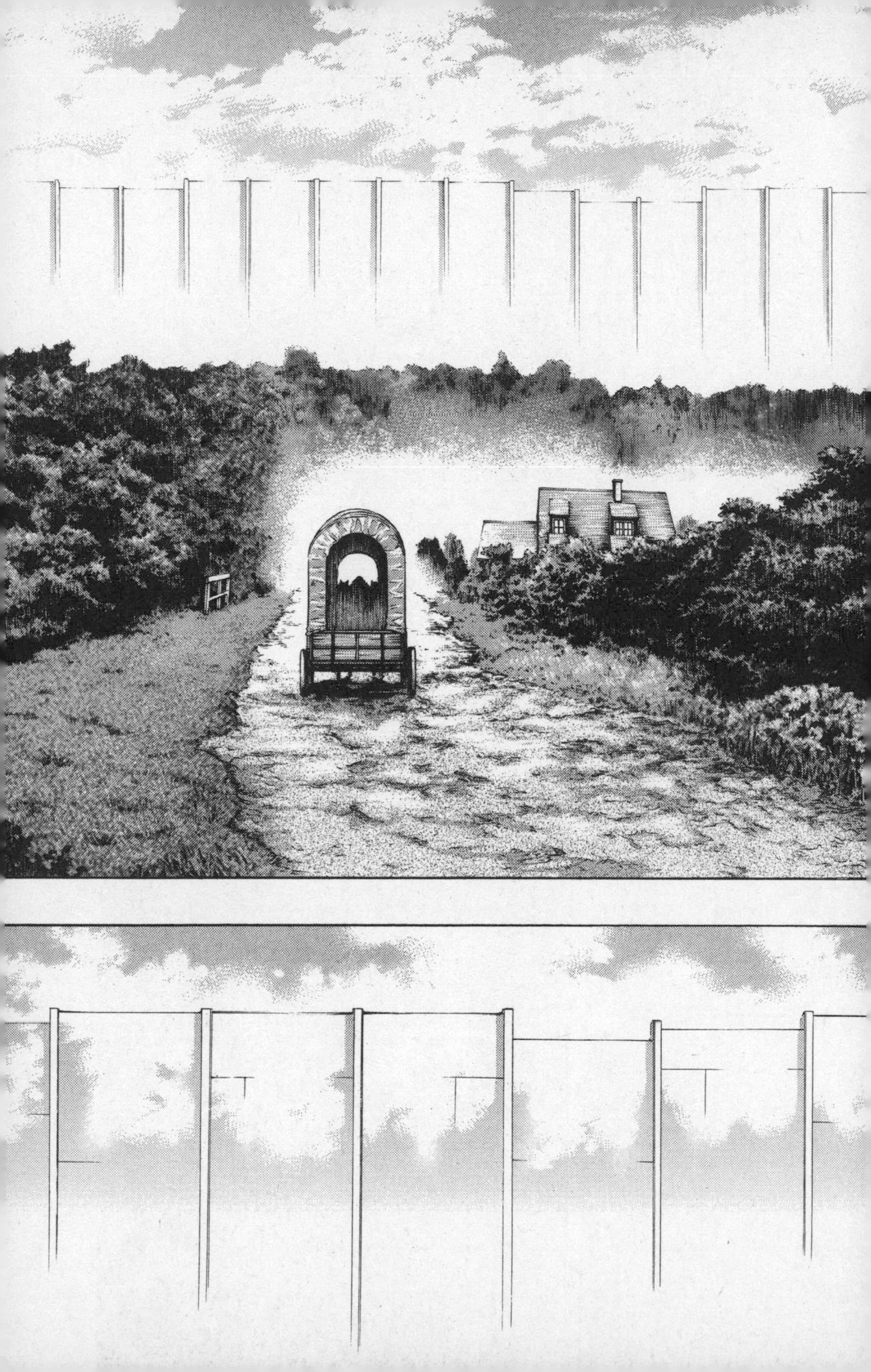

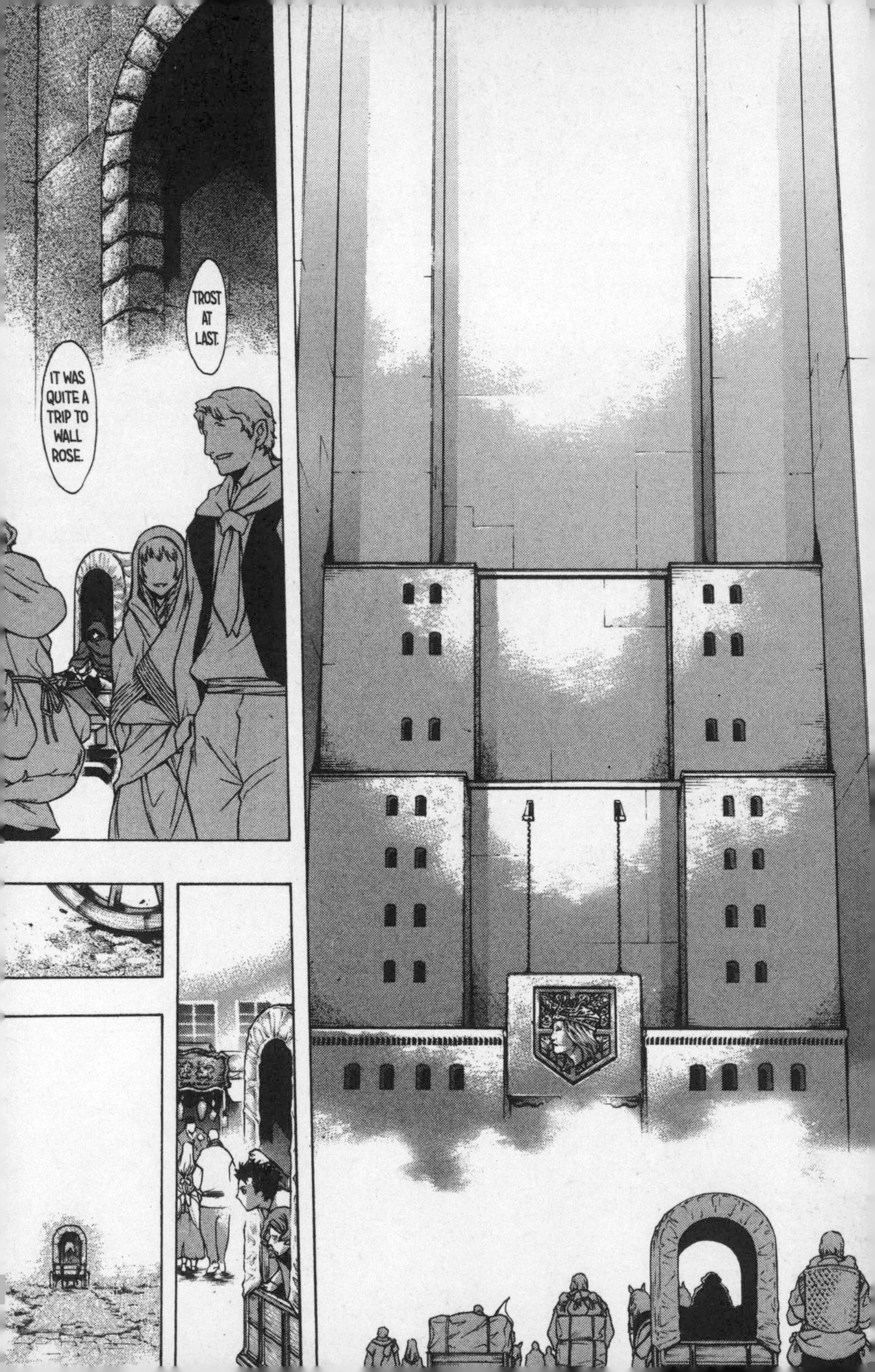
TROST AT LAST.
IT WAS QUITE A TRIP TO WALL ROSE.

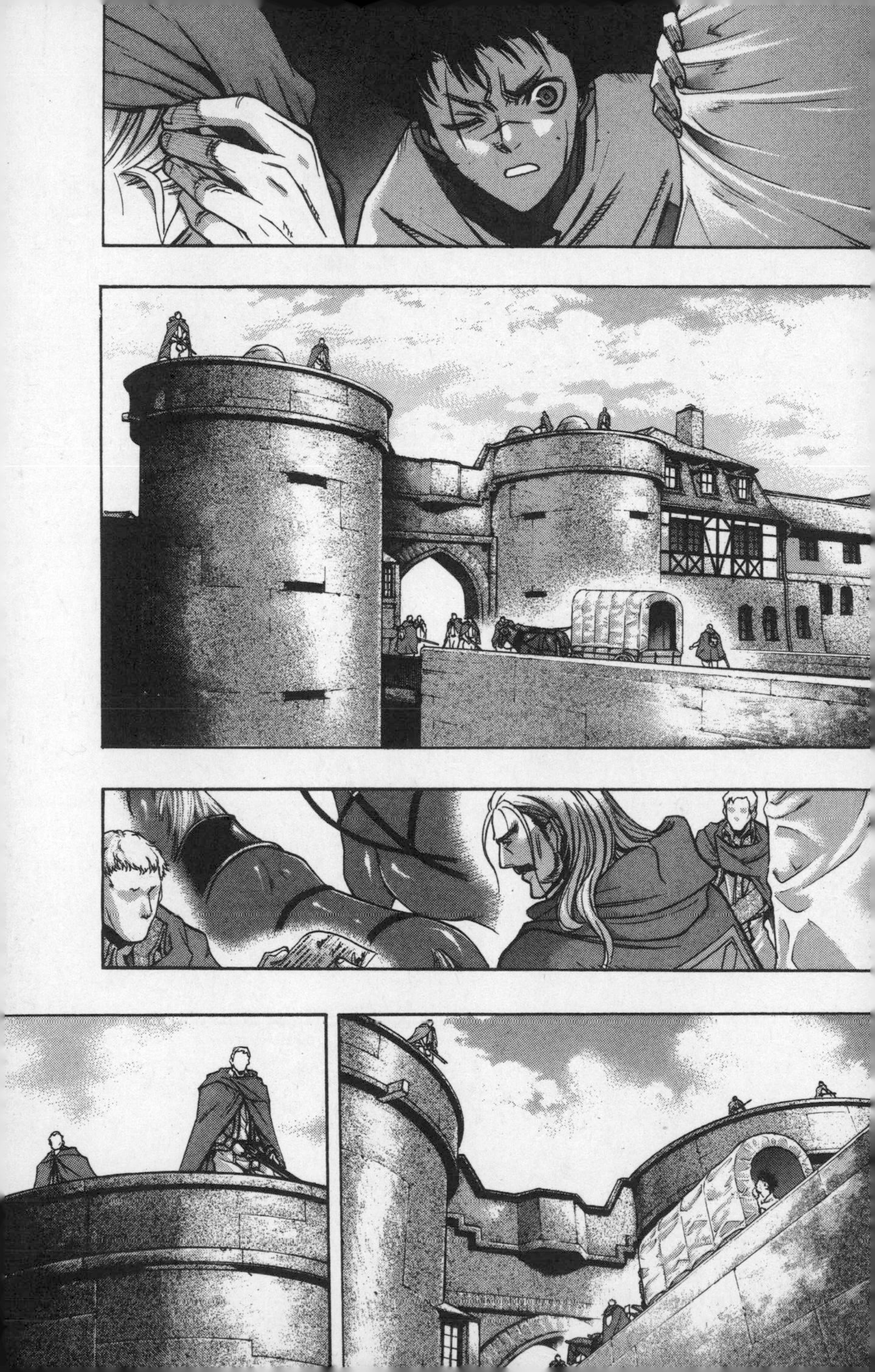

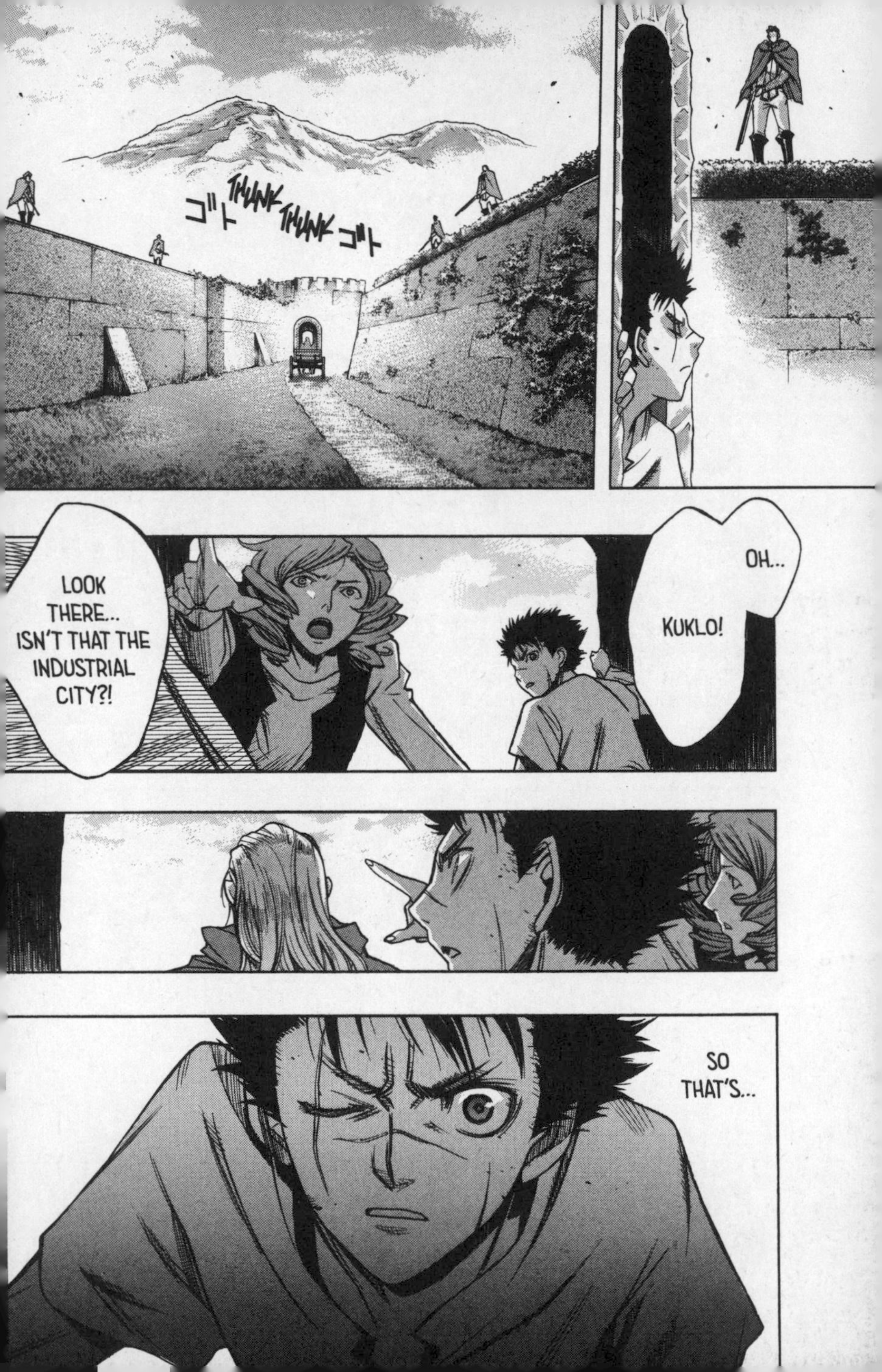
ゴト
THUNK
THUNK
ゴト
OH... KUKLO!
LOOK THERE... ISN'T THAT THE INDUSTRIAL CITY?!
SO THAT'S...

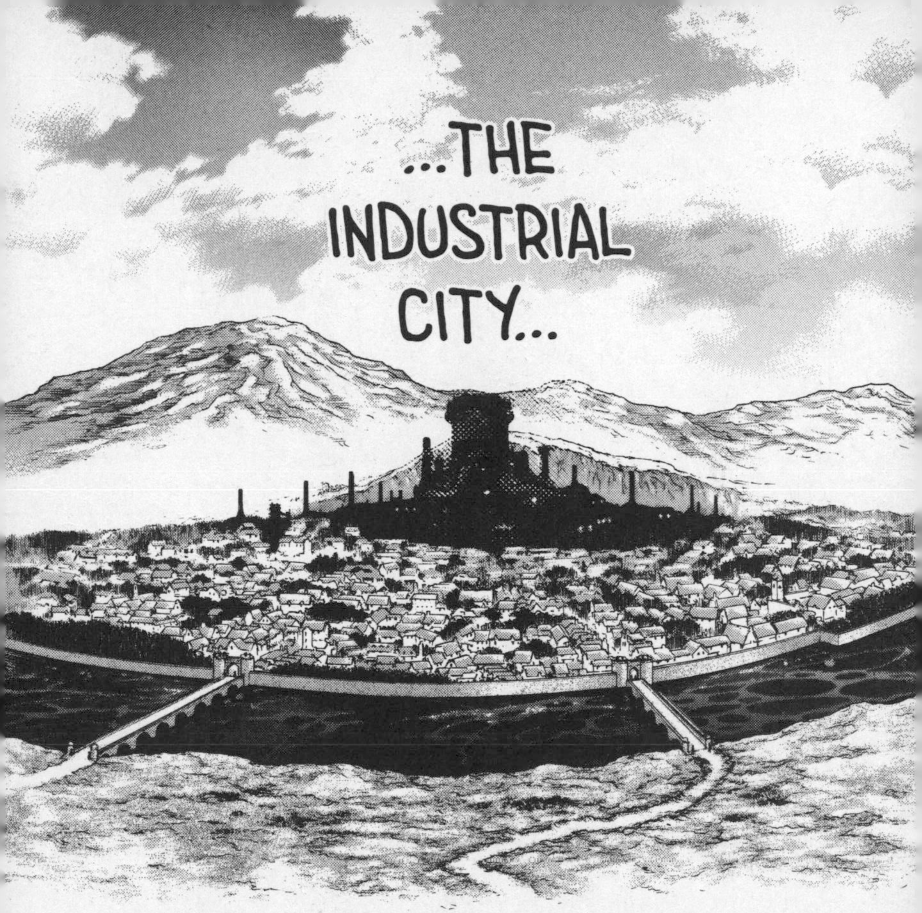
...THE INDUSTRIAL CITY...
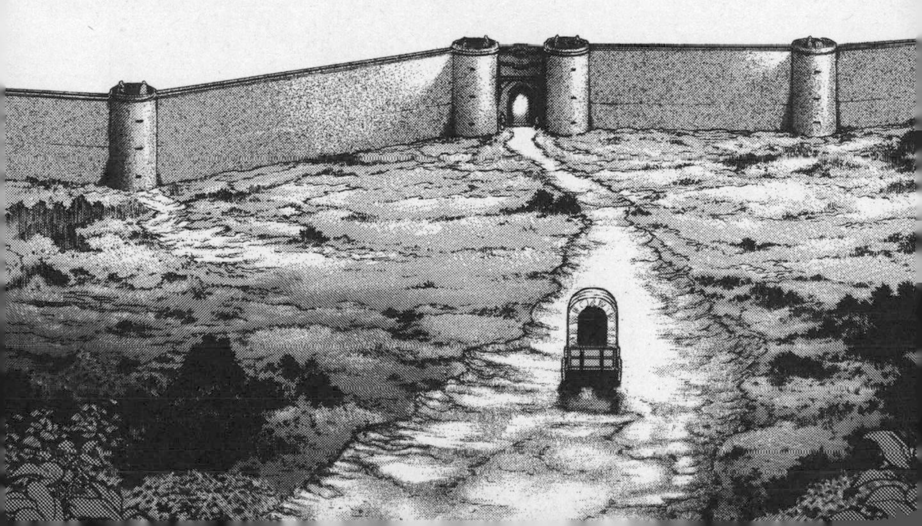

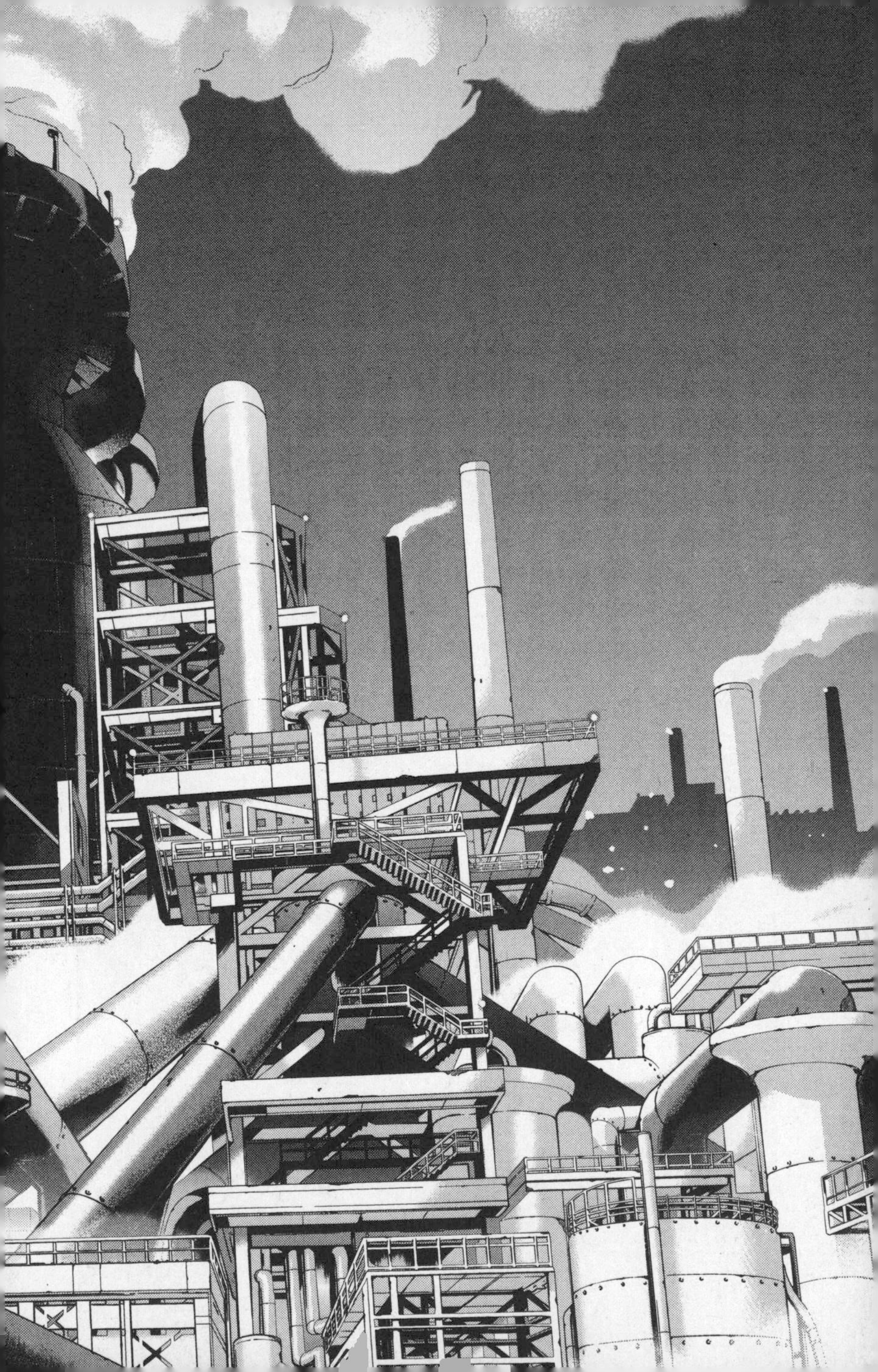

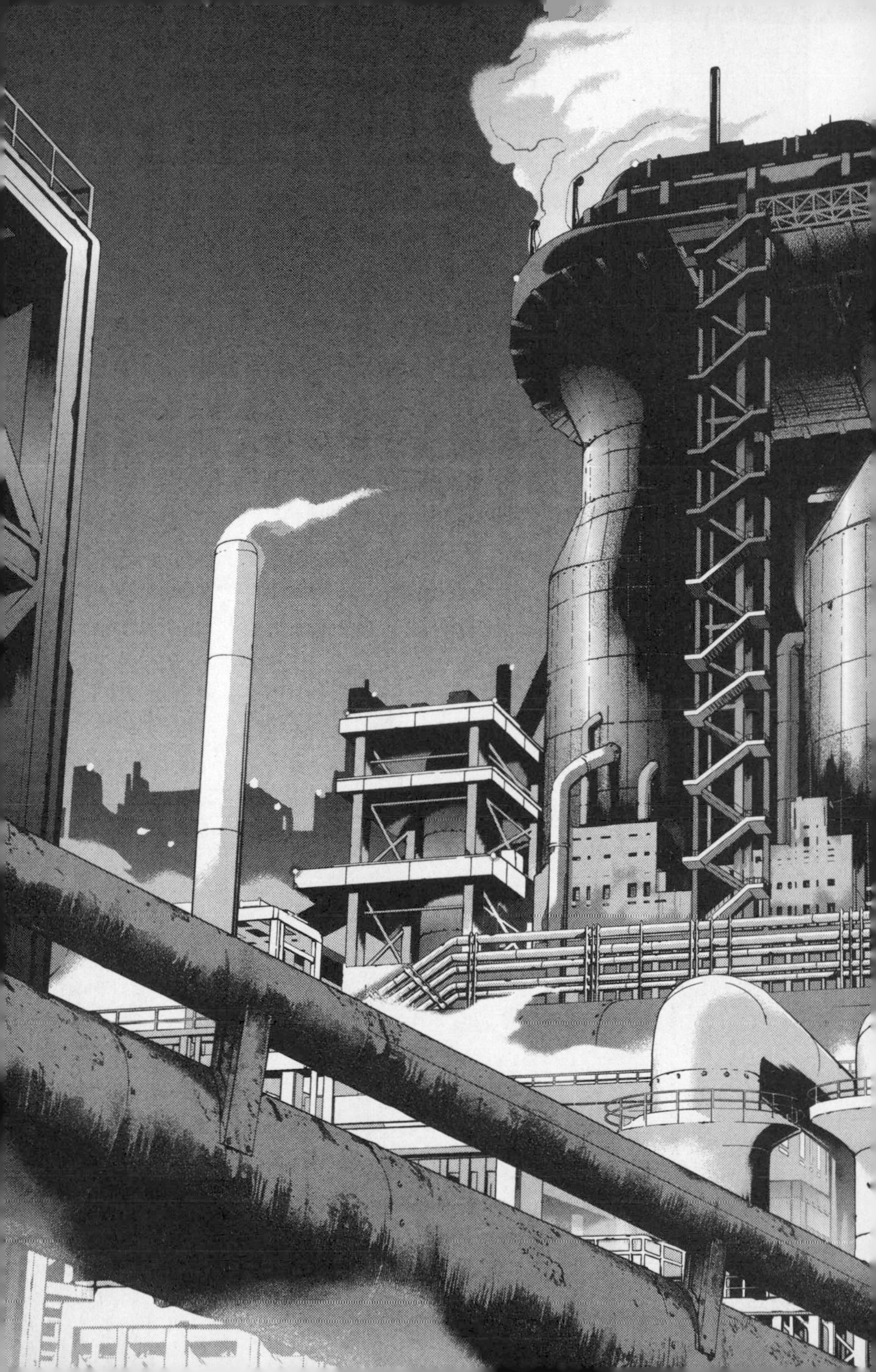

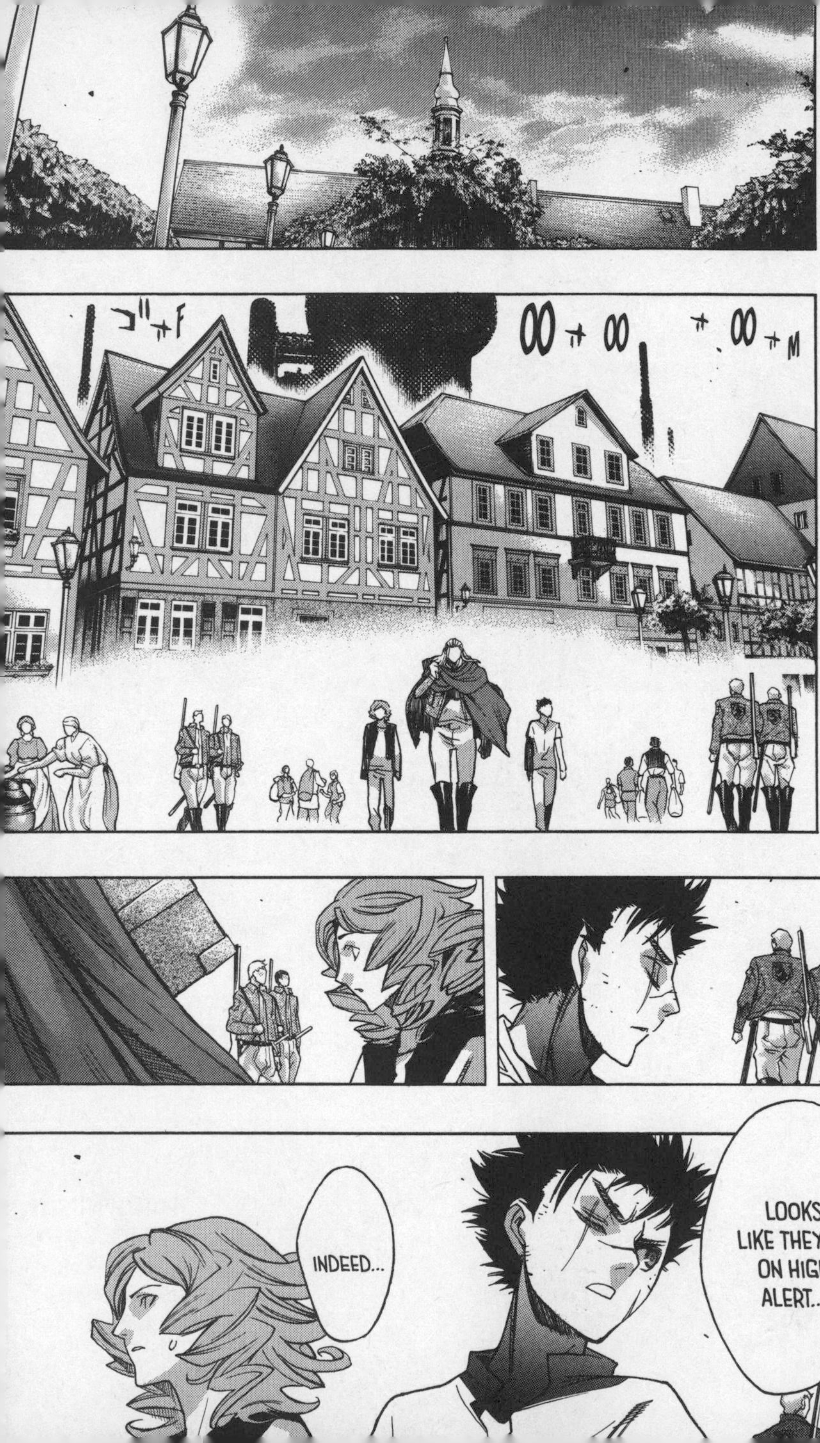
LOOKS LIKE THEY'RE ON HIGH ALERT...
INDEED...

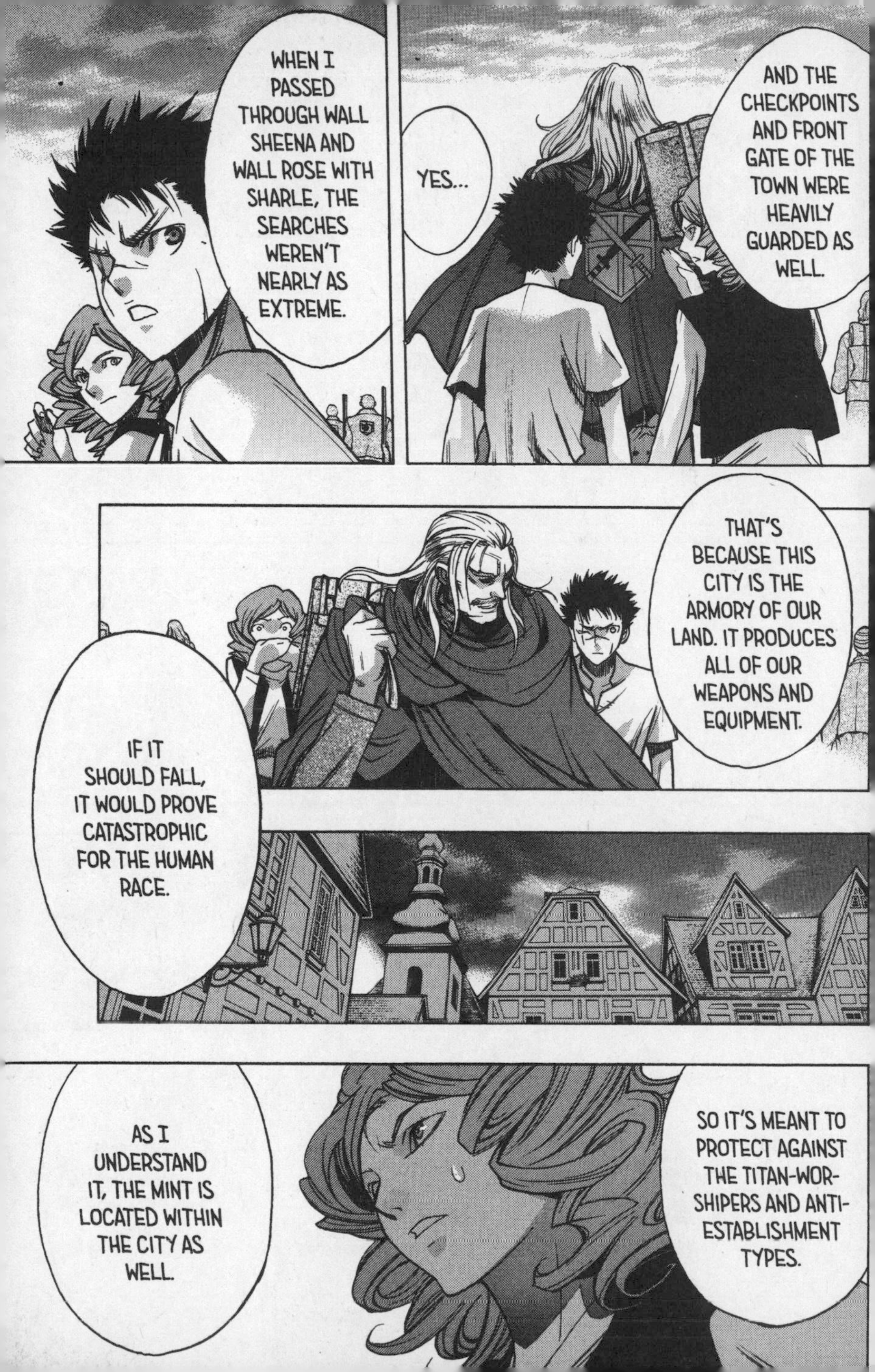
AND THE CHECKPOINTS AND FRONT GATE OF THE TOWN WERE HEAVILY GUARDED AS WELL.
YES...
WHEN I PASSED THROUGH WALL SHEENA AND WALL ROSE WITH SHARLE, THE SEARCHES WEREN'T NEARLY AS EXTREME.
THAT'S BECAUSE THIS CITY IS THE ARMORY OF OUR LAND. IT PRODUCES ALL OF OUR WEAPONS AND EQUIPMENT.
IF IT SHOULD FALL, IT WOULD PROVE CATASTROPHIC FOR THE HUMAN RACE.
SO IT'S MEANT TO PROTECT AGAINST THE TITAN-WORSHIPERS AND ANTI-ESTABLISHMENT TYPES.
AS I UNDERSTAND IT, THE MINT IS LOCATED WITHIN THE CITY AS WELL.

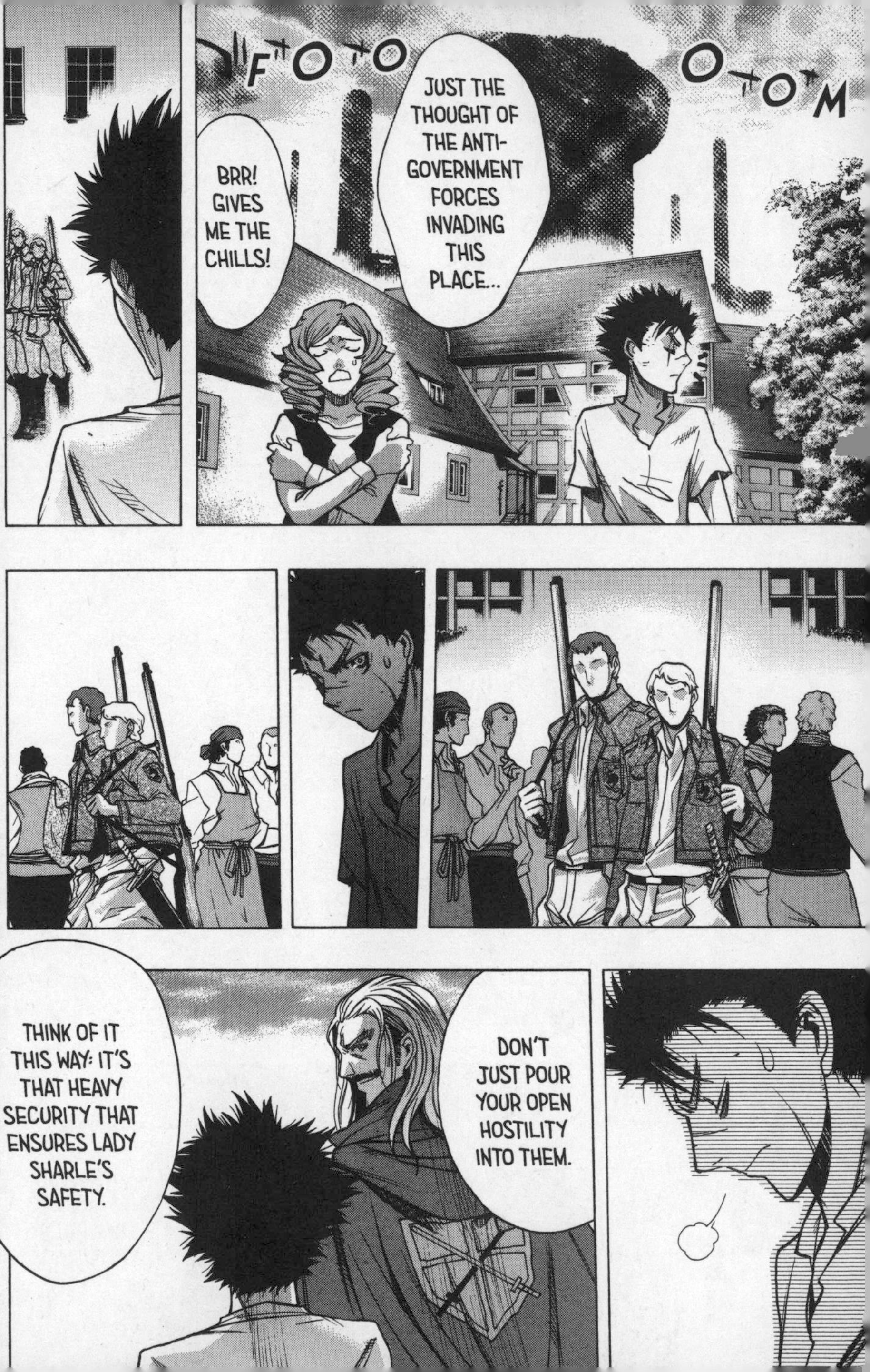
JUST THE THOUGHT OF THE ANTI-GOVERNMENT FORCES INVADING THIS PLACE...
BRR! GIVES ME THE CHILLS!
DON'T JUST POUR YOUR OPEN HOSTILITY INTO THEM.
THINK OF IT THIS WAY: IT'S THAT HEAVY SECURITY THAT ENSURES LADY SHARLE'S SAFETY.

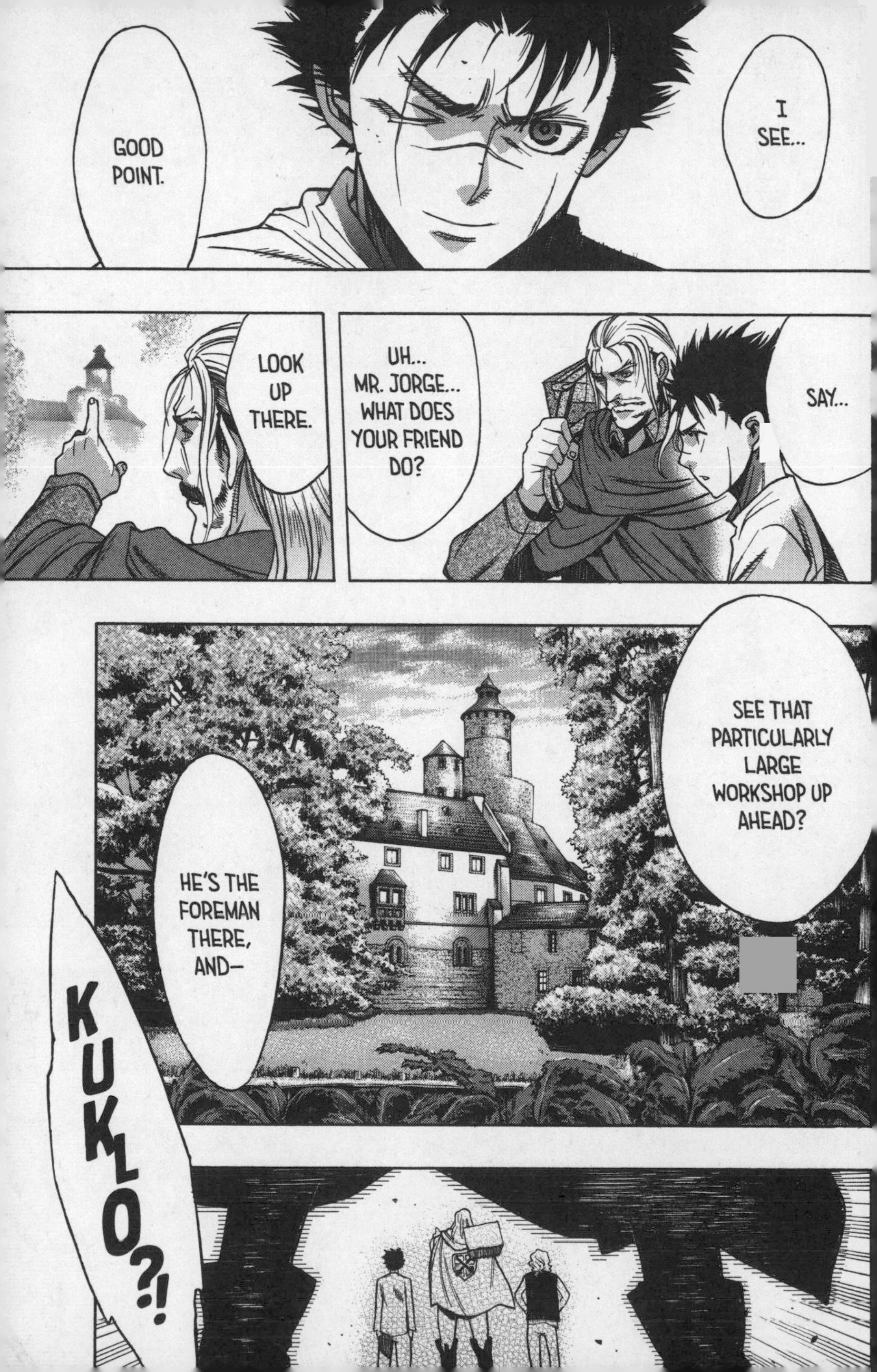
I SEE...
GOOD POINT.
SAY...
UH... MR. JORGE... WHAT DOES YOUR FRIEND DO?
LOOK UP THERE.
SEE THAT PARTICULARLY LARGE WORKSHOP UP AHEAD?
HE'S THE FOREMAN THERE, AND—
KUKLO?!

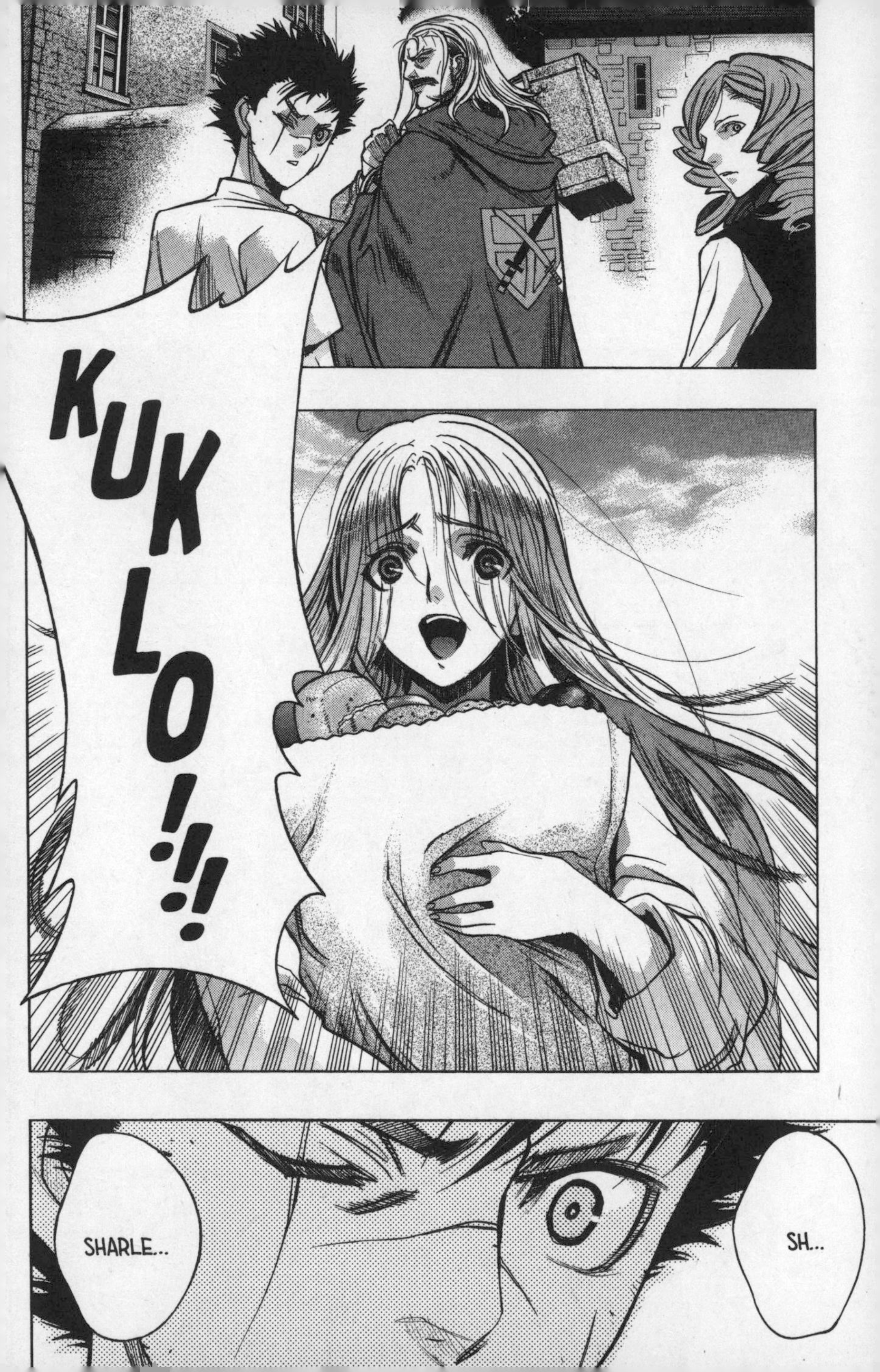
KUKLO!!!
SH...
SHARLE...

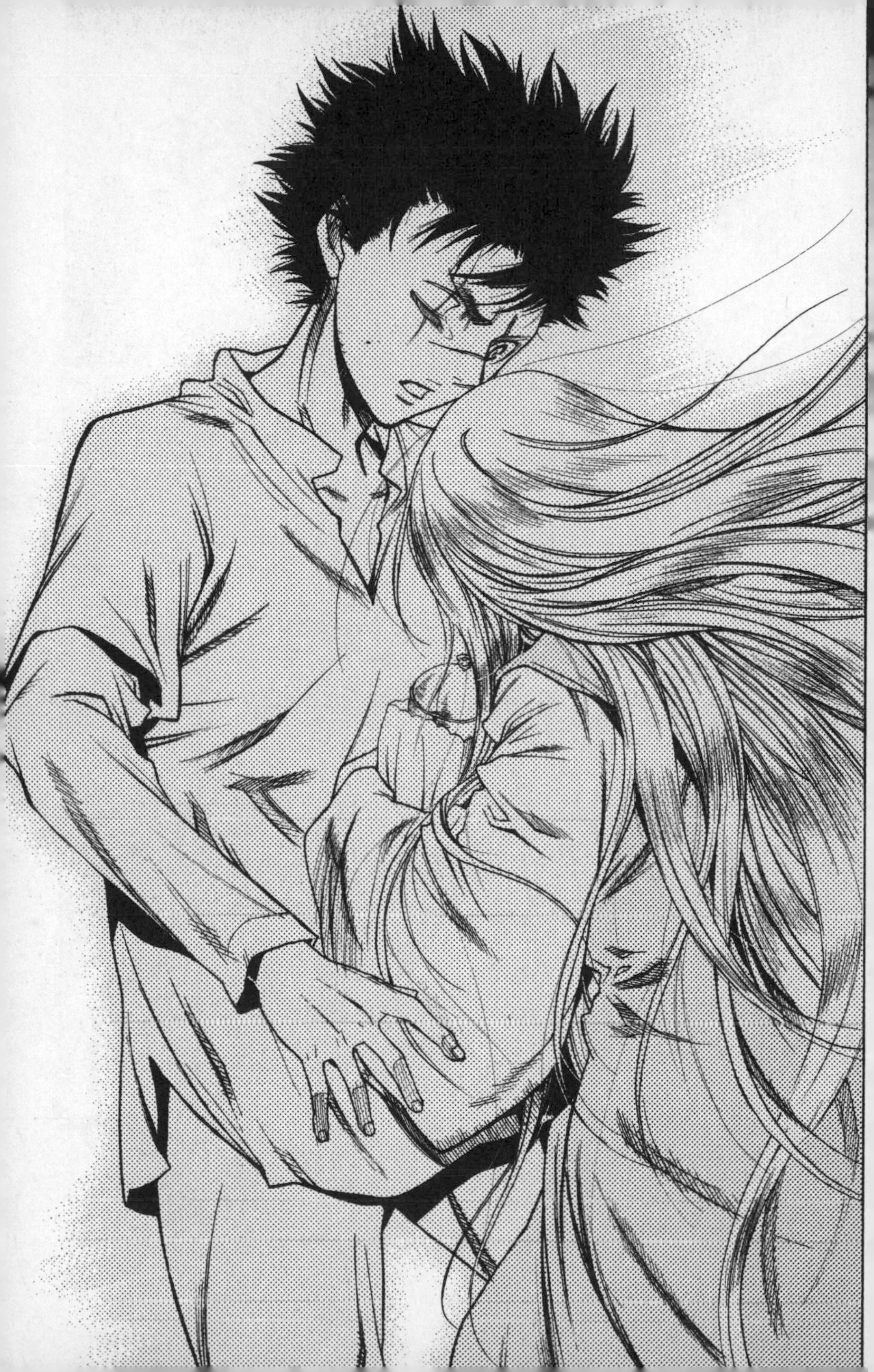

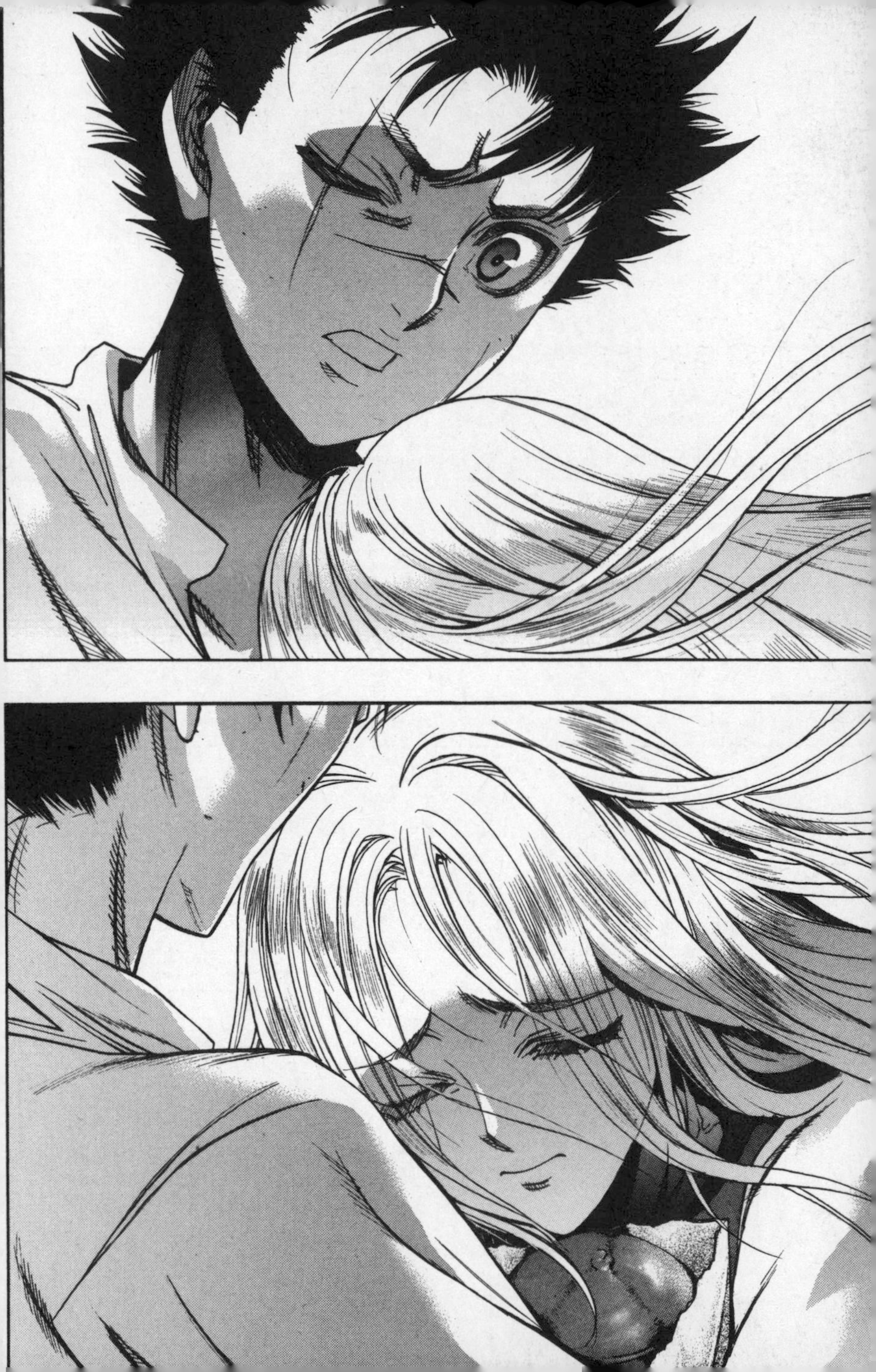

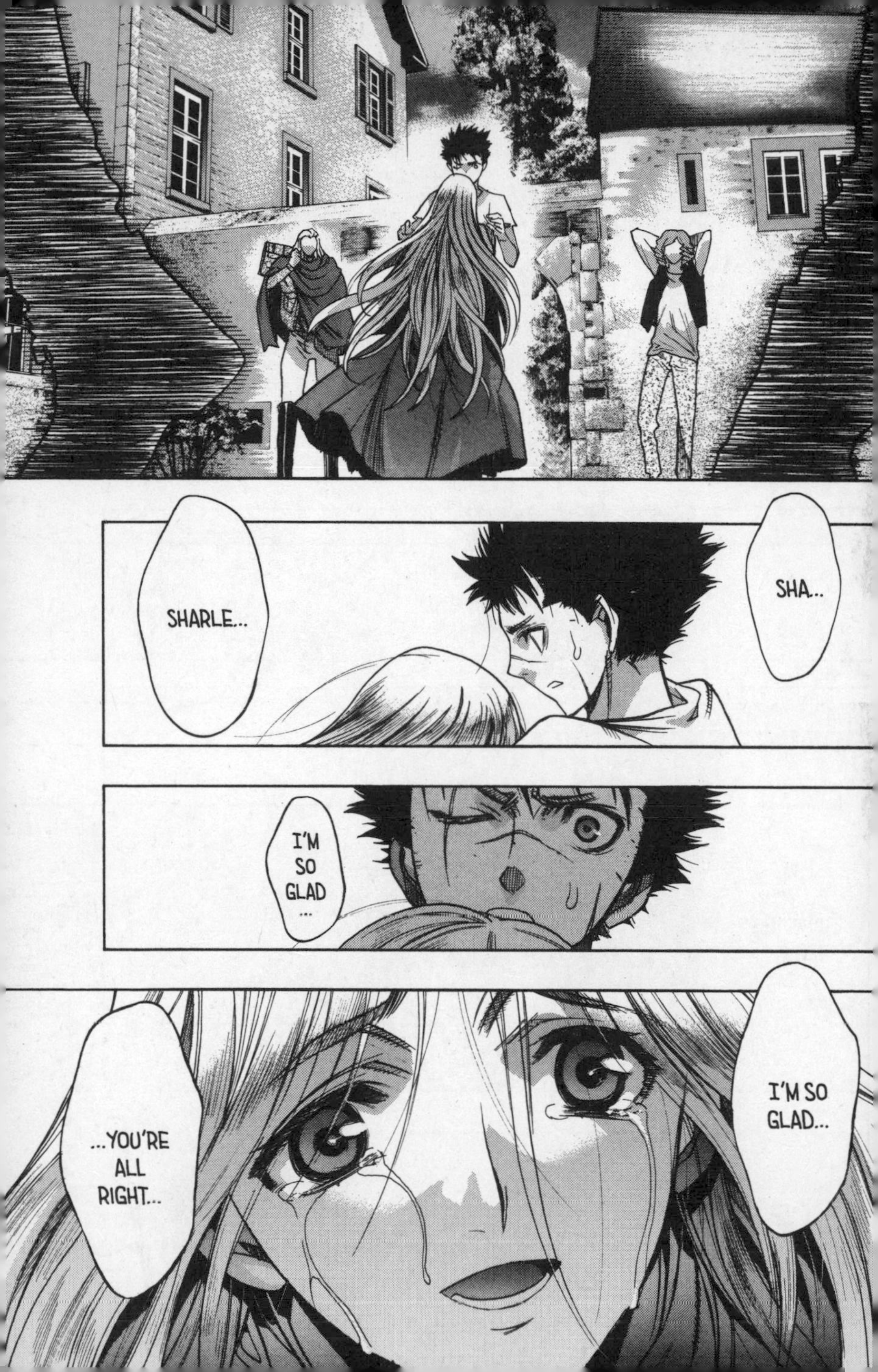
SHA...
SHARLE...
I'M SO GLAD ...
I'M SO GLAD...
...YOU'RE ALL RIGHT...

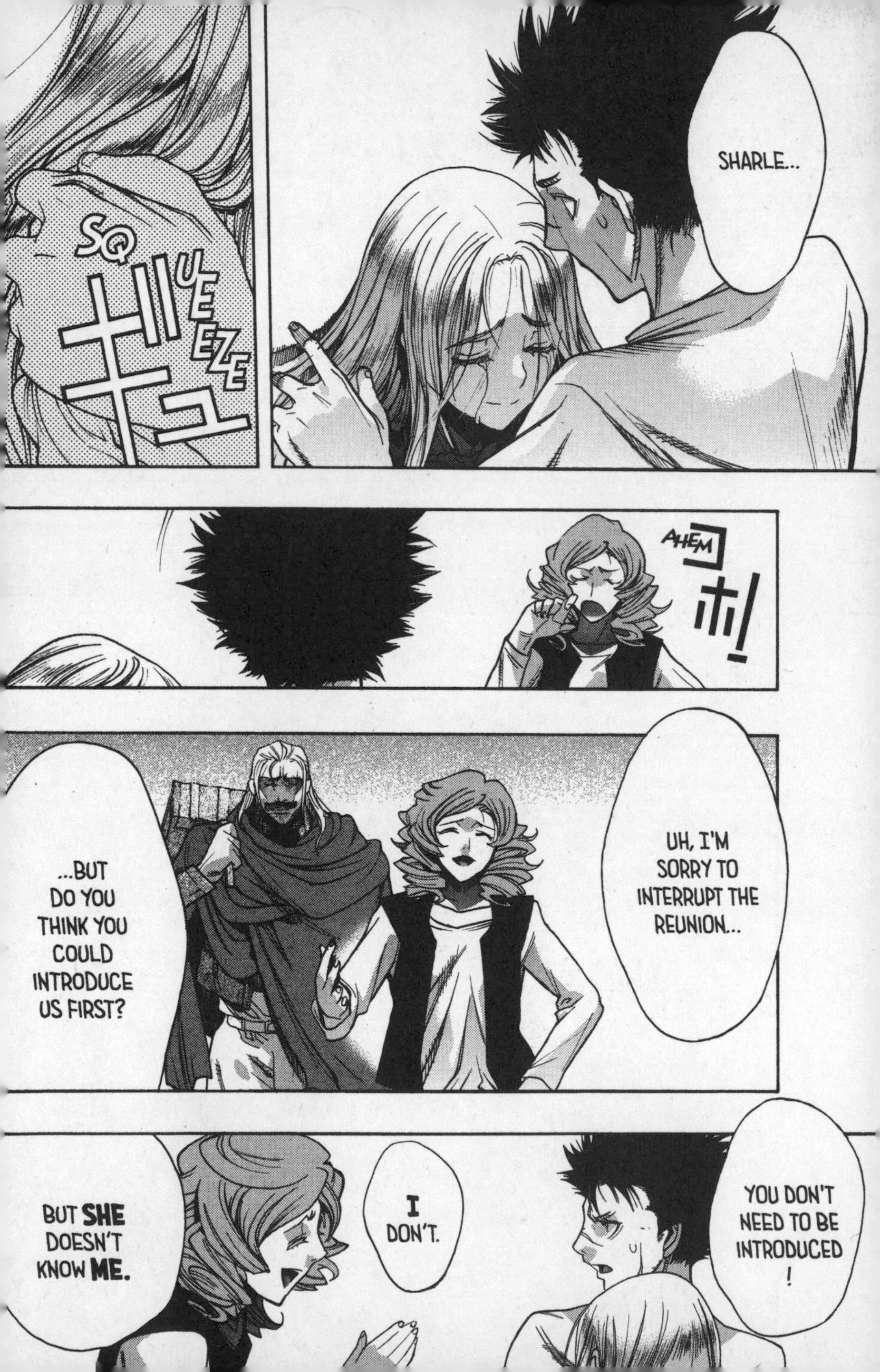
SHARLE...
SQUEEZE
キュ
AHEM
コホ!
UH, I'M SORRY TO INTERRUPT THE REUNION...
...BUT DO YOU THINK YOU COULD INTRODUCE US FIRST?
YOU DON'T NEED TO BE INTRODUCED!
I DON'T.
BUT **SHE** DOESN'T KNOW **ME.**

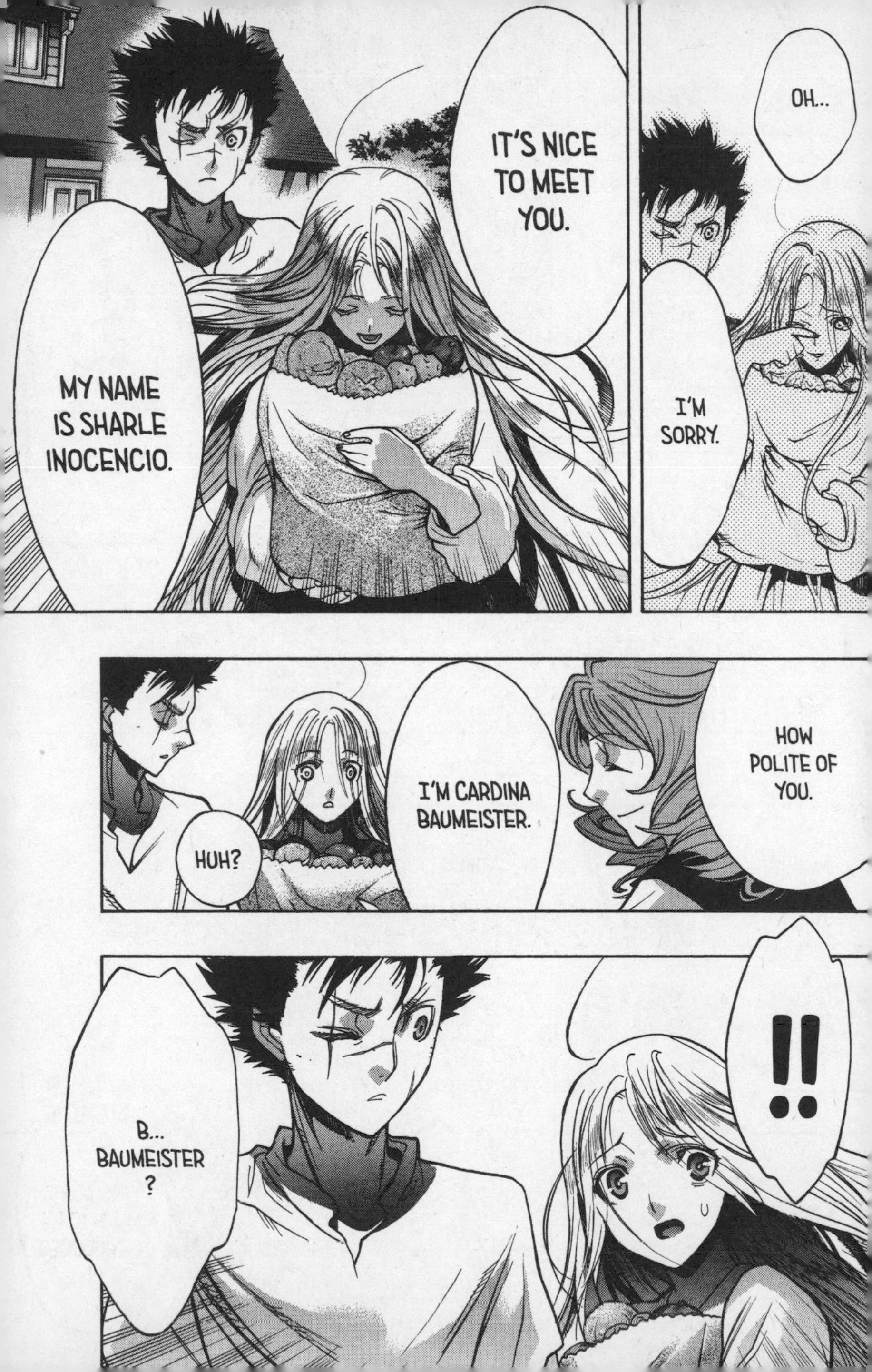
OH...
I'M SORRY.
IT'S NICE TO MEET YOU.
MY NAME IS SHARLE INOCENCIO.
HOW POLITE OF YOU.
I'M CARDINA BAUMEISTER.
HUH?
!!
B... BAUMEISTER?

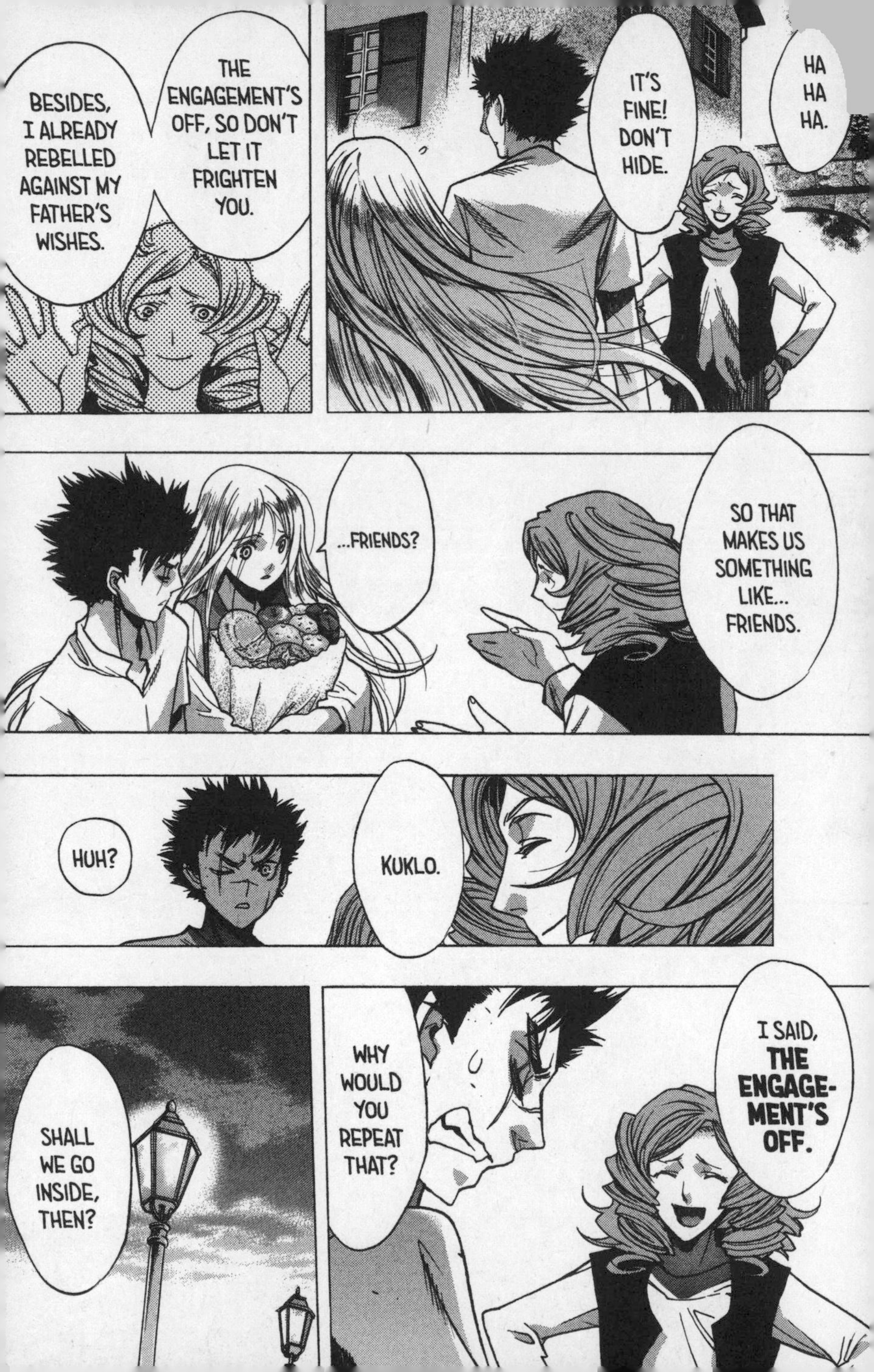
HA HA HA.
IT'S FINE! DON'T HIDE.
THE ENGAGEMENT'S OFF, SO DON'T LET IT FRIGHTEN YOU.
BESIDES, I ALREADY REBELLED AGAINST MY FATHER'S WISHES.
SO THAT MAKES US SOMETHING LIKE... FRIENDS.
...FRIENDS?
KUKLO.
HUH?
I SAID, **THE ENGAGEMENT'S OFF.**
WHY WOULD YOU REPEAT THAT?
SHALL WE GO INSIDE, THEN?

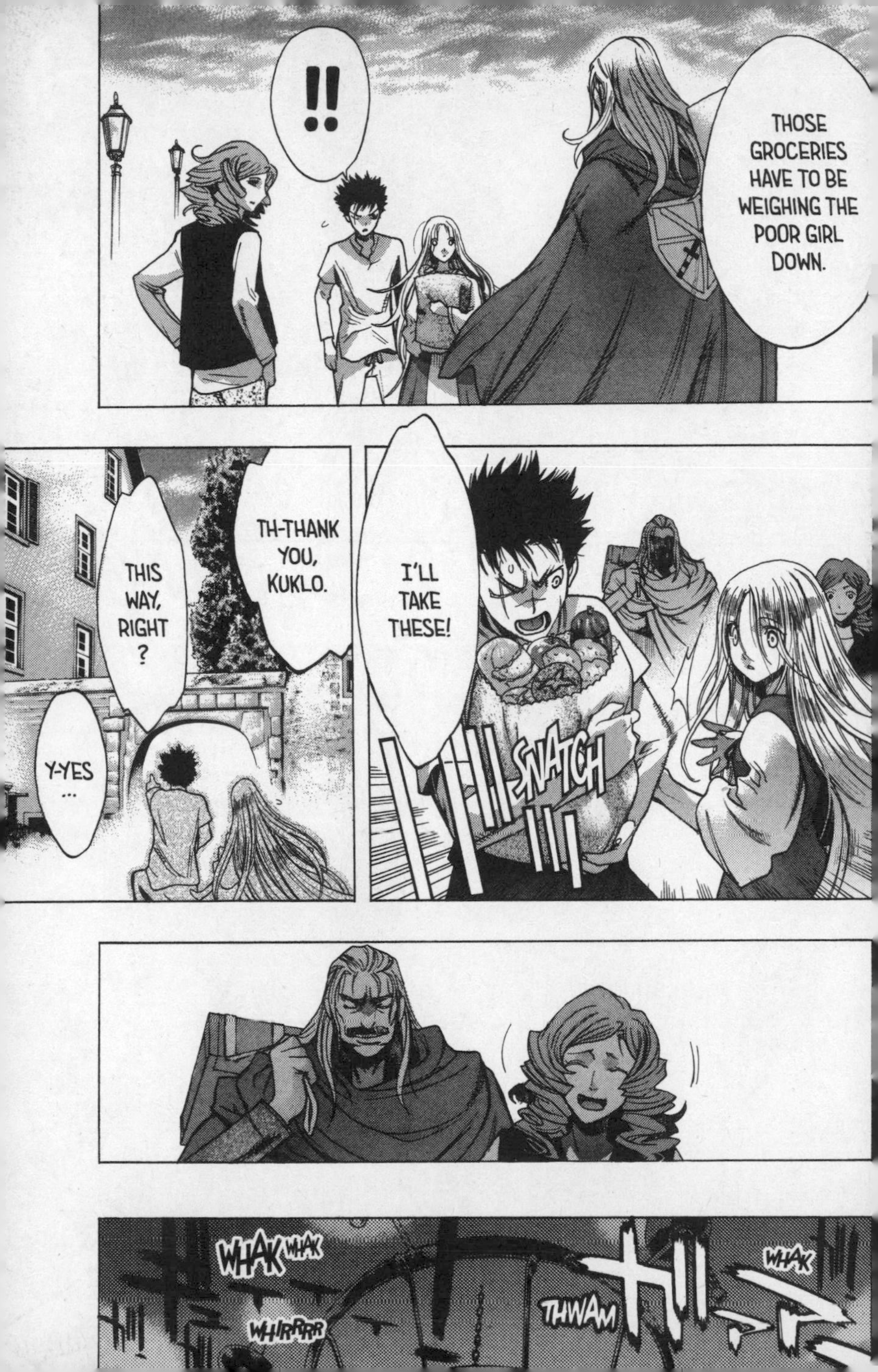
THOSE GROCERIES HAVE TO BE WEIGHING THE POOR GIRL DOWN.
!!
I'LL TAKE THESE!
SNATCH
TH-THANK YOU, KUKLO.
THIS WAY, RIGHT?
Y-YES ...
WHAK
THWAM
WHAK WHAK
WHIRRRR

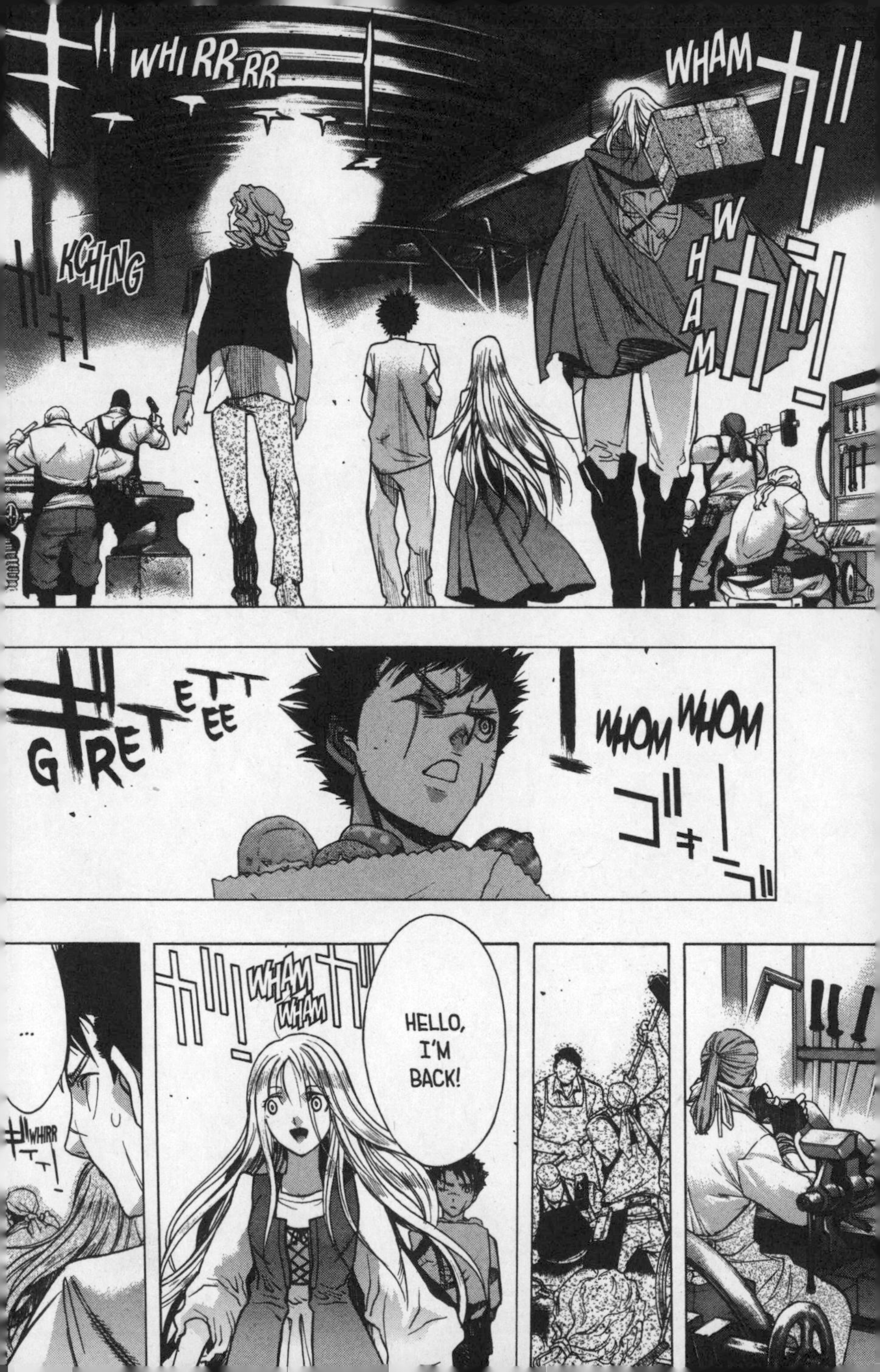
WHAM
WHAM
WHIRR-RR
KCHING
WHOM WHOM
GRETETTEE
WHAM WHAM
HELLO, I'M BACK!
...
WHIRR

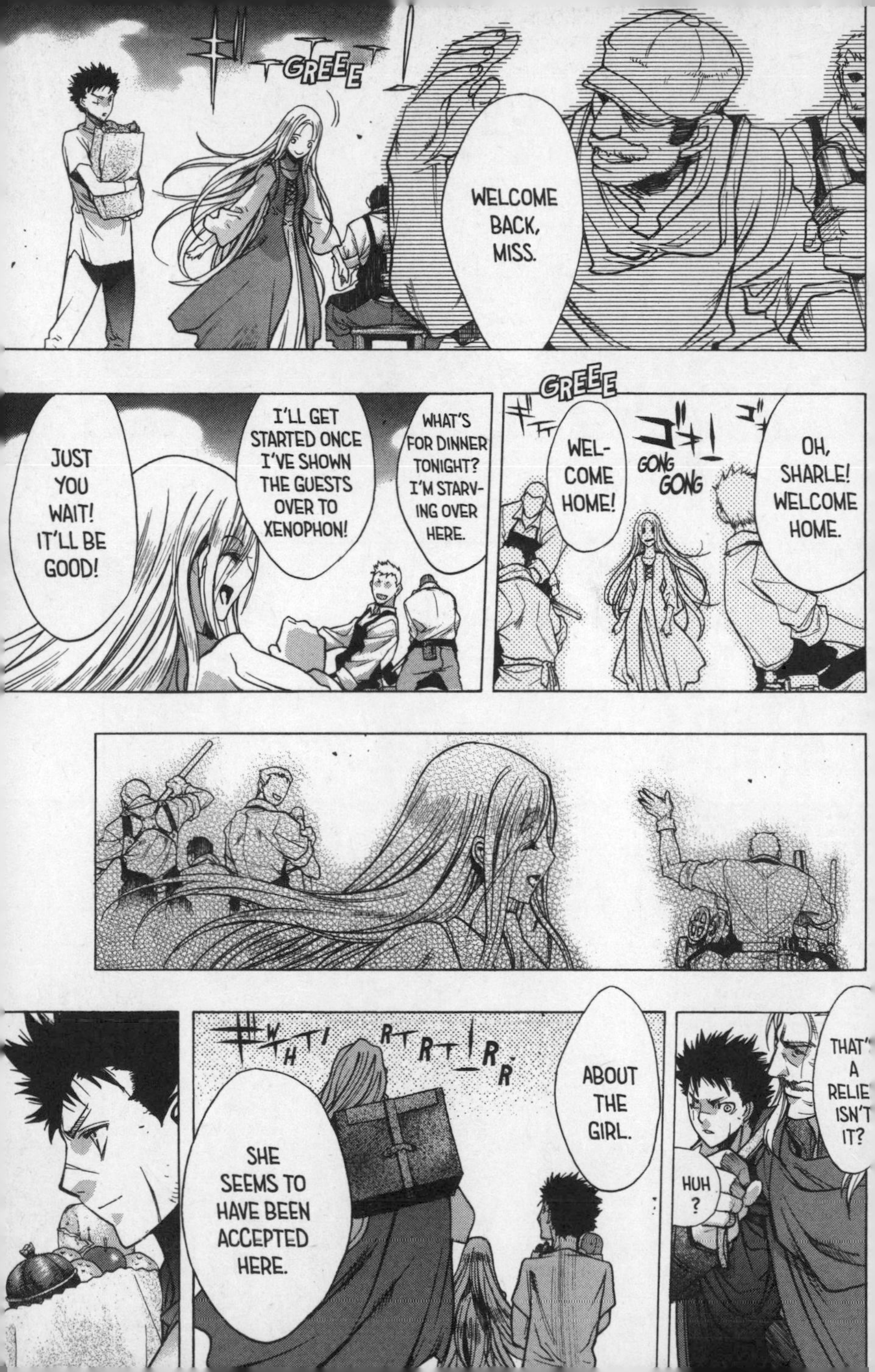
GREEE
WELCOME BACK, MISS.
OH, SHARLE! WELCOME HOME.
GONG GONG
WEL-COME HOME!
GREEE
WHAT'S FOR DINNER TONIGHT? I'M STARV-ING OVER HERE.
I'LL GET STARTED ONCE I'VE SHOWN THE GUESTS OVER TO XENOPHON!
JUST YOU WAIT! IT'LL BE GOOD!
THAT' A RELIE ISN'T IT?
HUH?
ABOUT THE GIRL.
WHIRRR
SHE SEEMS TO HAVE BEEN ACCEPTED HERE.

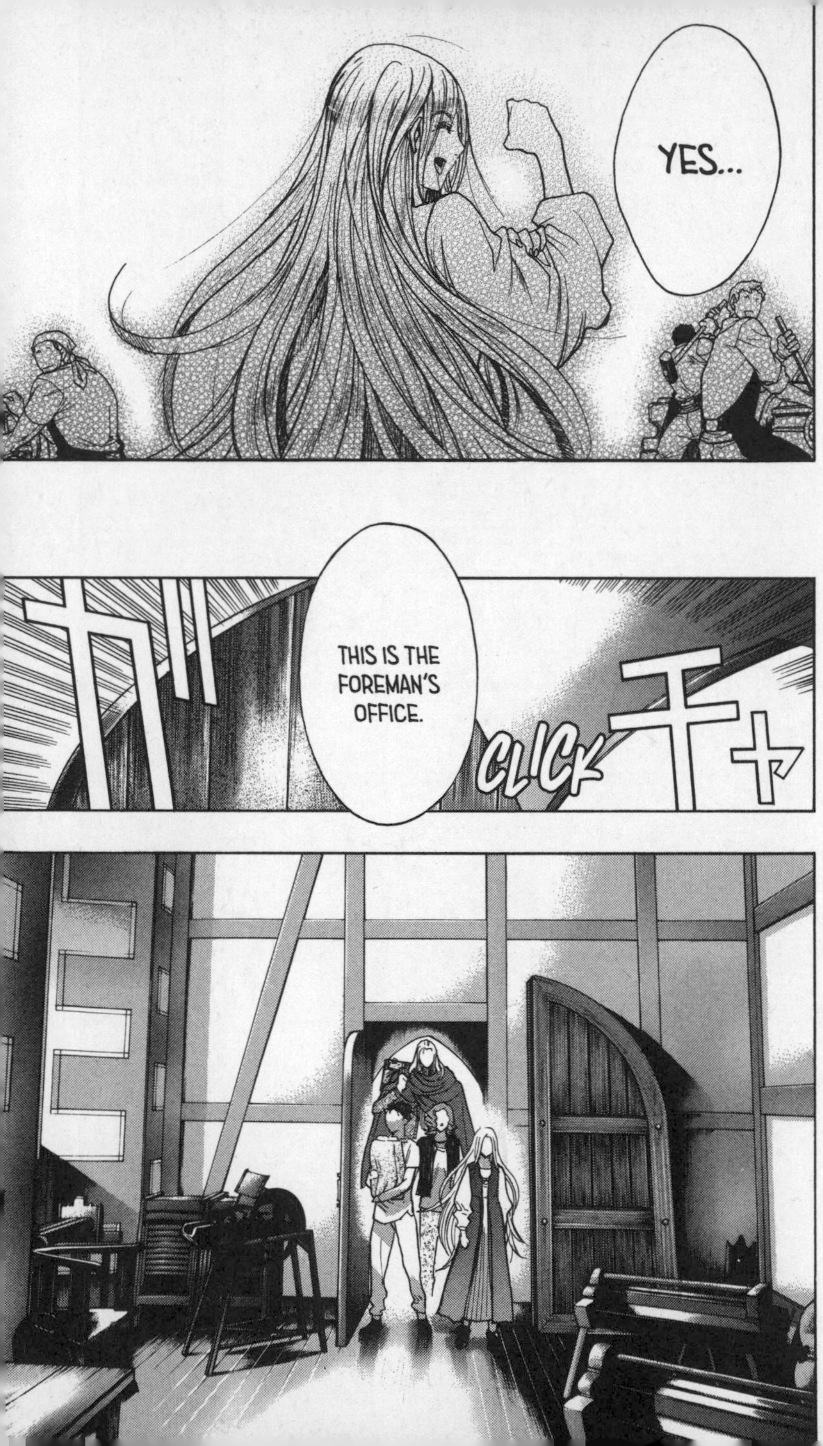
YES...
THIS IS THE FOREMAN'S OFFICE.
ガチャ
CLICK

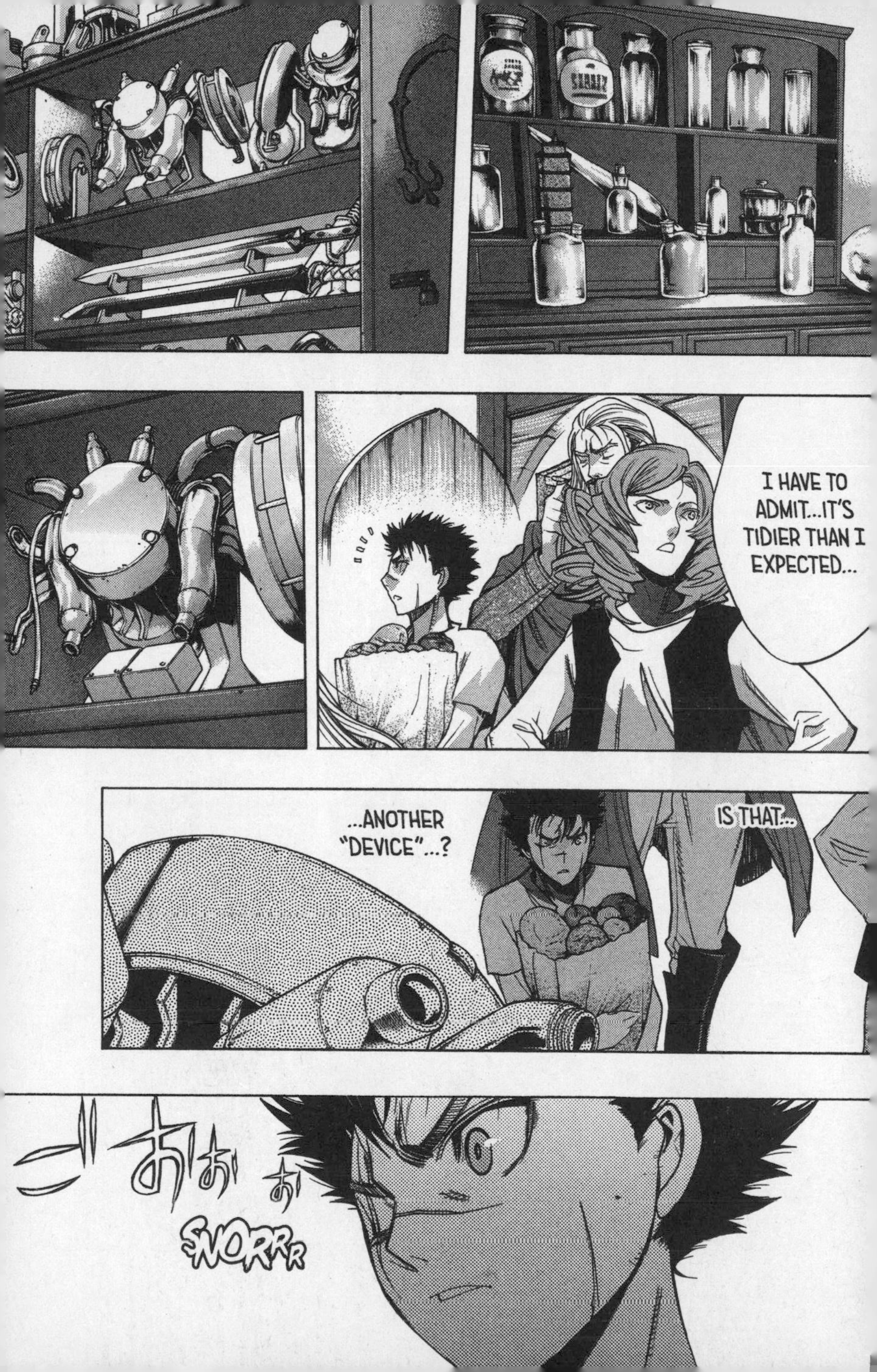
I HAVE TO ADMIT...IT'S TIDIER THAN I EXPECTED...
IS THAT...
...ANOTHER "DEVICE"...?
SNORRR

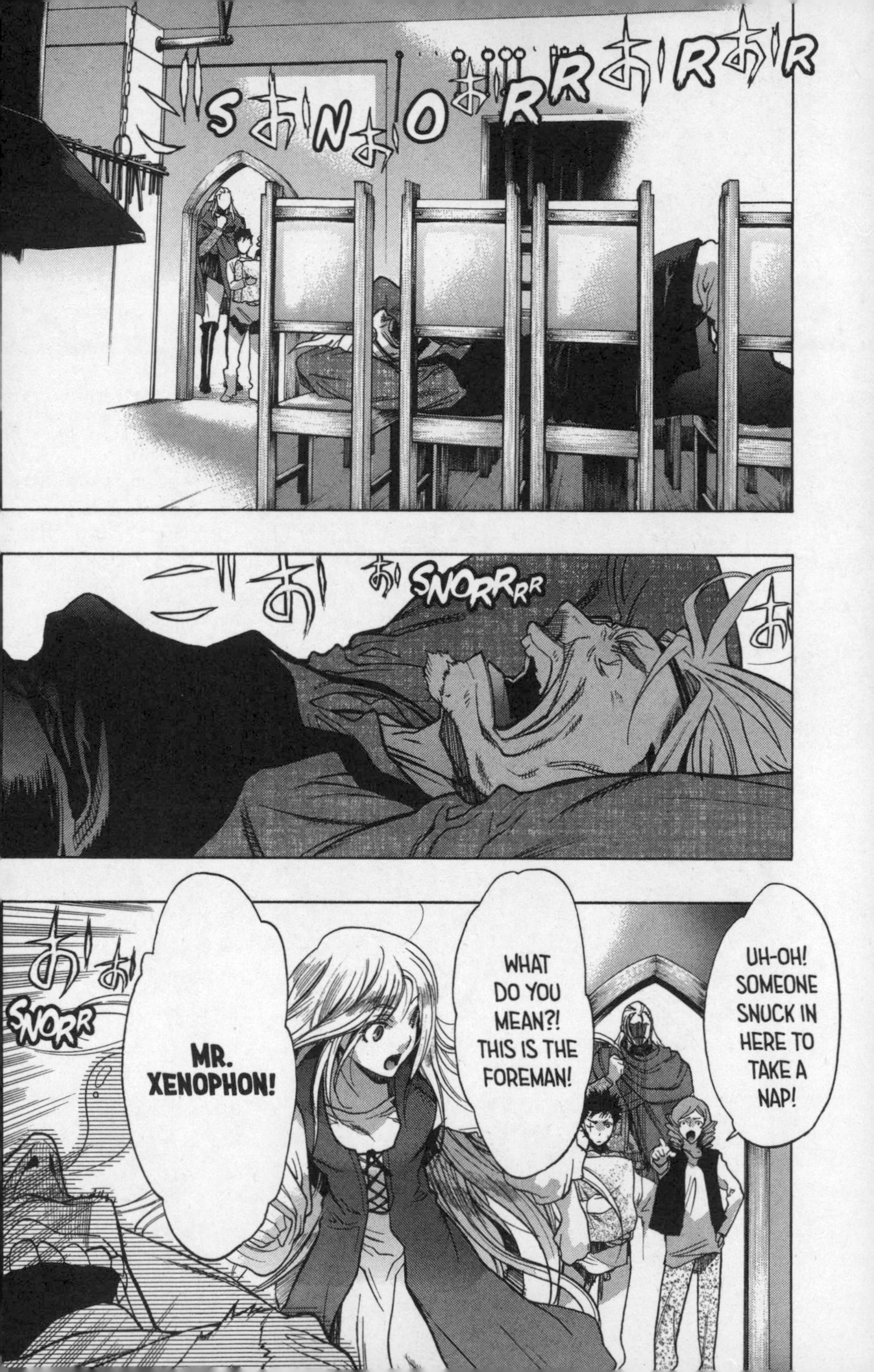
SNORRRR
SNORRRR
UH-OH! SOMEONE SNUCK IN HERE TO TAKE A NAP!
WHAT DO YOU MEAN?! THIS IS THE FOREMAN!
MR. XENOPHON!
SNORR

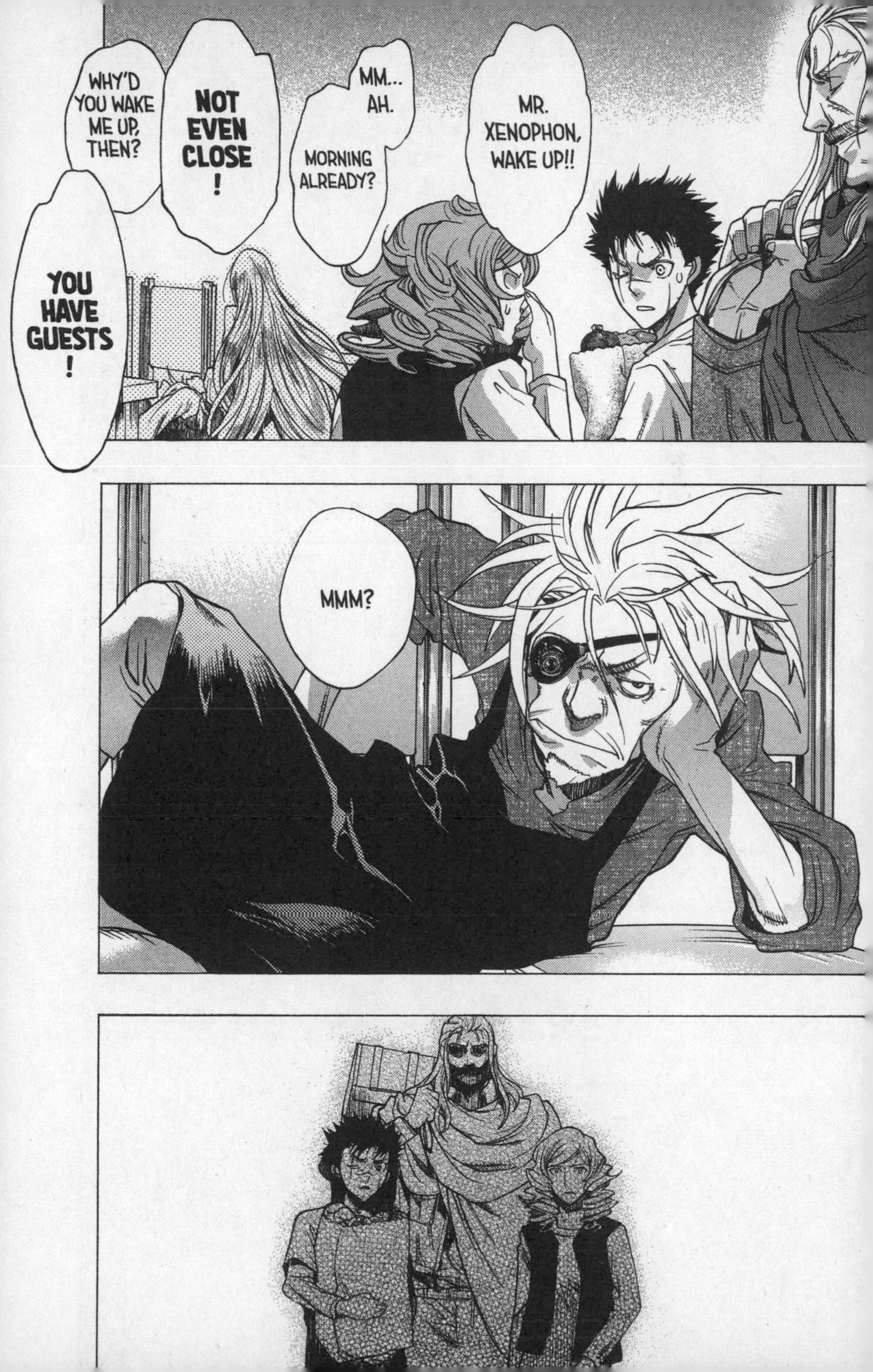
MR. XENOPHON, WAKE UP!!
MM... AH.
MORNING ALREADY?
NOT EVEN CLOSE!
WHY'D YOU WAKE ME UP, THEN?
YOU HAVE GUESTS!
MMM?

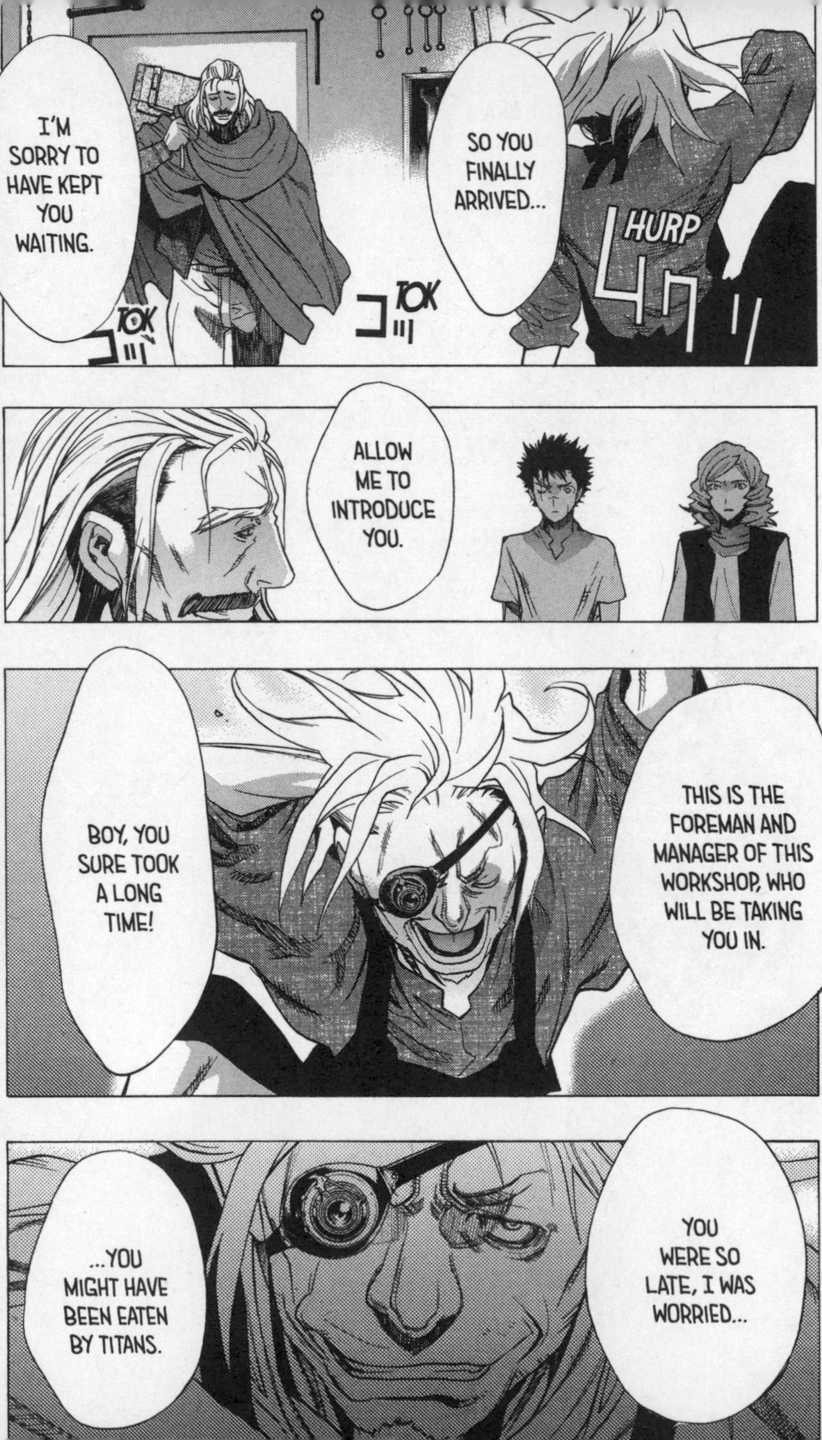
HURP
SO YOU FINALLY ARRIVED...
TOK
I'M SORRY TO HAVE KEPT YOU WAITING.
TOK
ALLOW ME TO INTRODUCE YOU.
THIS IS THE FOREMAN AND MANAGER OF THIS WORKSHOP, WHO WILL BE TAKING YOU IN.
BOY, YOU SURE TOOK A LONG TIME!
YOU WERE SO LATE, I WAS WORRIED...
...YOU MIGHT HAVE BEEN EATEN BY TITANS.

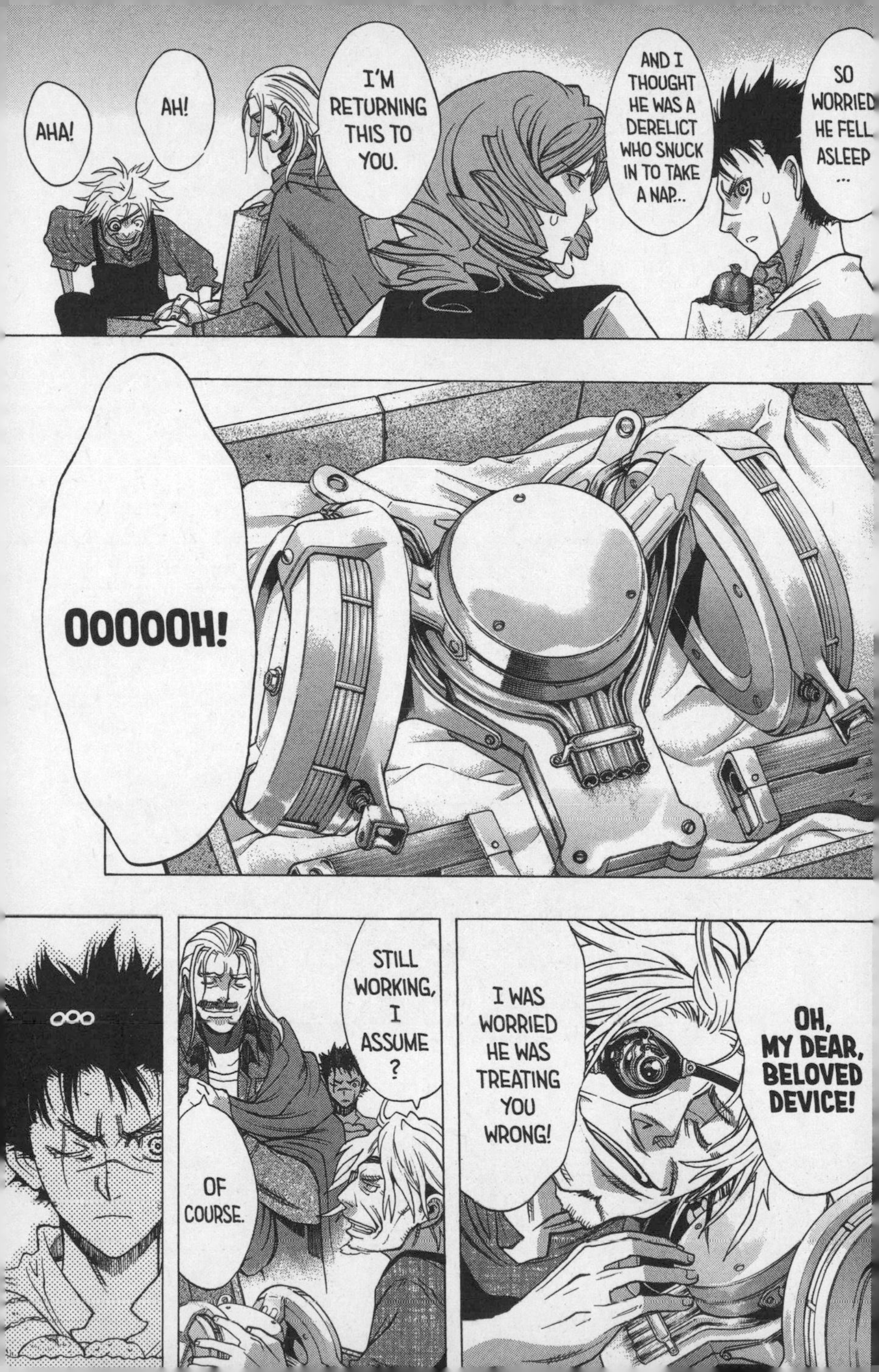
SO WORRIED HE FELL ASLEEP ...
AND I THOUGHT HE WAS A DERELICT WHO SNUCK IN TO TAKE A NAP...
I'M RETURNING THIS TO YOU.
AH!
AHA!
OOOOOH!
OH, MY DEAR, BELOVED DEVICE!
I WAS WORRIED HE WAS TREATING YOU WRONG!
STILL WORKING, I ASSUME?
OF COURSE.

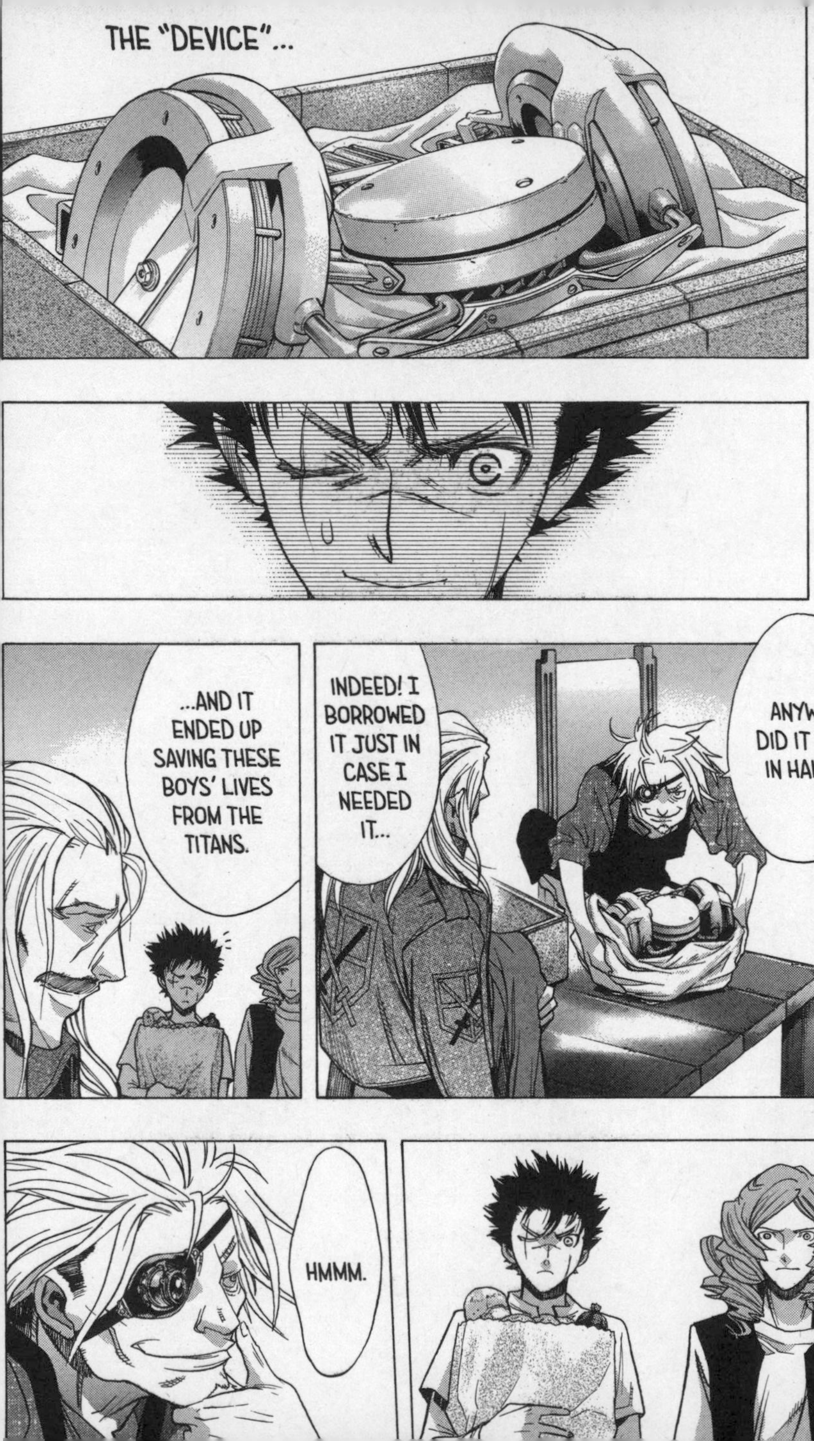
THE "DEVICE"...
ANYWAY... DID IT COME IN HANDY?
INDEED! I BORROWED IT JUST IN CASE I NEEDED IT...
...AND IT ENDED UP SAVING THESE BOYS' LIVES FROM THE TITANS.
HMMM.

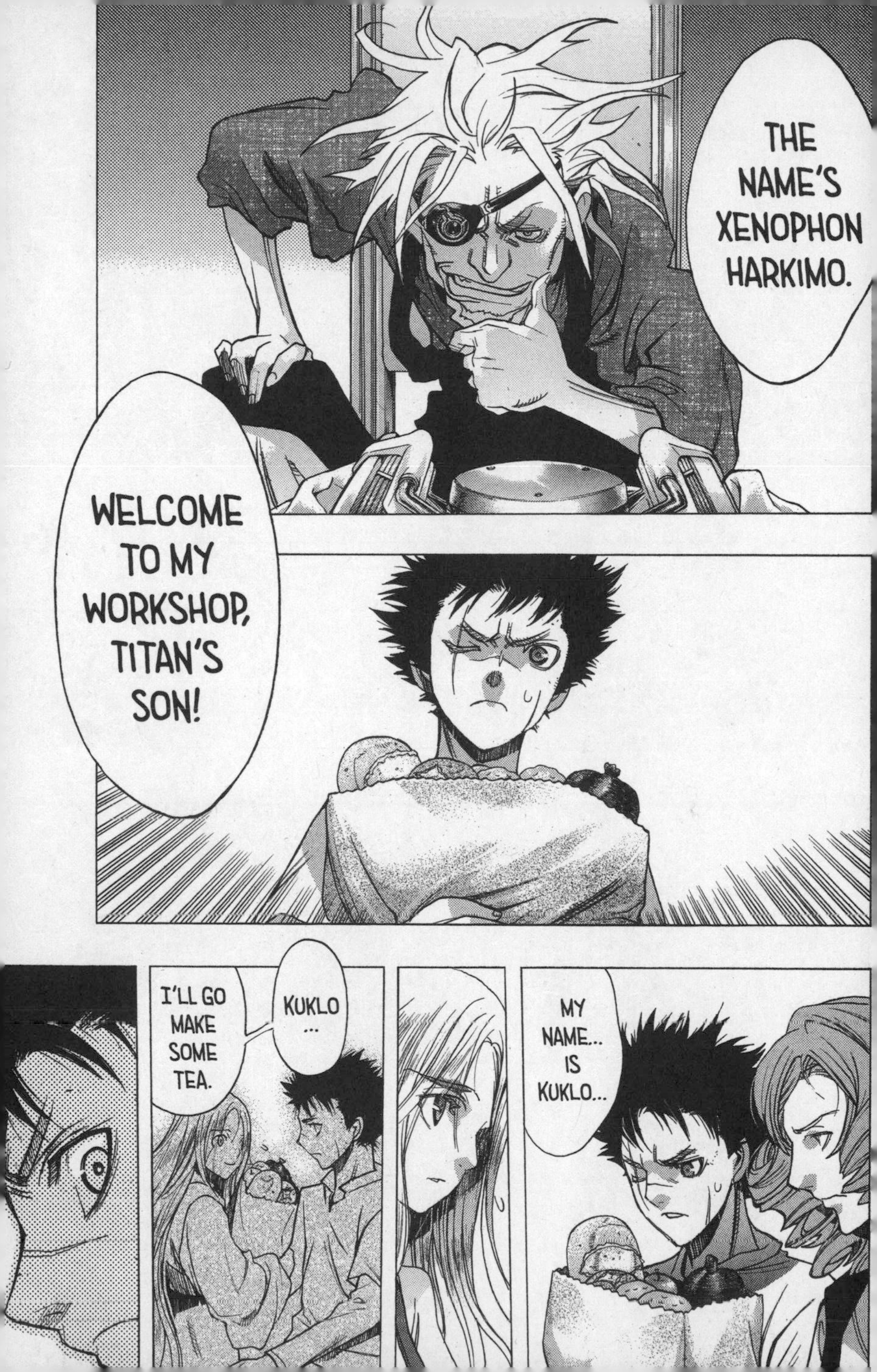
THE NAME'S XENOPHON HARKIMO.
WELCOME TO MY WORKSHOP, TITAN'S SON!
MY NAME... IS KUKLO...
KUKLO ...
I'LL GO MAKE SOME TEA.

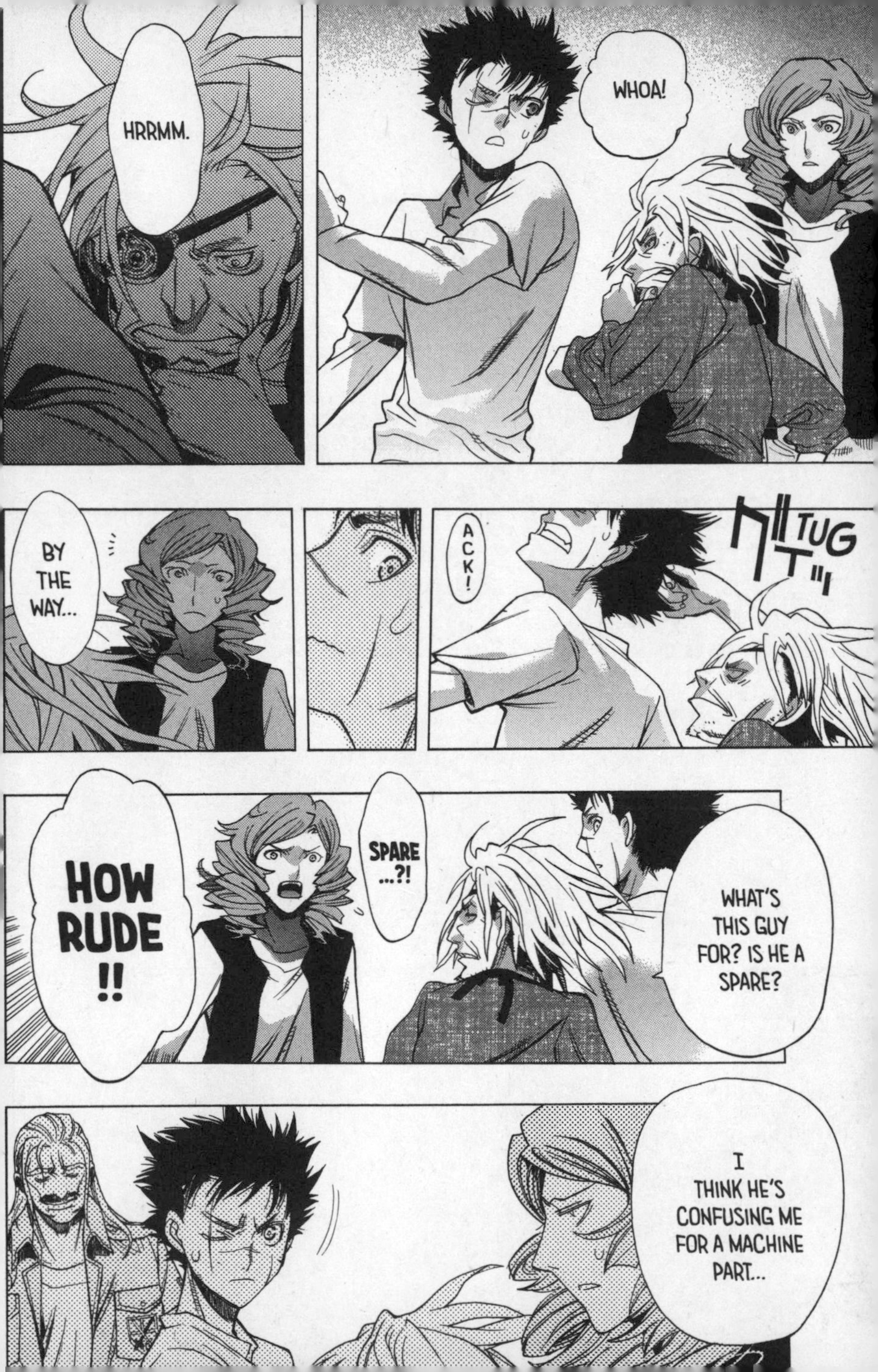
WHOA!
HRRMM.
TUG
ACK!
BY THE WAY...
WHAT'S THIS GUY FOR? IS HE A SPARE?
SPARE ...?!
HOW RUDE !!
I THINK HE'S CONFUSING ME FOR A MACHINE PART...

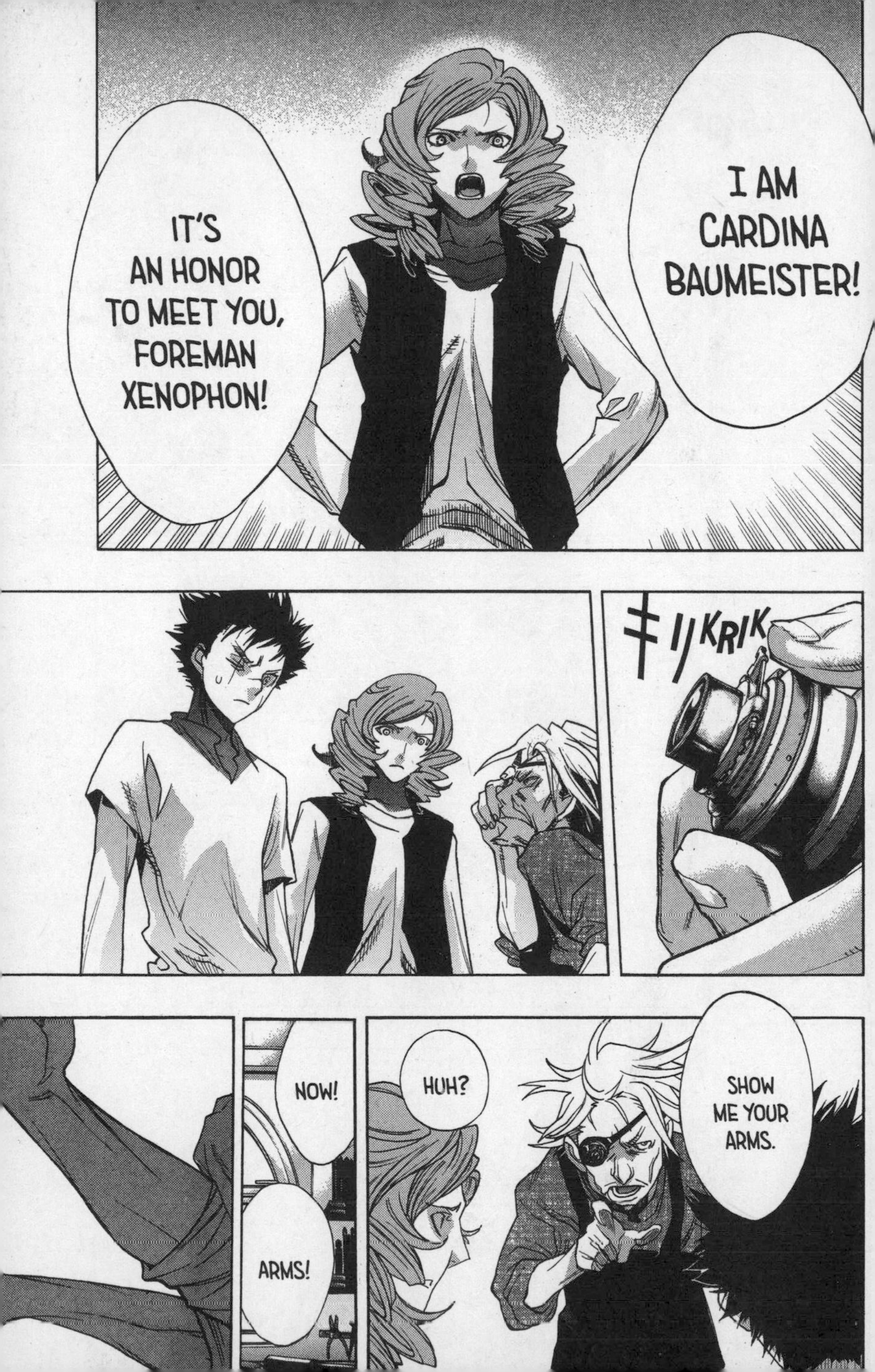
I AM CARDINA BAUMEISTER!
IT'S AN HONOR TO MEET YOU, FOREMAN XENOPHON!
KRIK
SHOW ME YOUR ARMS.
HUH?
NOW!
ARMS!

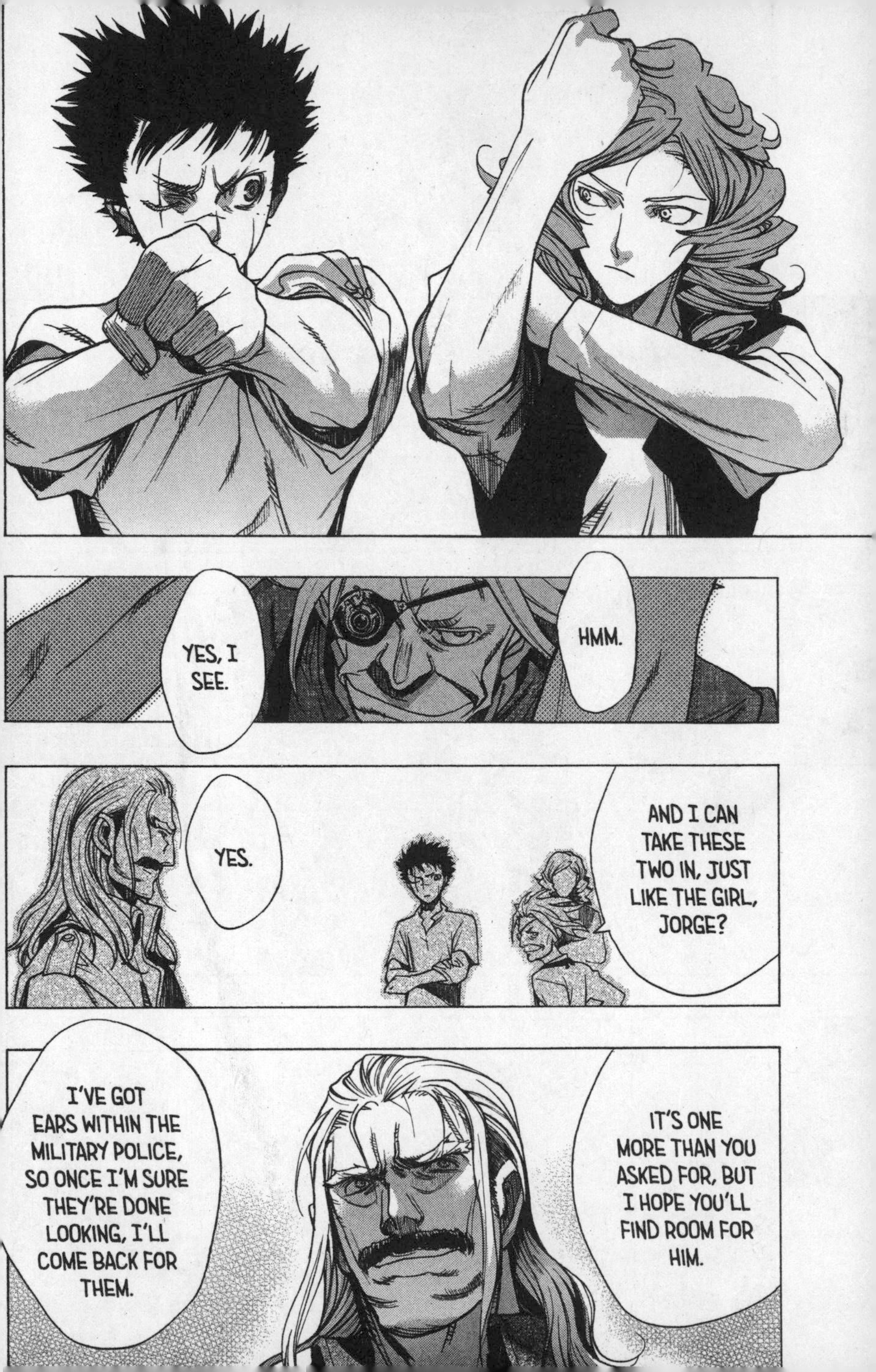
HMM.
YES, I SEE.
AND I CAN TAKE THESE TWO IN, JUST LIKE THE GIRL, JORGE?
YES.
IT'S ONE MORE THAN YOU ASKED FOR, BUT I HOPE YOU'LL FIND ROOM FOR HIM.
I'VE GOT EARS WITHIN THE MILITARY POLICE, SO ONCE I'M SURE THEY'RE DONE LOOKING, I'LL COME BACK FOR THEM.

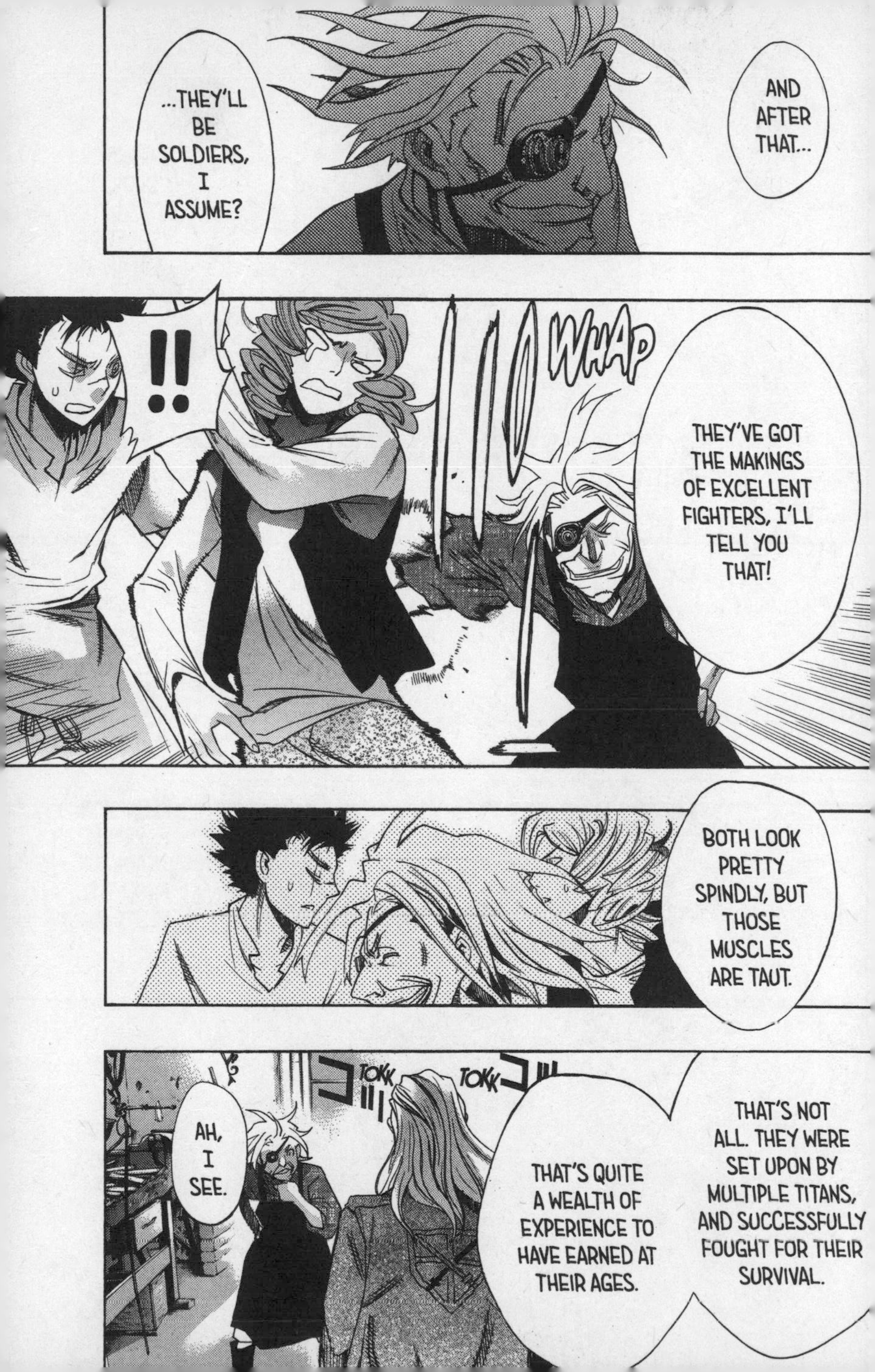
AND AFTER THAT...
...THEY'LL BE SOLDIERS, I ASSUME?
THEY'VE GOT THE MAKINGS OF EXCELLENT FIGHTERS, I'LL TELL YOU THAT!
WHAP
!!
BOTH LOOK PRETTY SPINDLY, BUT THOSE MUSCLES ARE TAUT.
TOKK
TOKK
THAT'S NOT ALL. THEY WERE SET UPON BY MULTIPLE TITANS, AND SUCCESSFULLY FOUGHT FOR THEIR SURVIVAL.
THAT'S QUITE A WEALTH OF EXPERIENCE TO HAVE EARNED AT THEIR AGES.
AH, I SEE.

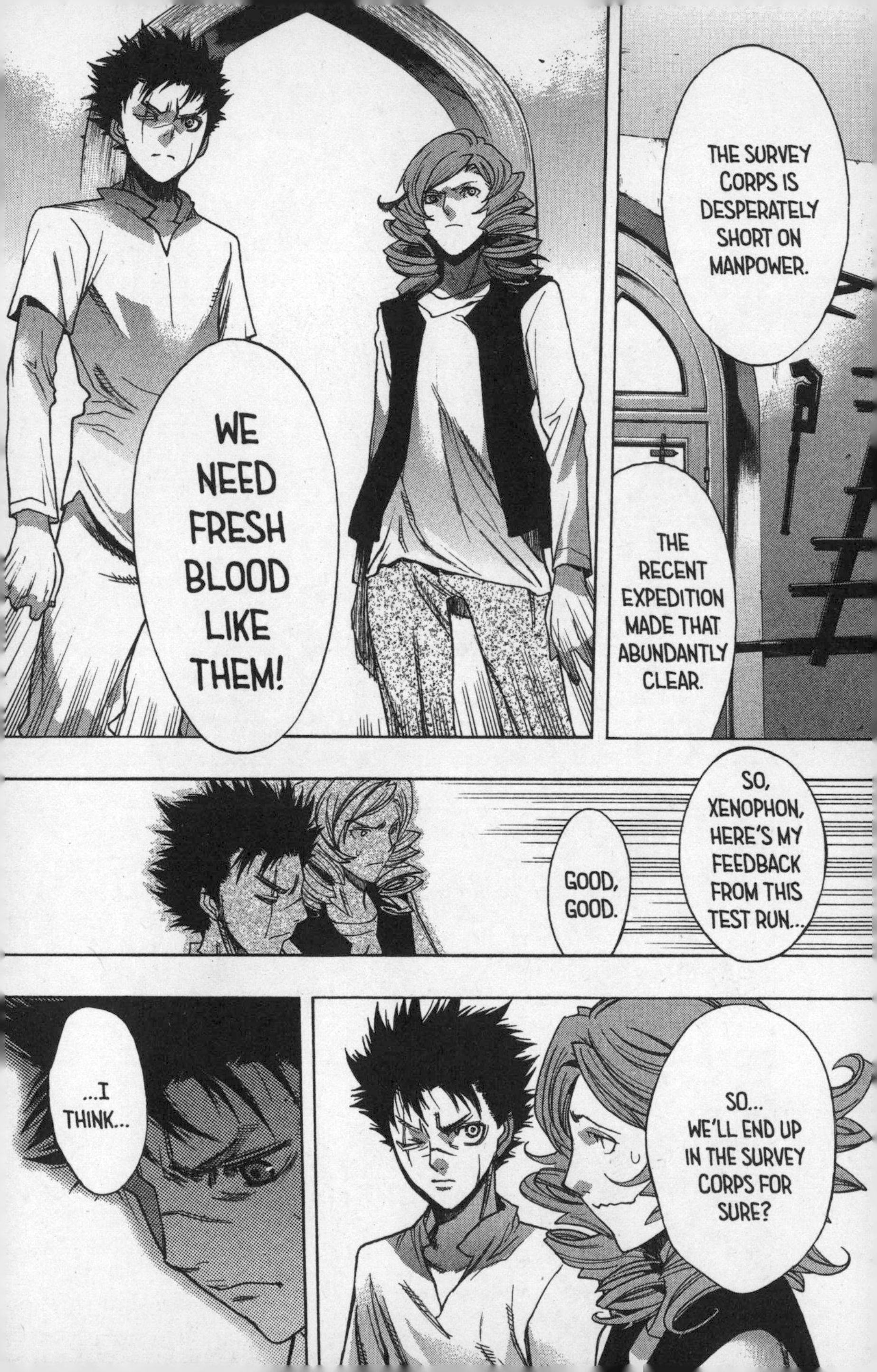
THE SURVEY CORPS IS DESPERATELY SHORT ON MANPOWER.
THE RECENT EXPEDITION MADE THAT ABUNDANTLY CLEAR.
WE NEED FRESH BLOOD LIKE THEM!
SO, XENOPHON, HERE'S MY FEEDBACK FROM THIS TEST RUN...
GOOD, GOOD.
SO... WE'LL END UP IN THE SURVEY CORPS FOR SURE?
...I THINK...

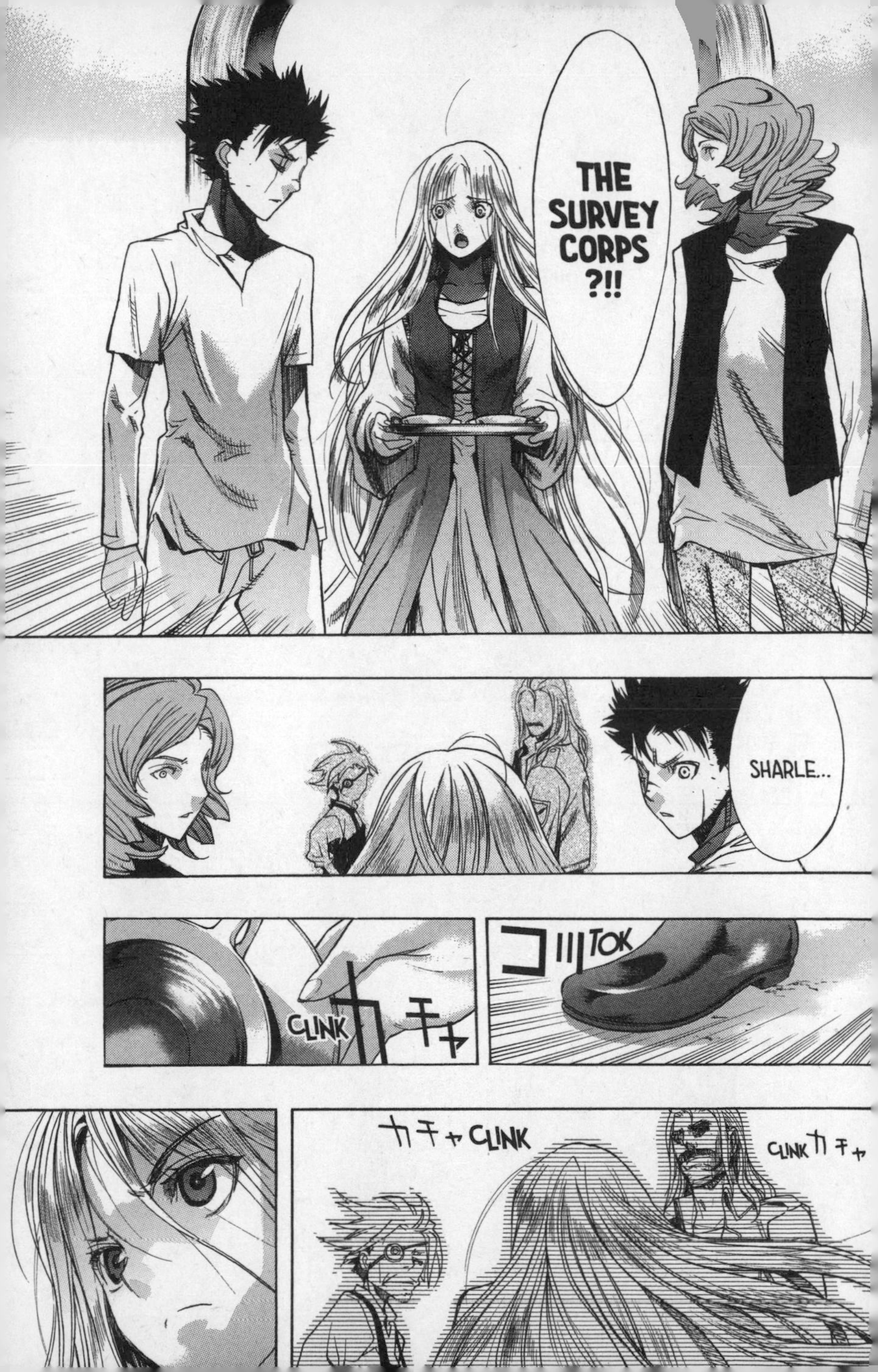
THE SURVEY CORPS ?!!
SHARLE...
TOK
CLINK カチャ
CLINK カチャ
カチャ CLINK

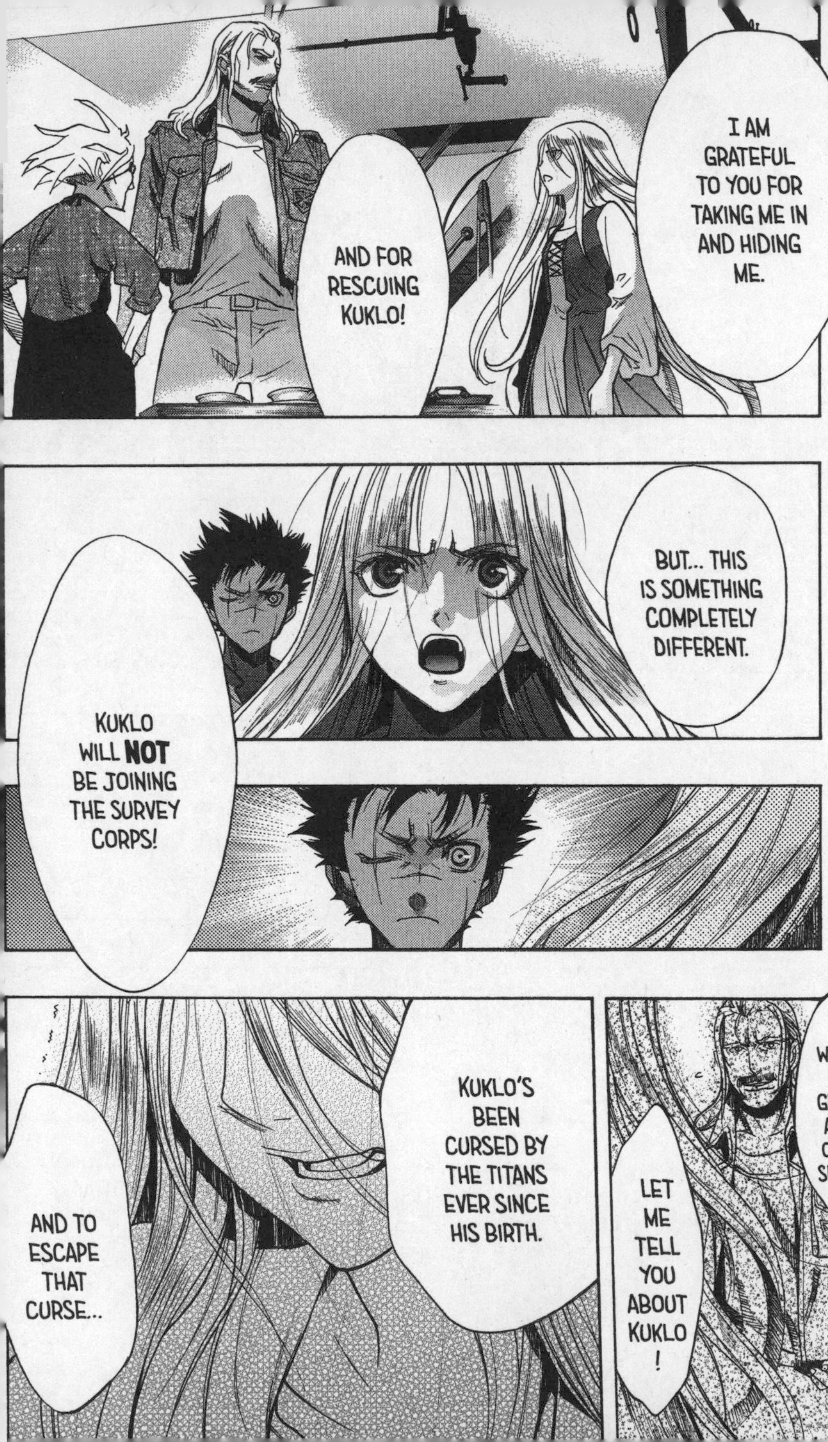
I AM GRATEFUL TO YOU FOR TAKING ME IN AND HIDING ME.
AND FOR RESCUING KUKLO!
BUT... THIS IS SOMETHING COMPLETELY DIFFERENT.
KUKLO WILL **NOT** BE JOINING THE SURVEY CORPS!
ER... WE HAVE BEEN GETTING AHEAD OF OUR SELVES—
LET ME TELL YOU ABOUT KUKLO!
KUKLO'S BEEN CURSED BY THE TITANS EVER SINCE HIS BIRTH.
AND TO ESCAPE THAT CURSE...

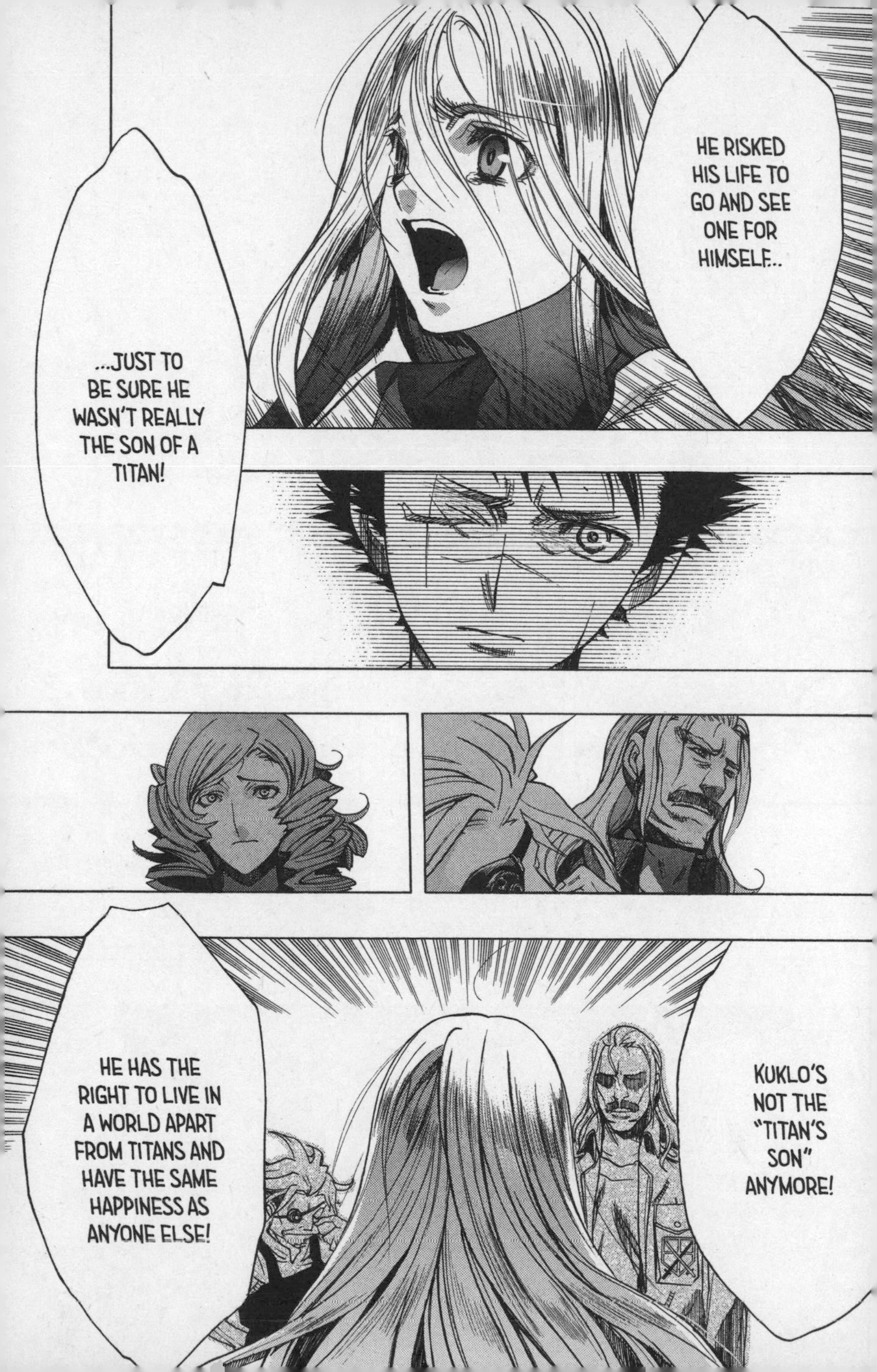
HE RISKED HIS LIFE TO GO AND SEE ONE FOR HIMSELF...
...JUST TO BE SURE HE WASN'T REALLY THE SON OF A TITAN!
KUKLO'S NOT THE "TITAN'S SON" ANYMORE!
HE HAS THE RIGHT TO LIVE IN A WORLD APART FROM TITANS AND HAVE THE SAME HAPPINESS AS ANYONE ELSE!

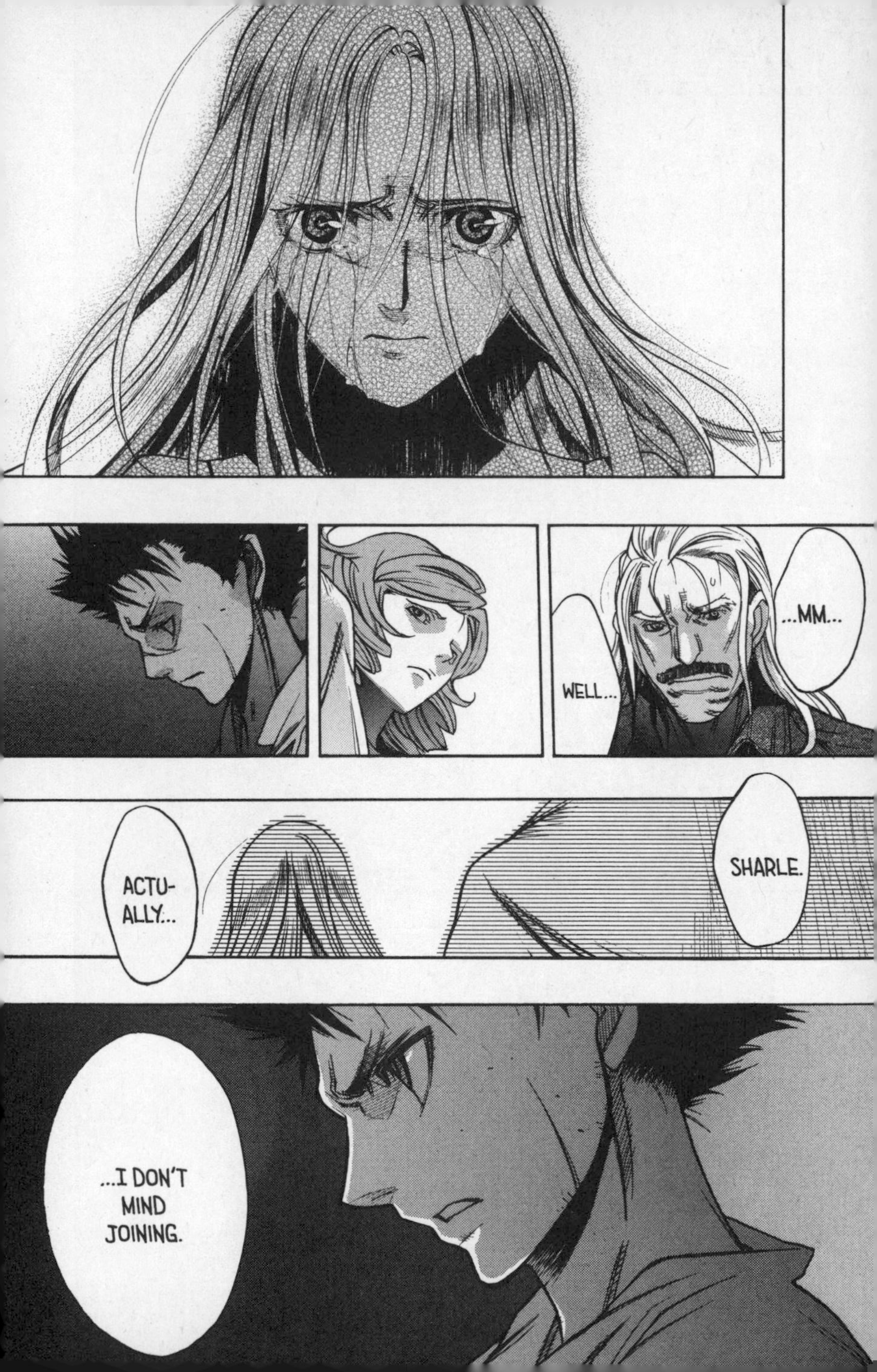
...MM...
WELL...
SHARLE.
ACTU-ALLY...
...I DON'T MIND JOINING.

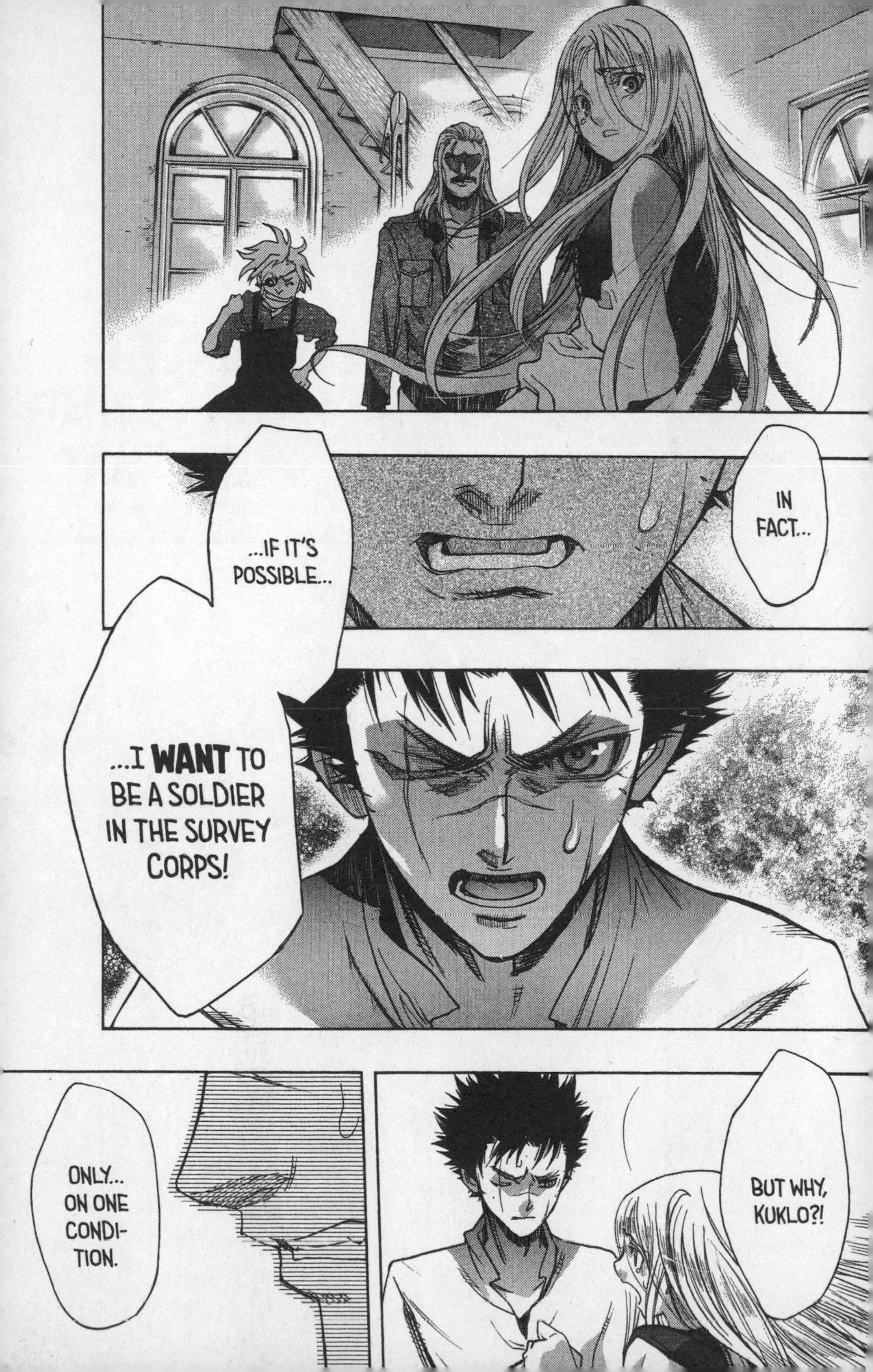
IN FACT...
...IF IT'S POSSIBLE...
...I **WANT** TO BE A SOLDIER IN THE SURVEY CORPS!
BUT WHY, KUKLO?!
ONLY... ON ONE CONDITION.

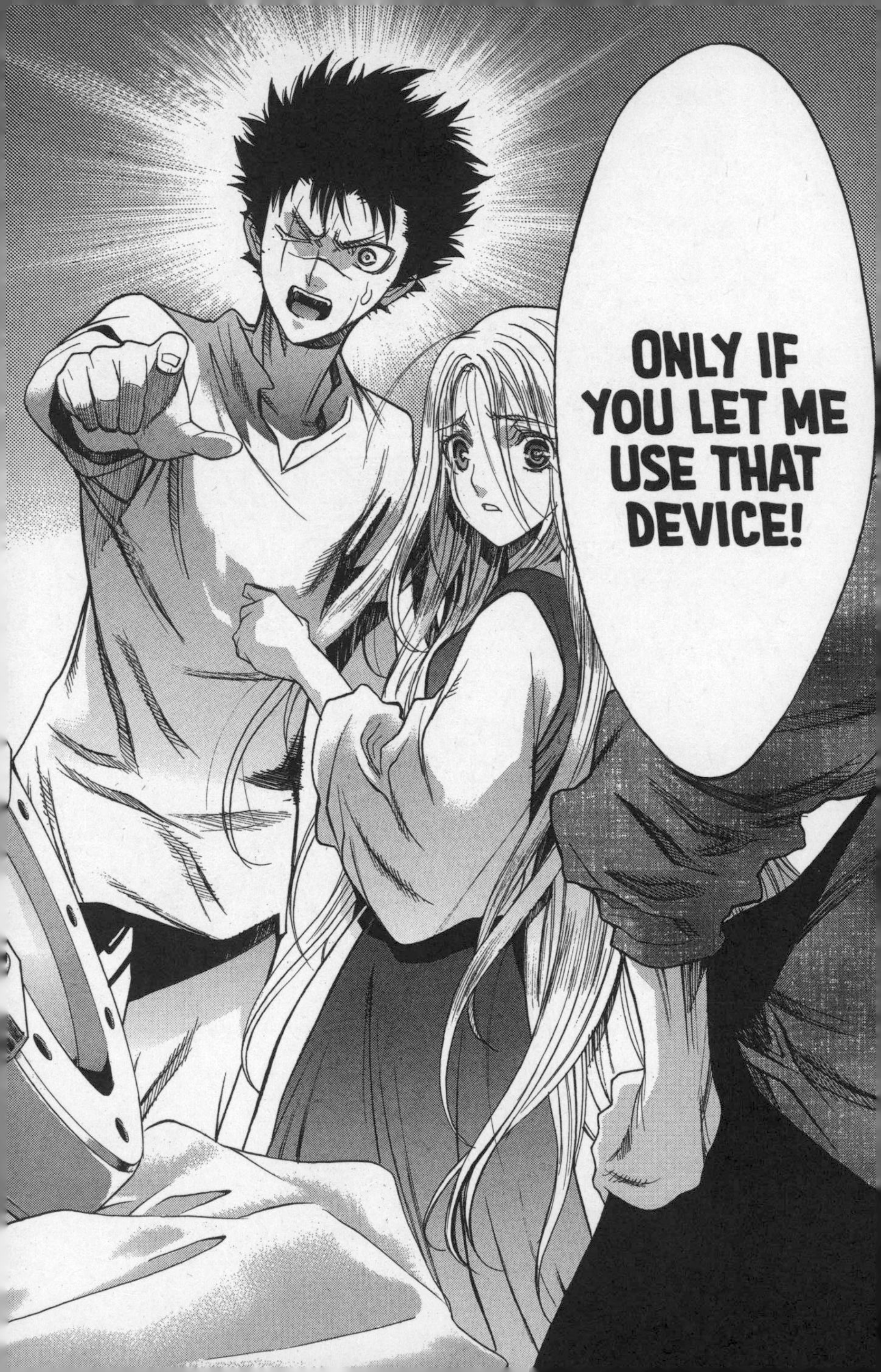
ONLY IF YOU LET ME USE THAT DEVICE!

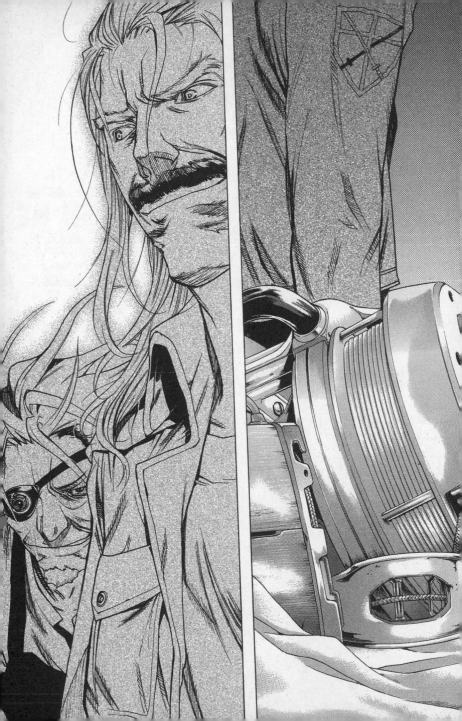

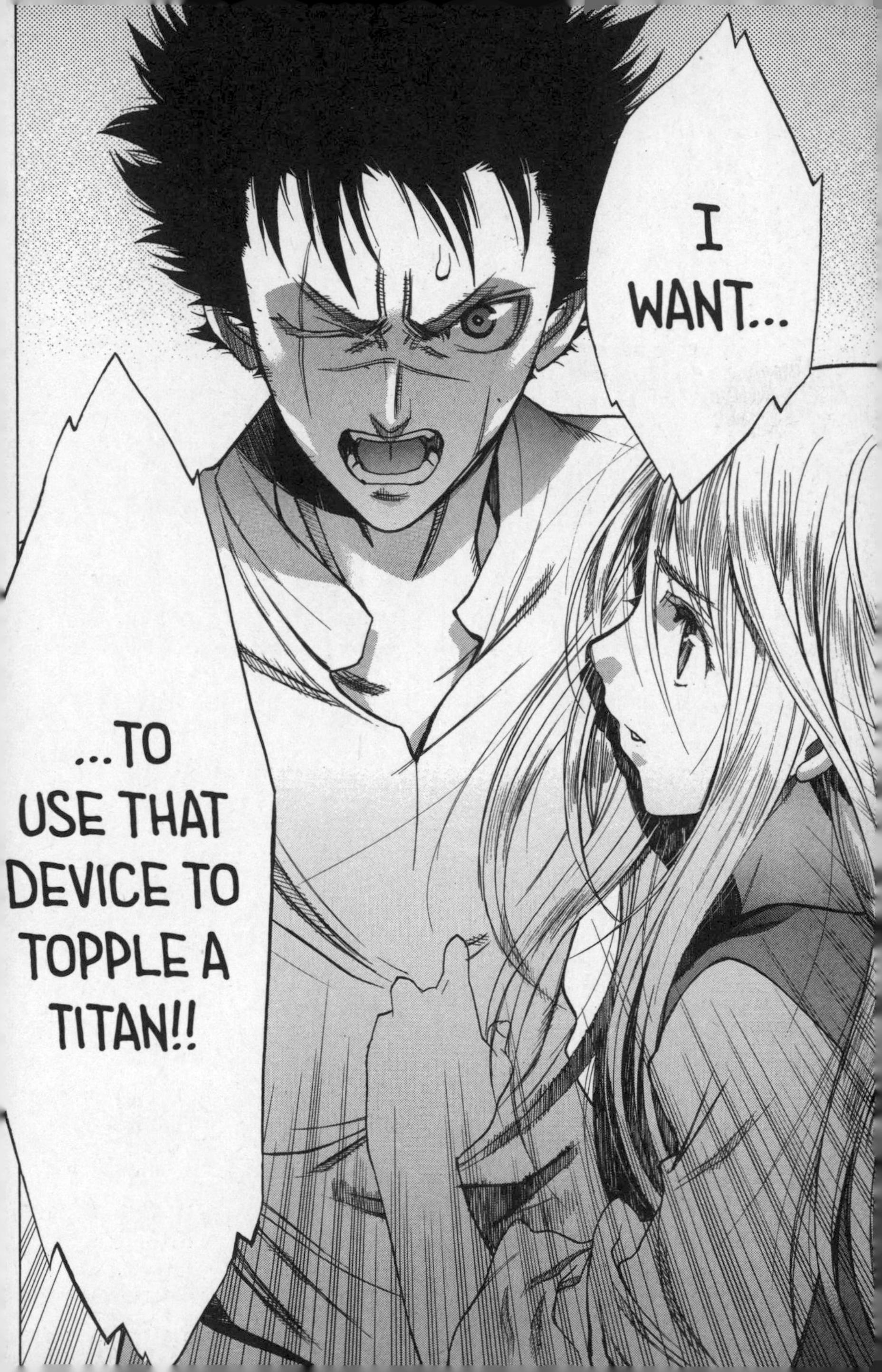
I WANT...
...TO USE THAT DEVICE TO TOPPLE A TITAN!!

Chapter 14: Visitors to the Industrial City · End

ATTACK on TITAN

BEFORE THE FALL

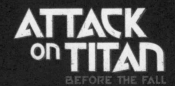

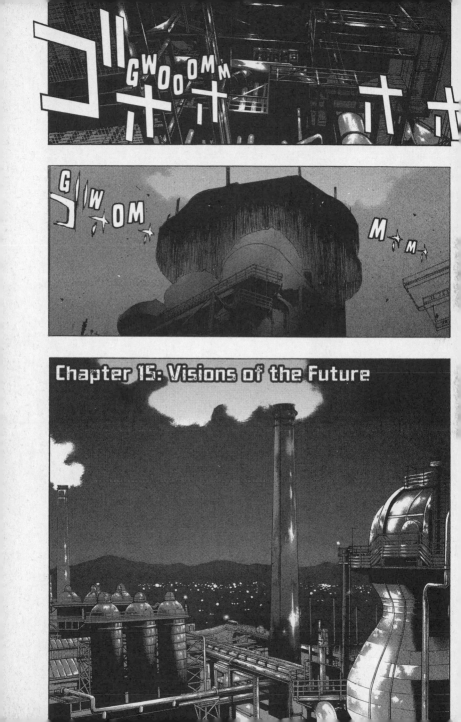

Chapter 15: Visions of the Future

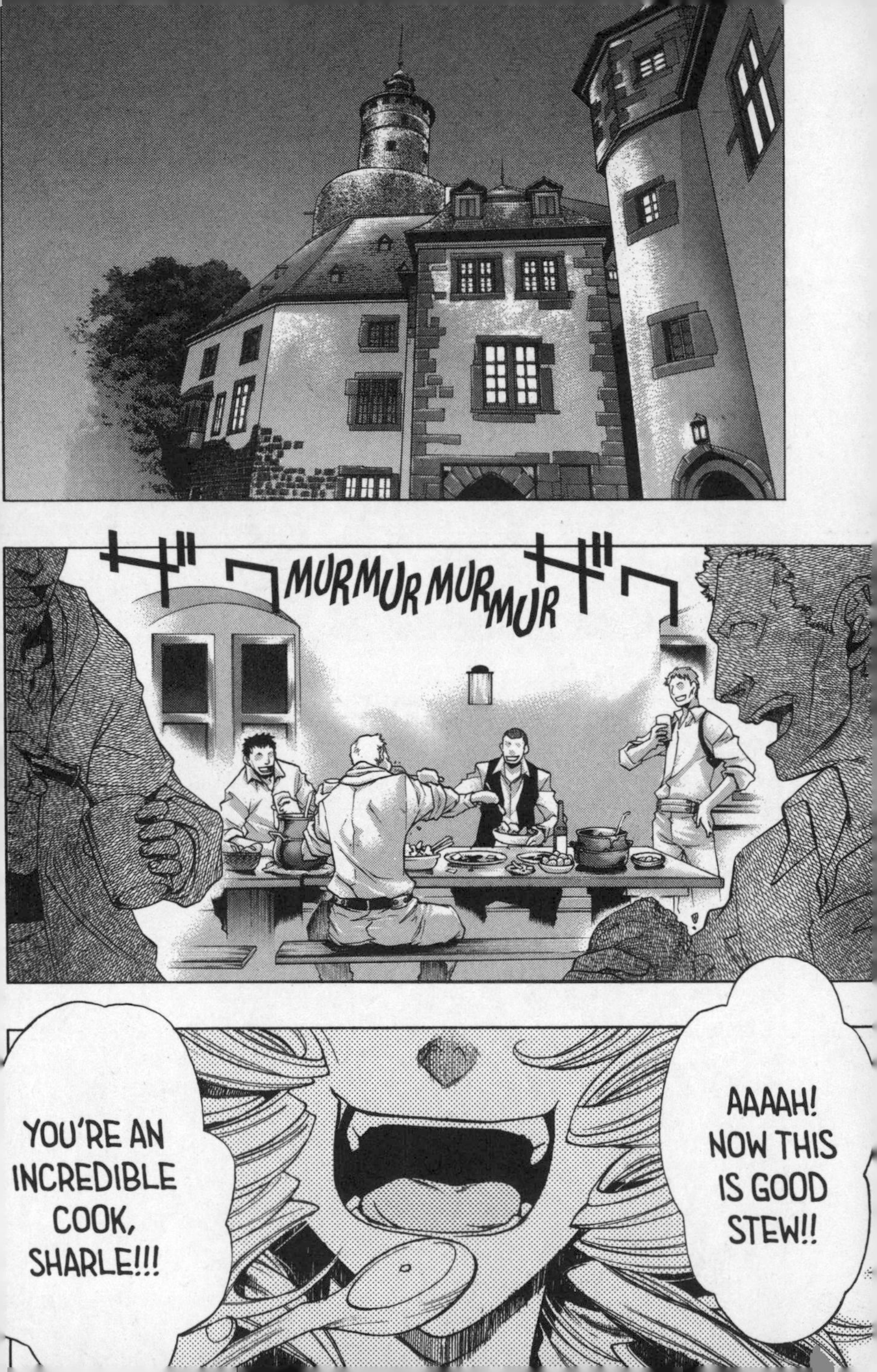
ザワ
MURMUR MURMUR
ザワ
AAAAH! NOW THIS IS GOOD STEW!!
YOU'RE AN INCREDIBLE COOK, SHARLE!!!

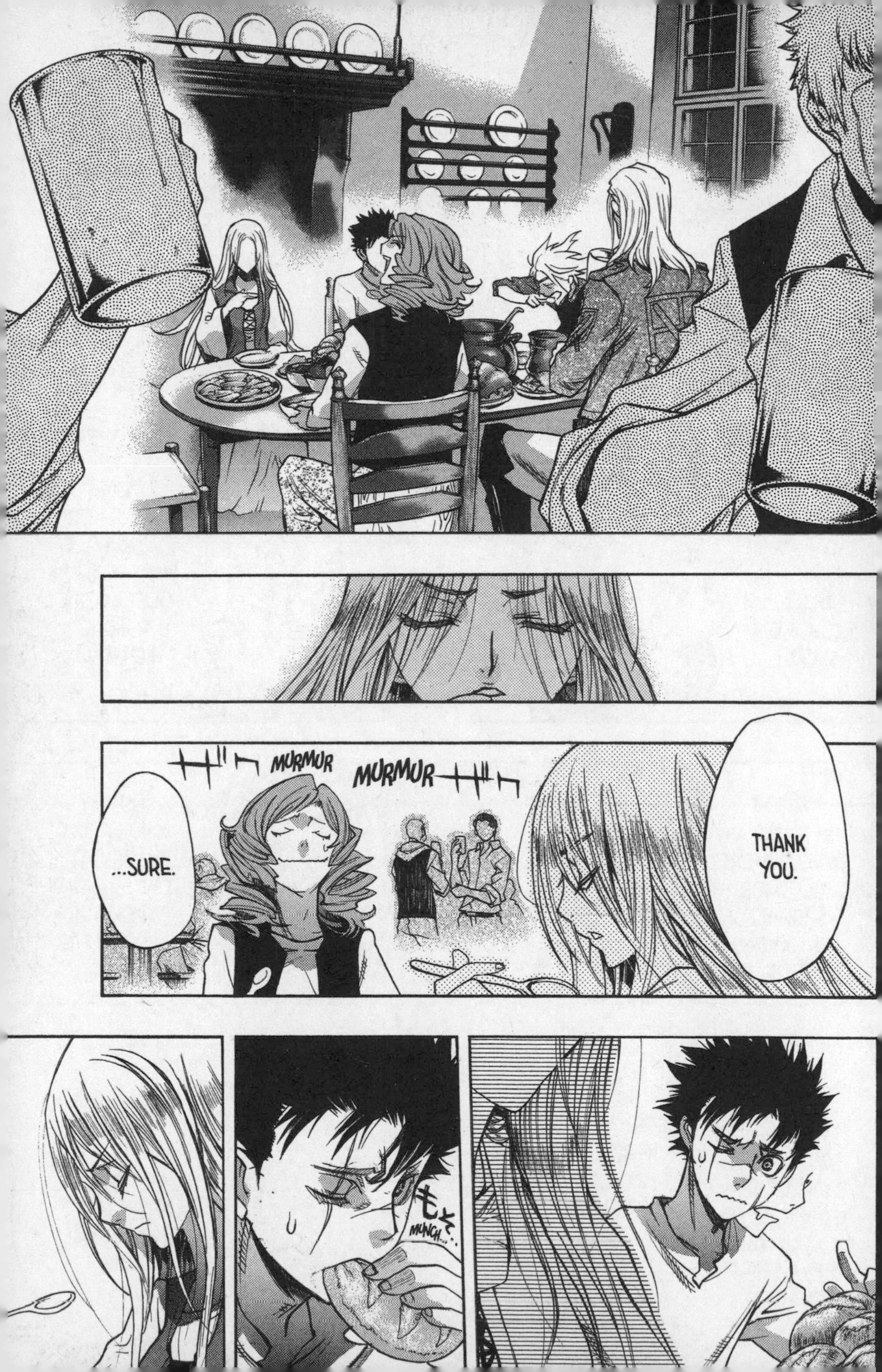
THANK YOU.
MURMUR
MURMUR
...SURE.
MUNCH...

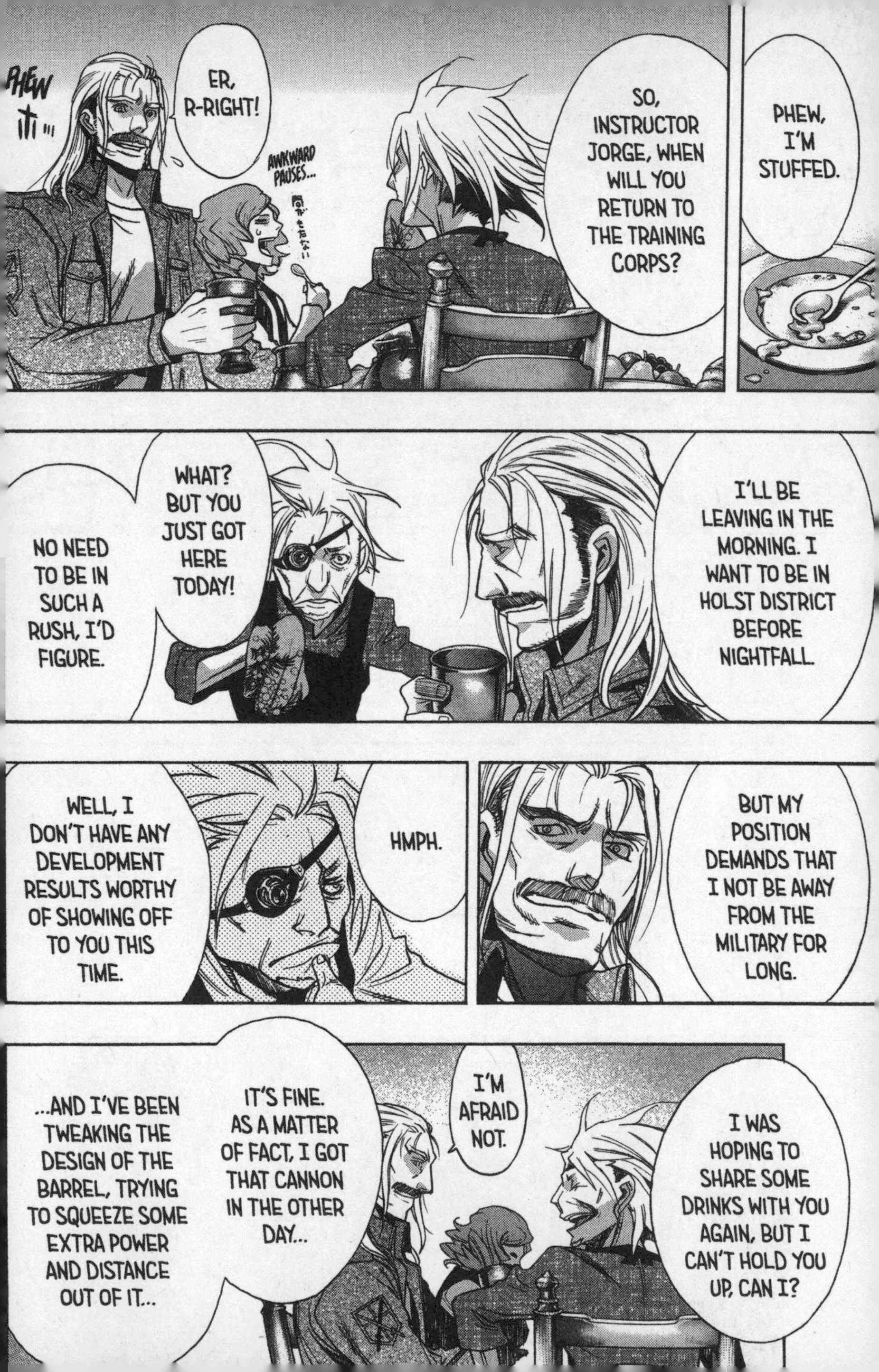
PHEW, I'M STUFFED.
SO, INSTRUCTOR JORGE, WHEN WILL YOU RETURN TO THE TRAINING CORPS?
ER, R-RIGHT!
PHEW
AWKWARD PAUSES...
間がもたない
I'LL BE LEAVING IN THE MORNING. I WANT TO BE IN HOLST DISTRICT BEFORE NIGHTFALL.
WHAT? BUT YOU JUST GOT HERE TODAY!
NO NEED TO BE IN SUCH A RUSH, I'D FIGURE.
BUT MY POSITION DEMANDS THAT I NOT BE AWAY FROM THE MILITARY FOR LONG.
HMPH.
WELL, I DON'T HAVE ANY DEVELOPMENT RESULTS WORTHY OF SHOWING OFF TO YOU THIS TIME.
I WAS HOPING TO SHARE SOME DRINKS WITH YOU AGAIN, BUT I CAN'T HOLD YOU UP, CAN I?
I'M AFRAID NOT.
IT'S FINE. AS A MATTER OF FACT, I GOT THAT CANNON IN THE OTHER DAY...
...AND I'VE BEEN TWEAKING THE DESIGN OF THE BARREL, TRYING TO SQUEEZE SOME EXTRA POWER AND DISTANCE OUT OF IT...

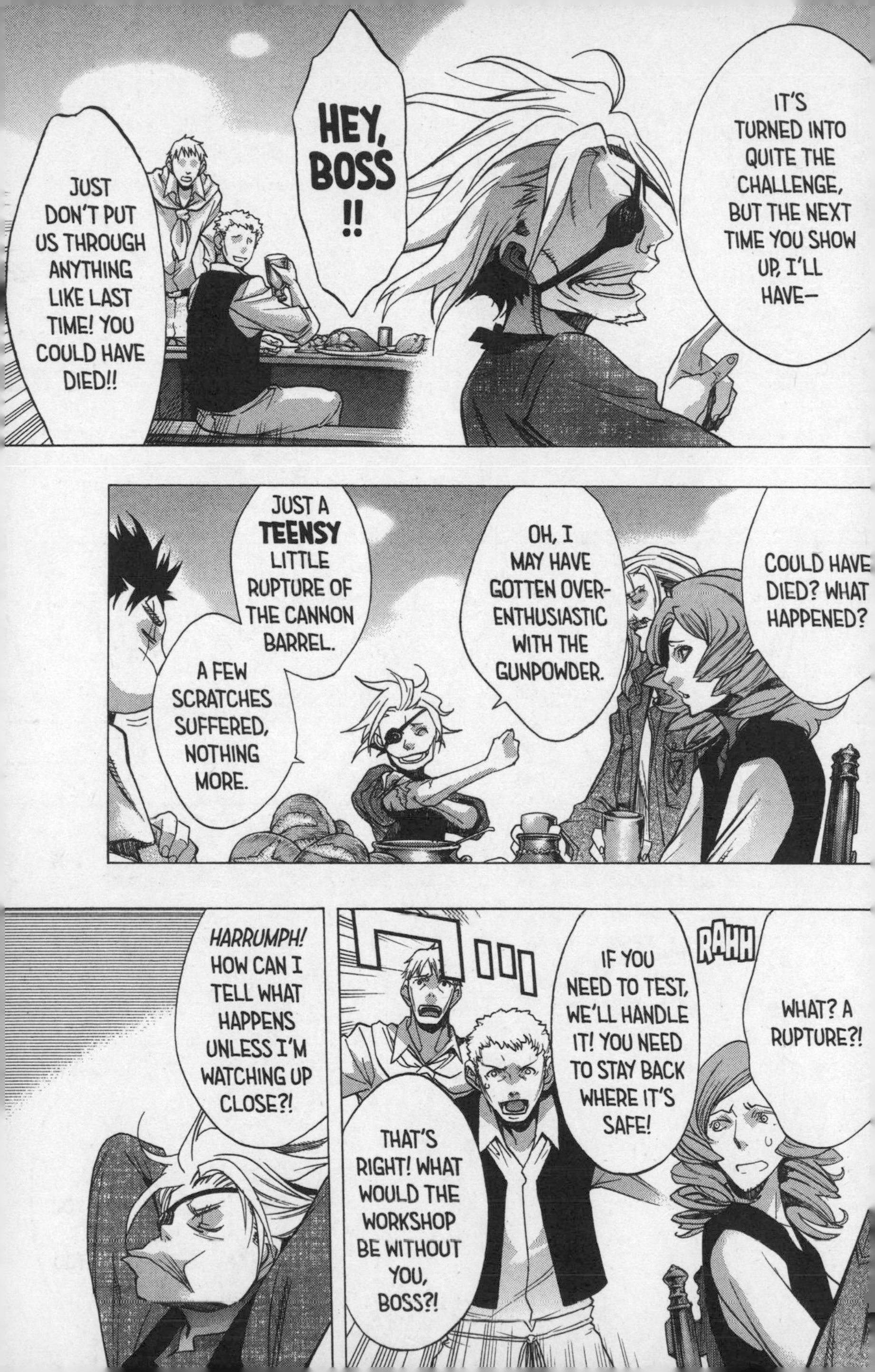
IT'S TURNED INTO QUITE THE CHALLENGE, BUT THE NEXT TIME YOU SHOW UP, I'LL HAVE—
HEY, BOSS!!
JUST DON'T PUT US THROUGH ANYTHING LIKE LAST TIME! YOU COULD HAVE DIED!!
COULD HAVE DIED? WHAT HAPPENED?
OH, I MAY HAVE GOTTEN OVER-ENTHUSIASTIC WITH THE GUNPOWDER.
JUST A **TEENSY** LITTLE RUPTURE OF THE CANNON BARREL.
A FEW SCRATCHES SUFFERED, NOTHING MORE.
WHAT? A RUPTURE?!
RAHH
IF YOU NEED TO TEST, WE'LL HANDLE IT! YOU NEED TO STAY BACK WHERE IT'S SAFE!
THAT'S RIGHT! WHAT WOULD THE WORKSHOP BE WITHOUT YOU, BOSS?!
HARRUMPH! HOW CAN I TELL WHAT HAPPENS UNLESS I'M WATCHING UP CLOSE?!

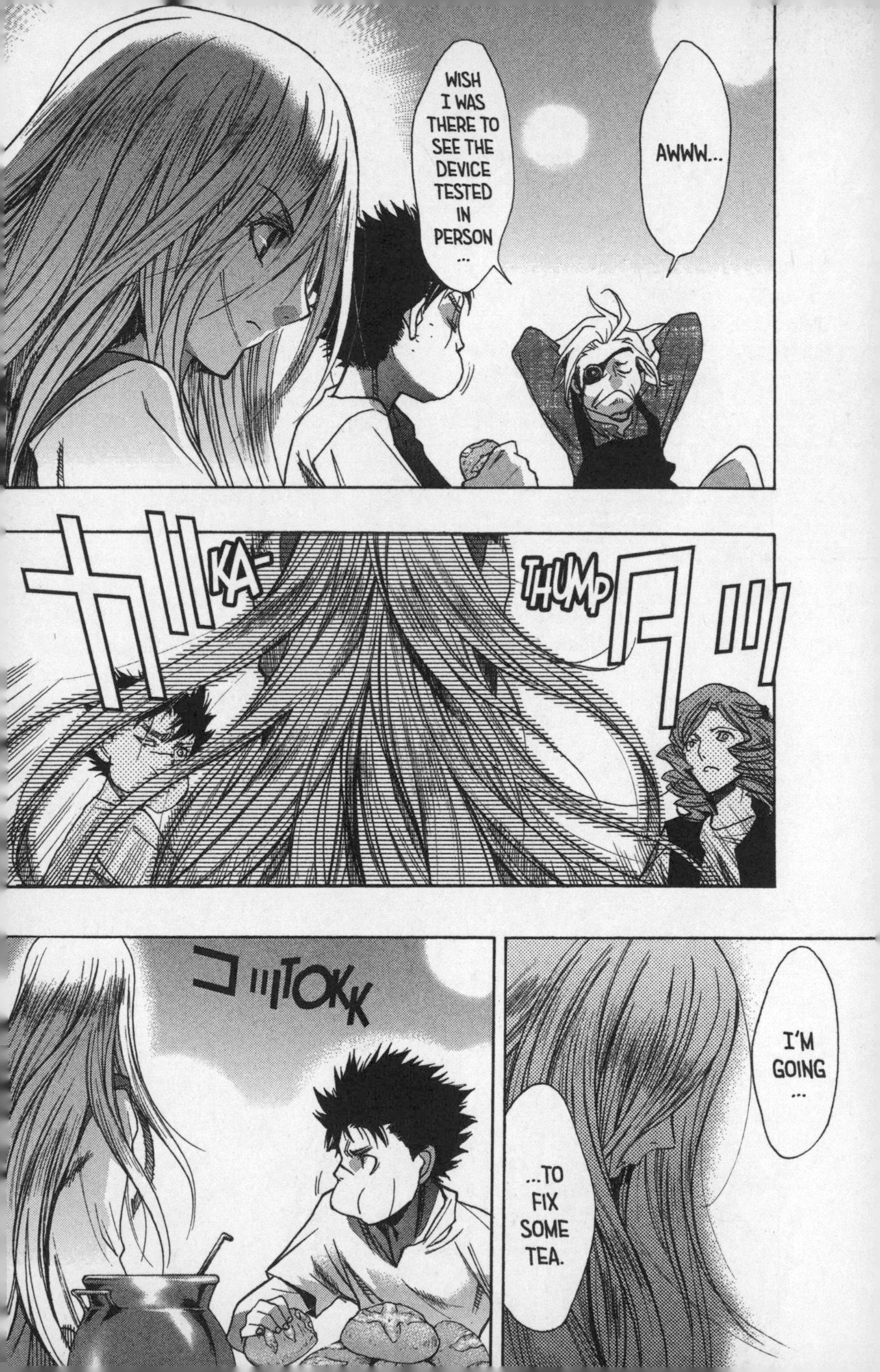
AWWW...
WISH I WAS THERE TO SEE THE DEVICE TESTED IN PERSON ...
タッ THUMP
カリ KA-
I'M GOING ...
...TO FIX SOME TEA.
コッ TOKK

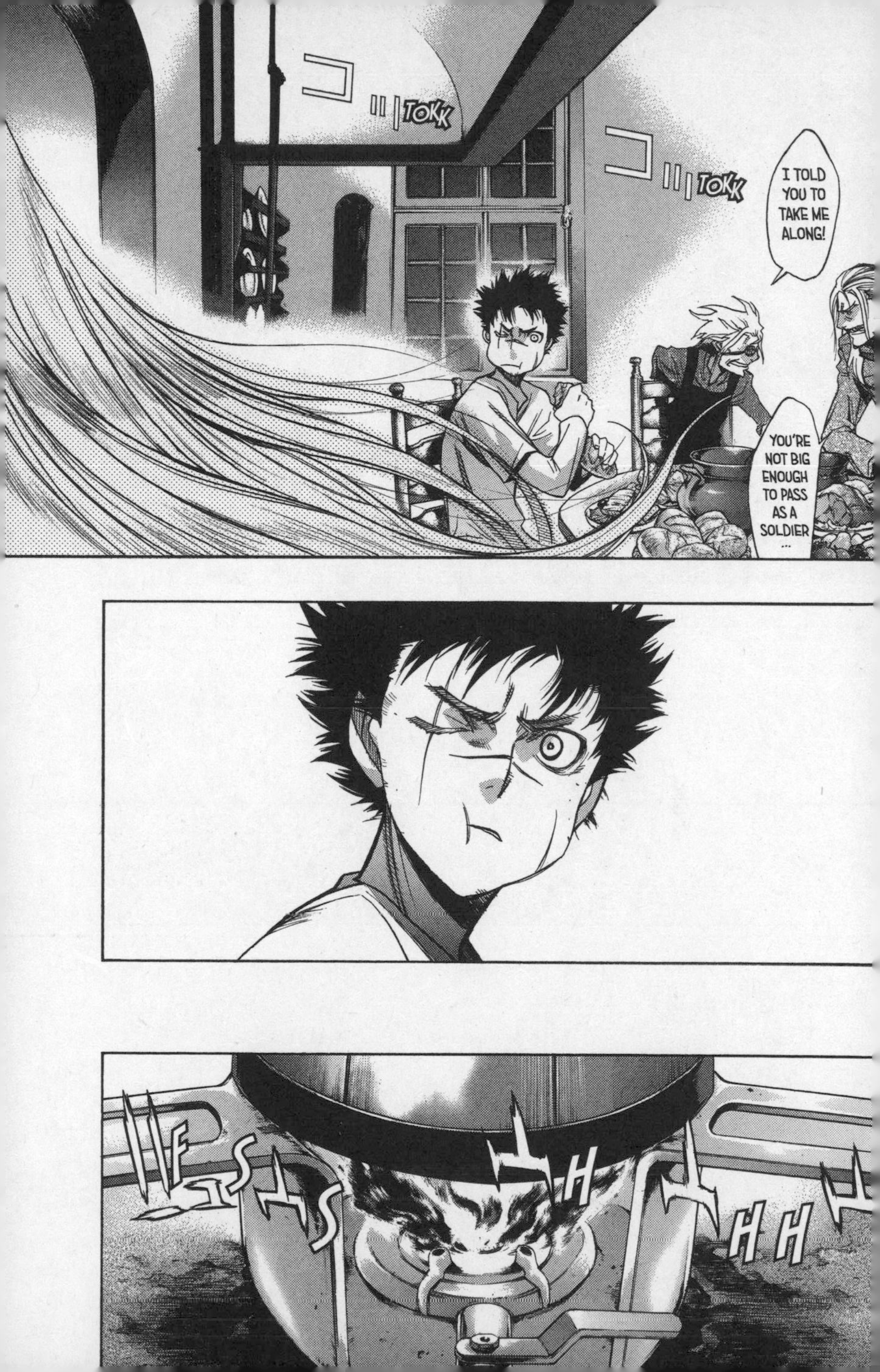
I TOLD YOU TO TAKE ME ALONG!
TOKK
TOKK
YOU'RE NOT BIG ENOUGH TO PASS AS A SOLDIER ...
FSSSHHH

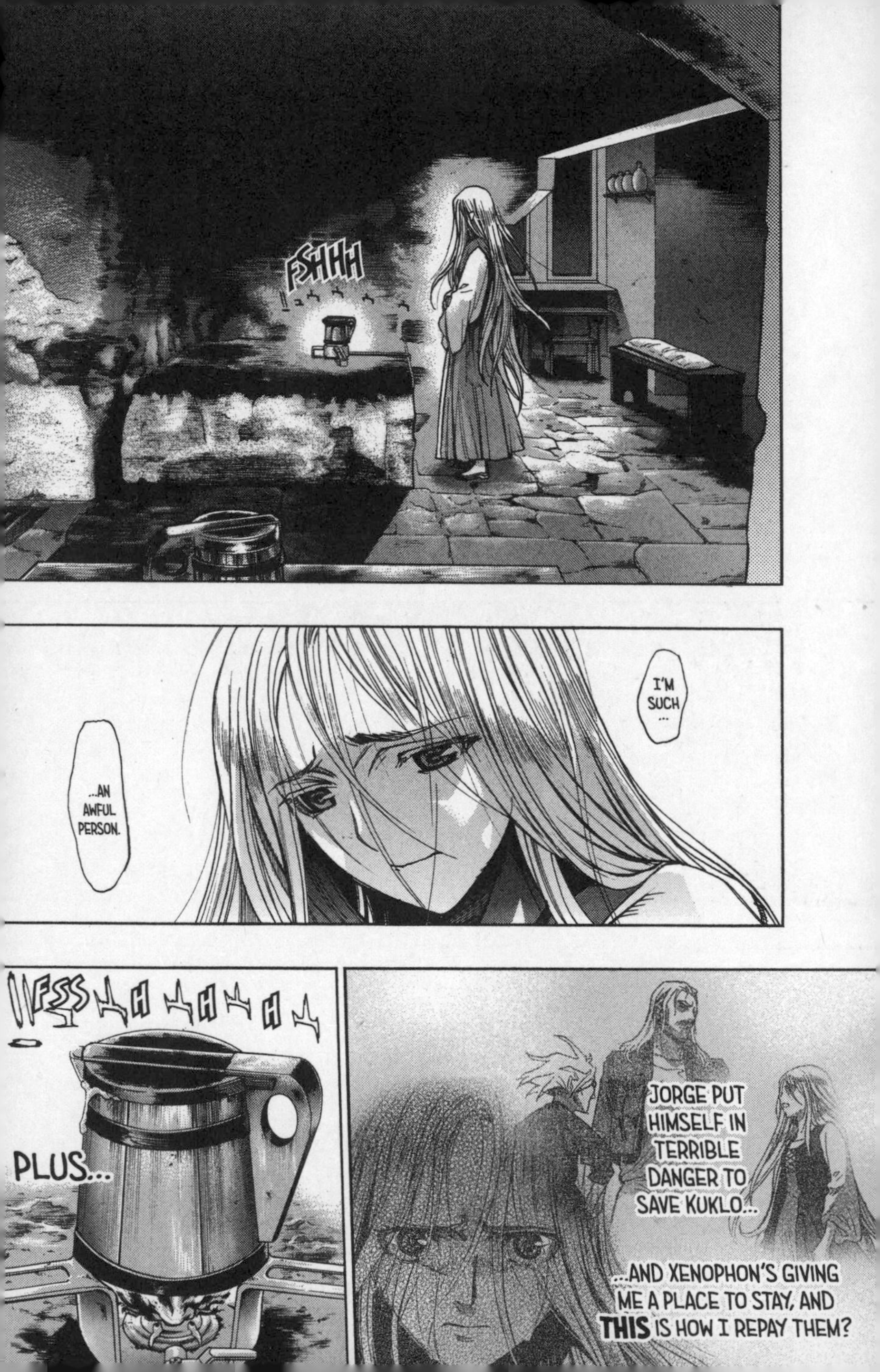
FSHHH
I'M SUCH...
...AN AWFUL PERSON.
JORGE PUT HIMSELF IN TERRIBLE DANGER TO SAVE KUKLO...
...AND XENOPHON'S GIVING ME A PLACE TO STAY, AND THIS IS HOW I REPAY THEM?
FSSHHHH
PLUS...

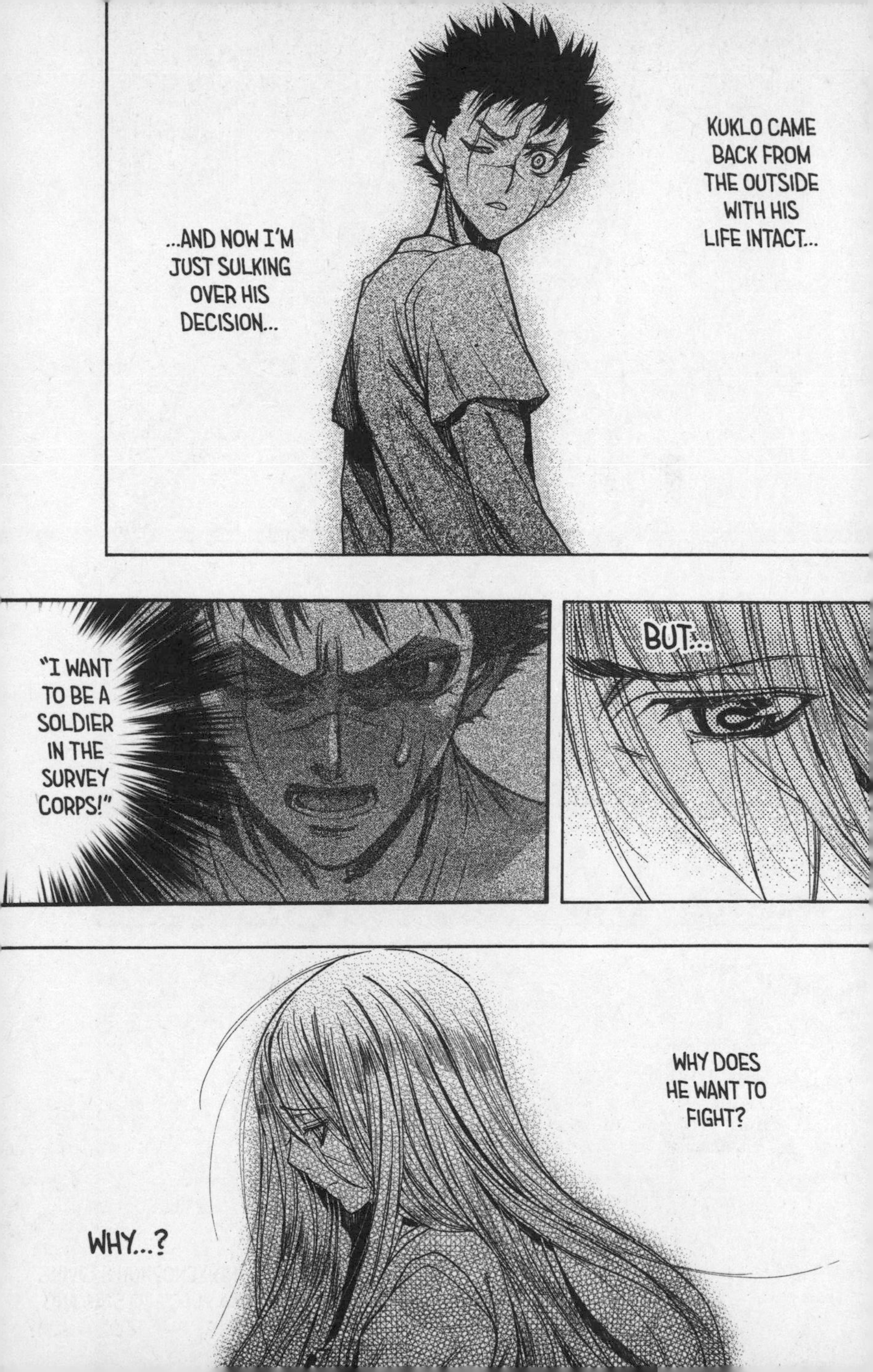
KUKLO CAME BACK FROM THE OUTSIDE WITH HIS LIFE INTACT...
...AND NOW I'M JUST SULKING OVER HIS DECISION...
BUT...
"I WANT TO BE A SOLDIER IN THE SURVEY CORPS!"
WHY DOES HE WANT TO FIGHT?
WHY...?

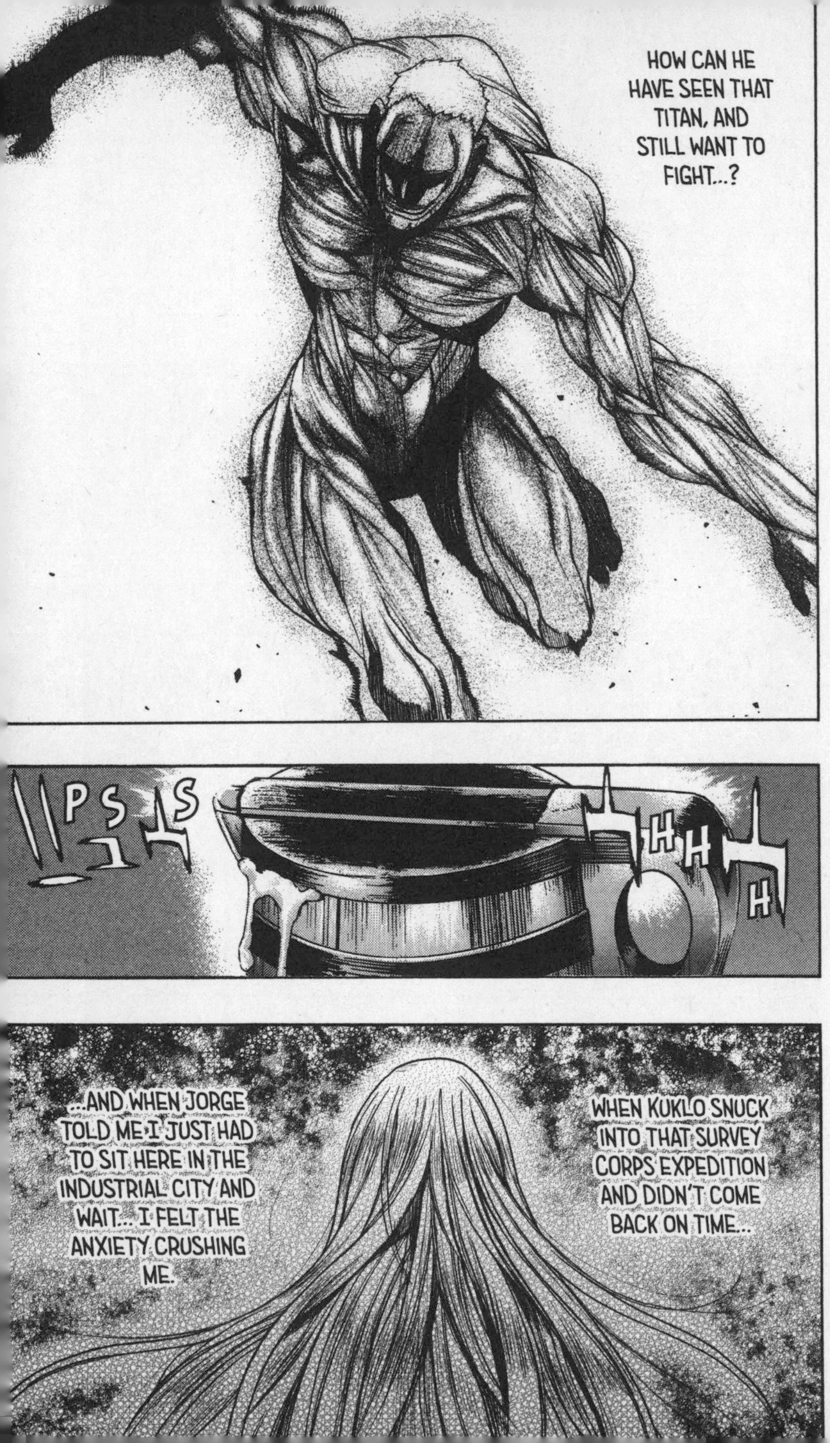
HOW CAN HE HAVE SEEN THAT TITAN, AND STILL WANT TO FIGHT...?
PSSHHHH
WHEN KUKLO SNUCK INTO THAT SURVEY CORPS EXPEDITION AND DIDN'T COME BACK ON TIME...
...AND WHEN JORGE TOLD ME I JUST HAD TO SIT HERE IN THE INDUSTRIAL CITY AND WAIT... I FELT THE ANXIETY CRUSHING ME.

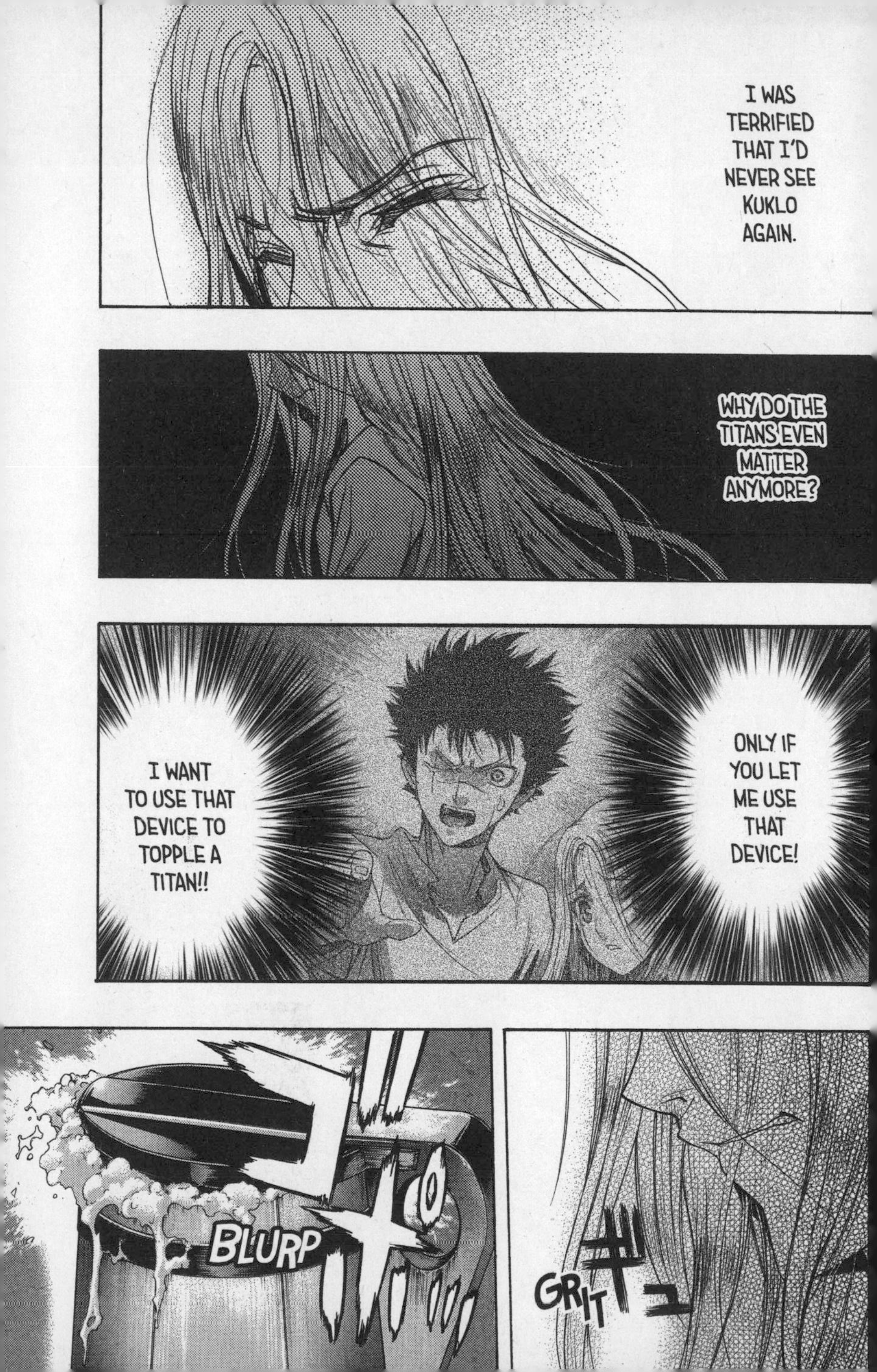
I WAS TERRIFIED THAT I'D NEVER SEE KUKLO AGAIN.
WHY DO THE TITANS EVEN MATTER ANYMORE?
ONLY IF YOU LET ME USE THAT DEVICE!
I WANT TO USE THAT DEVICE TO TOPPLE A TITAN!!
GRIT
BLURP

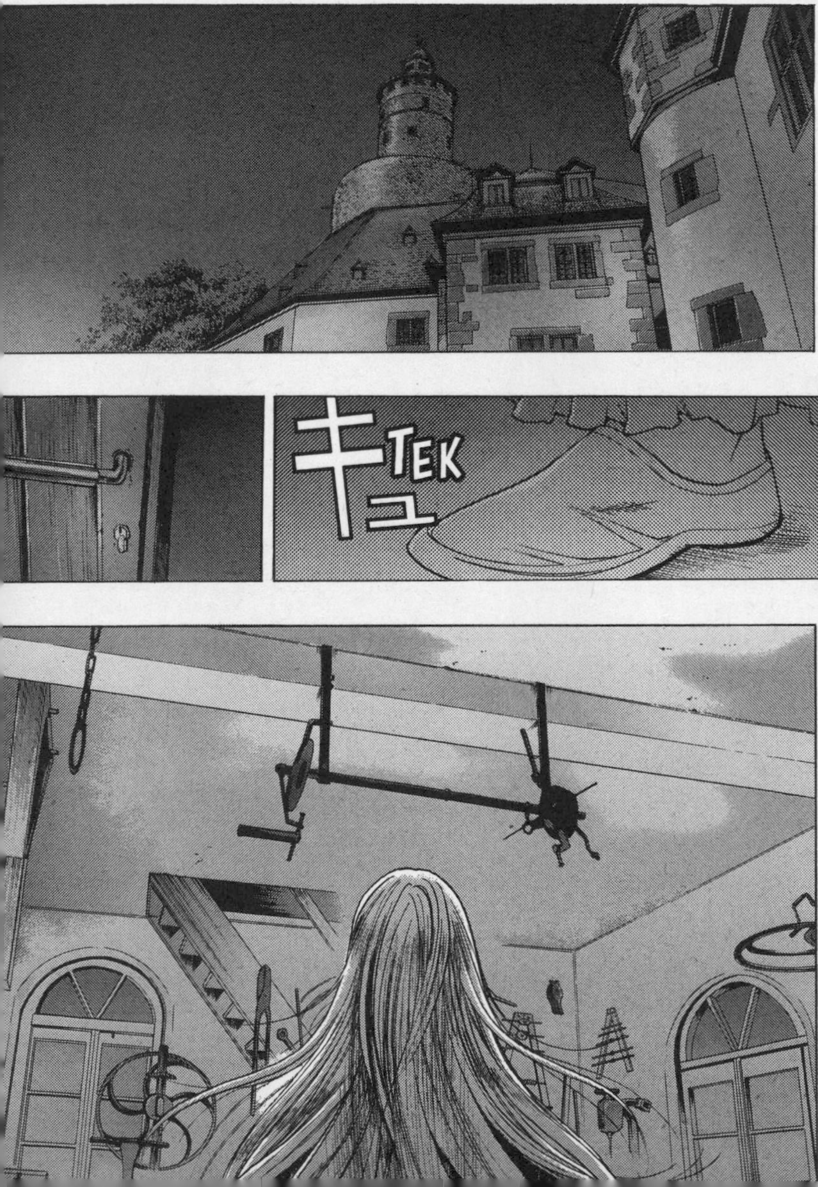
キュ
TEK

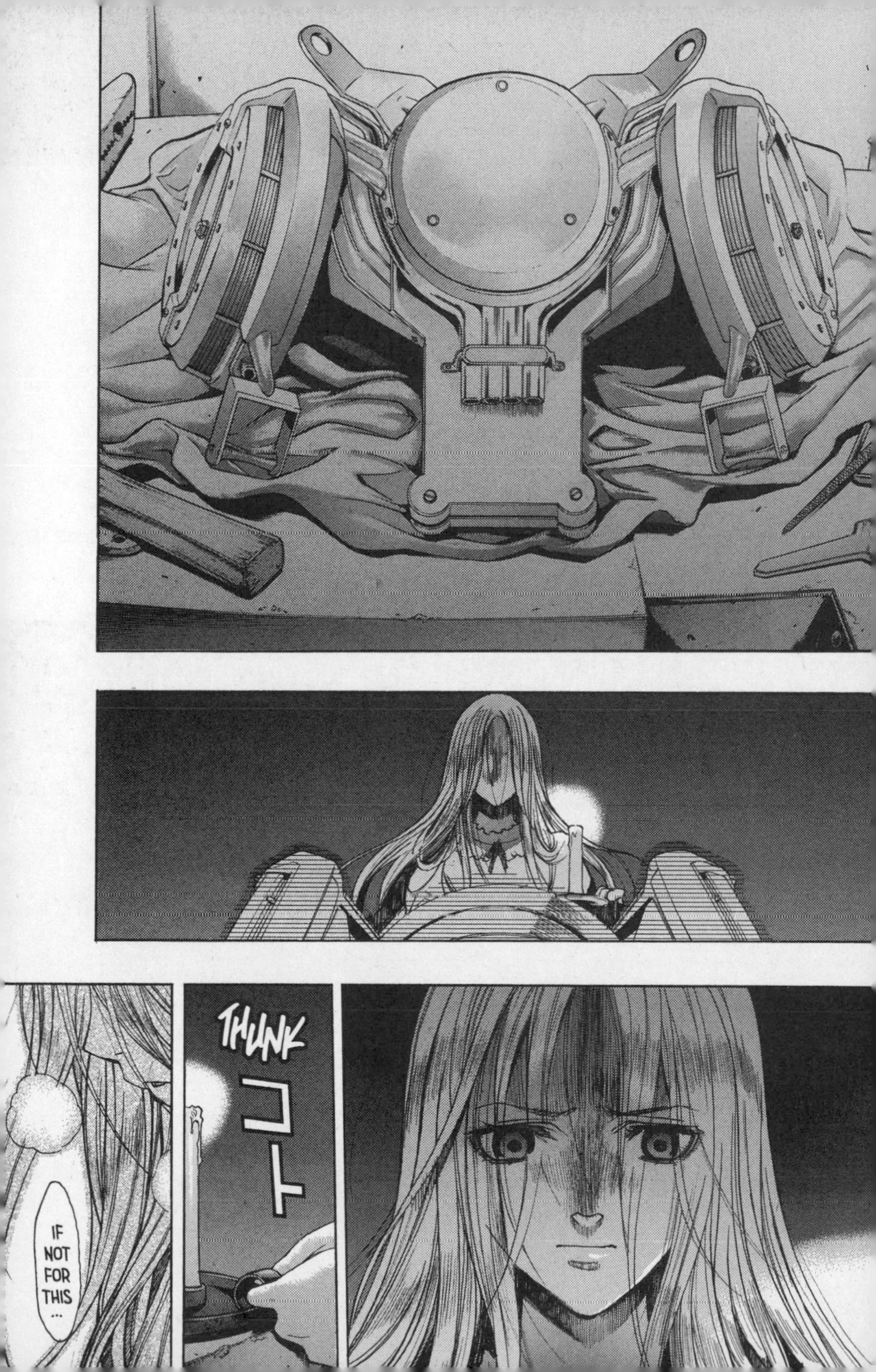
THUNK
コト
IF NOT FOR THIS ...

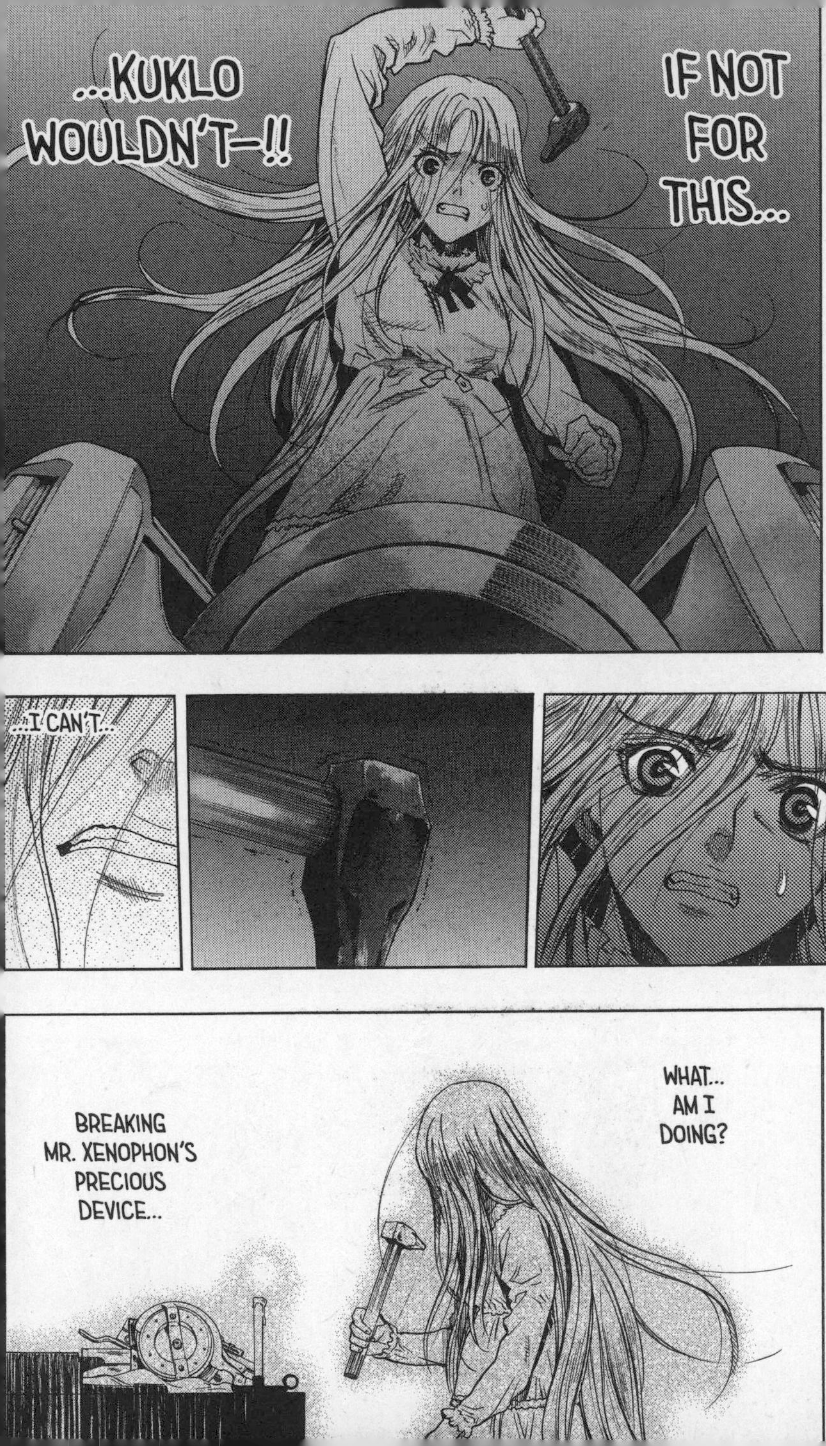
IF NOT FOR THIS...
...KUKLO WOULDN'T—!!
...I CAN'T...
WHAT... AM I DOING?
BREAKING MR. XENOPHON'S PRECIOUS DEVICE...

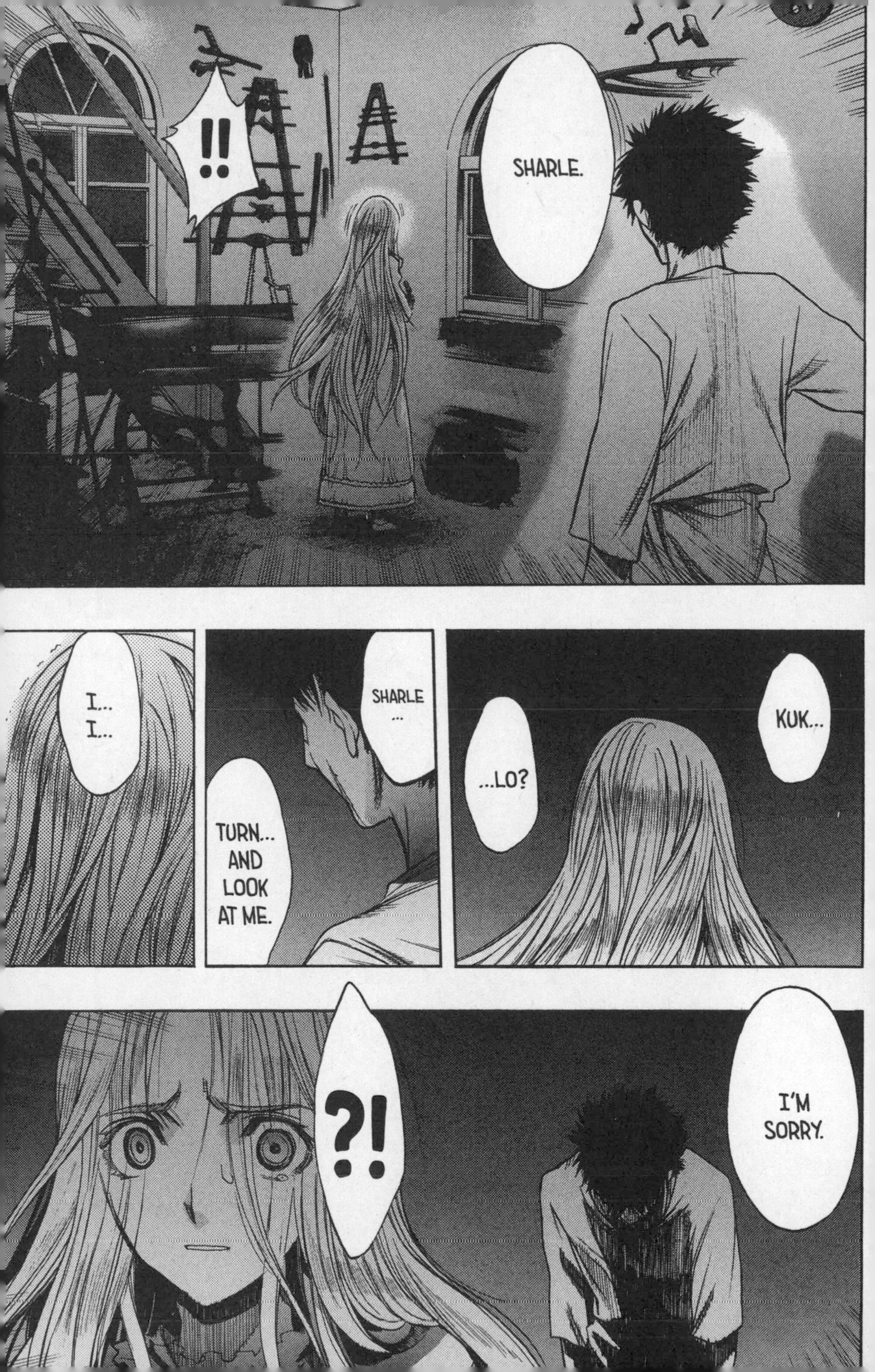
SHARLE.
!!
KUK...
...LO?
SHARLE ...
TURN... AND LOOK AT ME.
I... I...
I'M SORRY.
?!

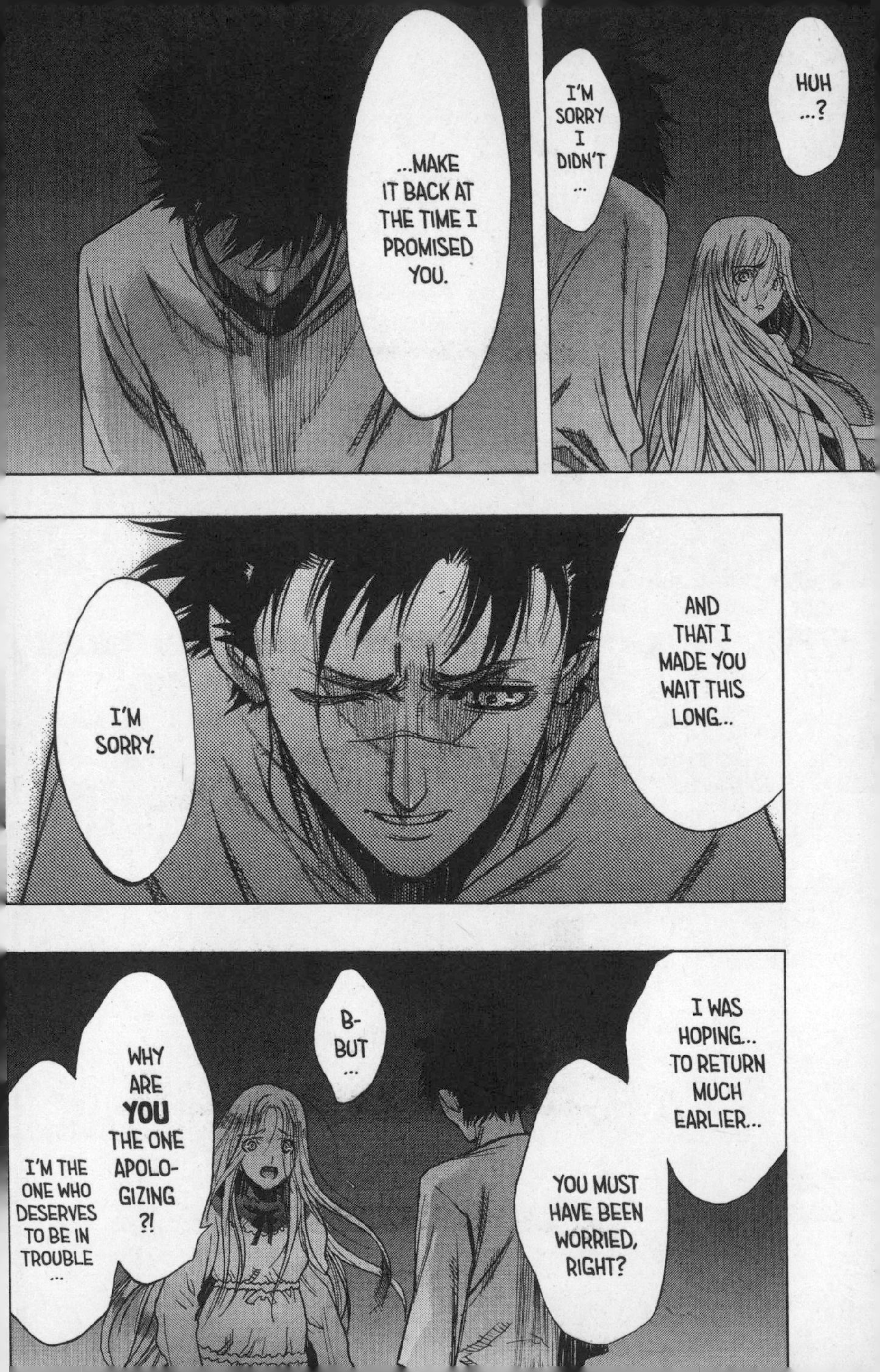
HUH ...?
I'M SORRY I DIDN'T ...
...MAKE IT BACK AT THE TIME I PROMISED YOU.
AND THAT I MADE YOU WAIT THIS LONG...
I'M SORRY.
I WAS HOPING... TO RETURN MUCH EARLIER...
YOU MUST HAVE BEEN WORRIED, RIGHT?
B-BUT ...
WHY ARE **YOU** THE ONE APOLOGIZING ?!
I'M THE ONE WHO DESERVES TO BE IN TROUBLE ...

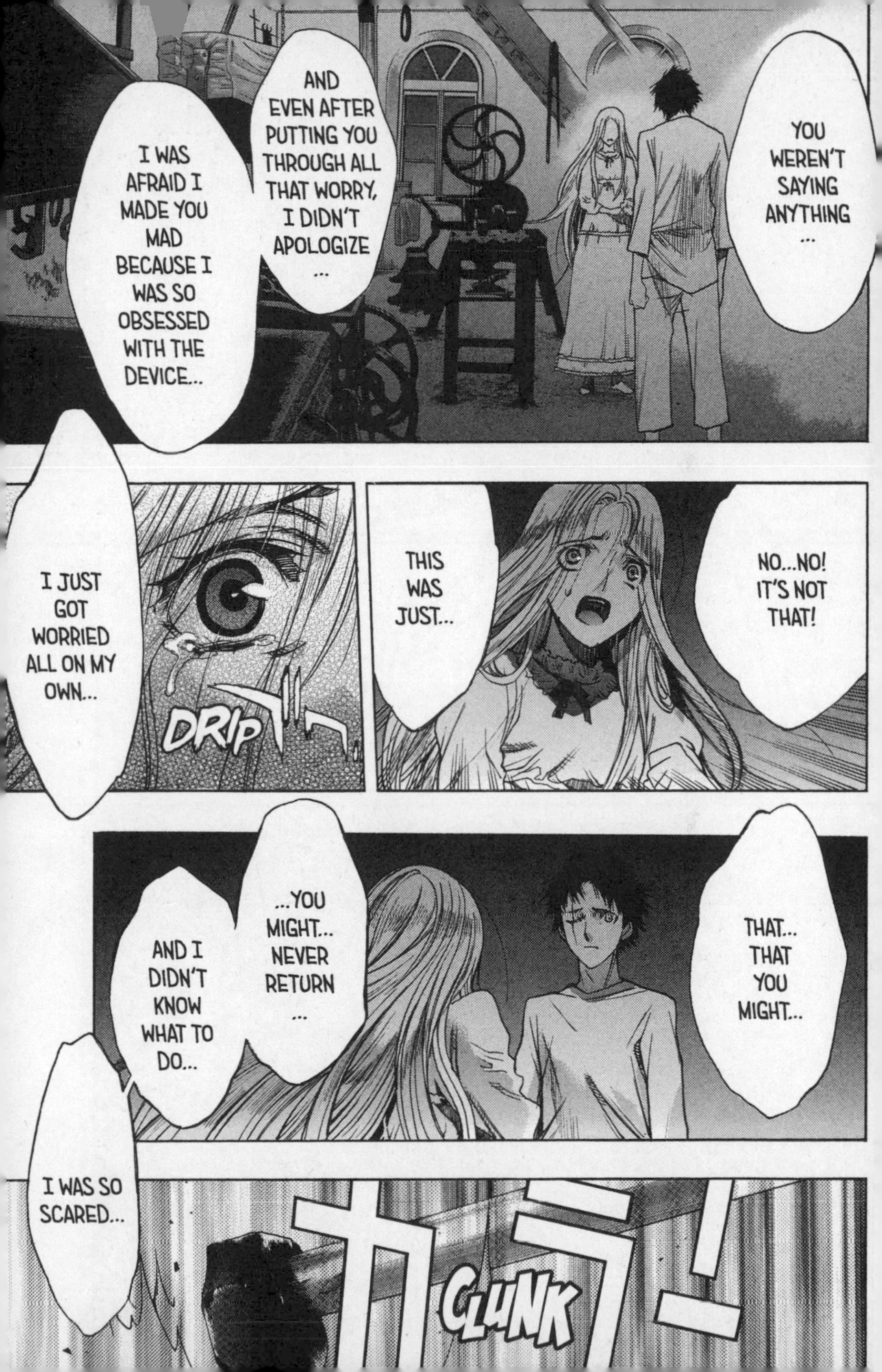
YOU WEREN'T SAYING ANYTHING ...
AND EVEN AFTER PUTTING YOU THROUGH ALL THAT WORRY, I DIDN'T APOLOGIZE ...
I WAS AFRAID I MADE YOU MAD BECAUSE I WAS SO OBSESSED WITH THE DEVICE...
NO...NO! IT'S NOT THAT!
THIS WAS JUST...
I JUST GOT WORRIED ALL ON MY OWN...
DRIP
THAT... THAT YOU MIGHT...
...YOU MIGHT... NEVER RETURN ...
AND I DIDN'T KNOW WHAT TO DO...
I WAS SO SCARED...
CLUNK

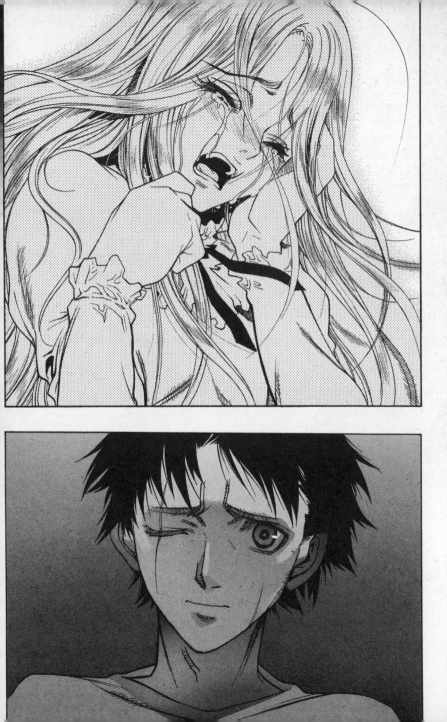

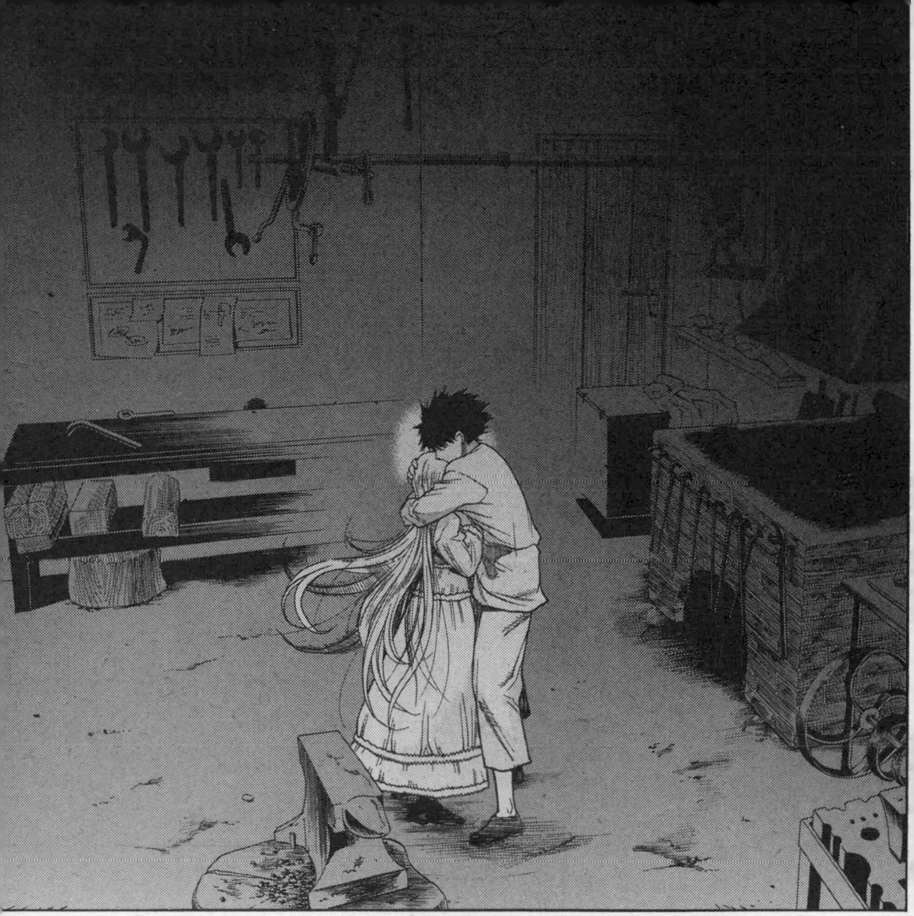

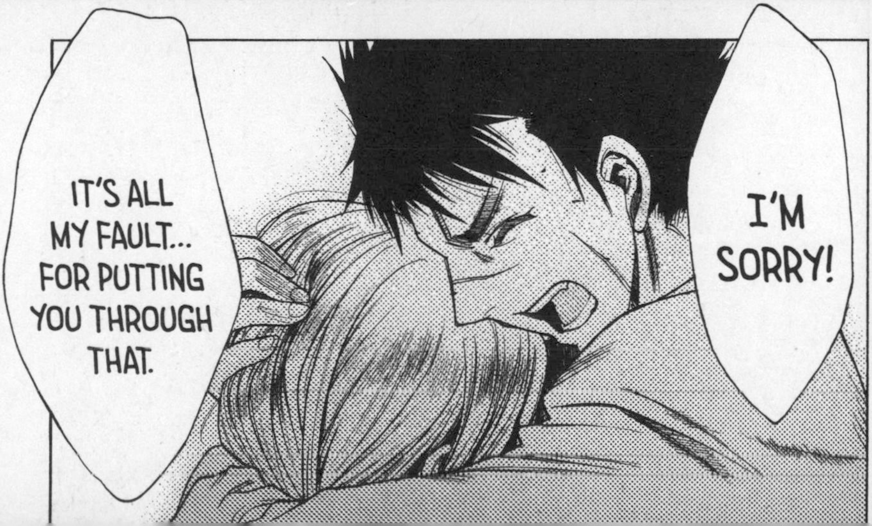
I'M SORRY!
IT'S ALL MY FAULT... FOR PUTTING YOU THROUGH THAT.

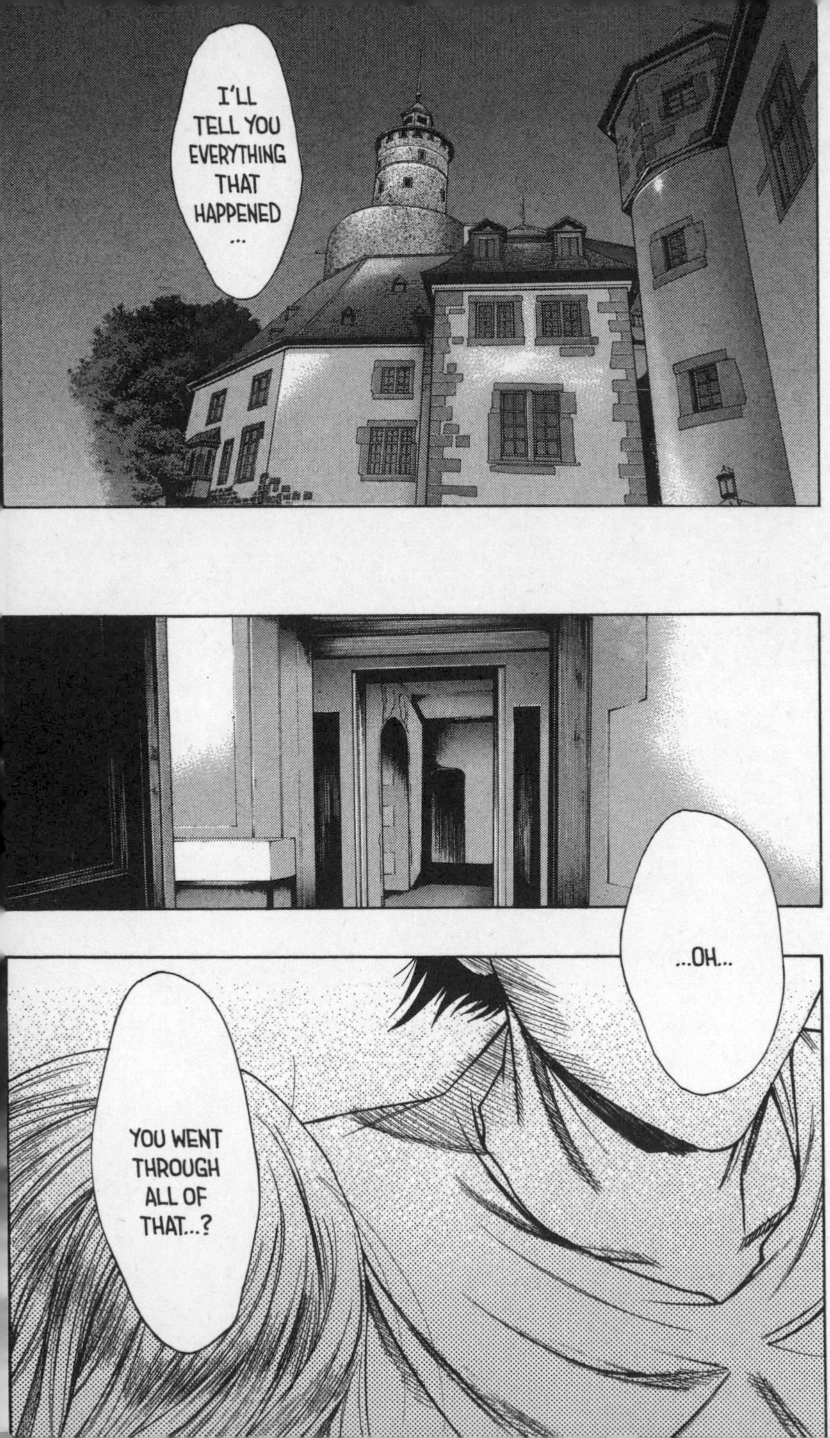
I'LL TELL YOU EVERYTHING THAT HAPPENED ...
...OH...
YOU WENT THROUGH ALL OF THAT...?

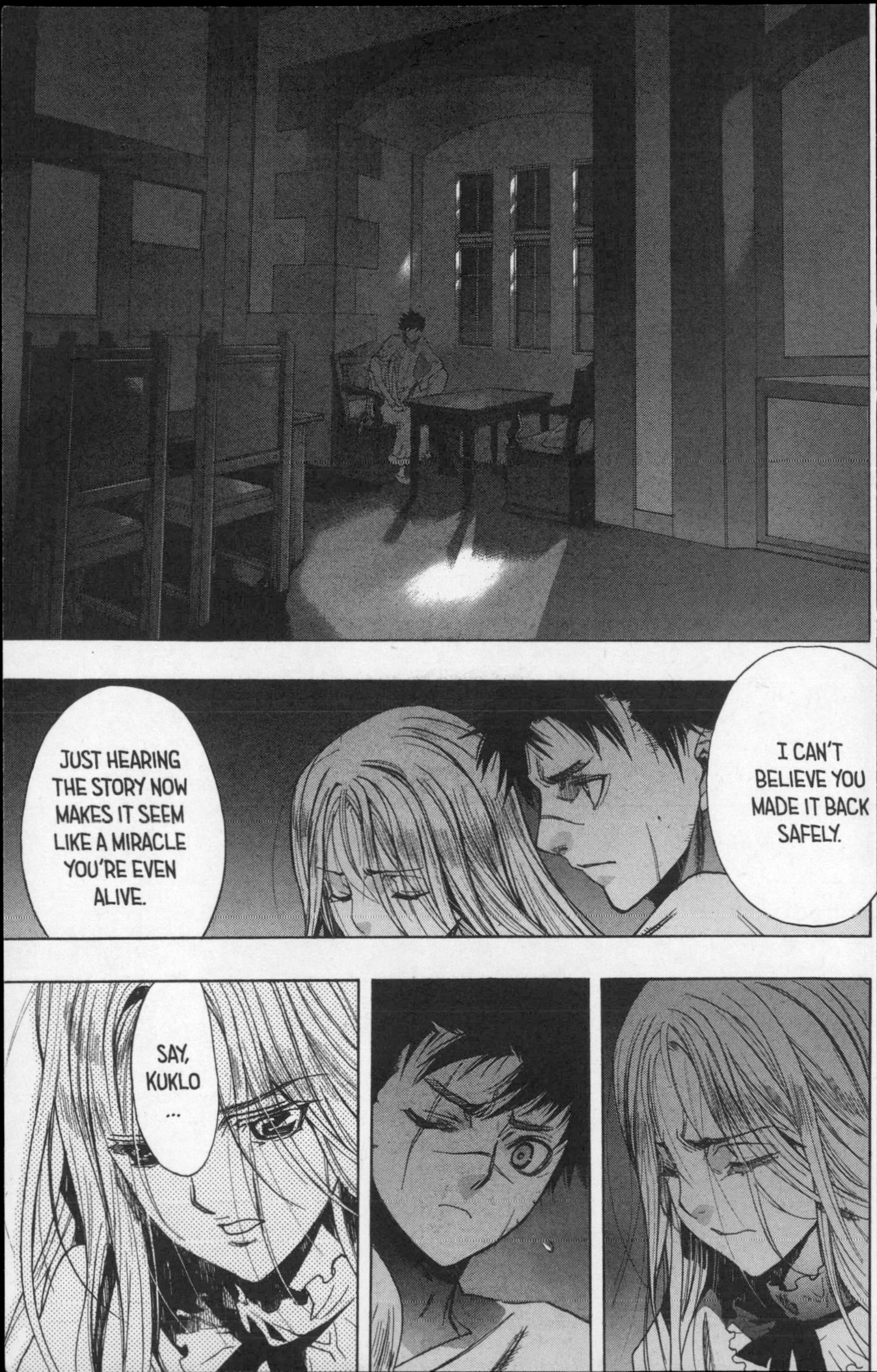
I CAN'T BELIEVE YOU MADE IT BACK SAFELY.
JUST HEARING THE STORY NOW MAKES IT SEEM LIKE A MIRACLE YOU'RE EVEN ALIVE.
SAY, KUKLO ...

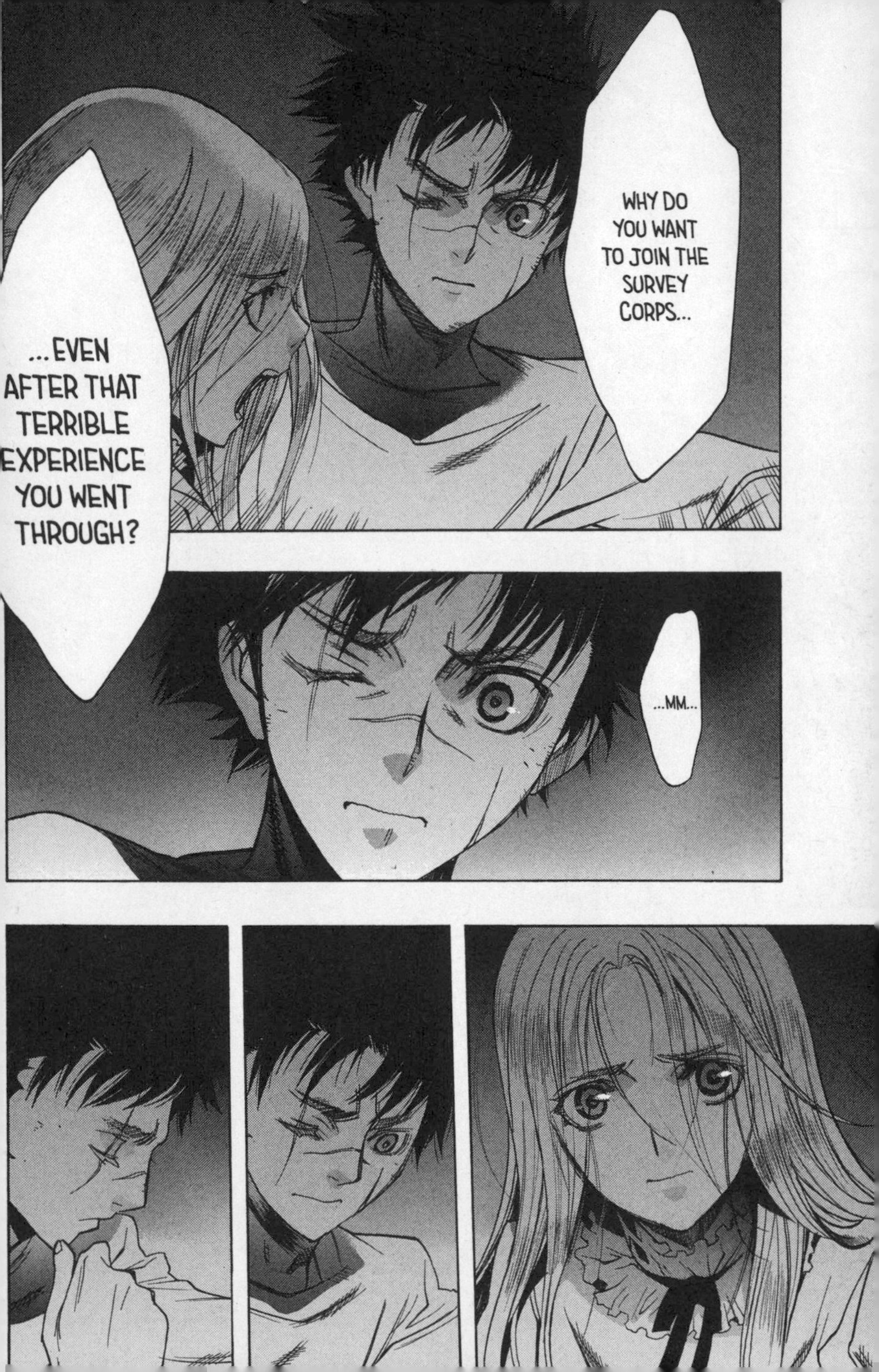
WHY DO YOU WANT TO JOIN THE SURVEY CORPS...
...EVEN AFTER THAT TERRIBLE EXPERIENCE YOU WENT THROUGH?
...MM...

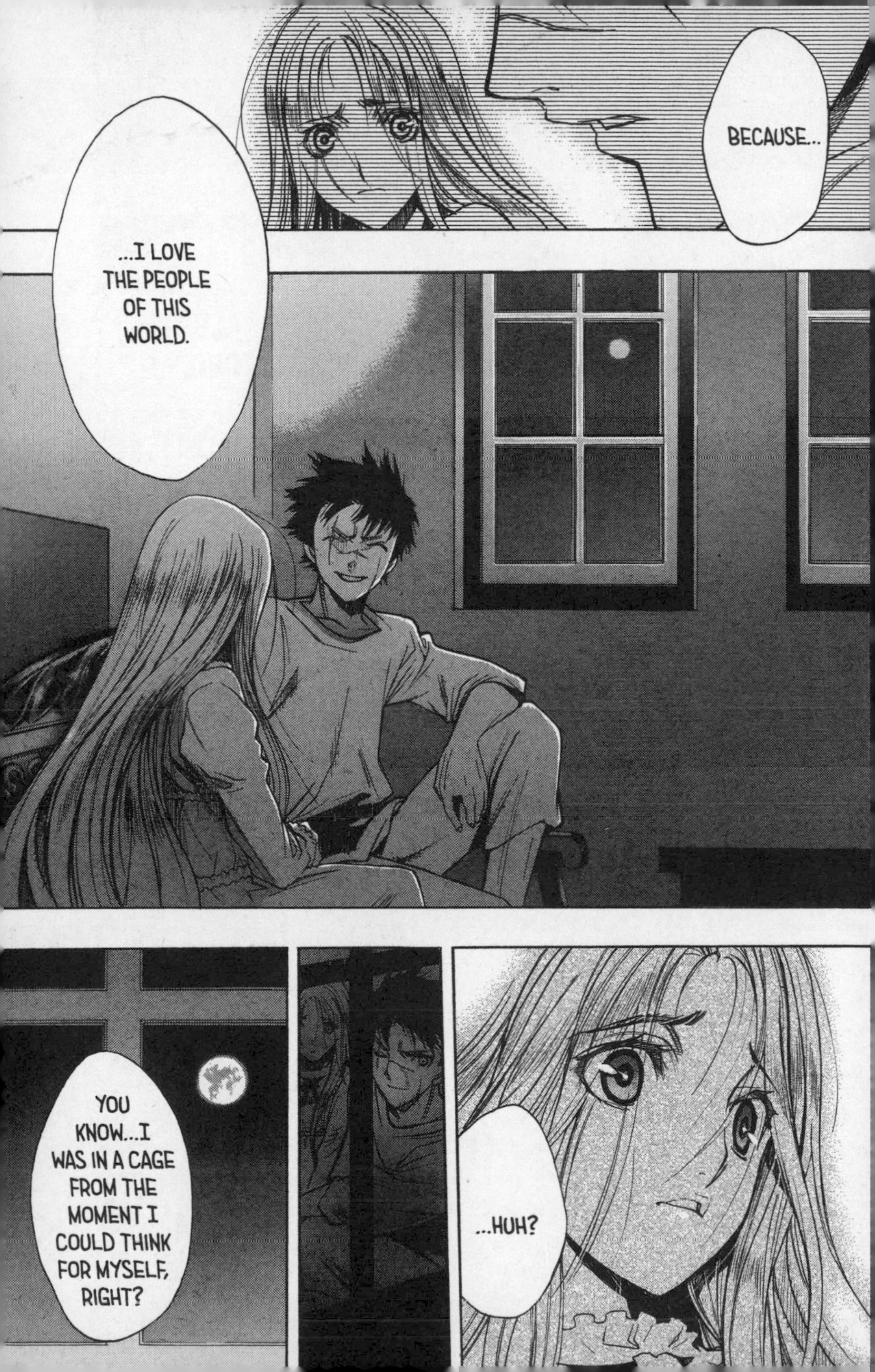
BECAUSE...
...I LOVE THE PEOPLE OF THIS WORLD.
...HUH?
YOU KNOW...I WAS IN A CAGE FROM THE MOMENT I COULD THINK FOR MYSELF, RIGHT?

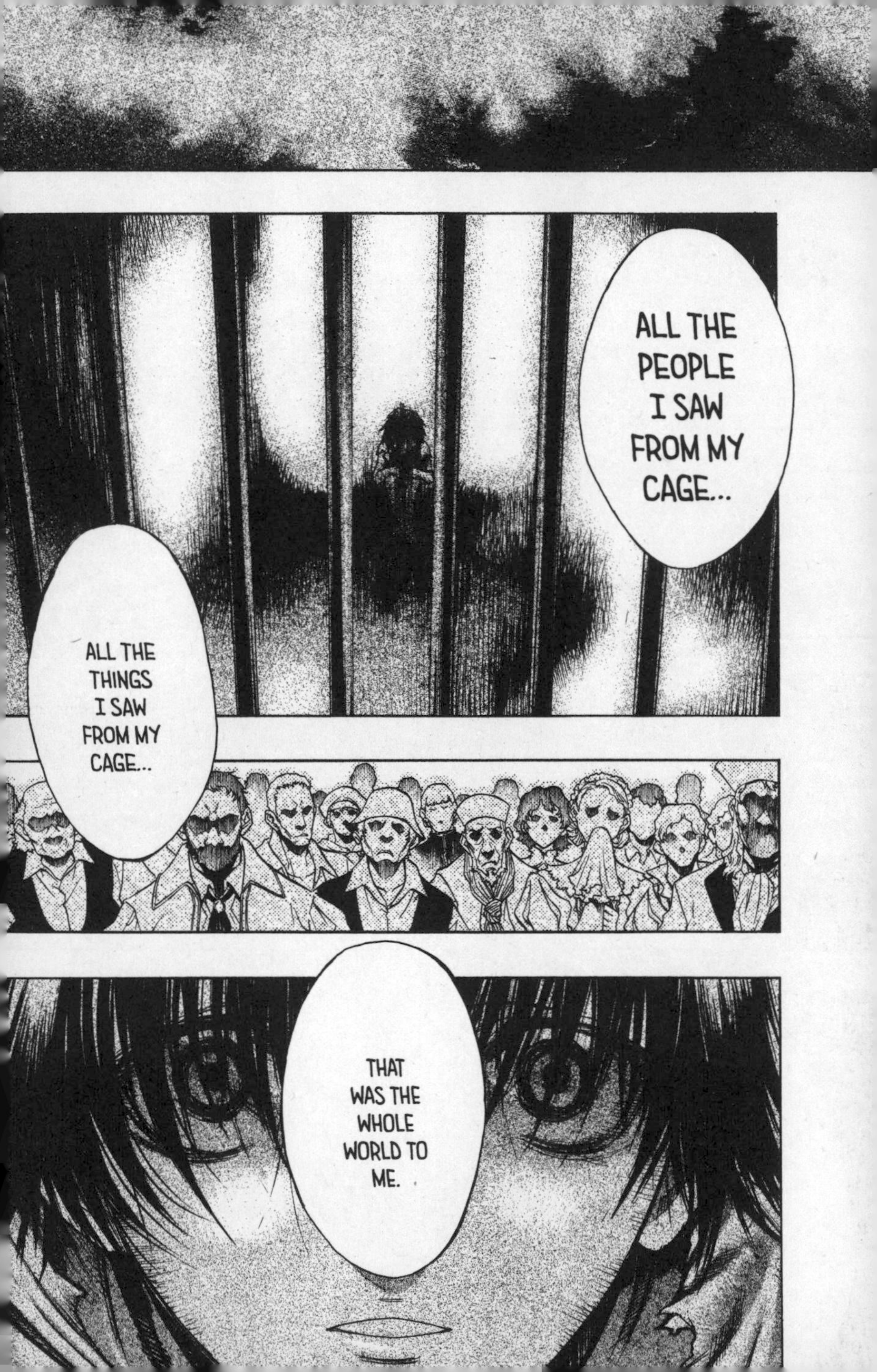
ALL THE PEOPLE I SAW FROM MY CAGE...
ALL THE THINGS I SAW FROM MY CAGE...
THAT WAS THE WHOLE WORLD TO ME.

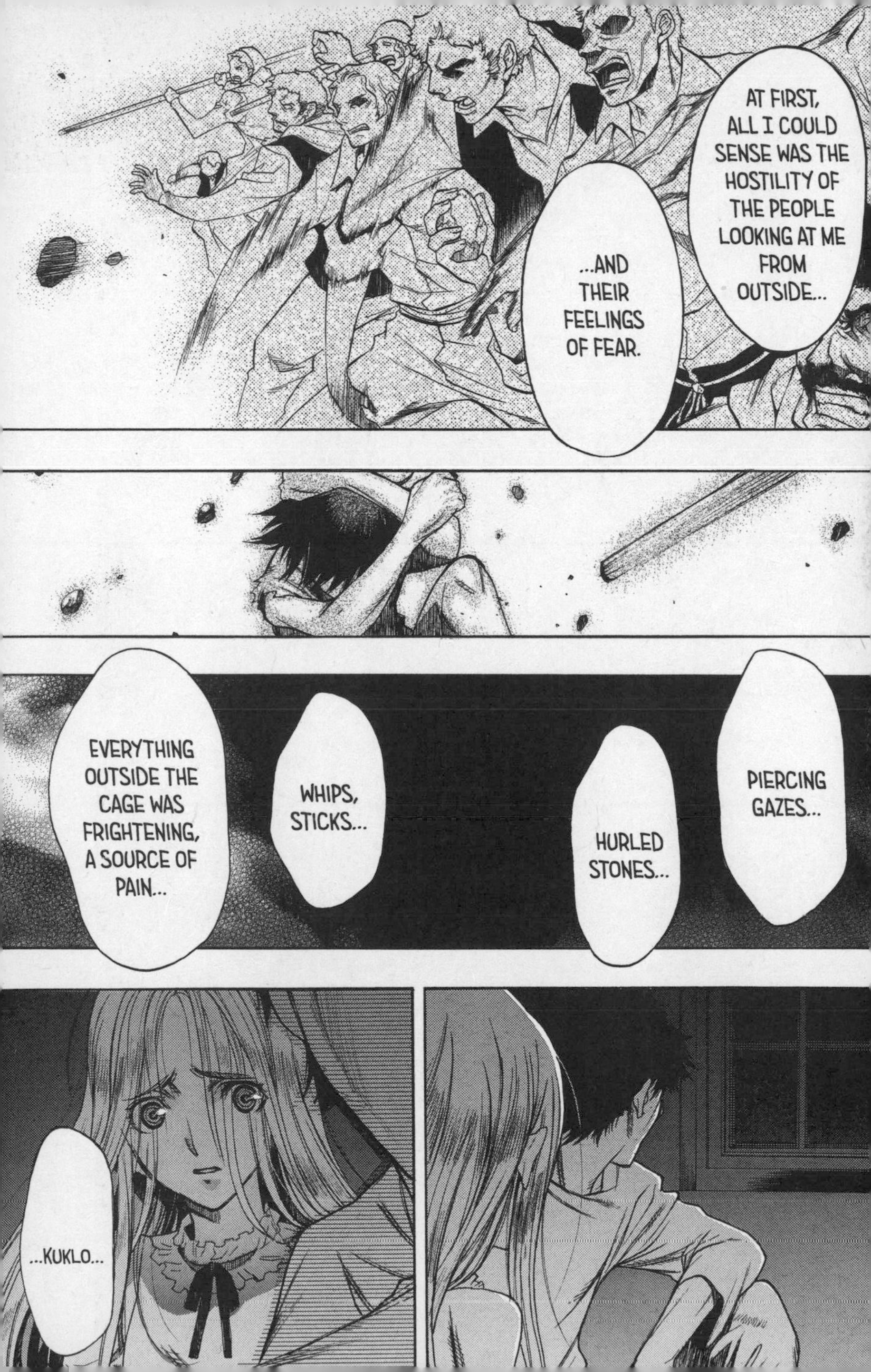
AT FIRST, ALL I COULD SENSE WAS THE HOSTILITY OF THE PEOPLE LOOKING AT ME FROM OUTSIDE...
...AND THEIR FEELINGS OF FEAR.
PIERCING GAZES...
HURLED STONES...
WHIPS, STICKS...
EVERYTHING OUTSIDE THE CAGE WAS FRIGHTENING, A SOURCE OF PAIN...
...KUKLO...

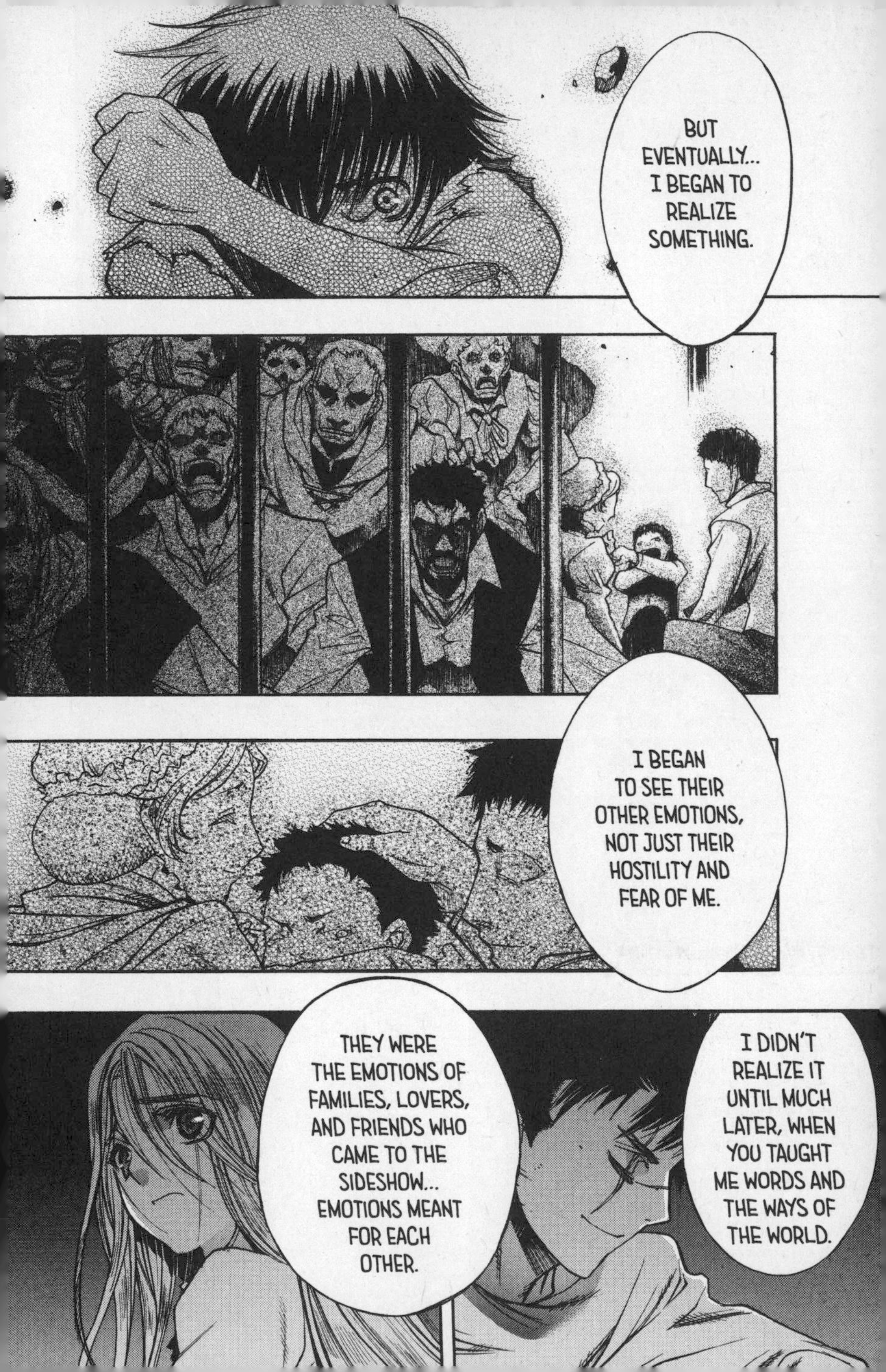
BUT EVENTUALLY... I BEGAN TO REALIZE SOMETHING.
I BEGAN TO SEE THEIR OTHER EMOTIONS, NOT JUST THEIR HOSTILITY AND FEAR OF ME.
THEY WERE THE EMOTIONS OF FAMILIES, LOVERS, AND FRIENDS WHO CAME TO THE SIDESHOW... EMOTIONS MEANT FOR EACH OTHER.
I DIDN'T REALIZE IT UNTIL MUCH LATER, WHEN YOU TAUGHT ME WORDS AND THE WAYS OF THE WORLD.

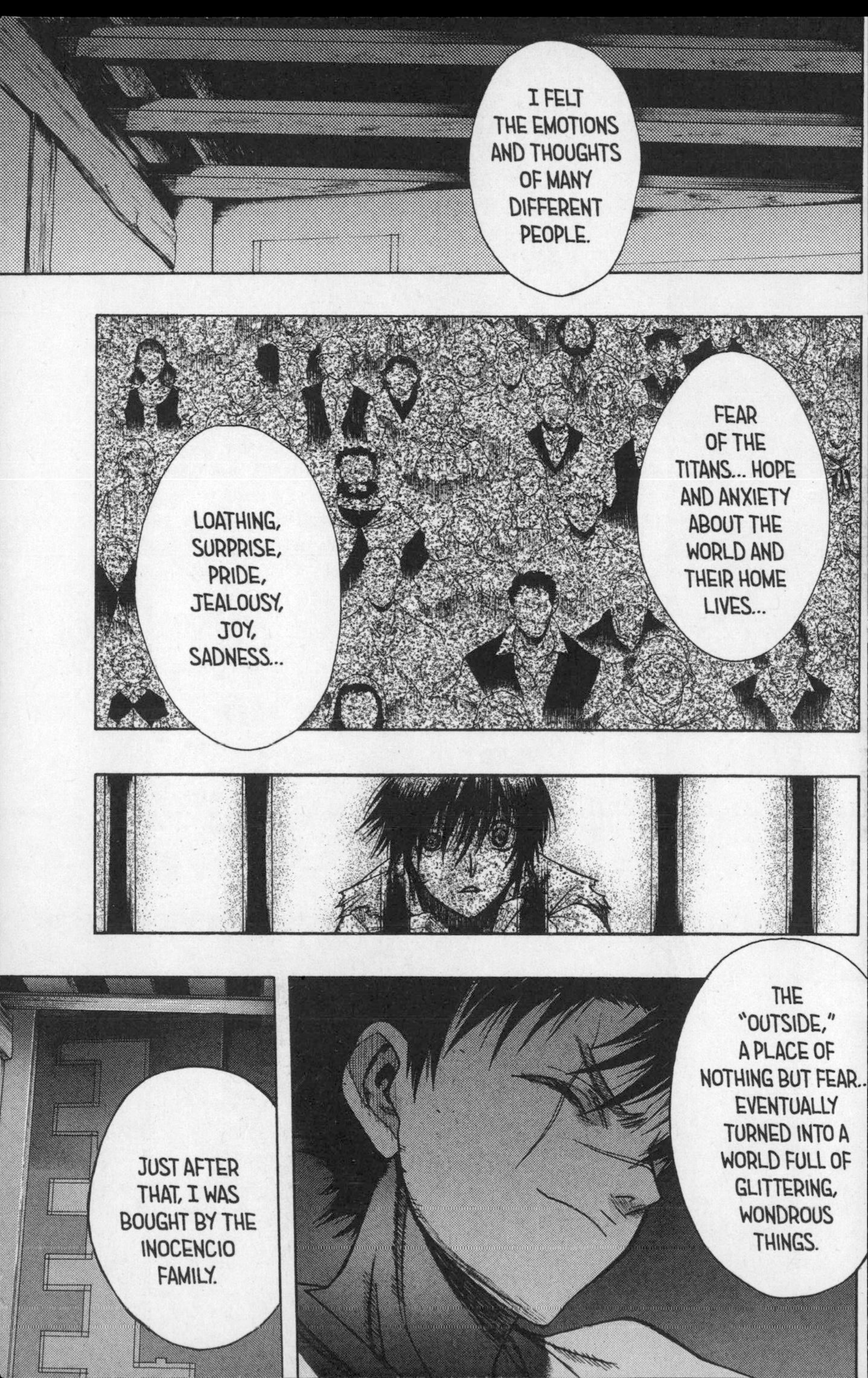
I FELT THE EMOTIONS AND THOUGHTS OF MANY DIFFERENT PEOPLE.
FEAR OF THE TITANS... HOPE AND ANXIETY ABOUT THE WORLD AND THEIR HOME LIVES...
LOATHING, SURPRISE, PRIDE, JEALOUSY, JOY, SADNESS...
THE "OUTSIDE," A PLACE OF NOTHING BUT FEAR... EVENTUALLY TURNED INTO A WORLD FULL OF GLITTERING, WONDROUS THINGS.
JUST AFTER THAT, I WAS BOUGHT BY THE INOCENCIO FAMILY.

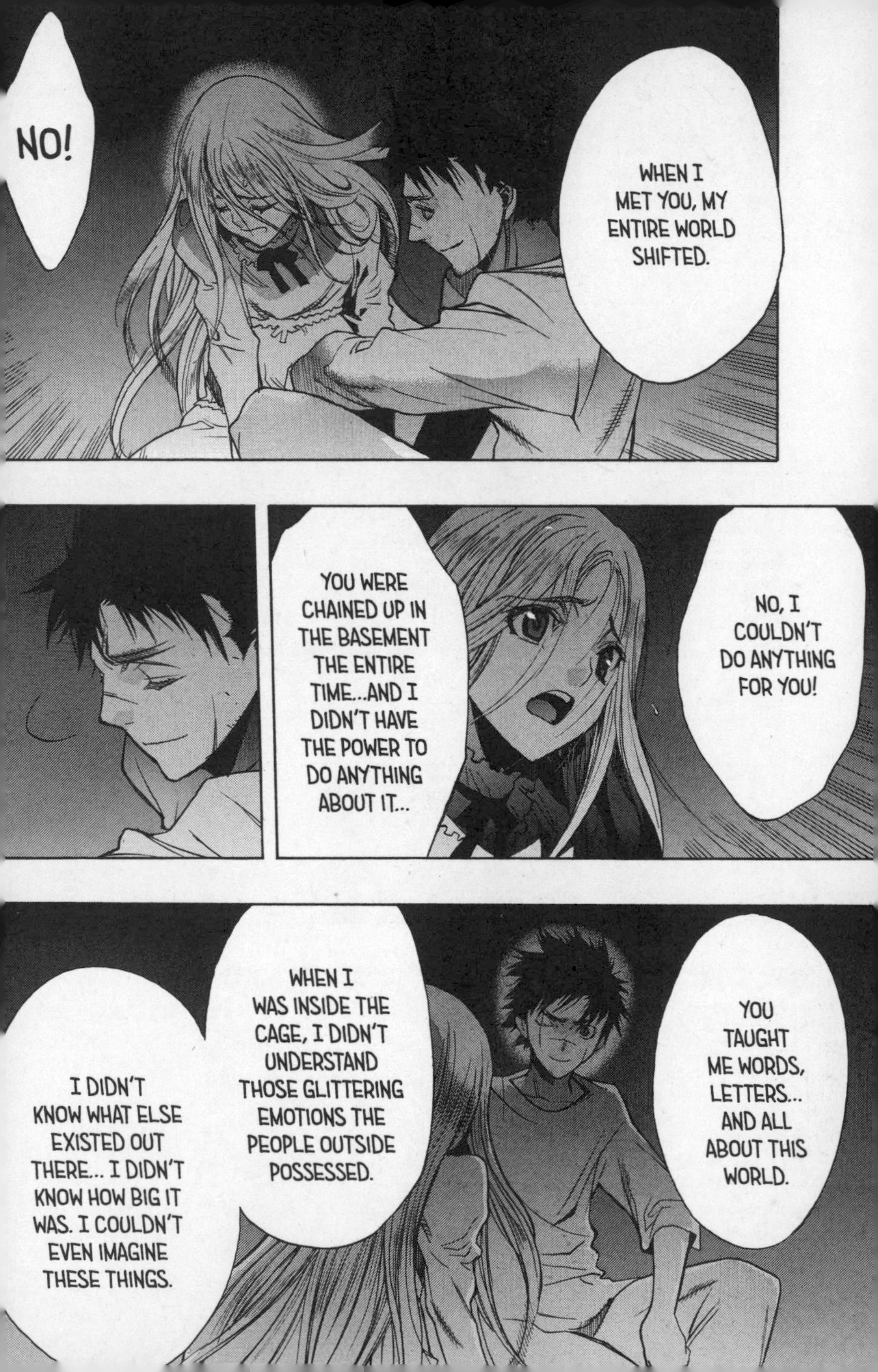
WHEN I MET YOU, MY ENTIRE WORLD SHIFTED.
NO!
NO, I COULDN'T DO ANYTHING FOR YOU!
YOU WERE CHAINED UP IN THE BASEMENT THE ENTIRE TIME...AND I DIDN'T HAVE THE POWER TO DO ANYTHING ABOUT IT...
YOU TAUGHT ME WORDS, LETTERS... AND ALL ABOUT THIS WORLD.
WHEN I WAS INSIDE THE CAGE, I DIDN'T UNDERSTAND THOSE GLITTERING EMOTIONS THE PEOPLE OUTSIDE POSSESSED.
I DIDN'T KNOW WHAT ELSE EXISTED OUT THERE... I DIDN'T KNOW HOW BIG IT WAS. I COULDN'T EVEN IMAGINE THESE THINGS.

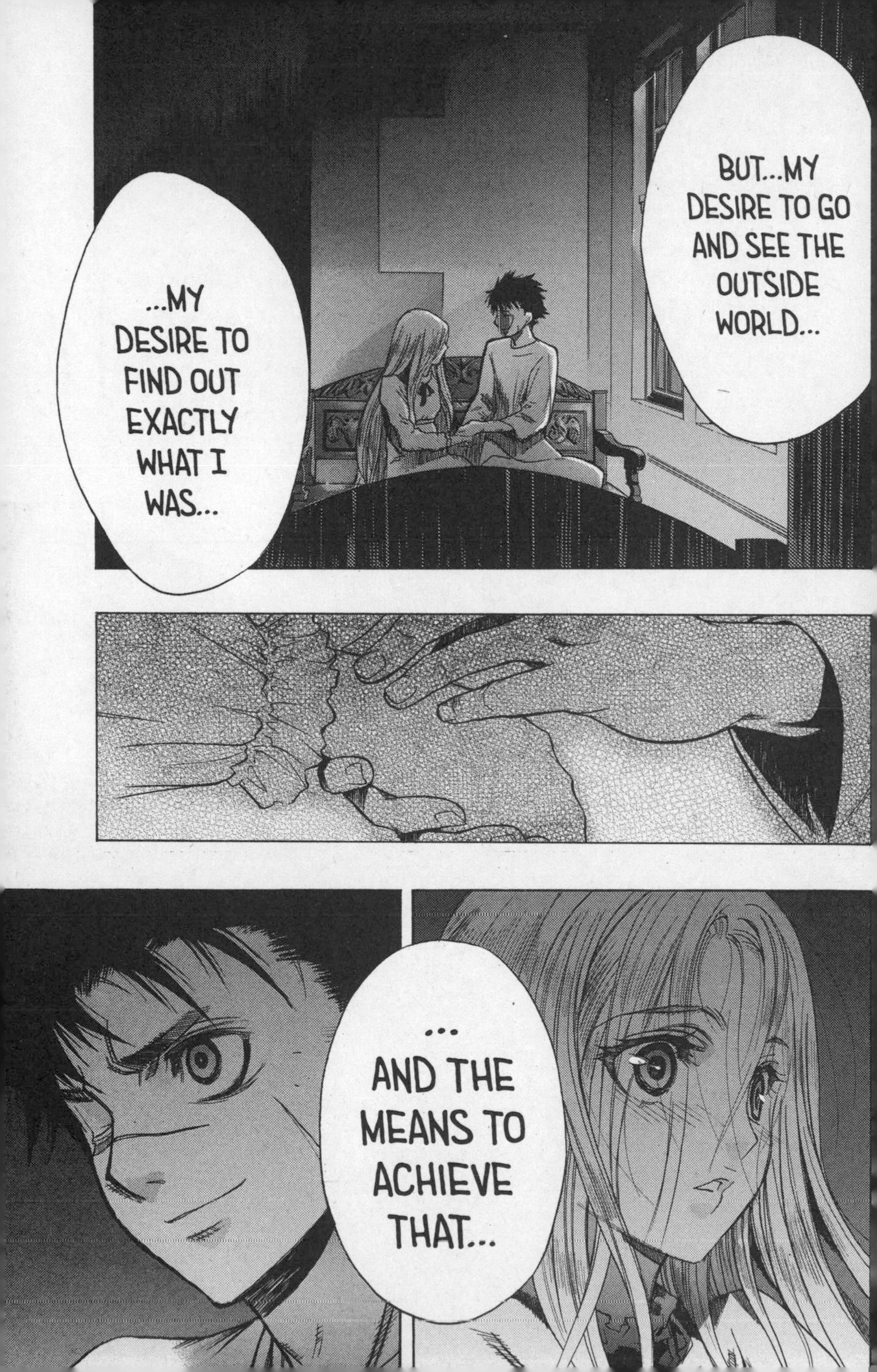
BUT...MY DESIRE TO GO AND SEE THE OUTSIDE WORLD...
...MY DESIRE TO FIND OUT EXACTLY WHAT I WAS...
...
AND THE MEANS TO ACHIEVE THAT...

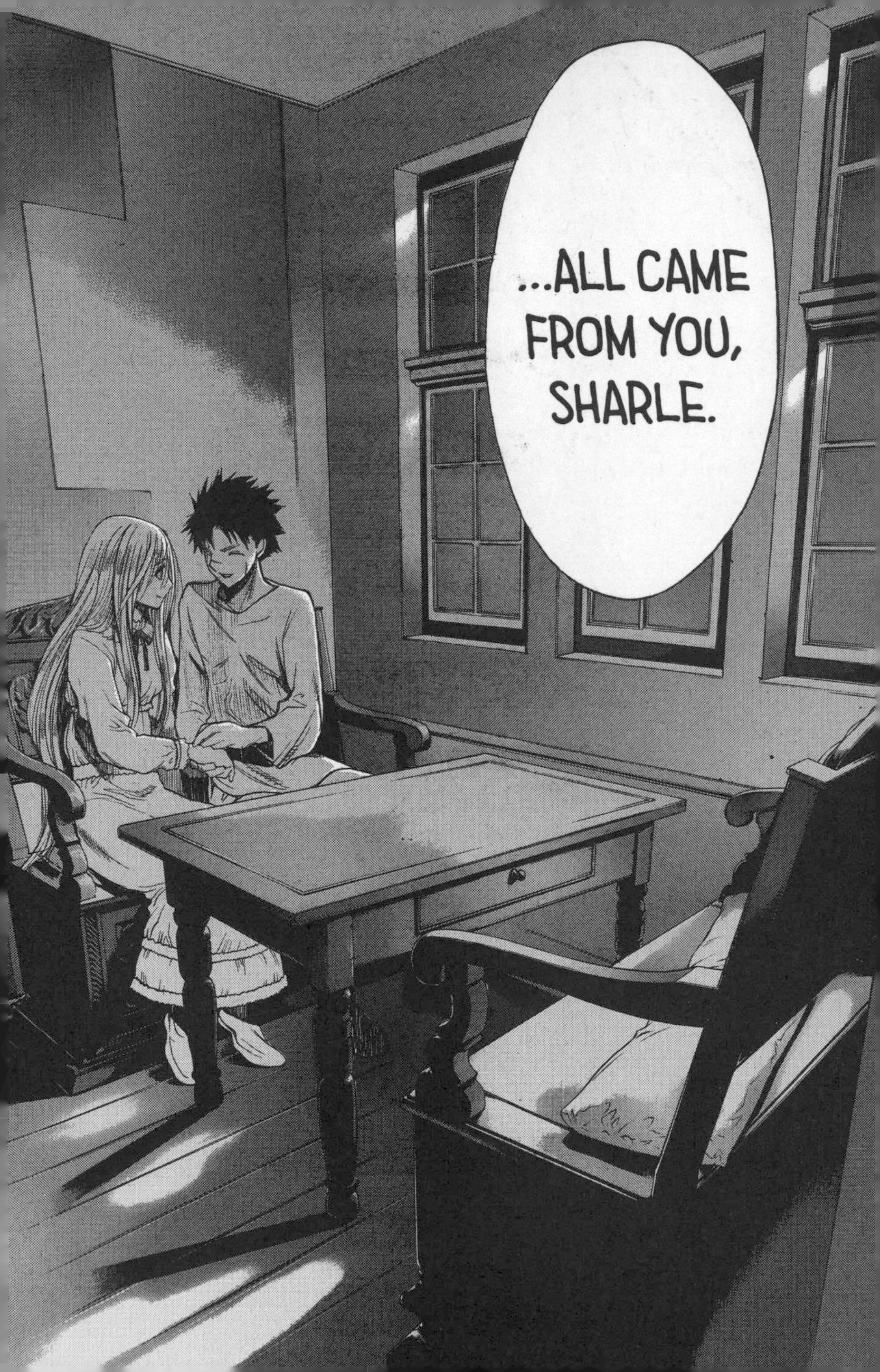
...ALL CAME FROM YOU, SHARLE.

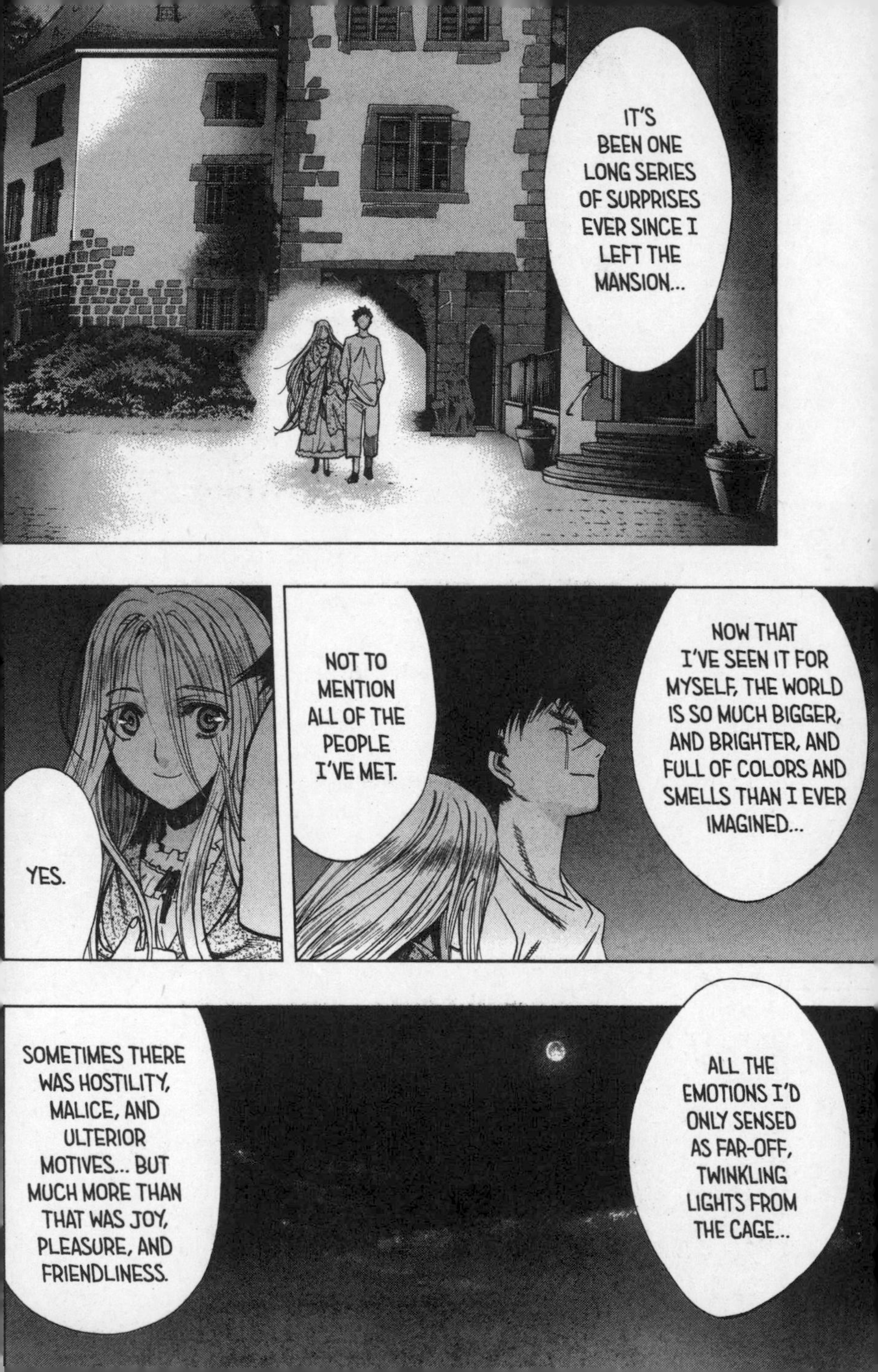
IT'S BEEN ONE LONG SERIES OF SURPRISES EVER SINCE I LEFT THE MANSION...
NOW THAT I'VE SEEN IT FOR MYSELF, THE WORLD IS SO MUCH BIGGER, AND BRIGHTER, AND FULL OF COLORS AND SMELLS THAN I EVER IMAGINED...
NOT TO MENTION ALL OF THE PEOPLE I'VE MET.
YES.
ALL THE EMOTIONS I'D ONLY SENSED AS FAR-OFF, TWINKLING LIGHTS FROM THE CAGE...
SOMETIMES THERE WAS HOSTILITY, MALICE, AND ULTERIOR MOTIVES... BUT MUCH MORE THAN THAT WAS JOY, PLEASURE, AND FRIENDLINESS.

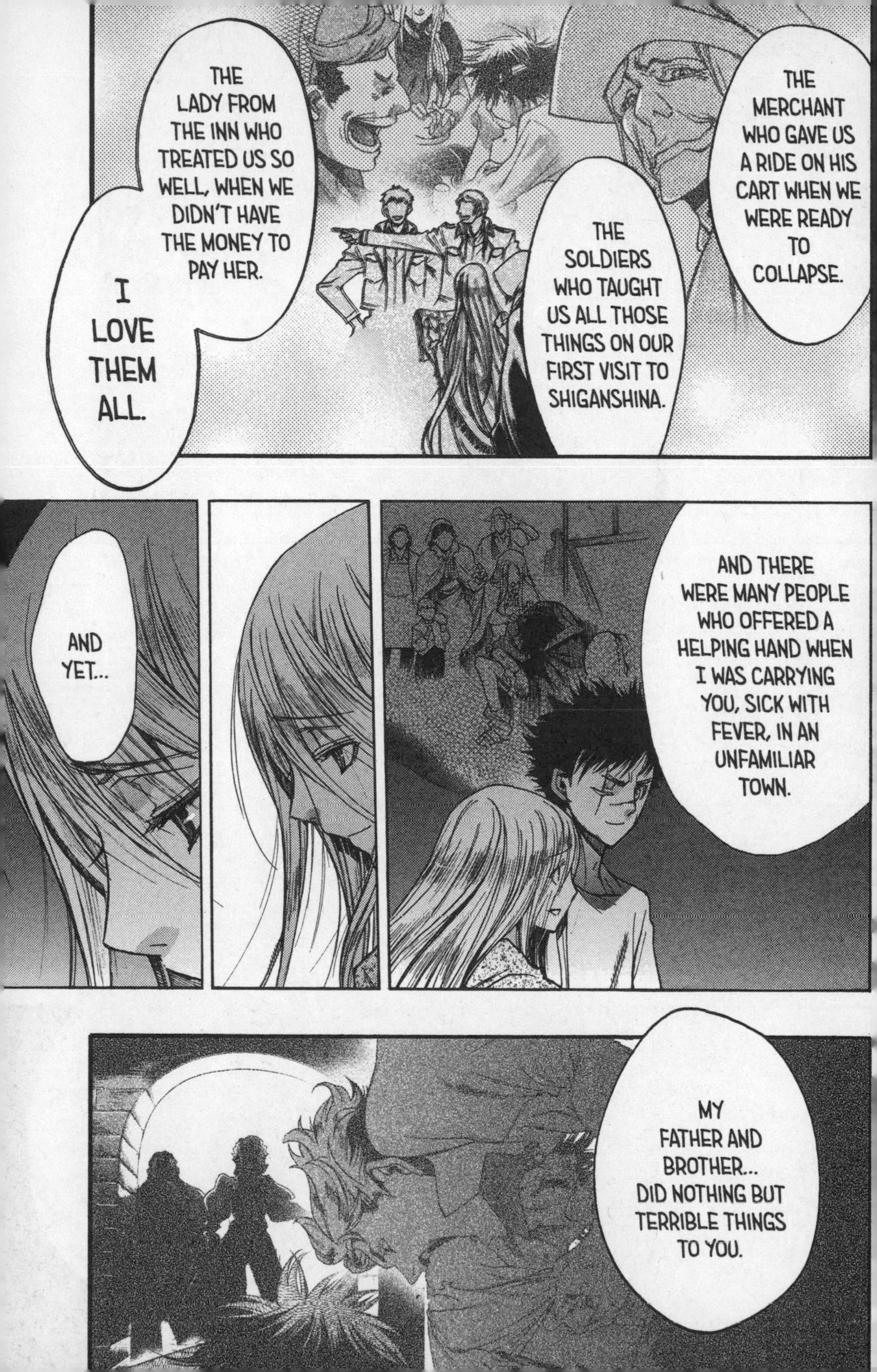
THE MERCHANT WHO GAVE US A RIDE ON HIS CART WHEN WE WERE READY TO COLLAPSE.
THE SOLDIERS WHO TAUGHT US ALL THOSE THINGS ON OUR FIRST VISIT TO SHIGANSHINA.
THE LADY FROM THE INN WHO TREATED US SO WELL, WHEN WE DIDN'T HAVE THE MONEY TO PAY HER.
I LOVE THEM ALL.
AND THERE WERE MANY PEOPLE WHO OFFERED A HELPING HAND WHEN I WAS CARRYING YOU, SICK WITH FEVER, IN AN UNFAMILIAR TOWN.
AND YET...
MY FATHER AND BROTHER... DID NOTHING BUT TERRIBLE THINGS TO YOU.

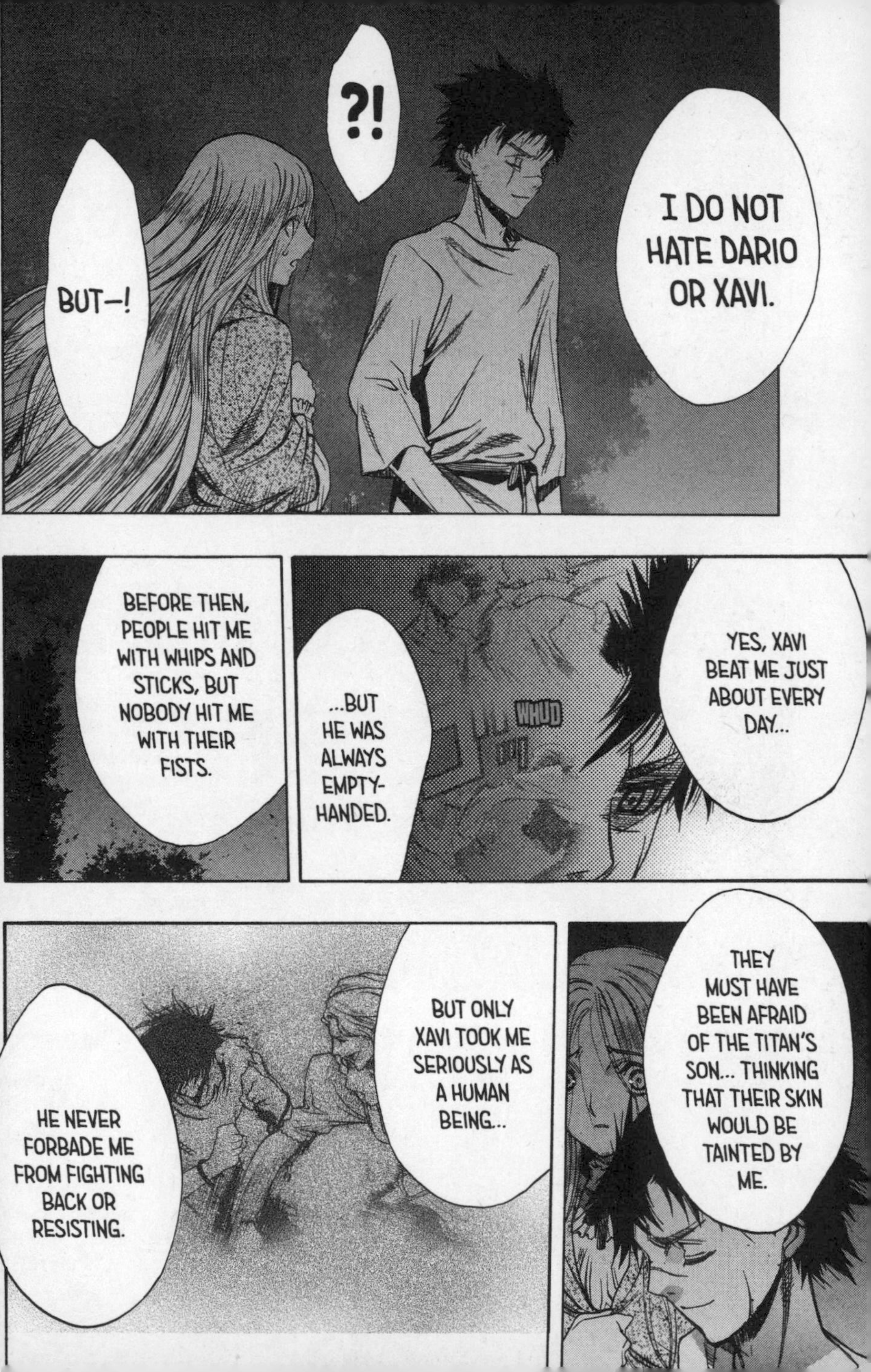
I DO NOT HATE DARIO OR XAVI.
?!
BUT—!
YES, XAVI BEAT ME JUST ABOUT EVERY DAY...
WHUD
...BUT HE WAS ALWAYS EMPTY-HANDED.
BEFORE THEN, PEOPLE HIT ME WITH WHIPS AND STICKS, BUT NOBODY HIT ME WITH THEIR FISTS.
THEY MUST HAVE BEEN AFRAID OF THE TITAN'S SON... THINKING THAT THEIR SKIN WOULD BE TAINTED BY ME.
BUT ONLY XAVI TOOK ME SERIOUSLY AS A HUMAN BEING...
HE NEVER FORBADE ME FROM FIGHTING BACK OR RESISTING.

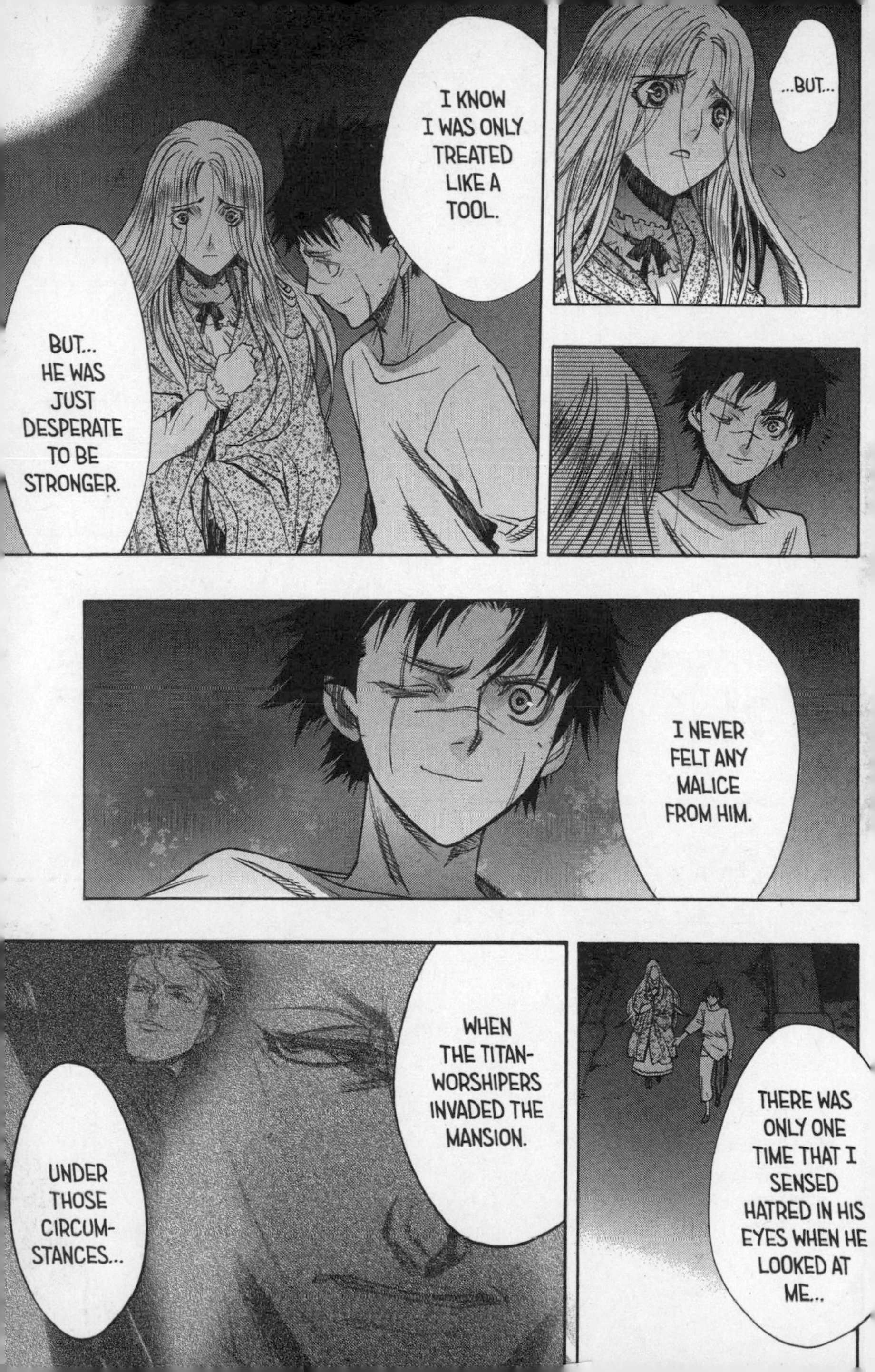
...BUT...
I KNOW I WAS ONLY TREATED LIKE A TOOL.
BUT... HE WAS JUST DESPERATE TO BE STRONGER.
I NEVER FELT ANY MALICE FROM HIM.
THERE WAS ONLY ONE TIME THAT I SENSED HATRED IN HIS EYES WHEN HE LOOKED AT ME...
WHEN THE TITAN-WORSHIPERS INVADED THE MANSION.
UNDER THOSE CIRCUM-STANCES...

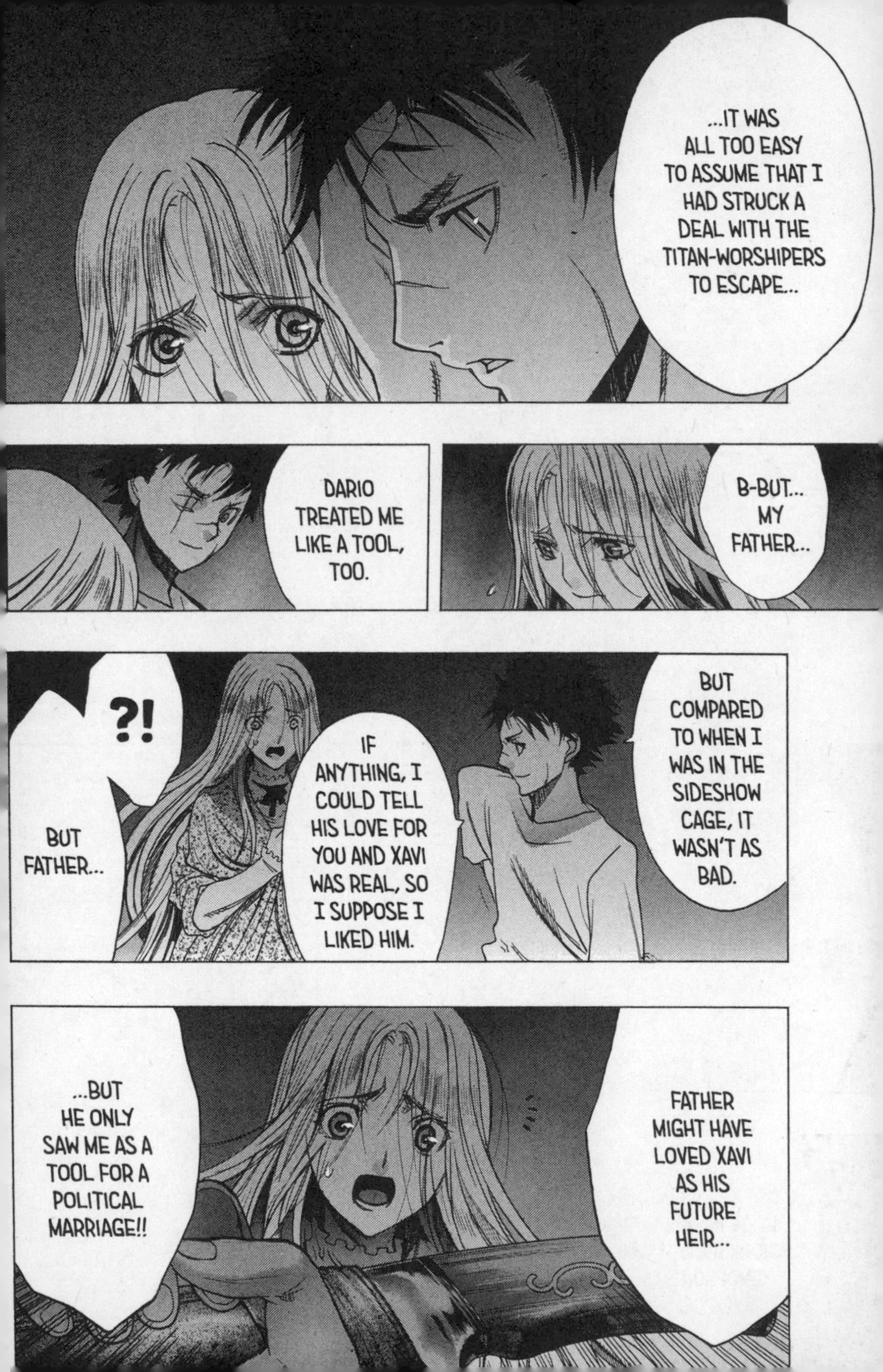
...IT WAS ALL TOO EASY TO ASSUME THAT I HAD STRUCK A DEAL WITH THE TITAN-WORSHIPERS TO ESCAPE...
B-BUT... MY FATHER...
DARIO TREATED ME LIKE A TOOL, TOO.
BUT COMPARED TO WHEN I WAS IN THE SIDESHOW CAGE, IT WASN'T AS BAD.
IF ANYTHING, I COULD TELL HIS LOVE FOR YOU AND XAVI WAS REAL, SO I SUPPOSE I LIKED HIM.
?!
BUT FATHER...
FATHER MIGHT HAVE LOVED XAVI AS HIS FUTURE HEIR...
...BUT HE ONLY SAW ME AS A TOOL FOR A POLITICAL MARRIAGE!!

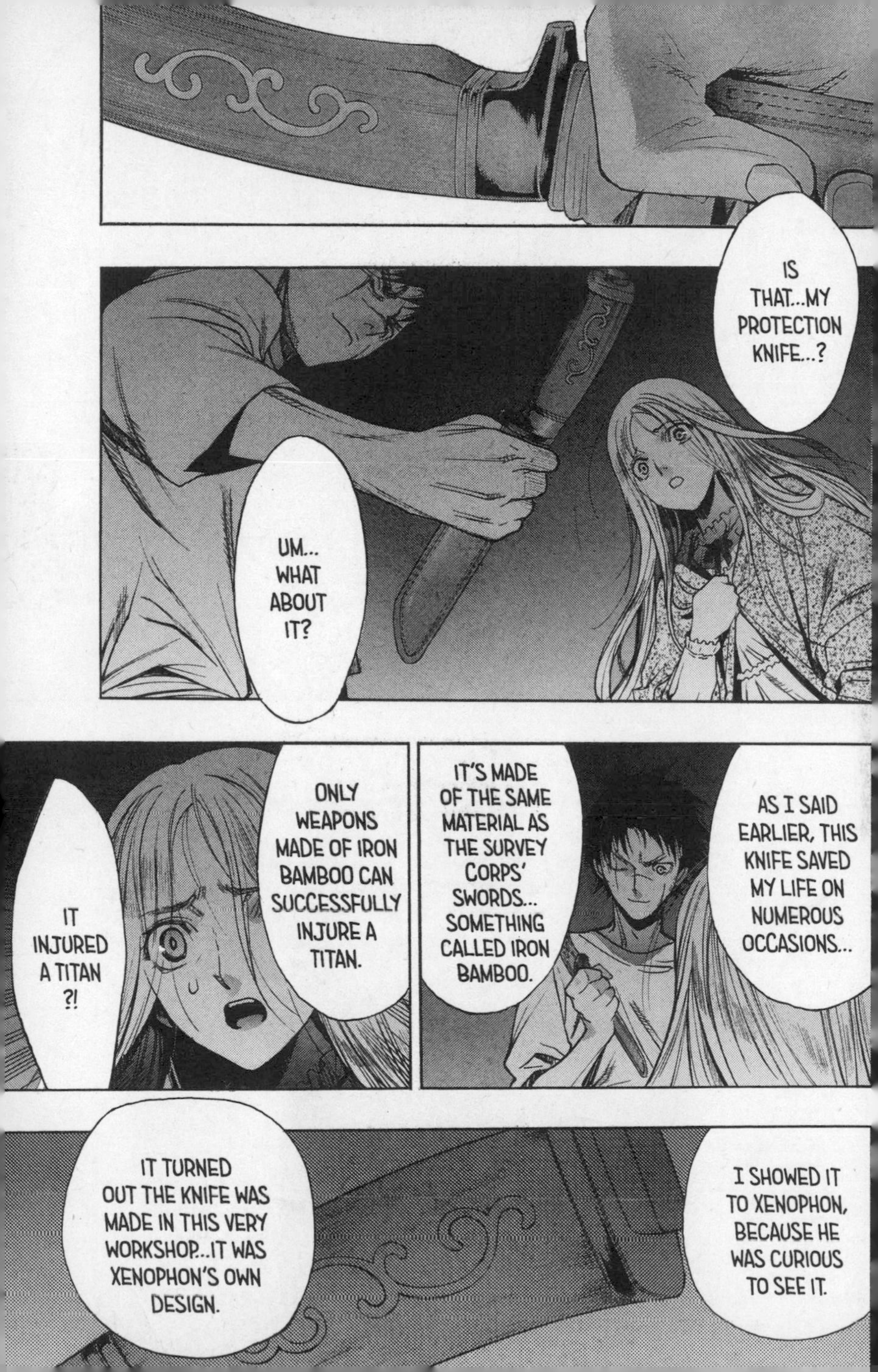
IS THAT...MY PROTECTION KNIFE...?
UM... WHAT ABOUT IT?
AS I SAID EARLIER, THIS KNIFE SAVED MY LIFE ON NUMEROUS OCCASIONS...
IT'S MADE OF THE SAME MATERIAL AS THE SURVEY CORPS' SWORDS... SOMETHING CALLED IRON BAMBOO.
ONLY WEAPONS MADE OF IRON BAMBOO CAN SUCCESSFULLY INJURE A TITAN.
IT INJURED A TITAN ?!
I SHOWED IT TO XENOPHON, BECAUSE HE WAS CURIOUS TO SEE IT.
IT TURNED OUT THE KNIFE WAS MADE IN THIS VERY WORKSHOP...IT WAS XENOPHON'S OWN DESIGN.

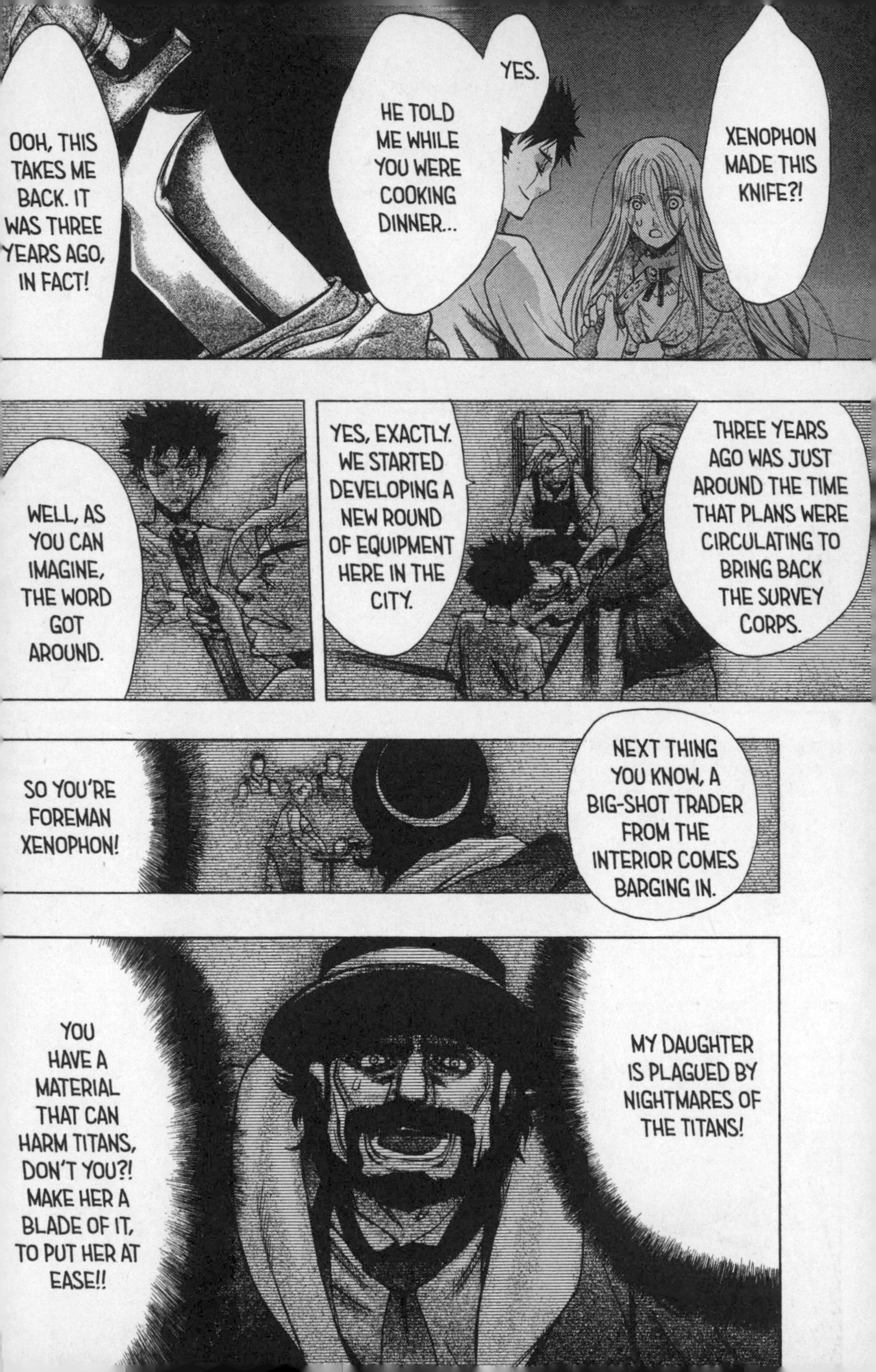
XENOPHON MADE THIS KNIFE?!
YES.
HE TOLD ME WHILE YOU WERE COOKING DINNER...
OOH, THIS TAKES ME BACK. IT WAS THREE YEARS AGO, IN FACT!
THREE YEARS AGO WAS JUST AROUND THE TIME THAT PLANS WERE CIRCULATING TO BRING BACK THE SURVEY CORPS.
YES, EXACTLY. WE STARTED DEVELOPING A NEW ROUND OF EQUIPMENT HERE IN THE CITY.
WELL, AS YOU CAN IMAGINE, THE WORD GOT AROUND.
NEXT THING YOU KNOW, A BIG-SHOT TRADER FROM THE INTERIOR COMES BARGING IN.
SO YOU'RE FOREMAN XENOPHON!
MY DAUGHTER IS PLAGUED BY NIGHTMARES OF THE TITANS!
YOU HAVE A MATERIAL THAT CAN HARM TITANS, DON'T YOU?! MAKE HER A BLADE OF IT, TO PUT HER AT EASE!!

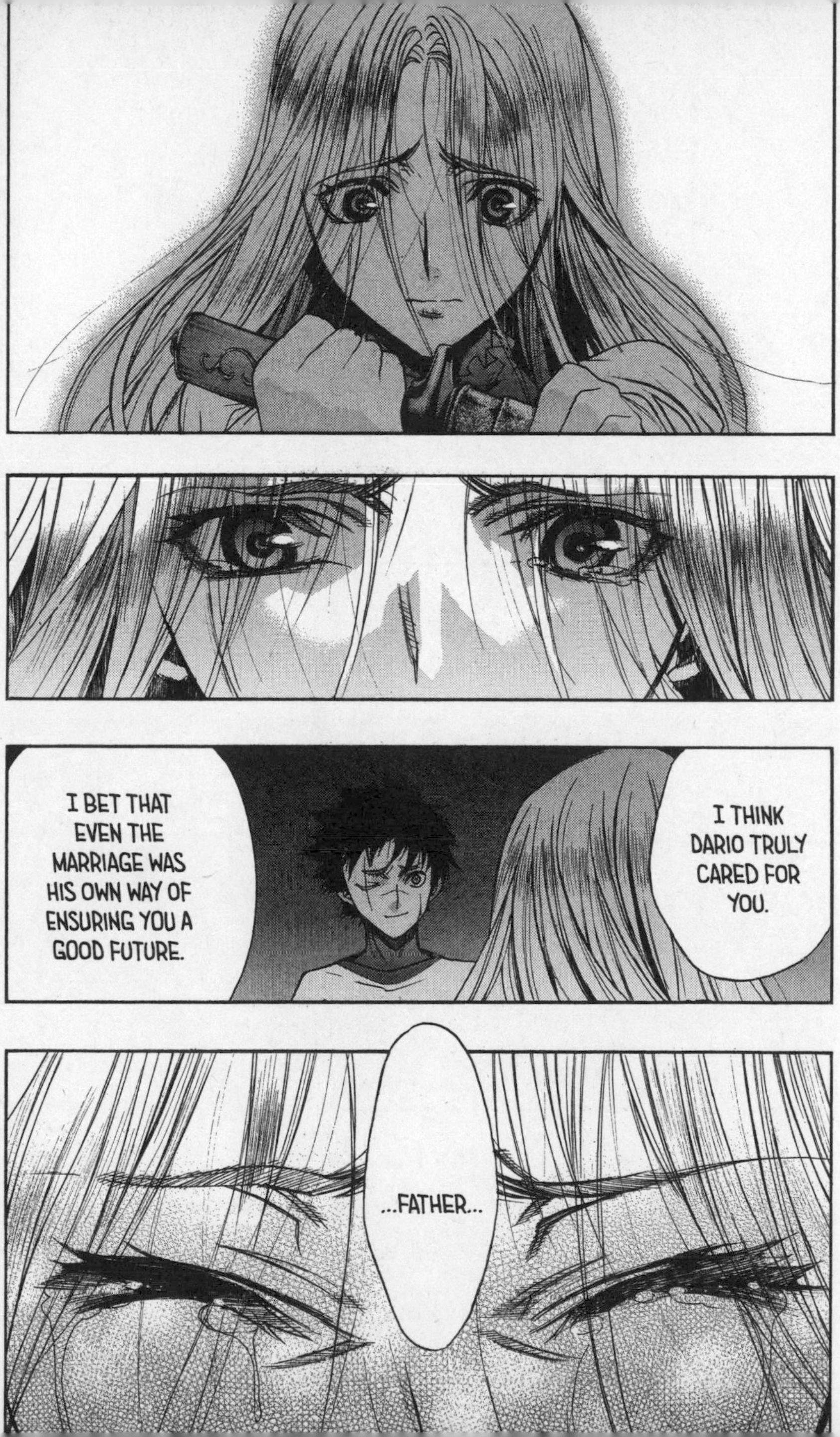
I THINK DARIO TRULY CARED FOR YOU.
I BET THAT EVEN THE MARRIAGE WAS HIS OWN WAY OF ENSURING YOU A GOOD FUTURE.
...FATHER...

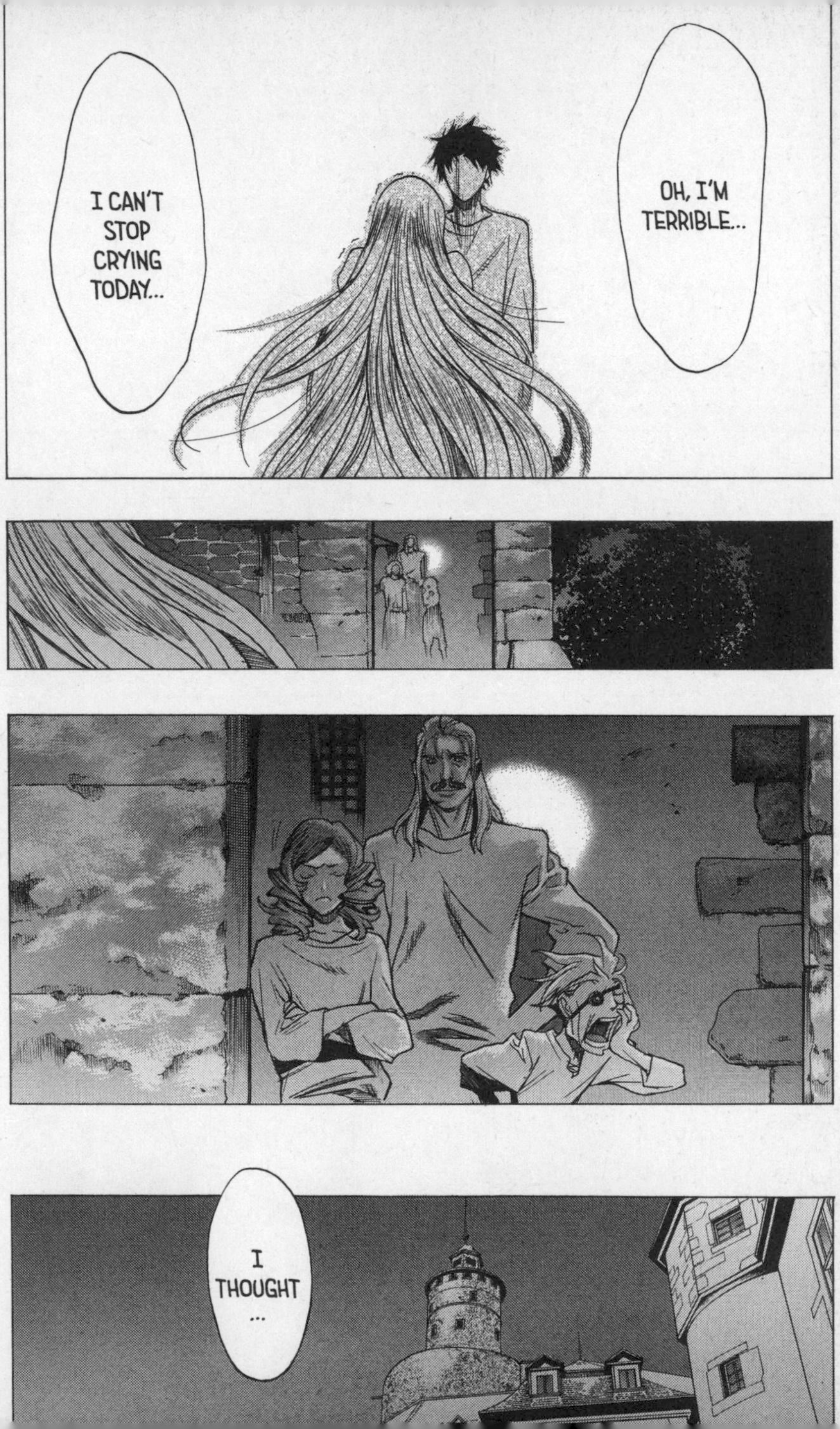
OH, I'M TERRIBLE...
I CAN'T STOP CRYING TODAY...
I THOUGHT ...

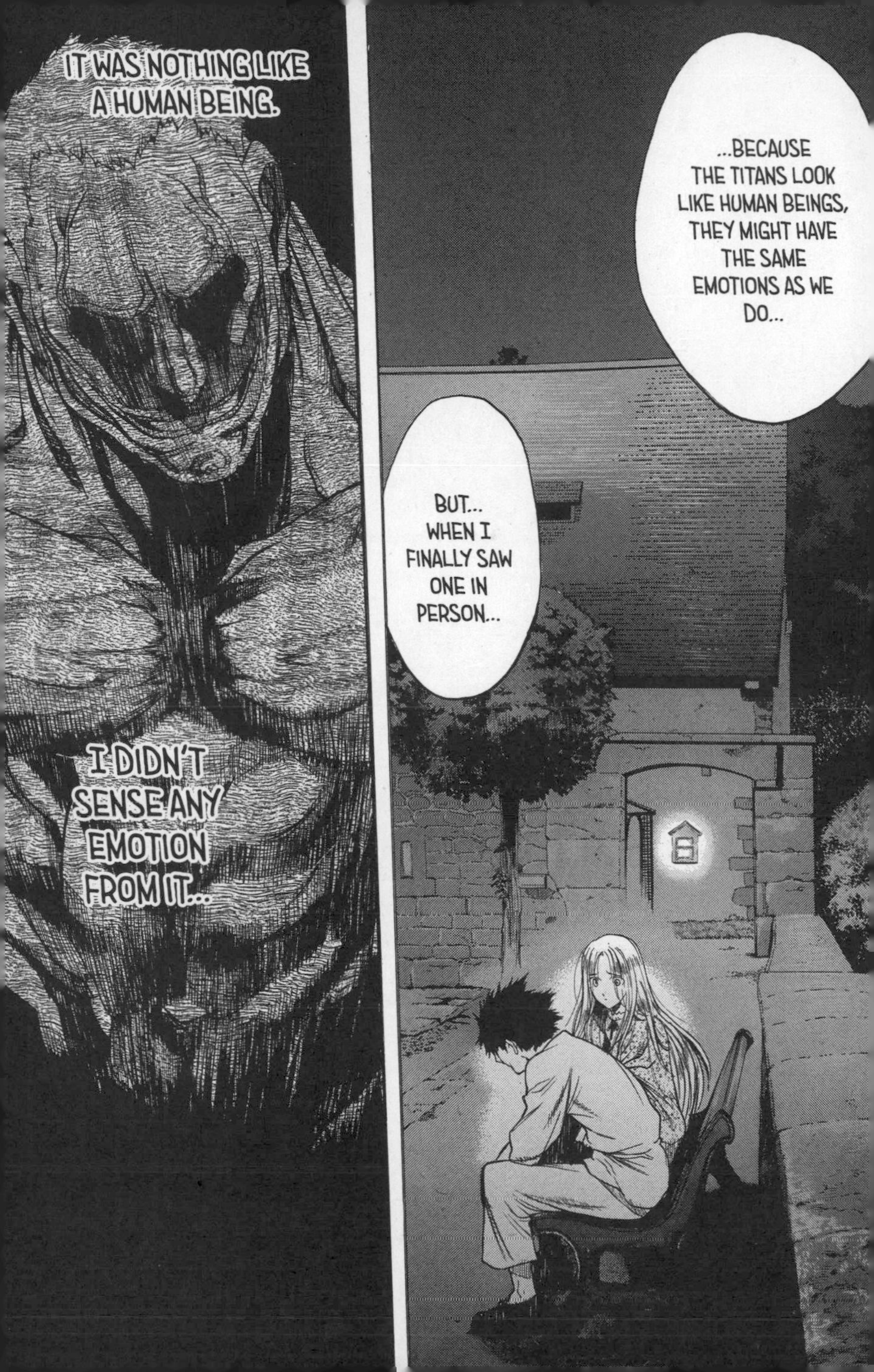
...BECAUSE THE TITANS LOOK LIKE HUMAN BEINGS, THEY MIGHT HAVE THE SAME EMOTIONS AS WE DO...
BUT... WHEN I FINALLY SAW ONE IN PERSON...
IT WAS NOTHING LIKE A HUMAN BEING.
I DIDN'T SENSE ANY EMOTION FROM IT...

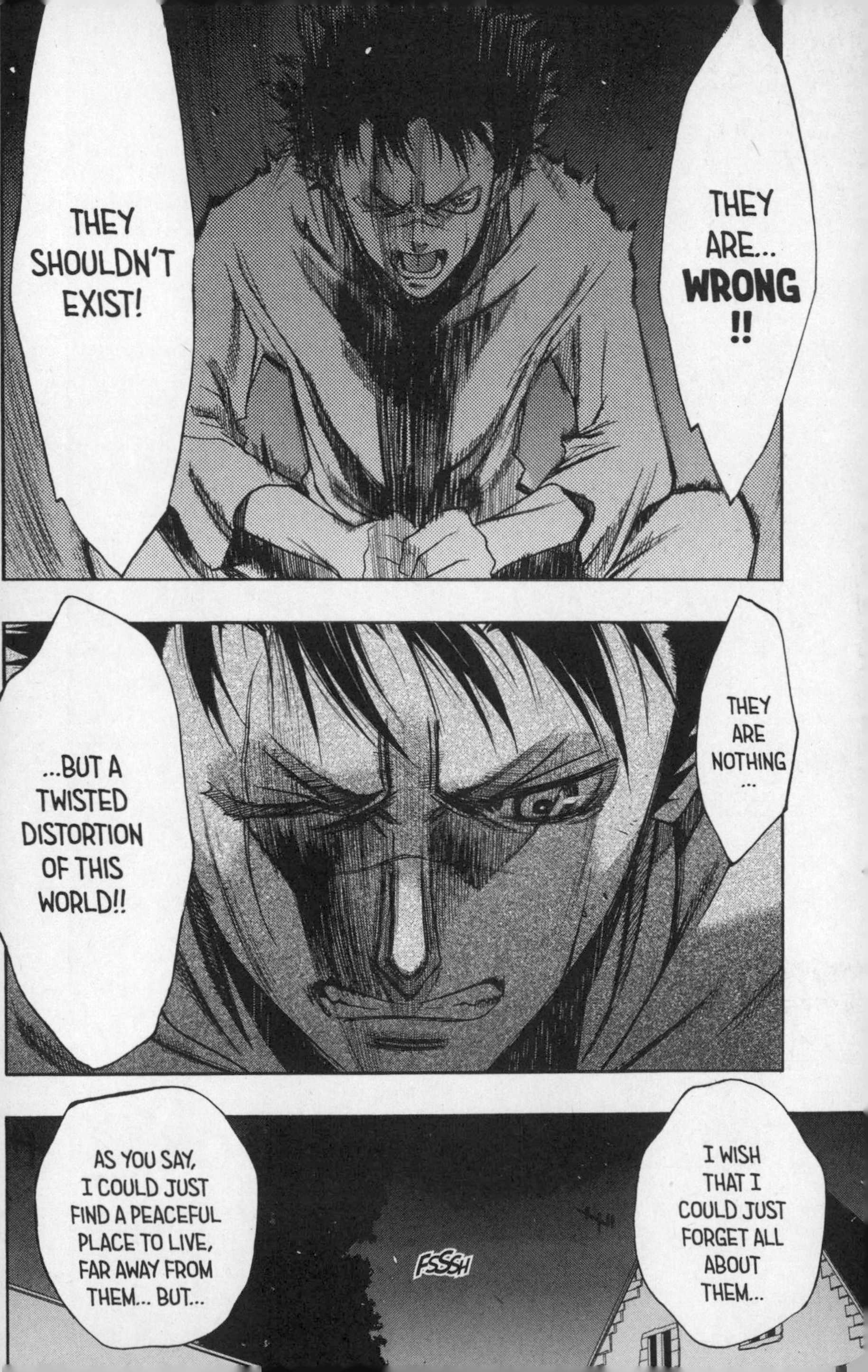
THEY ARE... WRONG !!
THEY SHOULDN'T EXIST!
THEY ARE NOTHING ...
...BUT A TWISTED DISTORTION OF THIS WORLD!!
I WISH THAT I COULD JUST FORGET ALL ABOUT THEM...
AS YOU SAY, I COULD JUST FIND A PEACEFUL PLACE TO LIVE, FAR AWAY FROM THEM... BUT...
FSSSH

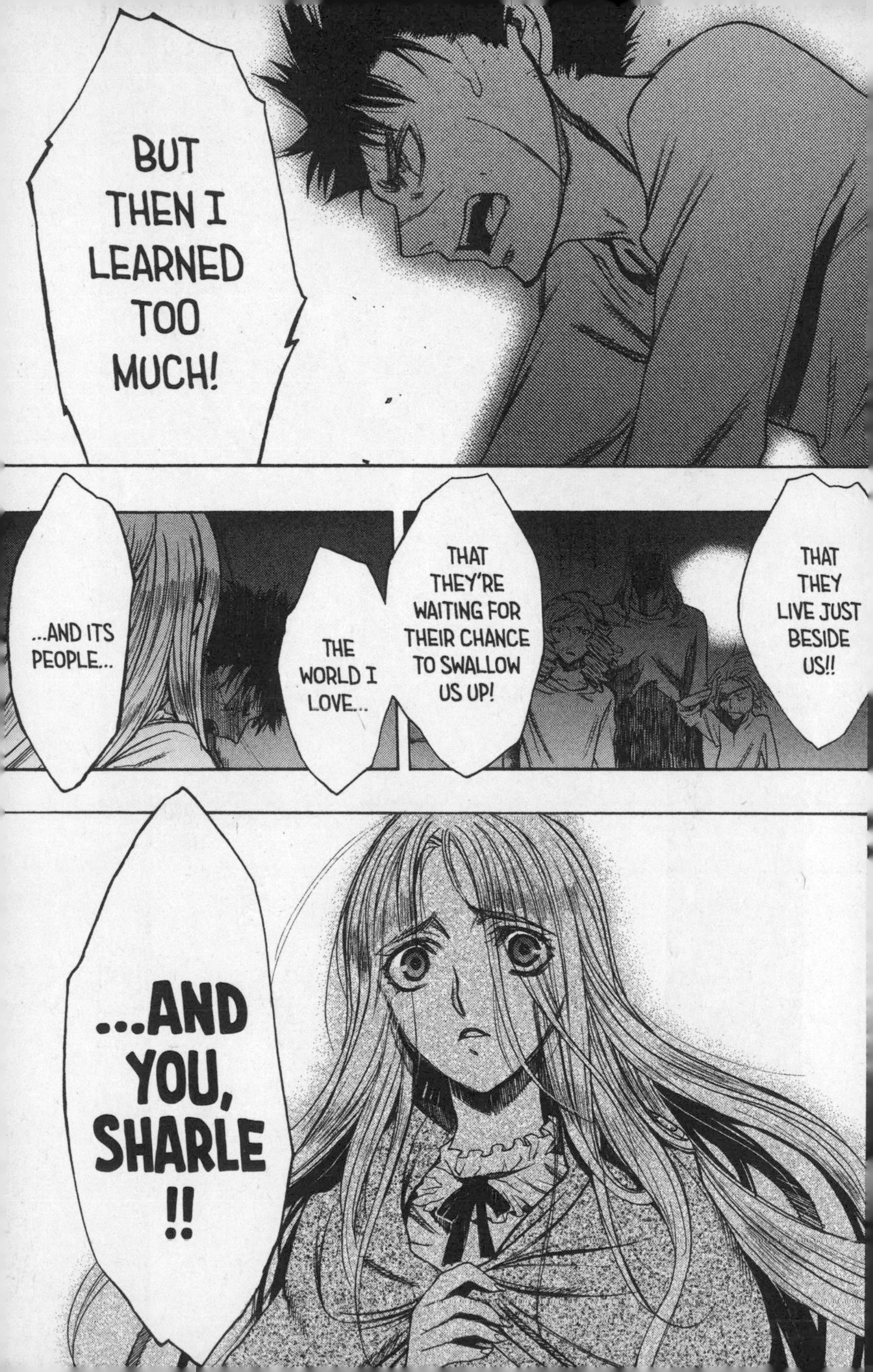
BUT THEN I LEARNED TOO MUCH!
THAT THEY LIVE JUST BESIDE US!!
THAT THEY'RE WAITING FOR THEIR CHANCE TO SWALLOW US UP!
THE WORLD I LOVE...
...AND ITS PEOPLE...
...AND YOU, SHARLE!!

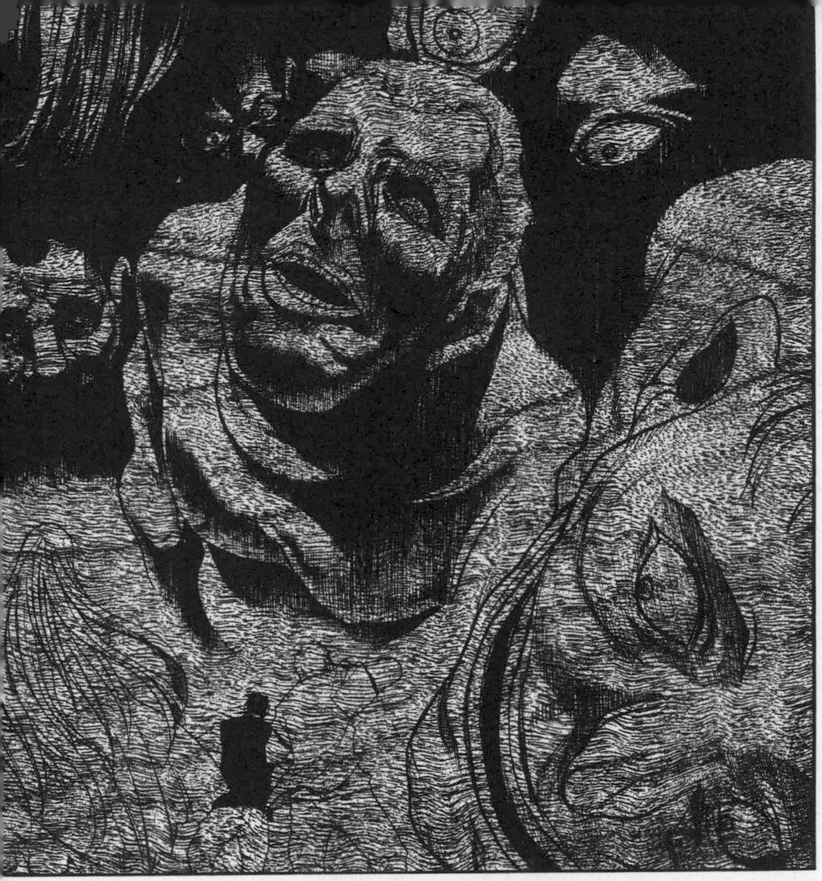

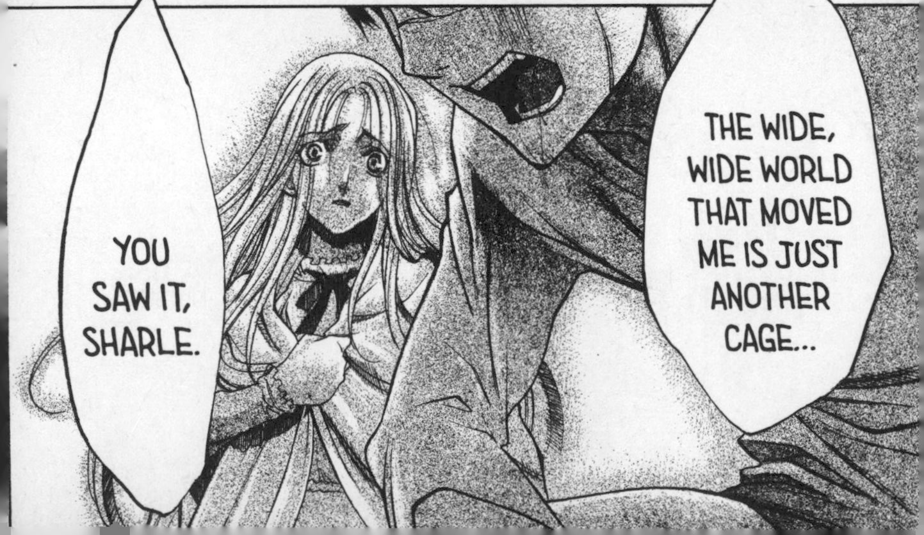
THE WIDE, WIDE WORLD THAT MOVED ME IS JUST ANOTHER CAGE...
YOU SAW IT, SHARLE.

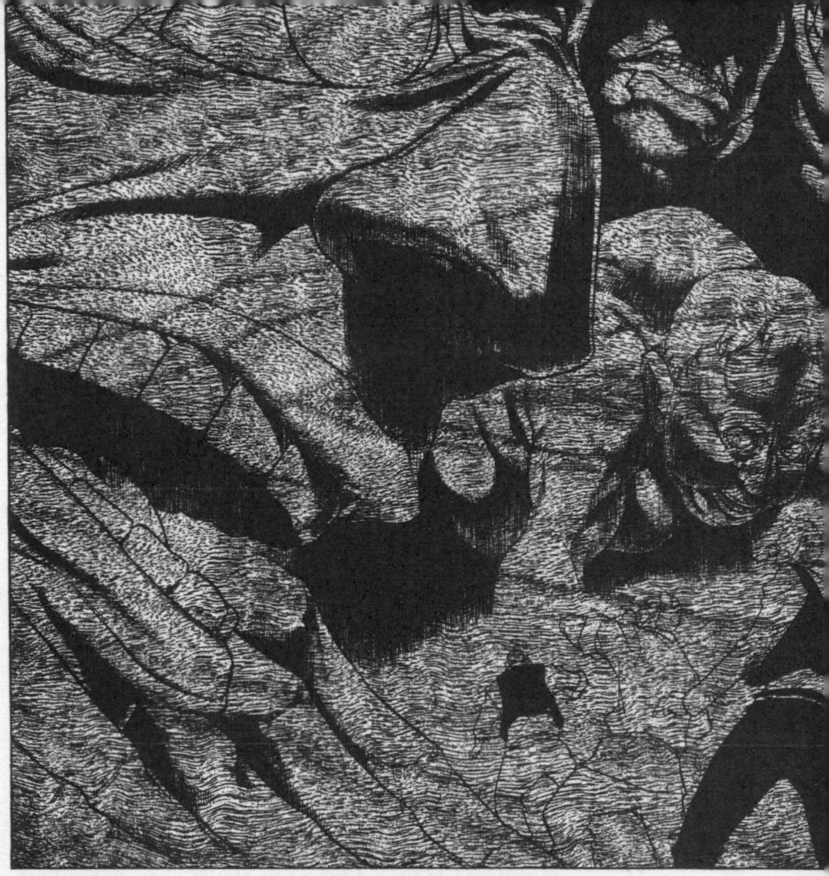

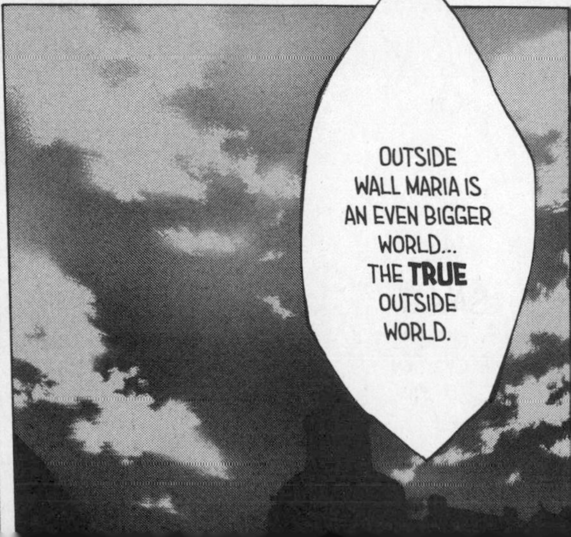
OUTSIDE WALL MARIA IS AN EVEN BIGGER WORLD... THE **TRUE** OUTSIDE WORLD.

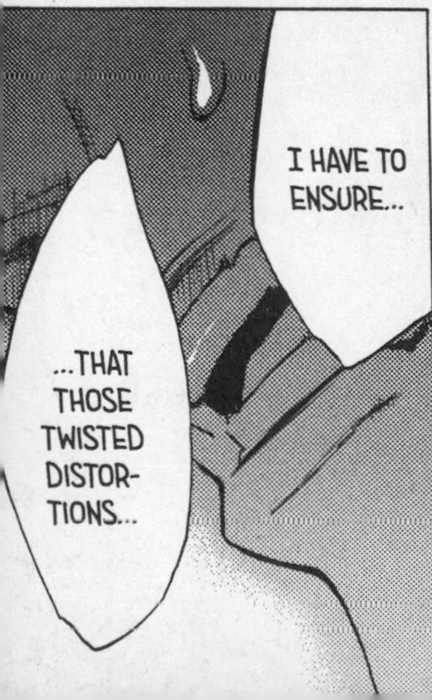
I HAVE TO ENSURE...
...THAT THOSE TWISTED DISTORTIONS...

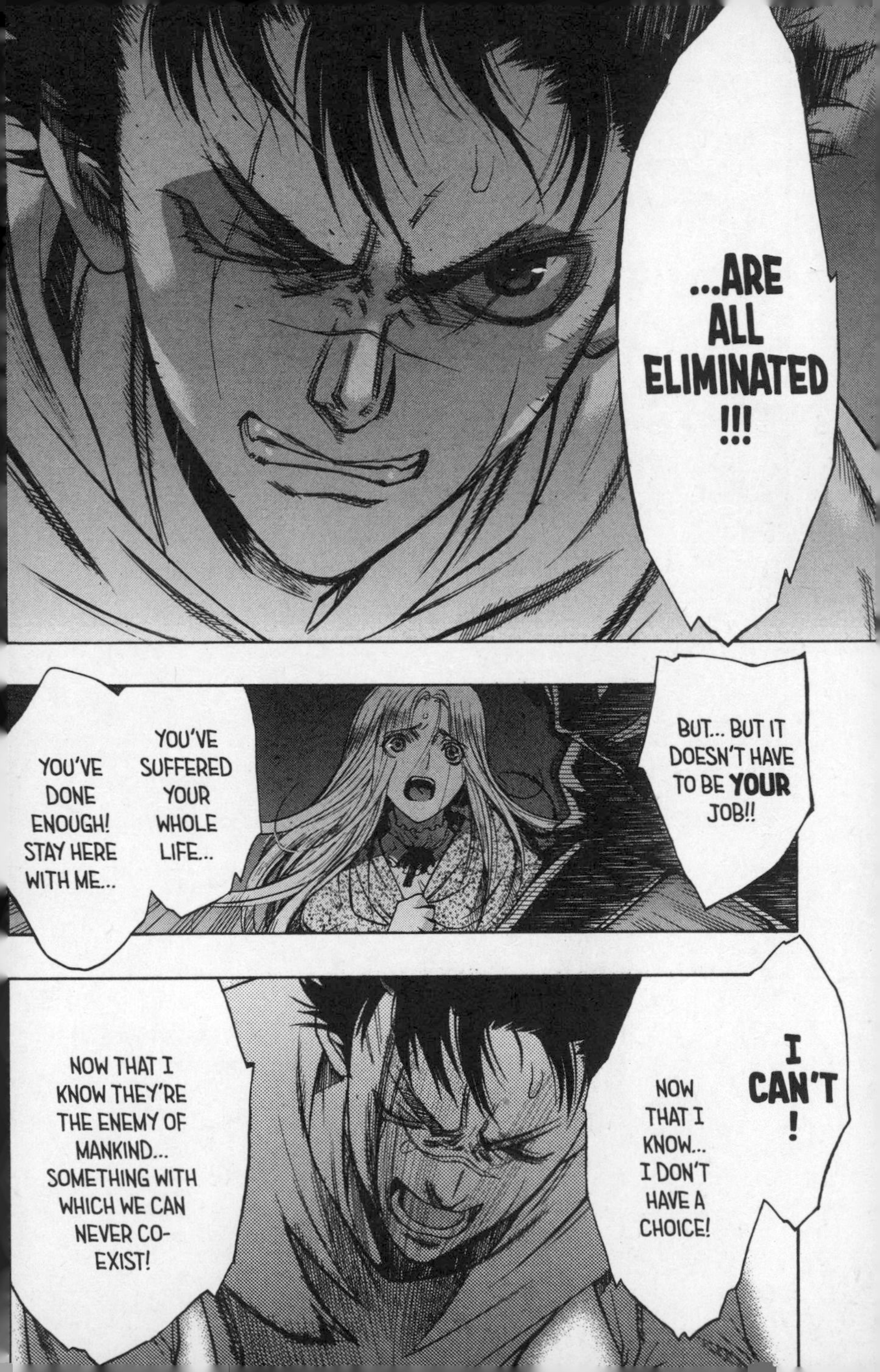
...ARE ALL ELIMINATED !!!
BUT... BUT IT DOESN'T HAVE TO BE **YOUR** JOB!!
YOU'VE SUFFERED YOUR WHOLE LIFE...
YOU'VE DONE ENOUGH! STAY HERE WITH ME...
I CAN'T !
NOW THAT I KNOW... I DON'T HAVE A CHOICE!
NOW THAT I KNOW THEY'RE THE ENEMY OF MANKIND... SOMETHING WITH WHICH WE CAN NEVER CO-EXIST!

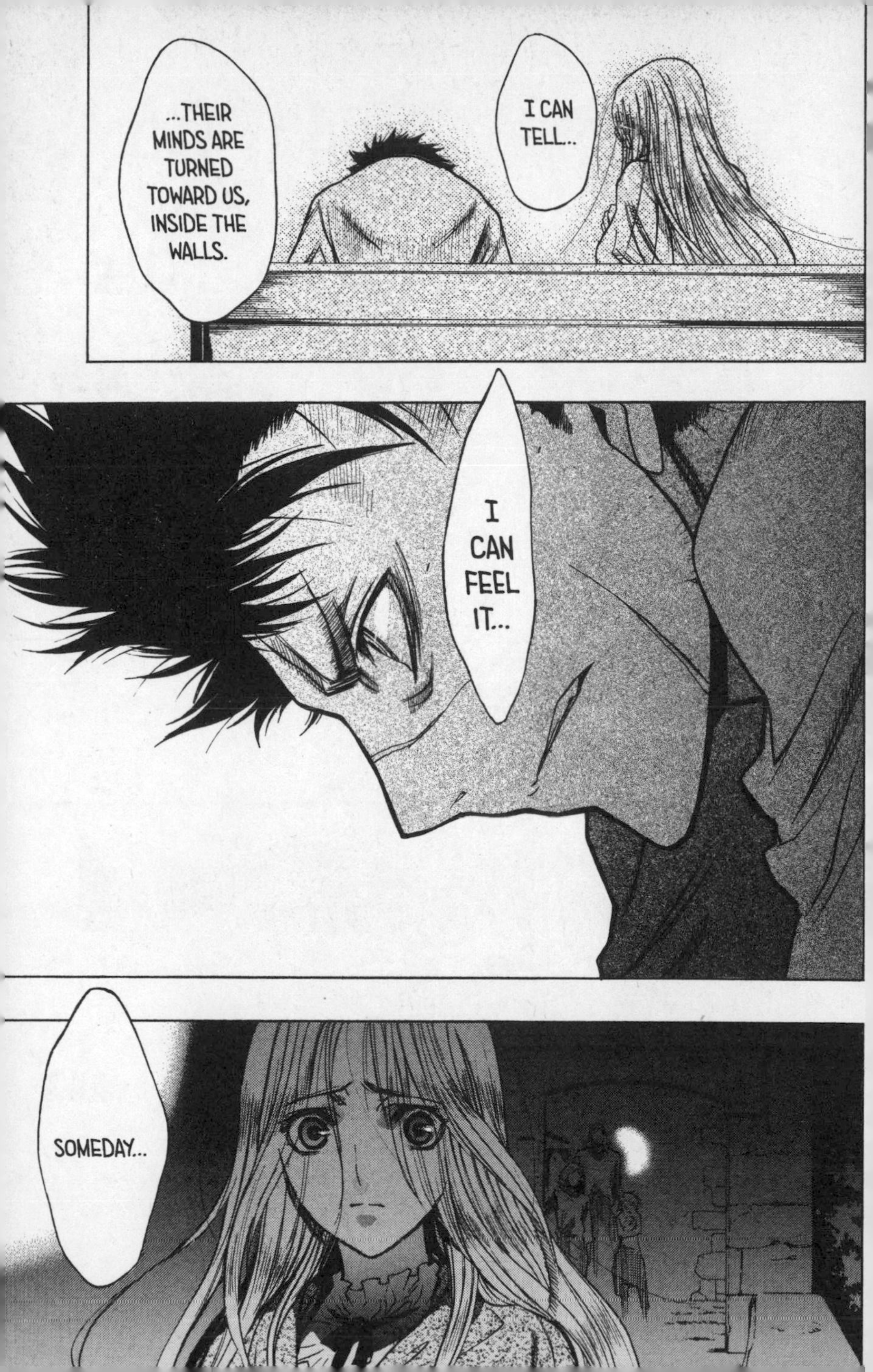
I CAN TELL...
...THEIR MINDS ARE TURNED TOWARD US, INSIDE THE WALLS.
I CAN FEEL IT...
SOMEDAY...

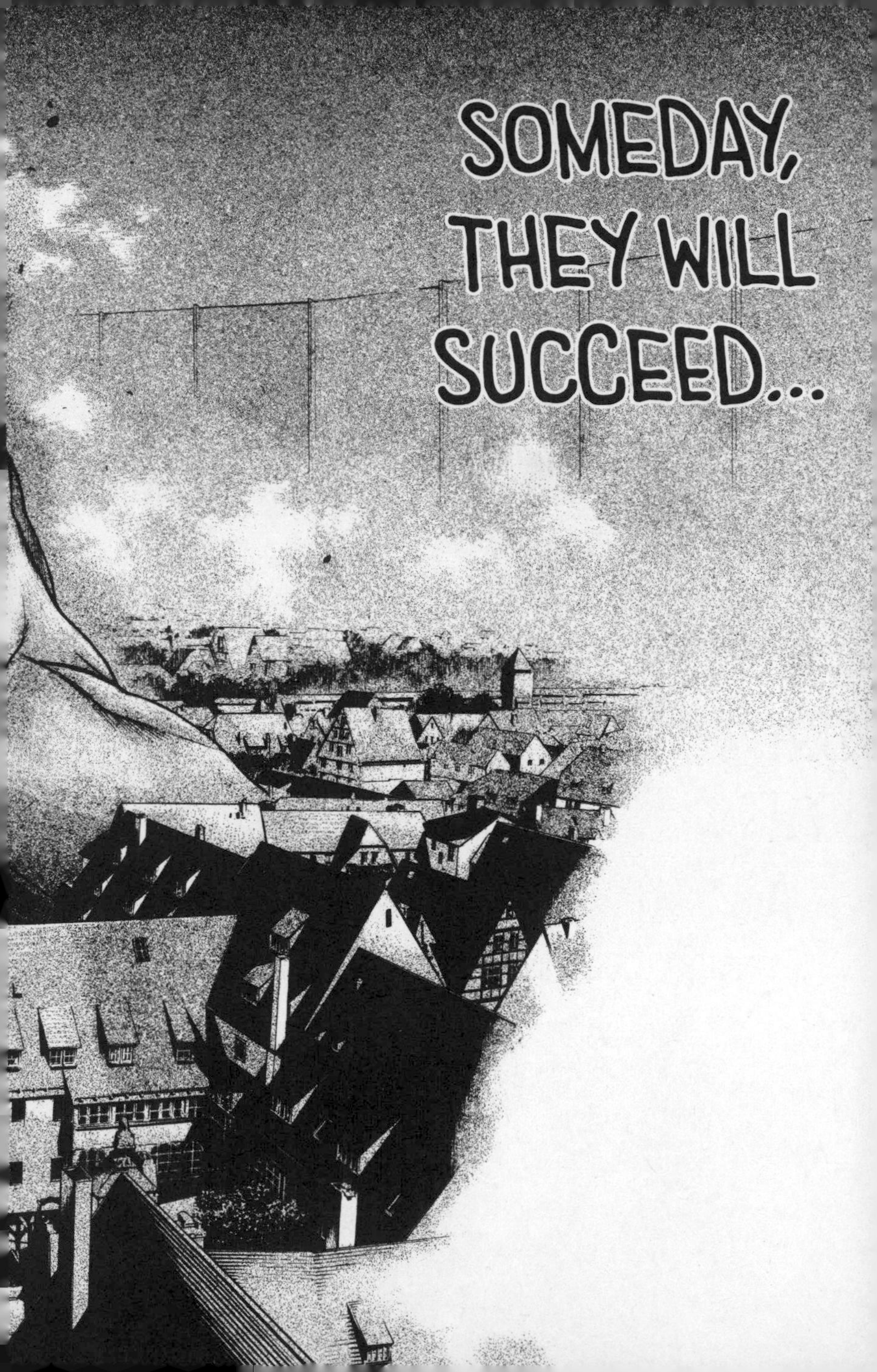
SOMEDAY, THEY WILL SUCCEED...

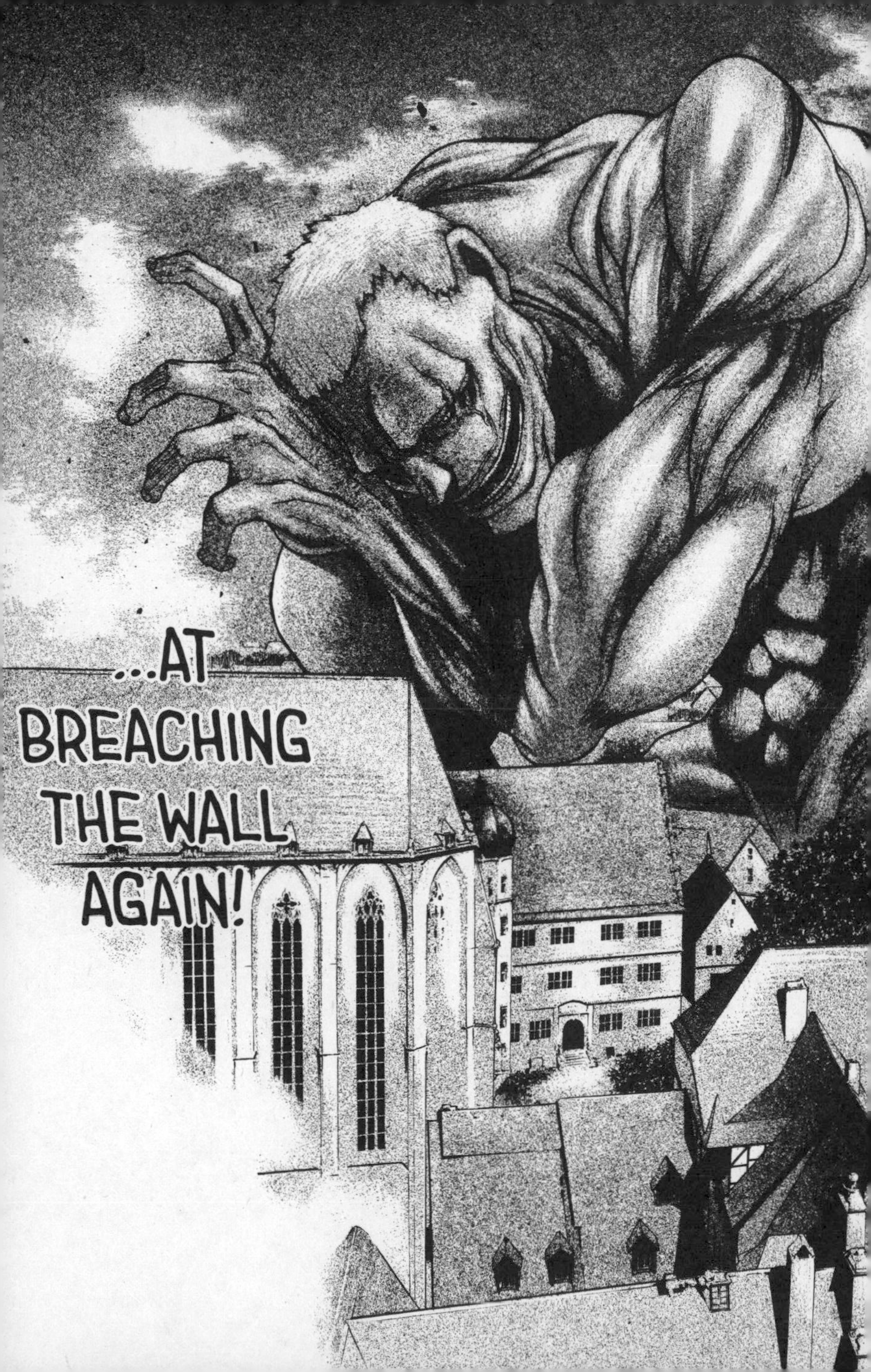
...AT BREACHING THE WALL AGAIN!

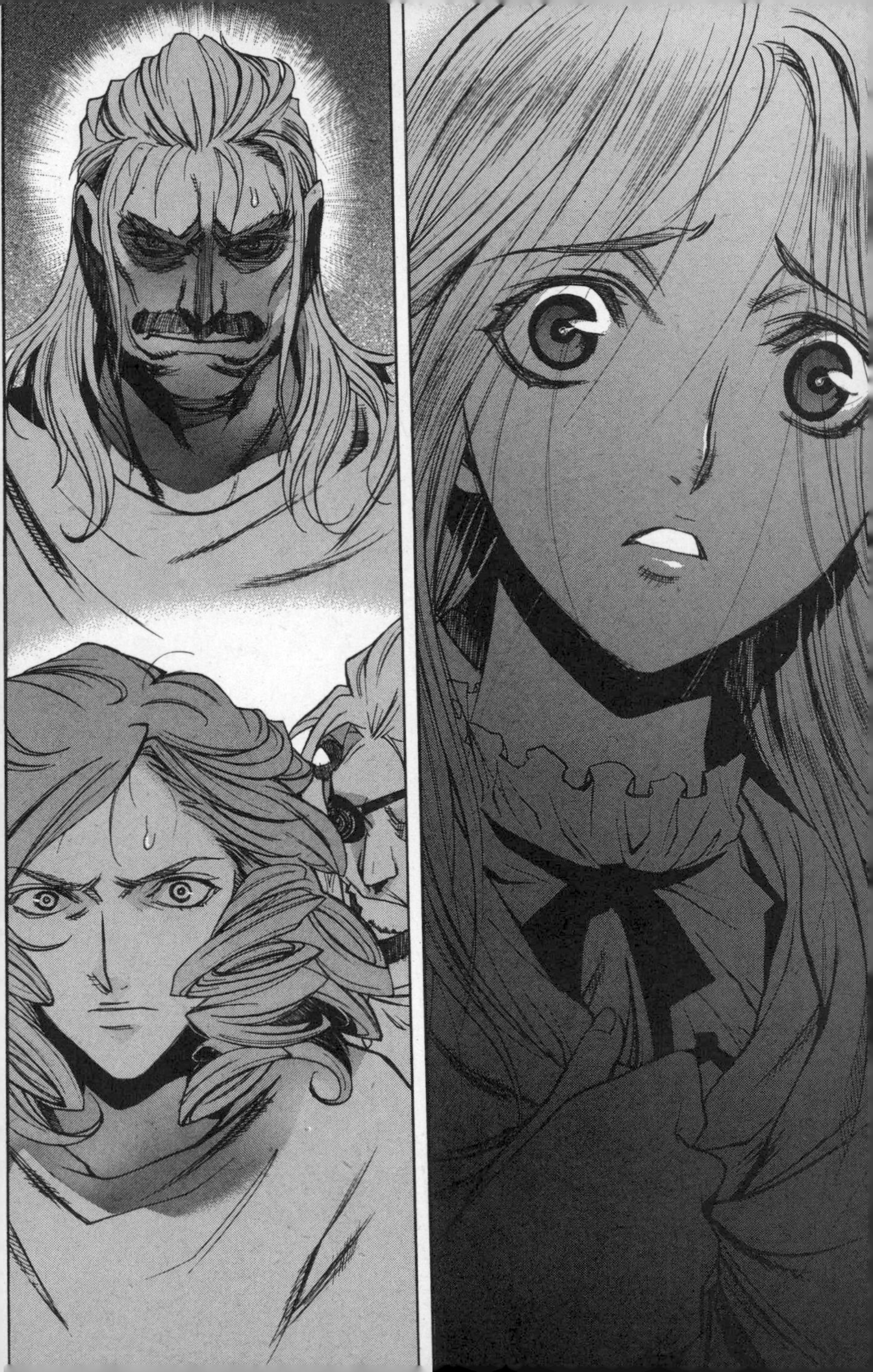

Chapter 15: Visions of the Future · End

ATTACK on TITAN

BEFORE THE FALL

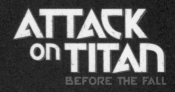

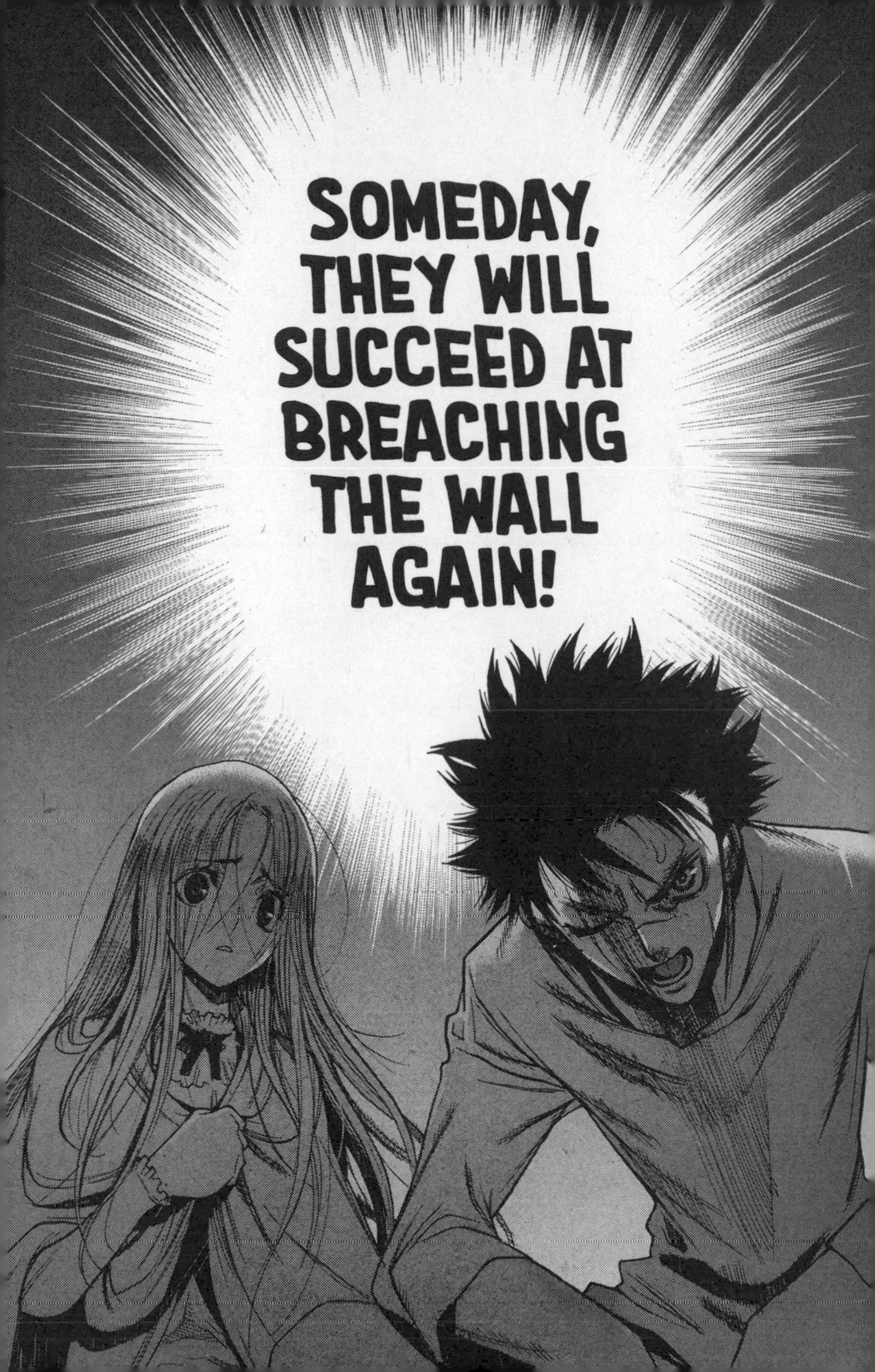
SOMEDAY, THEY WILL SUCCEED AT BREACHING THE WALL AGAIN!

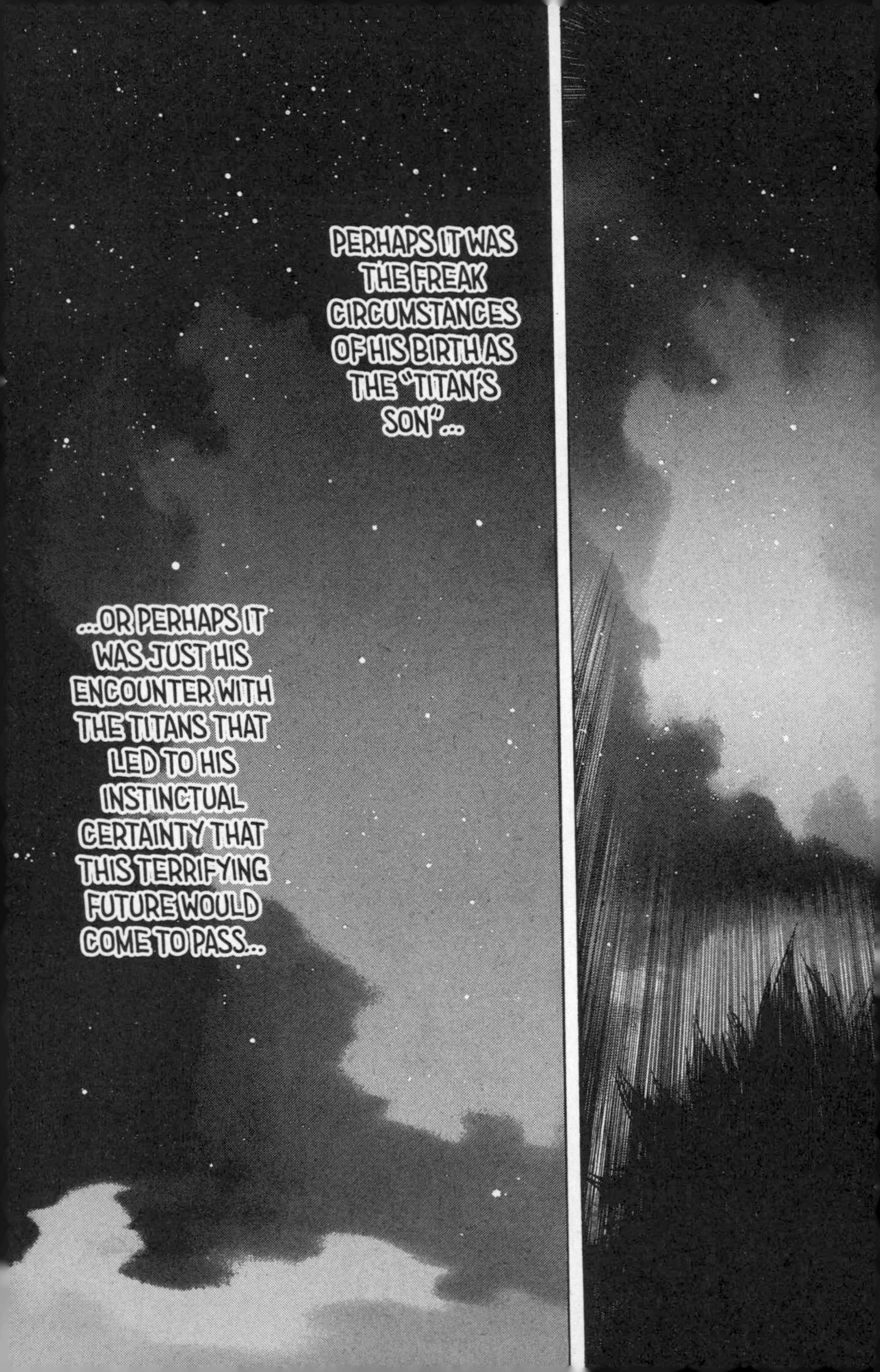
PERHAPS IT WAS THE FREAK CIRCUMSTANCES OF HIS BIRTH AS THE "TITAN'S SON"...
...OR PERHAPS IT WAS JUST HIS ENCOUNTER WITH THE TITANS THAT LED TO HIS INSTINCTUAL CERTAINTY THAT THIS TERRIFYING FUTURE WOULD COME TO PASS...

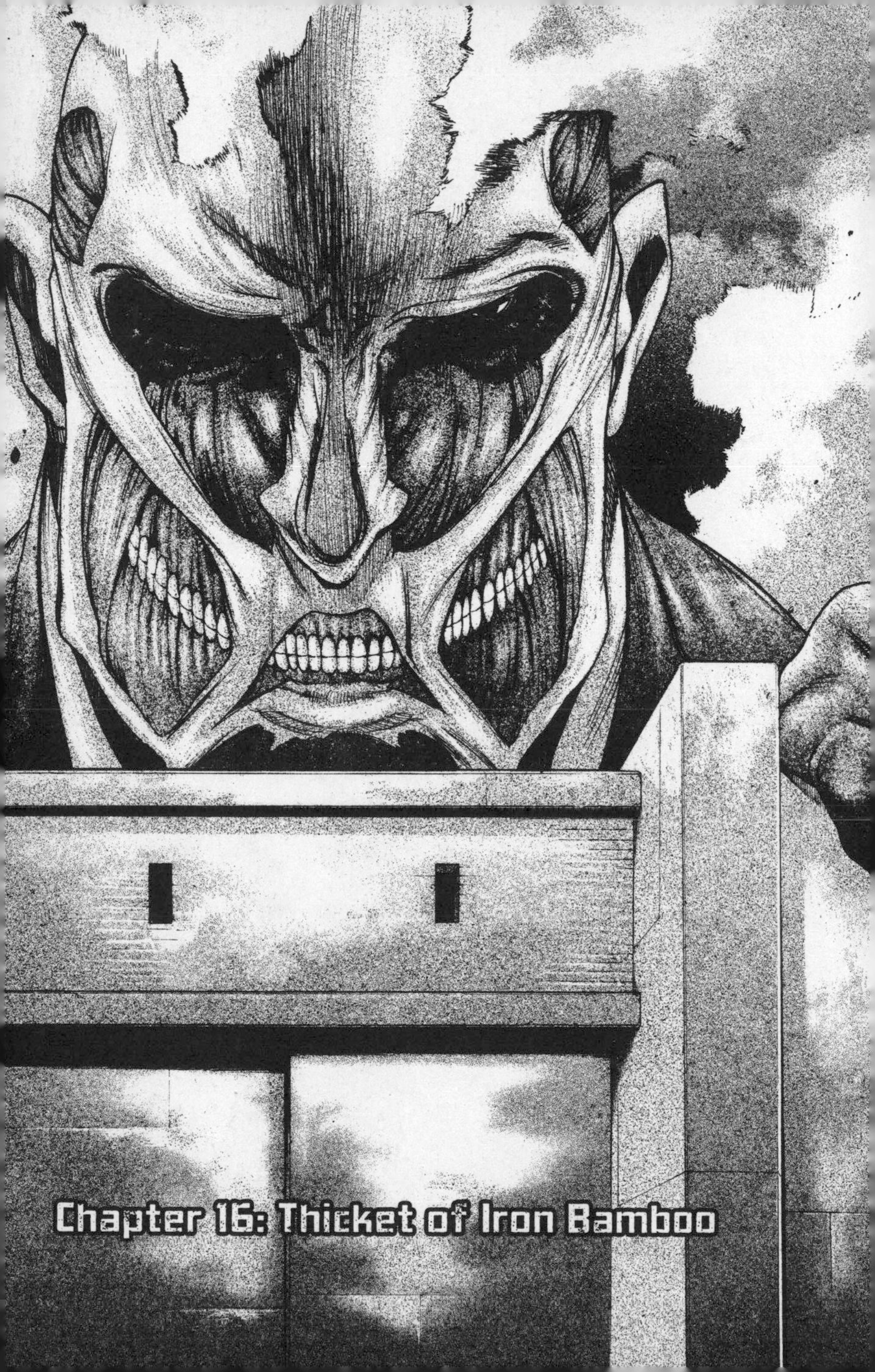
Chapter 16: Thicket of Iron Bamboo

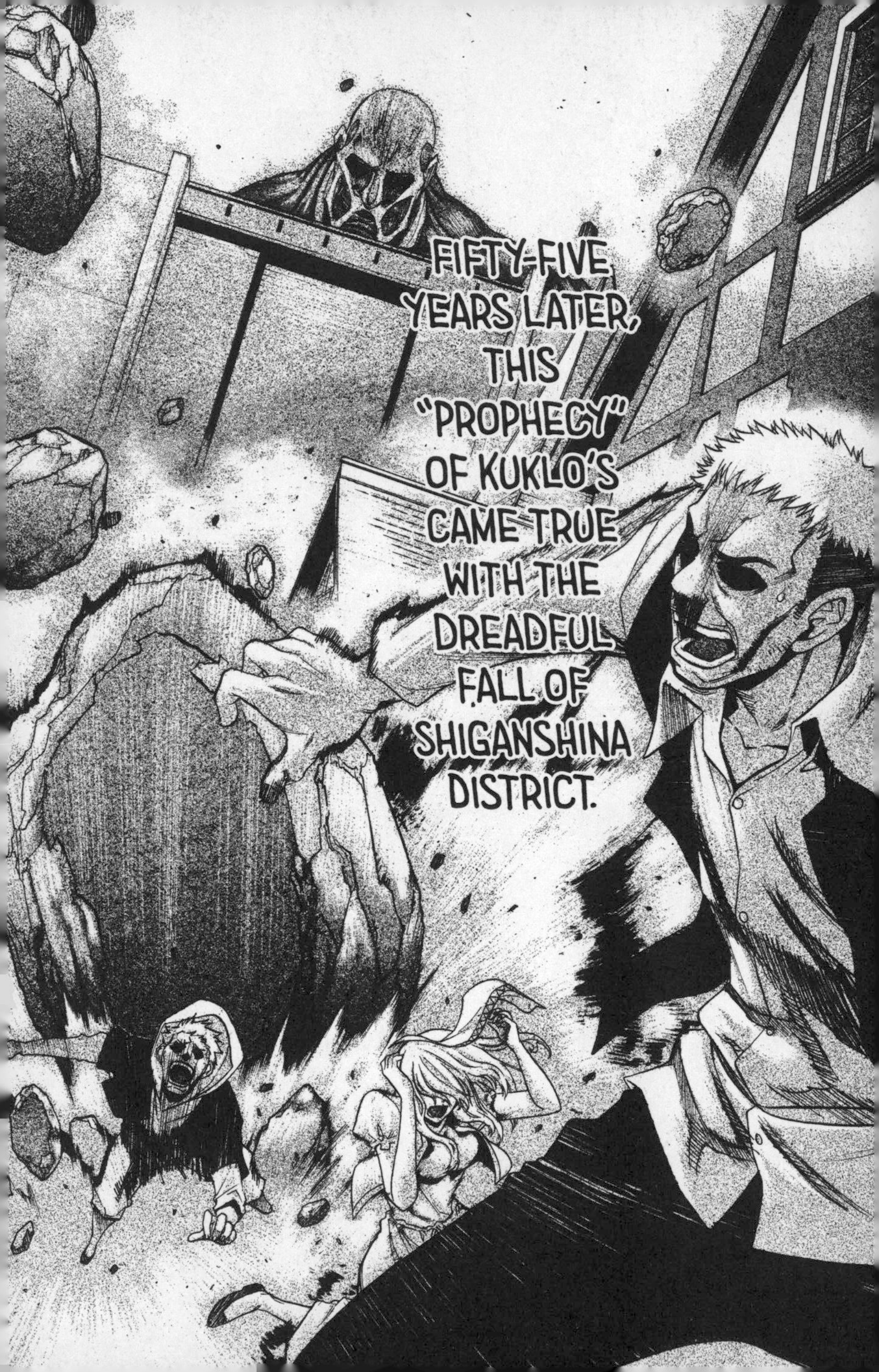
FIFTY-FIVE YEARS LATER, THIS "PROPHECY" OF KUKLO'S CAME TRUE WITH THE DREADFUL FALL OF SHIGANSHINA DISTRICT.

EVERY HUMAN BEING WHO HUDDLED FOR SAFETY WITHIN THE WALLS COULD HAVE SEEN THIS NIGHTMARISH DAY COMING...
...BUT THE IMAGE WAS SO TERRIFYING AND FULL OF DESPAIR THAT HUMANITY CHOSE TO HIDE THE THOUGHT IN ITS UNCONSCIOUS MIND AND IGNORE IT.

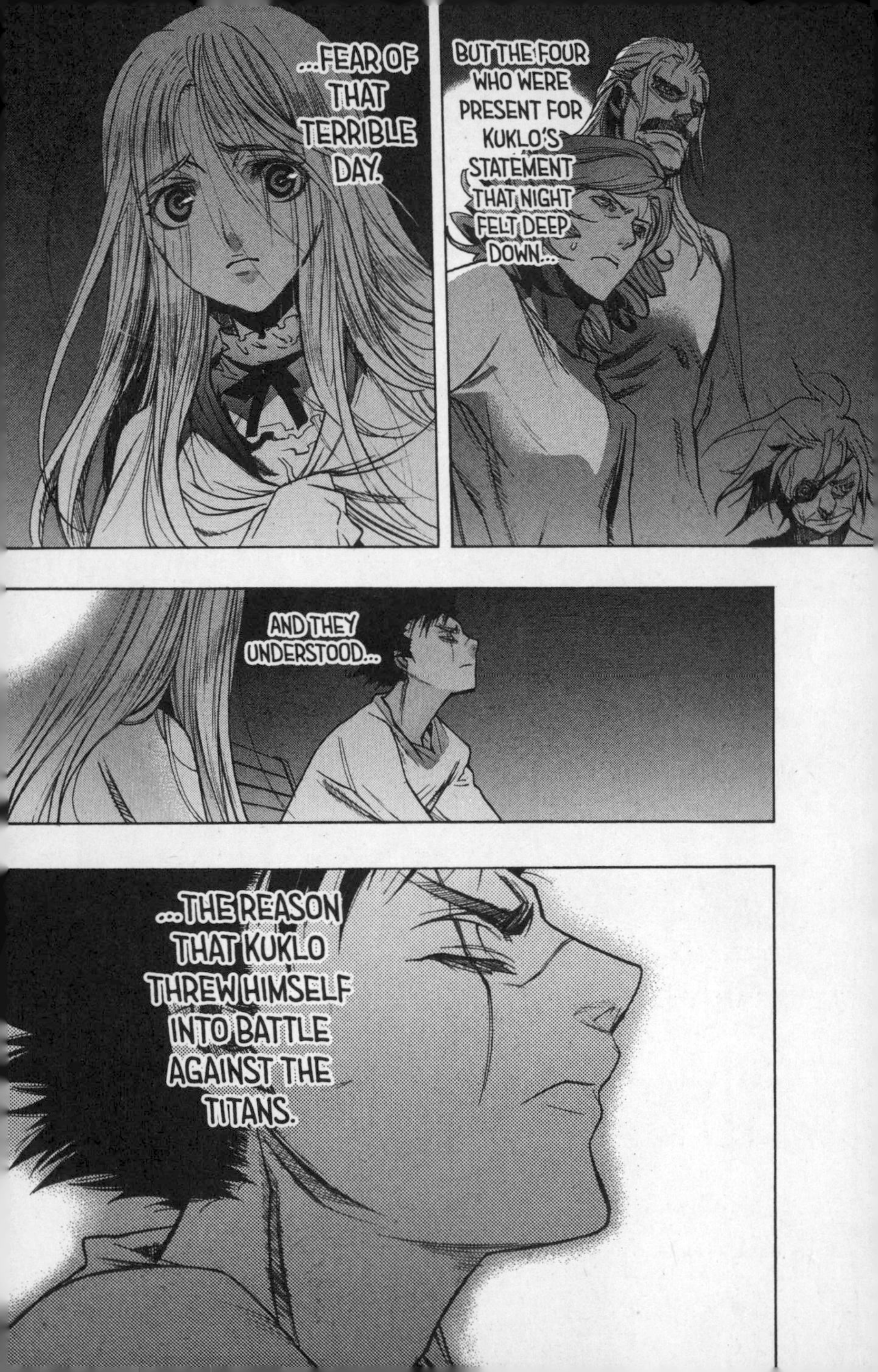
BUT THE FOUR WHO WERE PRESENT FOR KUKLO'S STATEMENT THAT NIGHT FELT DEEP DOWN...
...FEAR OF THAT TERRIBLE DAY.
AND THEY UNDERSTOOD...
...THE REASON THAT KUKLO THREW HIMSELF INTO BATTLE AGAINST THE TITANS.

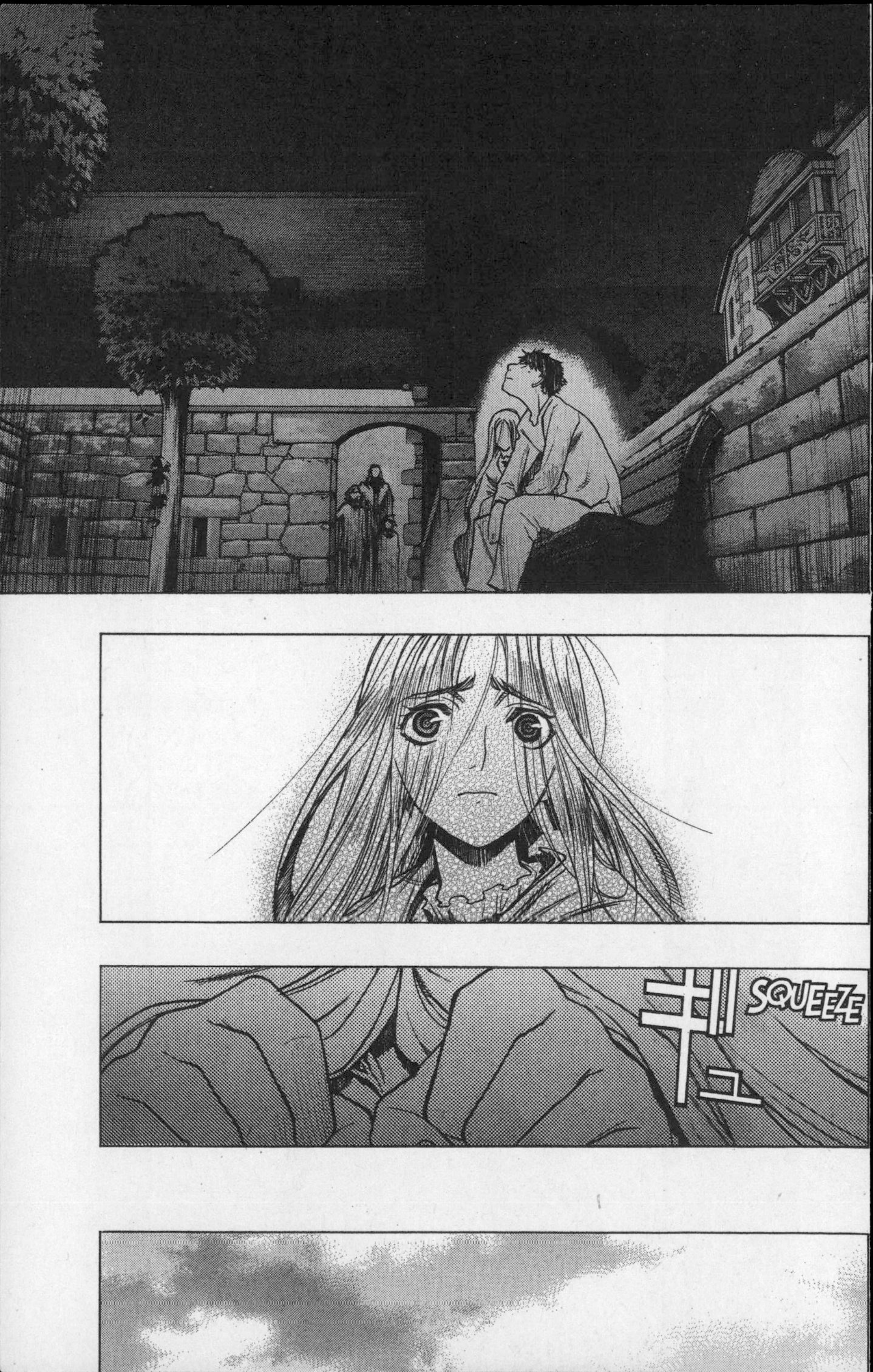
キュ
SQUEEZE

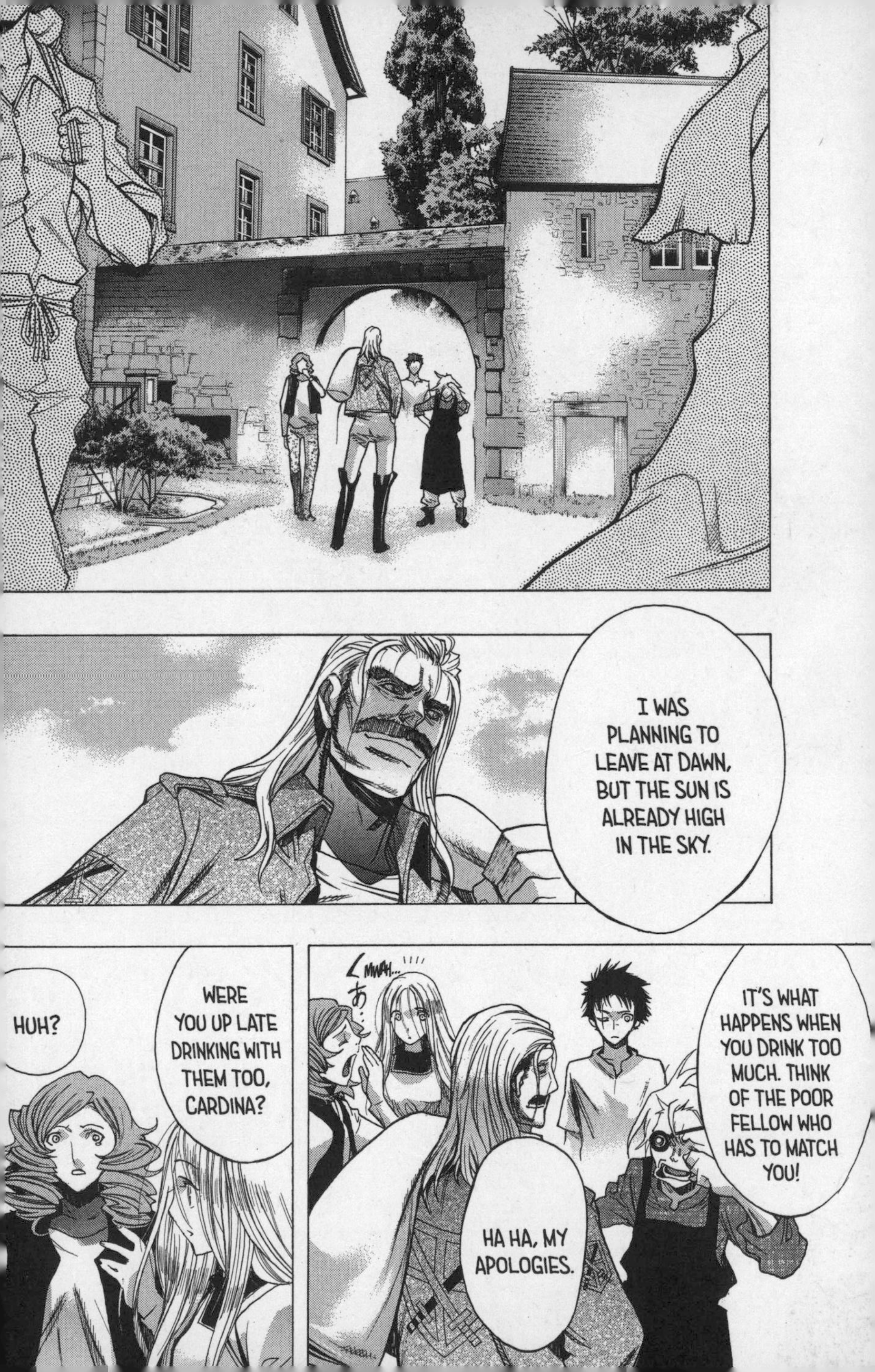
I WAS PLANNING TO LEAVE AT DAWN, BUT THE SUN IS ALREADY HIGH IN THE SKY.
IT'S WHAT HAPPENS WHEN YOU DRINK TOO MUCH. THINK OF THE POOR FELLOW WHO HAS TO MATCH YOU!
MWAH...
あ…
HA HA, MY APOLOGIES.
WERE YOU UP LATE DRINKING WITH THEM TOO, CARDINA?
HUH?

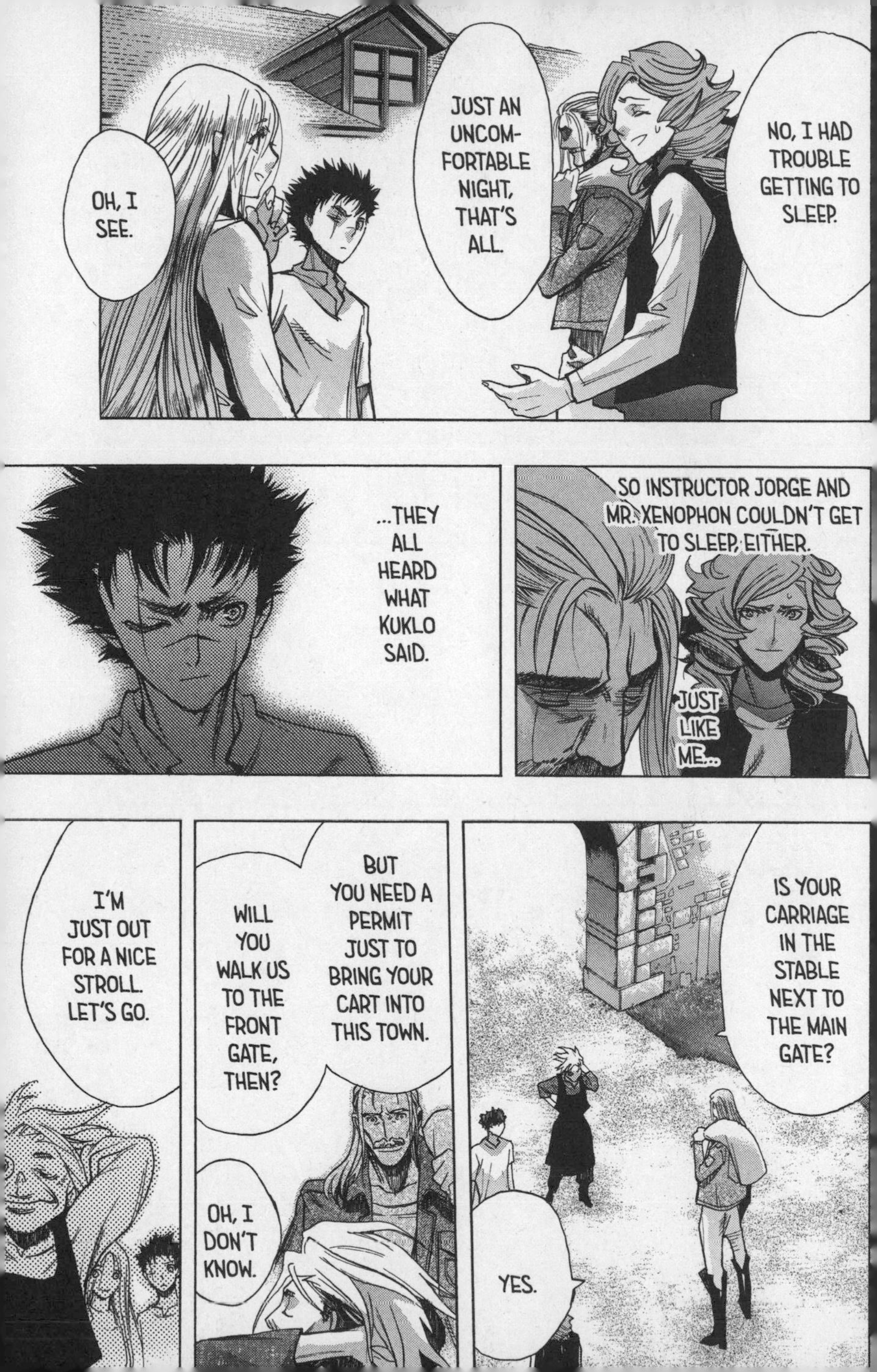
NO, I HAD TROUBLE GETTING TO SLEEP.
JUST AN UNCOMFORTABLE NIGHT, THAT'S ALL.
OH, I SEE.
SO INSTRUCTOR JORGE AND MR. XENOPHON COULDN'T GET TO SLEEP, EITHER.
JUST LIKE ME...
...THEY ALL HEARD WHAT KUKLO SAID.
IS YOUR CARRIAGE IN THE STABLE NEXT TO THE MAIN GATE?
YES.
BUT YOU NEED A PERMIT JUST TO BRING YOUR CART INTO THIS TOWN.
WILL YOU WALK US TO THE FRONT GATE, THEN?
OH, I DON'T KNOW.
I'M JUST OUT FOR A NICE STROLL. LET'S GO.

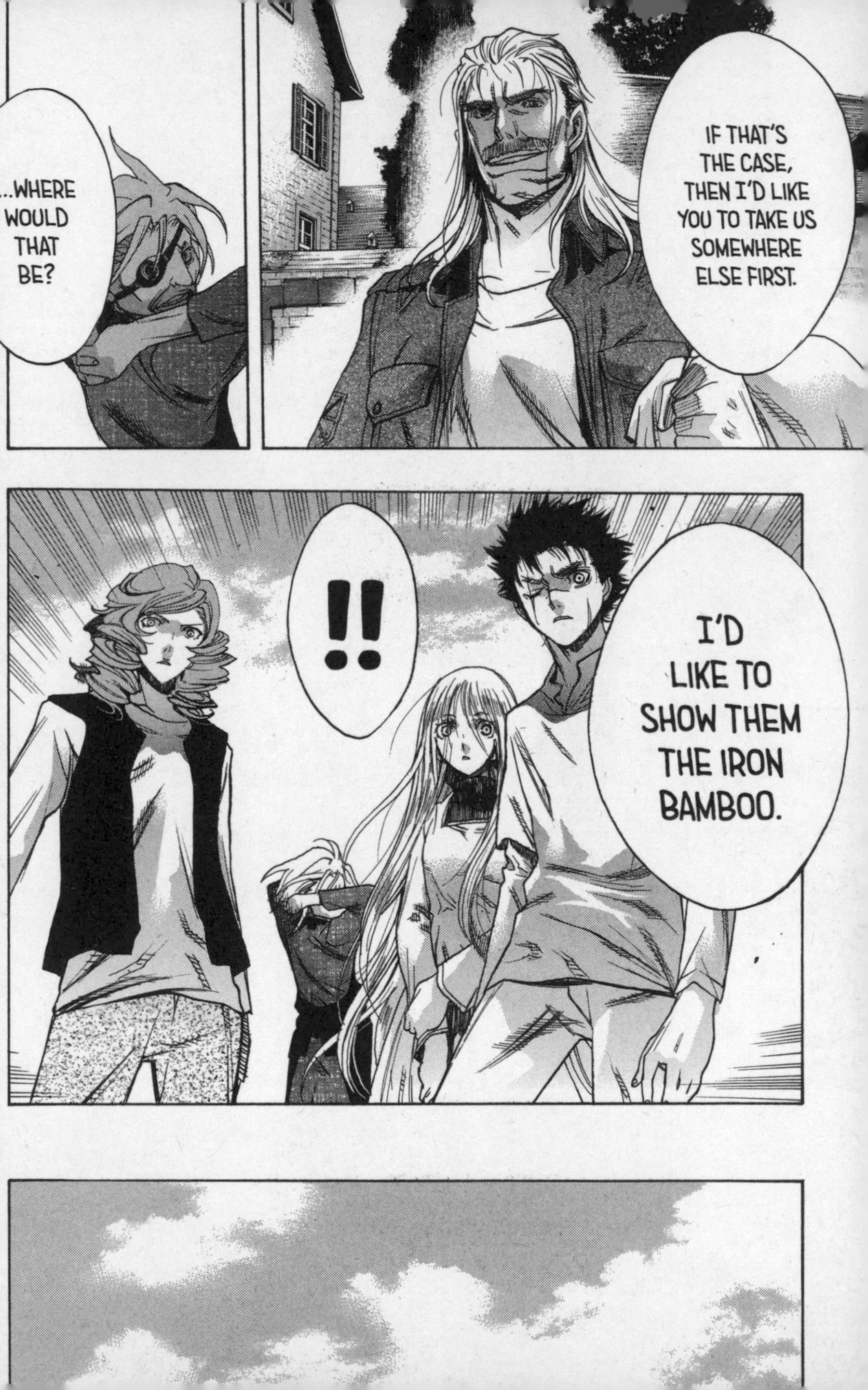
IF THAT'S THE CASE, THEN I'D LIKE YOU TO TAKE US SOMEWHERE ELSE FIRST.
...WHERE WOULD THAT BE?
I'D LIKE TO SHOW THEM THE IRON BAMBOO.
!!

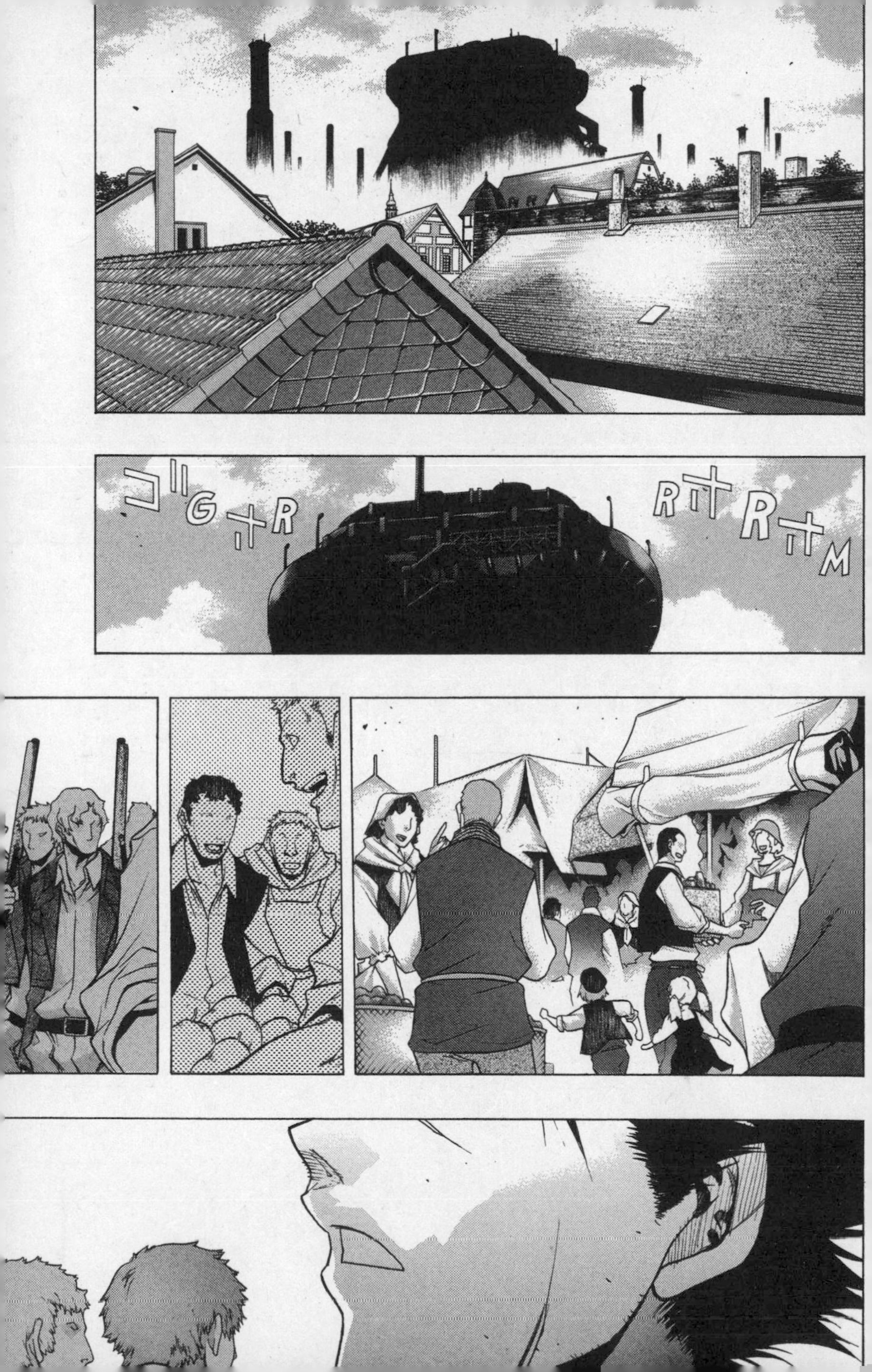
GR
RRM

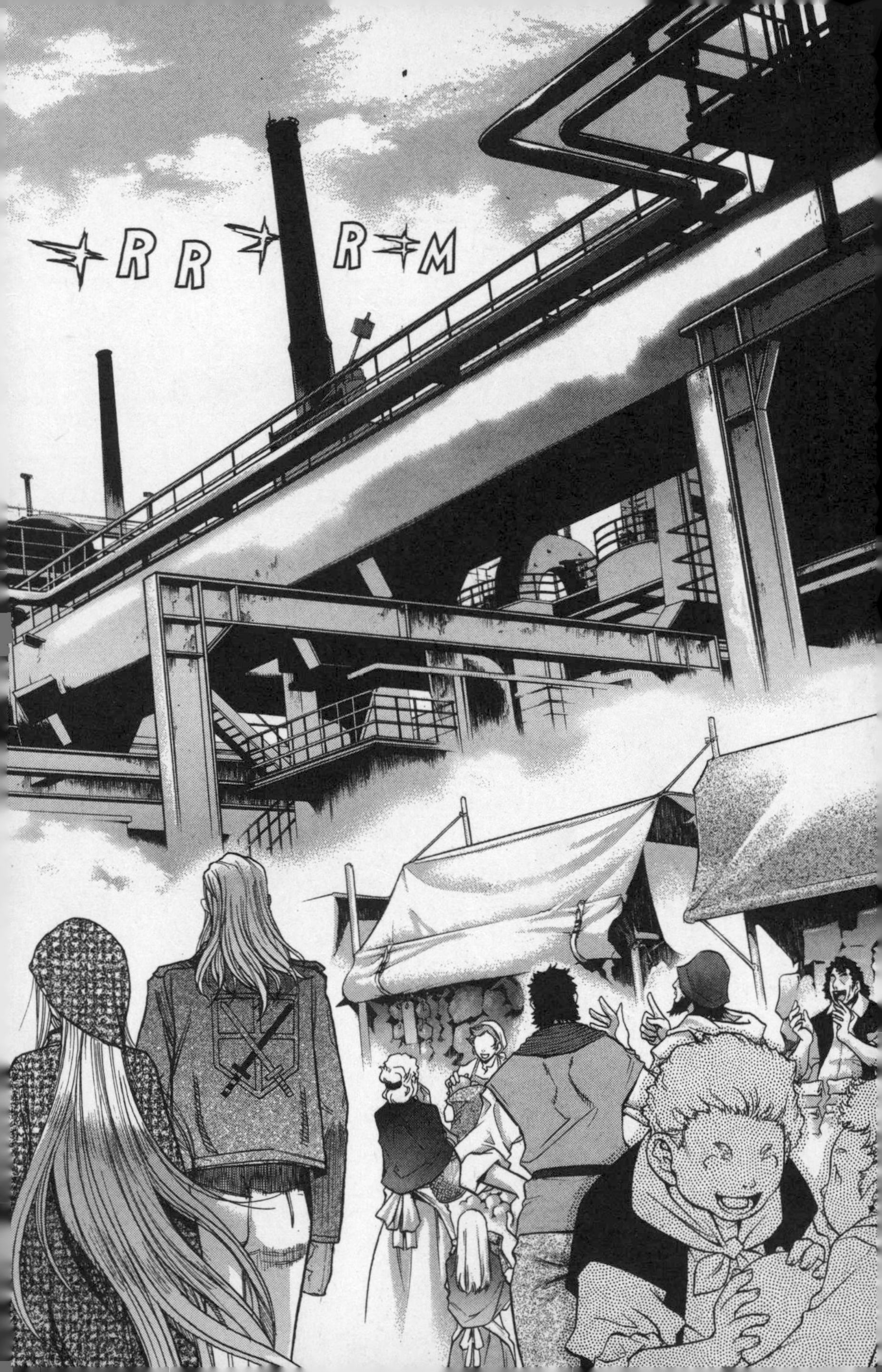
RR R M

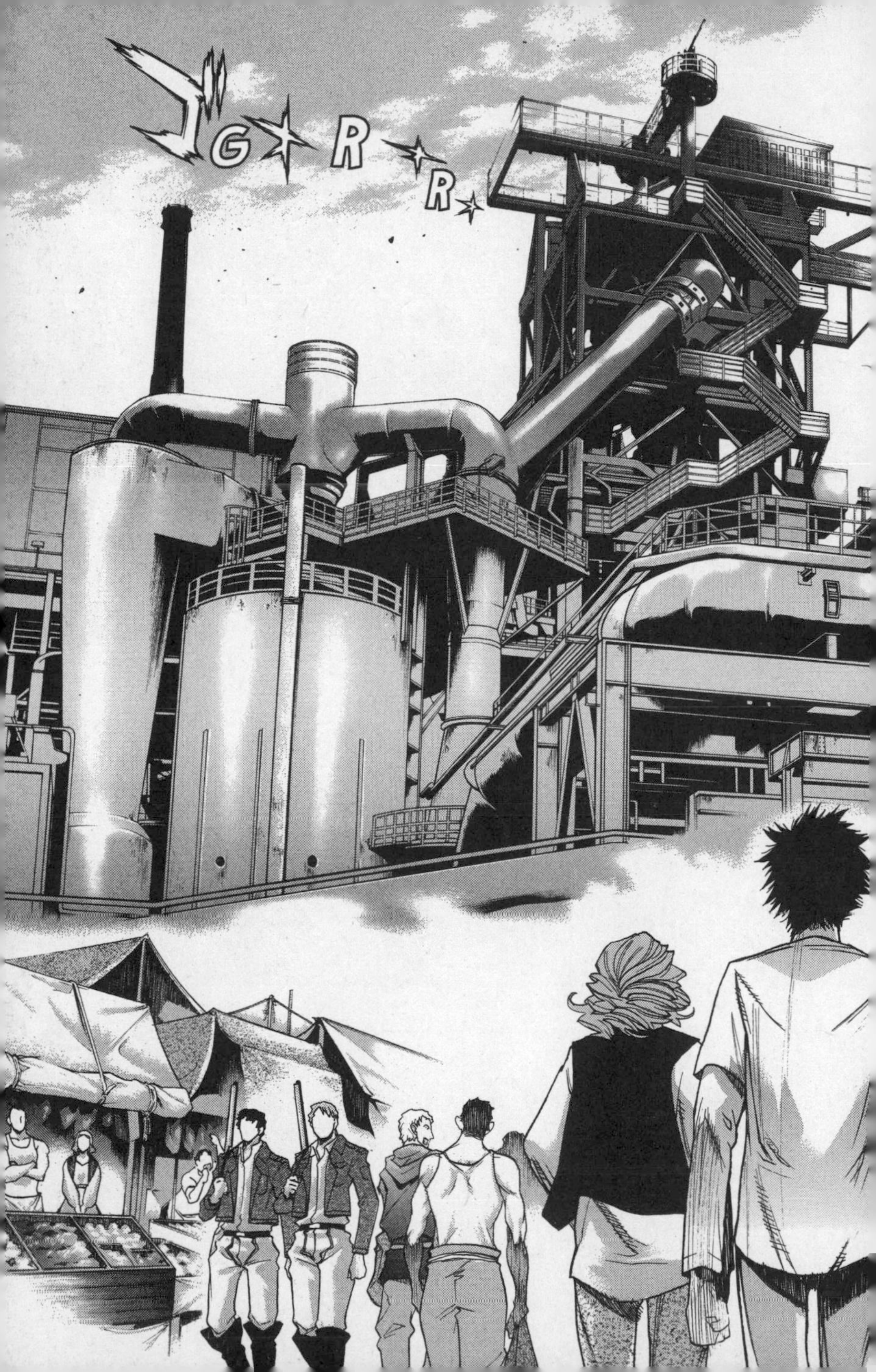
GRR

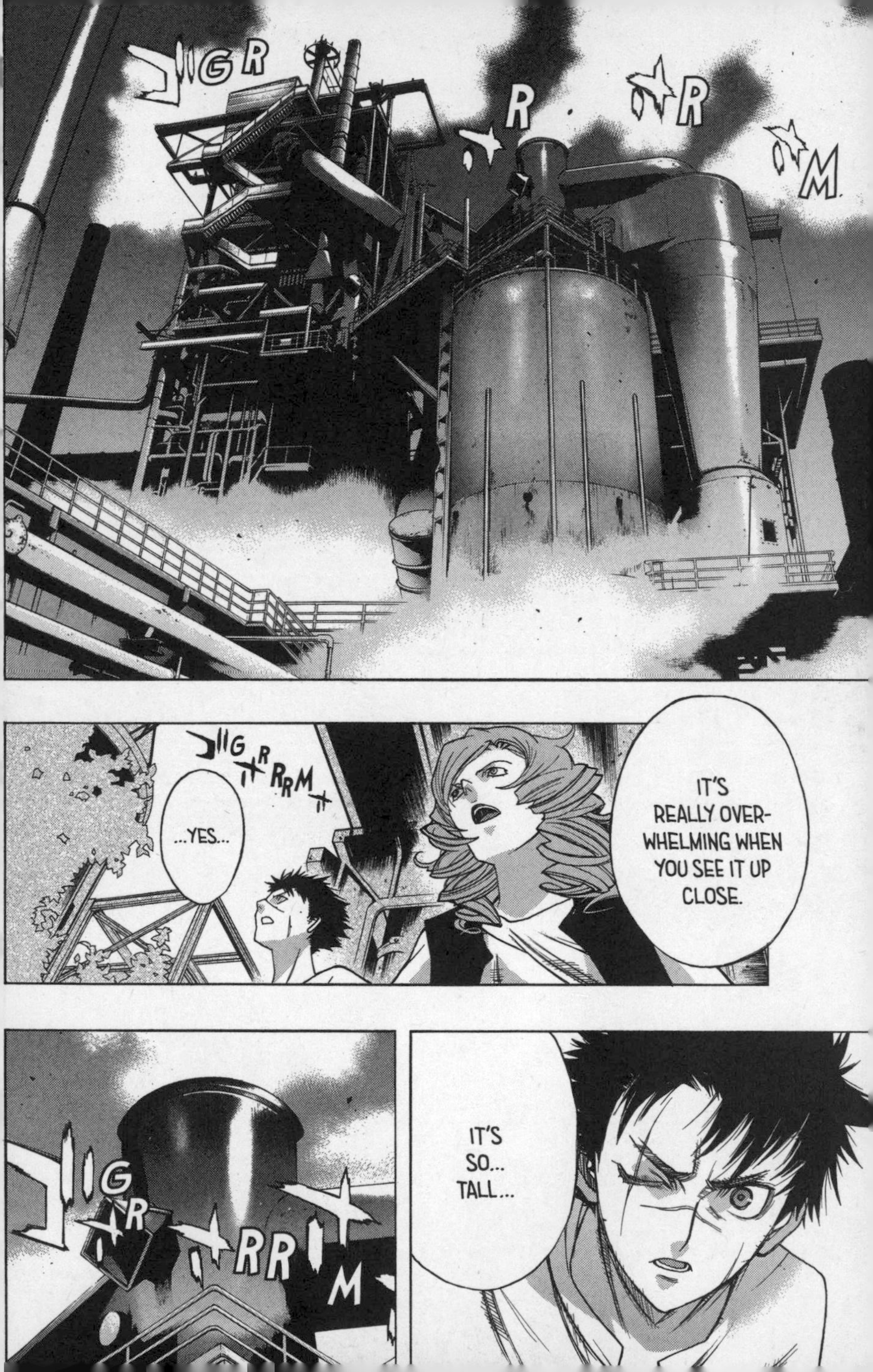
GRRRM
IT'S REALLY OVER-WHELMING WHEN YOU SEE IT UP CLOSE.
...YES...
GRRRM
IT'S SO... TALL...
GRRRM

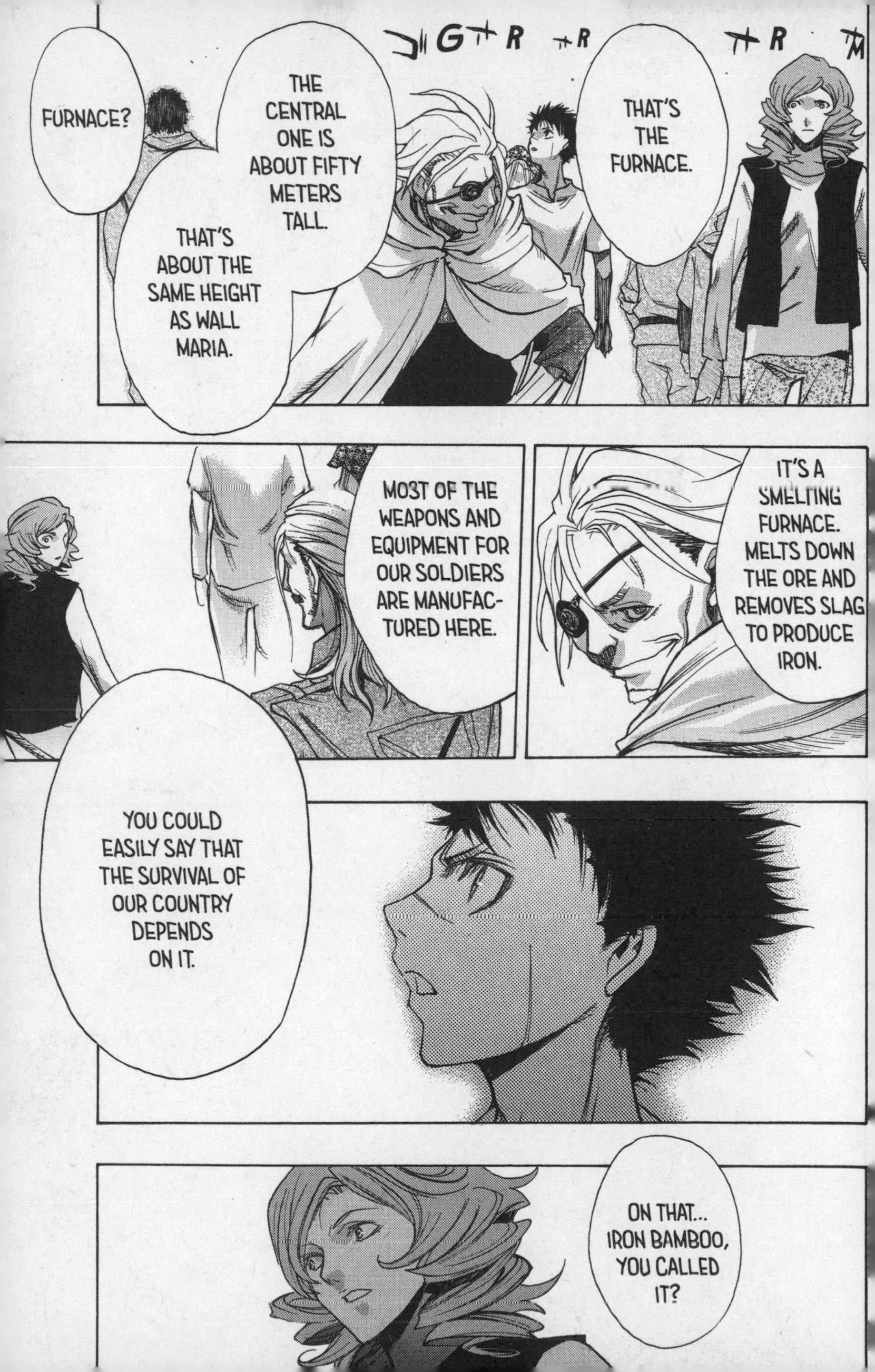
THAT'S THE FURNACE.
THE CENTRAL ONE IS ABOUT FIFTY METERS TALL.
FURNACE?
THAT'S ABOUT THE SAME HEIGHT AS WALL MARIA.
IT'S A SMELTING FURNACE. MELTS DOWN THE ORE AND REMOVES SLAG TO PRODUCE IRON.
MOST OF THE WEAPONS AND EQUIPMENT FOR OUR SOLDIERS ARE MANUFAC-TURED HERE.
YOU COULD EASILY SAY THAT THE SURVIVAL OF OUR COUNTRY DEPENDS ON IT.
ON THAT... IRON BAMBOO, YOU CALLED IT?

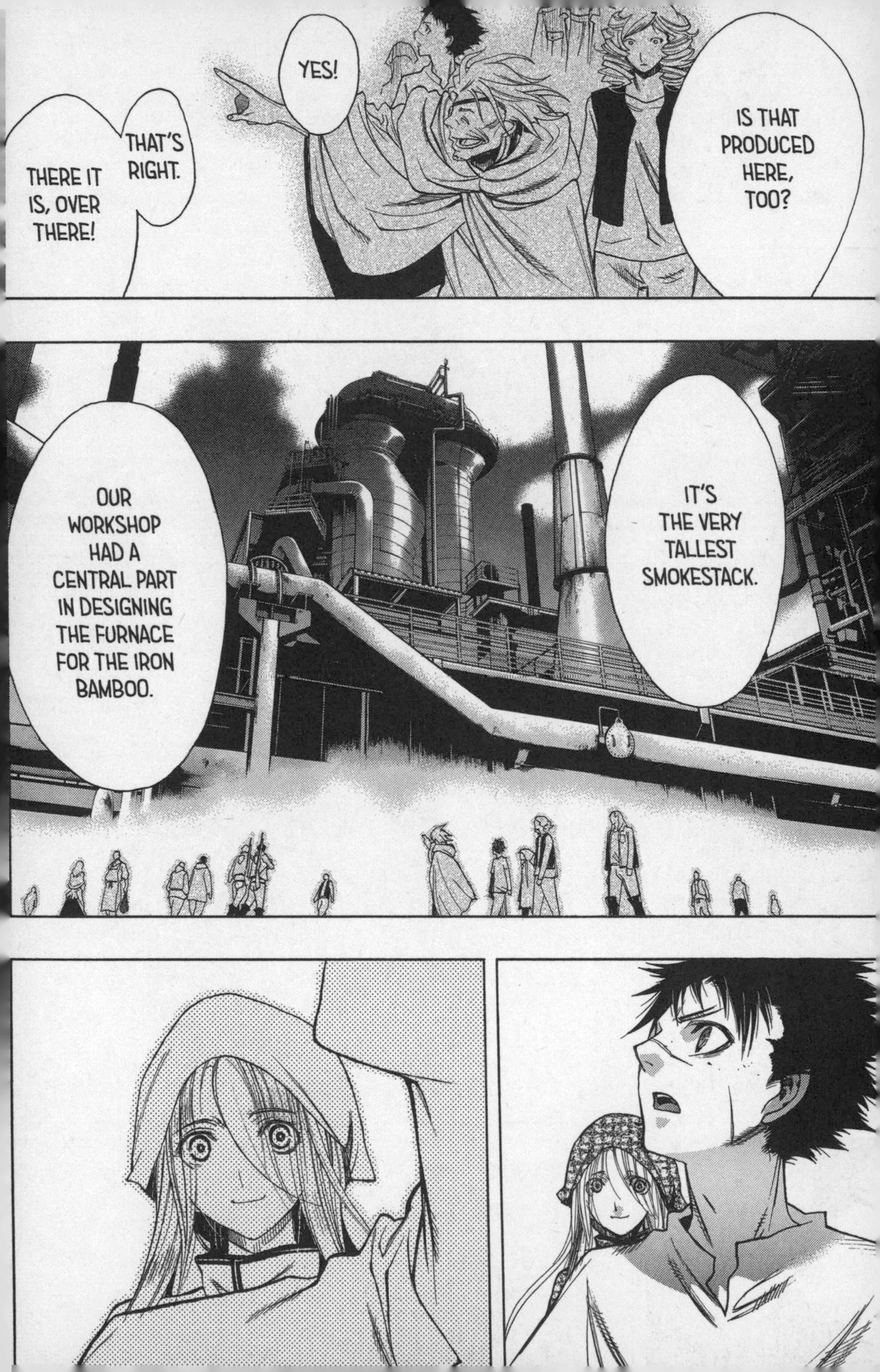
IS THAT PRODUCED HERE, TOO?
YES!
THAT'S RIGHT.
THERE IT IS, OVER THERE!
IT'S THE VERY TALLEST SMOKESTACK.
OUR WORKSHOP HAD A CENTRAL PART IN DESIGNING THE FURNACE FOR THE IRON BAMBOO.

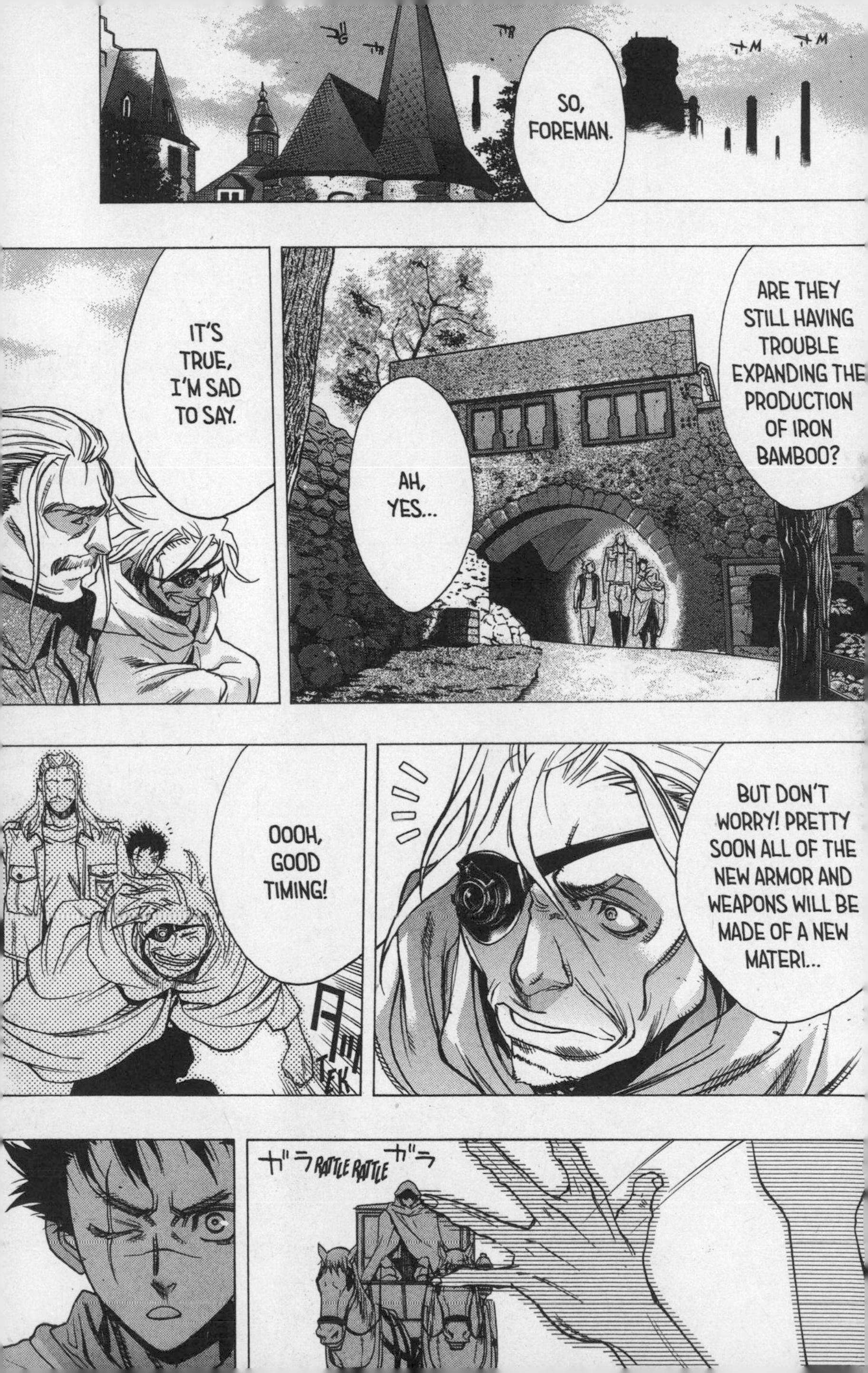
SO, FOREMAN.
ARE THEY STILL HAVING TROUBLE EXPANDING THE PRODUCTION OF IRON BAMBOO?
AH, YES...
IT'S TRUE, I'M SAD TO SAY.
BUT DON'T WORRY! PRETTY SOON ALL OF THE NEW ARMOR AND WEAPONS WILL BE MADE OF A NEW MATERI...
OOOH, GOOD TIMING!
TEK
ガラ RATTLE RATTLE ガラ

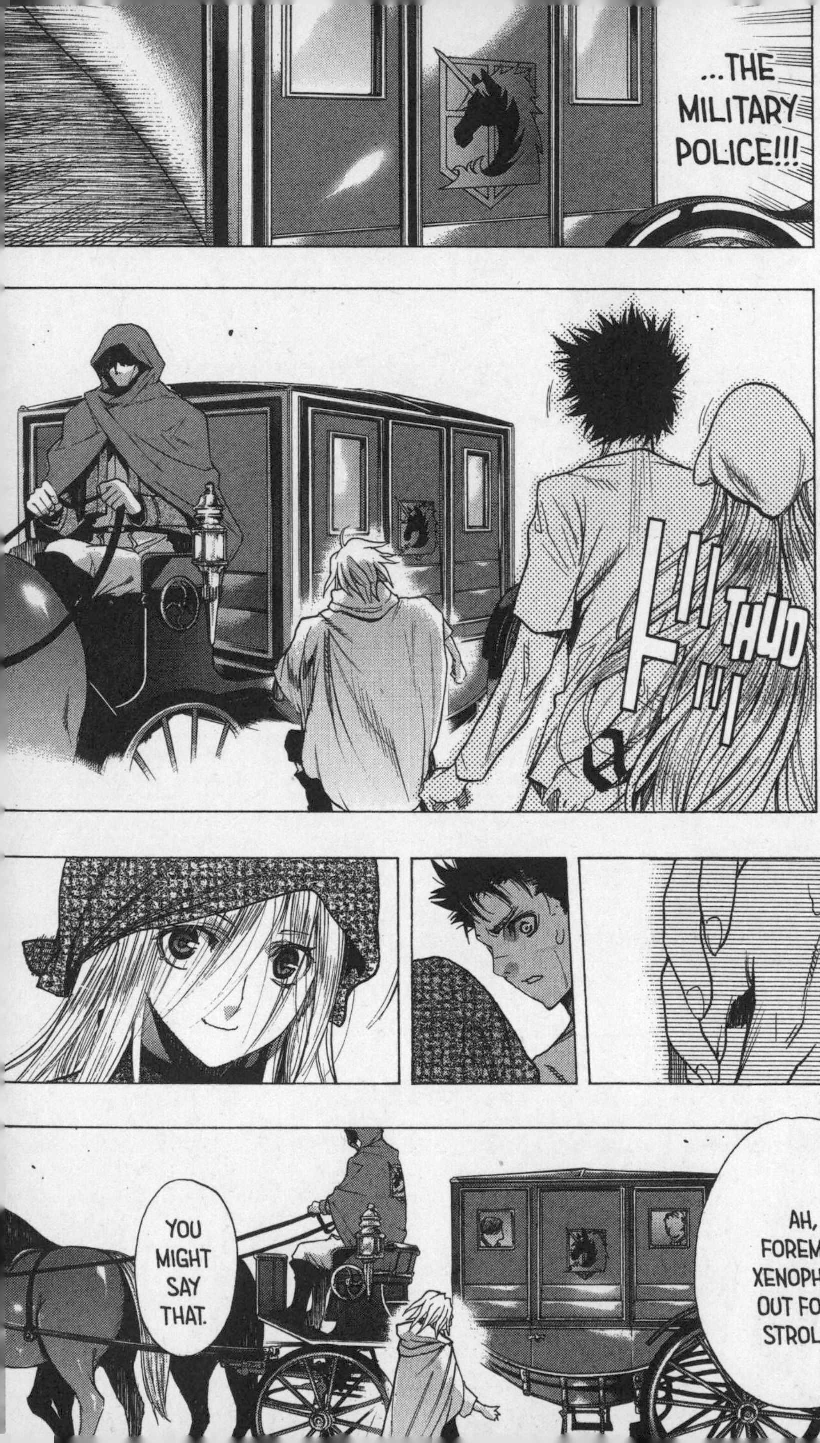
...THE MILITARY POLICE!!!
THUD
AH, FOREMAN XENOPHON! OUT FOR A STROLL?
YOU MIGHT SAY THAT.

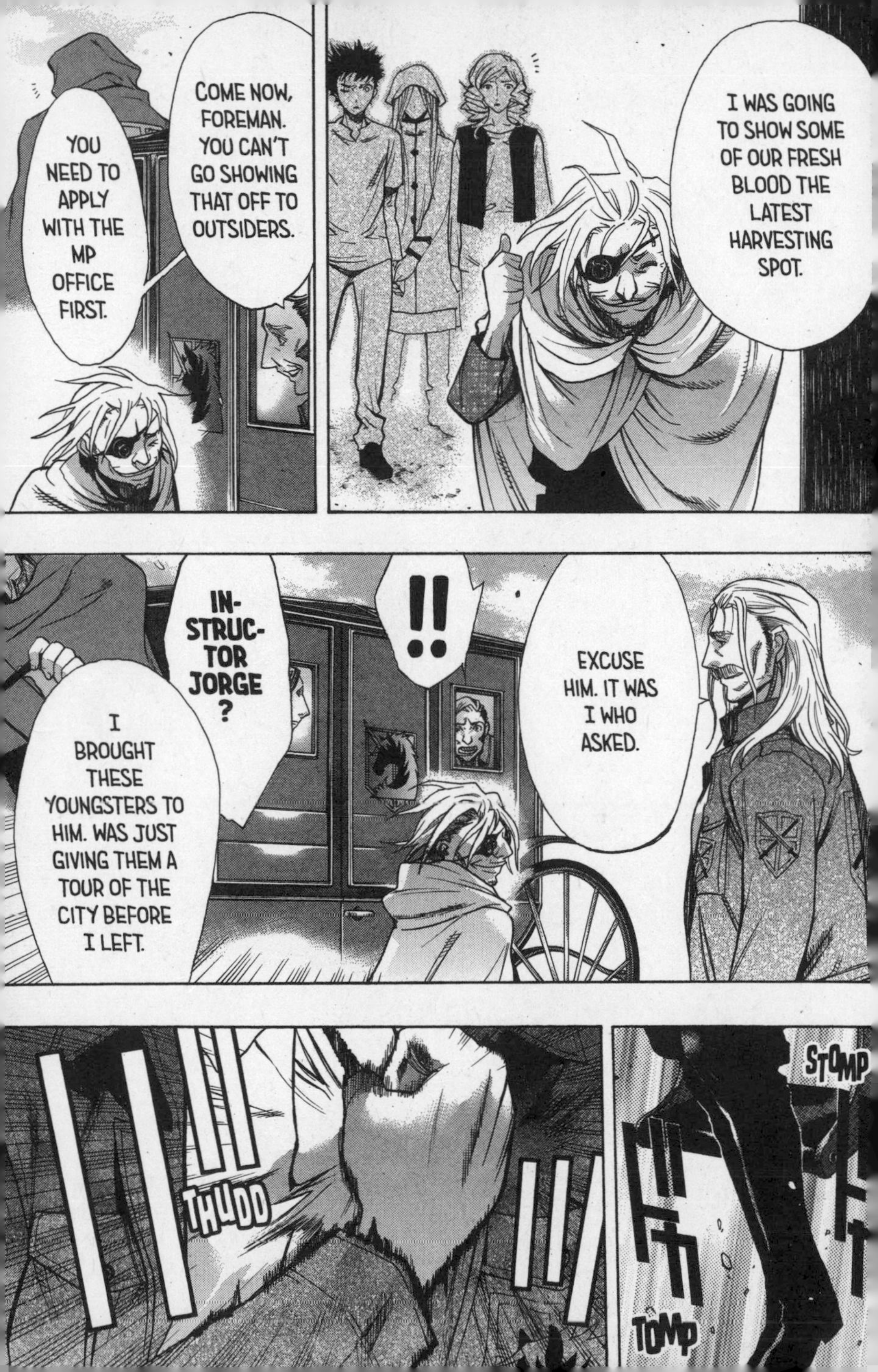
I WAS GOING TO SHOW SOME OF OUR FRESH BLOOD THE LATEST HARVESTING SPOT.
COME NOW, FOREMAN. YOU CAN'T GO SHOWING THAT OFF TO OUTSIDERS.
YOU NEED TO APPLY WITH THE MP OFFICE FIRST.
EXCUSE HIM. IT WAS I WHO ASKED.
!!
IN-STRUC-TOR JORGE?
I BROUGHT THESE YOUNGSTERS TO HIM. WAS JUST GIVING THEM A TOUR OF THE CITY BEFORE I LEFT.
STOMP
TOMP
THUDD

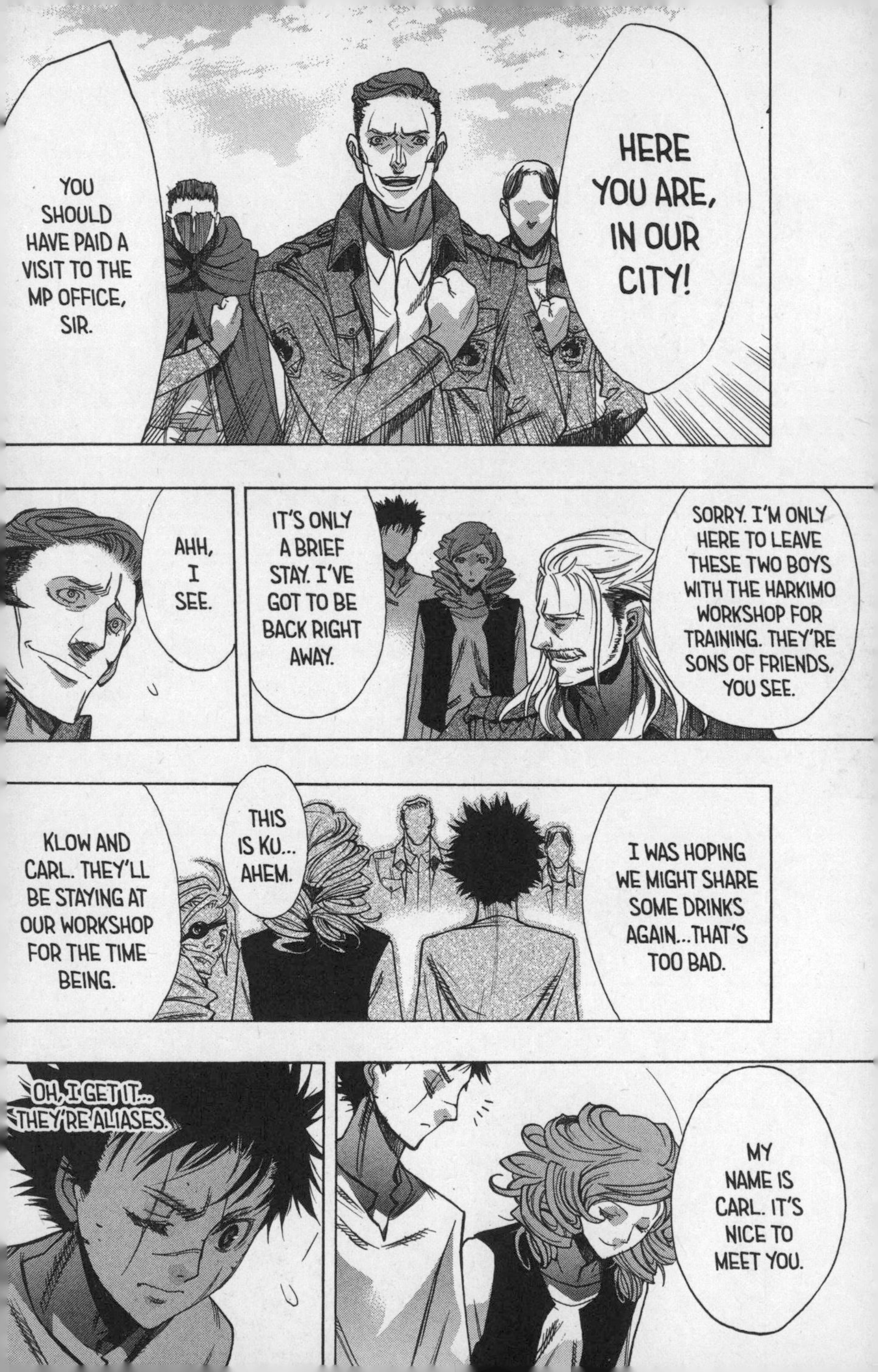
HERE YOU ARE, IN OUR CITY!
YOU SHOULD HAVE PAID A VISIT TO THE MP OFFICE, SIR.
SORRY. I'M ONLY HERE TO LEAVE THESE TWO BOYS WITH THE HARKIMO WORKSHOP FOR TRAINING. THEY'RE SONS OF FRIENDS, YOU SEE.
IT'S ONLY A BRIEF STAY. I'VE GOT TO BE BACK RIGHT AWAY.
AHH, I SEE.
I WAS HOPING WE MIGHT SHARE SOME DRINKS AGAIN...THAT'S TOO BAD.
THIS IS KU... AHEM.
KLOW AND CARL. THEY'LL BE STAYING AT OUR WORKSHOP FOR THE TIME BEING.
MY NAME IS CARL. IT'S NICE TO MEET YOU.
OH, I GET IT... THEY'RE ALIASES.

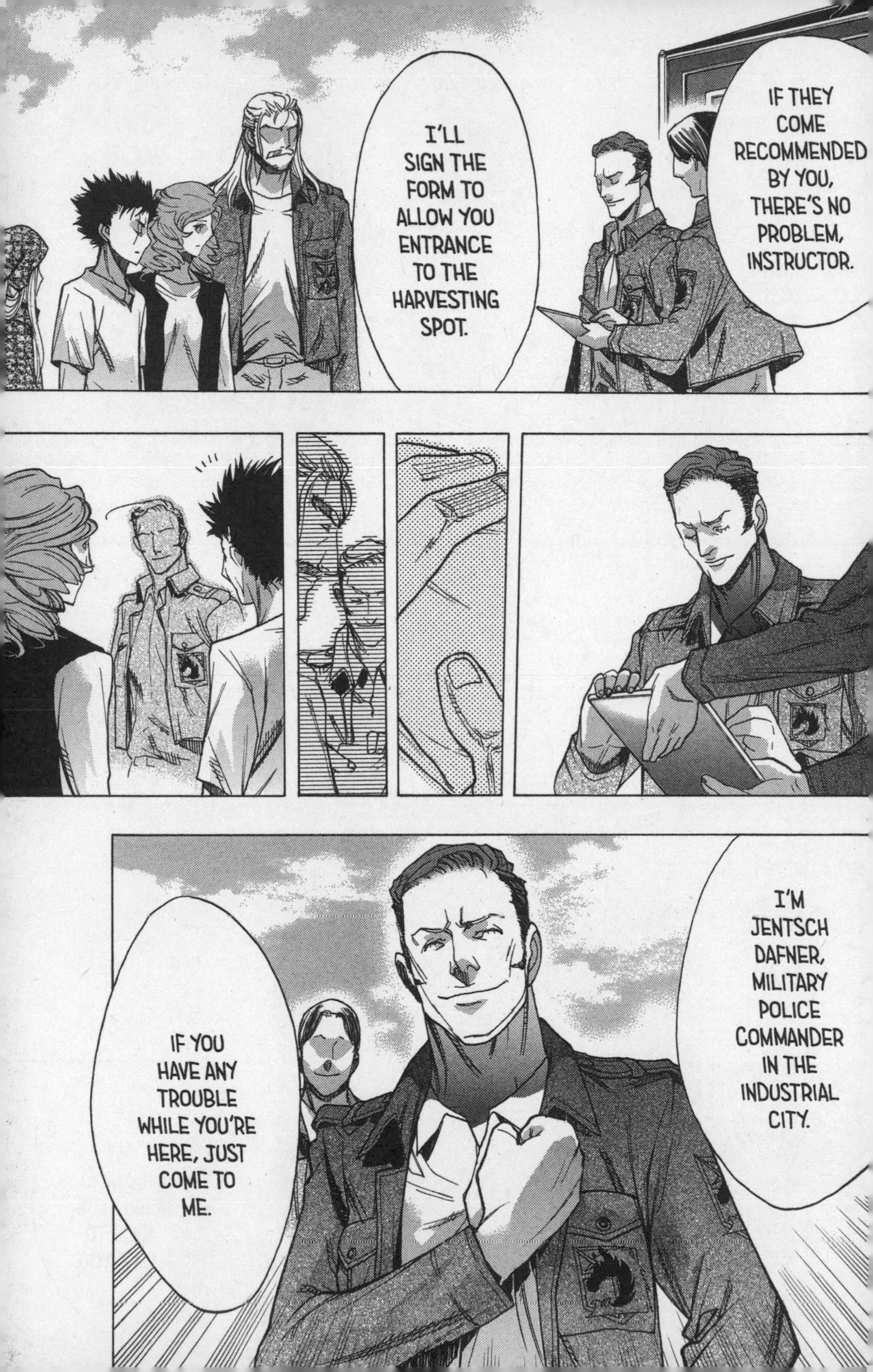
IF THEY COME RECOMMENDED BY YOU, THERE'S NO PROBLEM, INSTRUCTOR.
I'LL SIGN THE FORM TO ALLOW YOU ENTRANCE TO THE HARVESTING SPOT.
I'M JENTSCH DAFNER, MILITARY POLICE COMMANDER IN THE INDUSTRIAL CITY.
IF YOU HAVE ANY TROUBLE WHILE YOU'RE HERE, JUST COME TO ME.

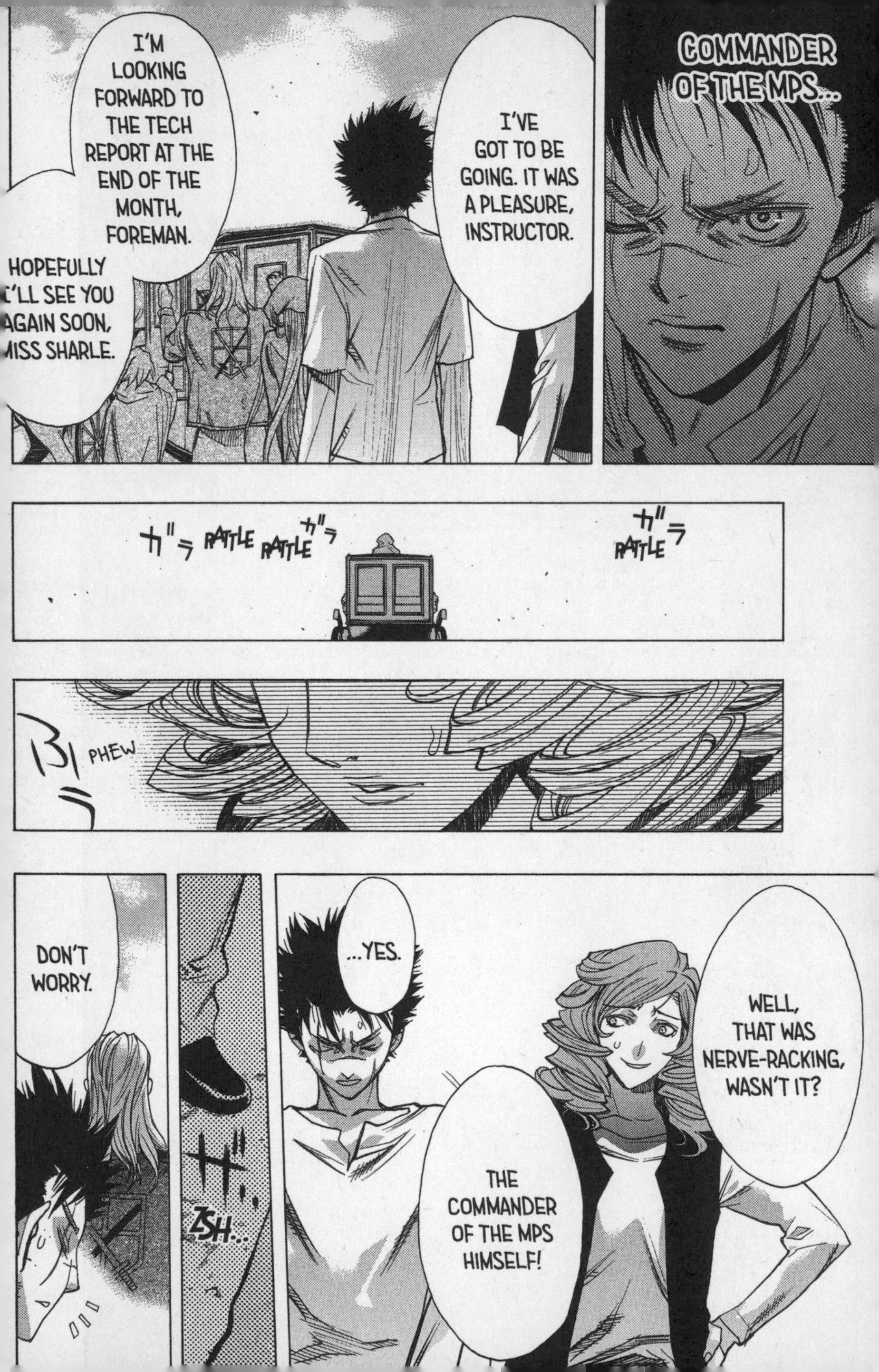
COMMANDER OF THE MPS...
I'VE GOT TO BE GOING. IT WAS A PLEASURE, INSTRUCTOR.
I'M LOOKING FORWARD TO THE TECH REPORT AT THE END OF THE MONTH, FOREMAN.
HOPEFULLY 'LL SEE YOU AGAIN SOON, MISS SHARLE.
ガラ RATTLE
ガラ RATTLE
ガラ RATTLE
ふぅ PHEW
WELL, THAT WAS NERVE-RACKING, WASN'T IT?
THE COMMANDER OF THE MPS HIMSELF!
...YES.
ZSH...
DON'T WORRY.

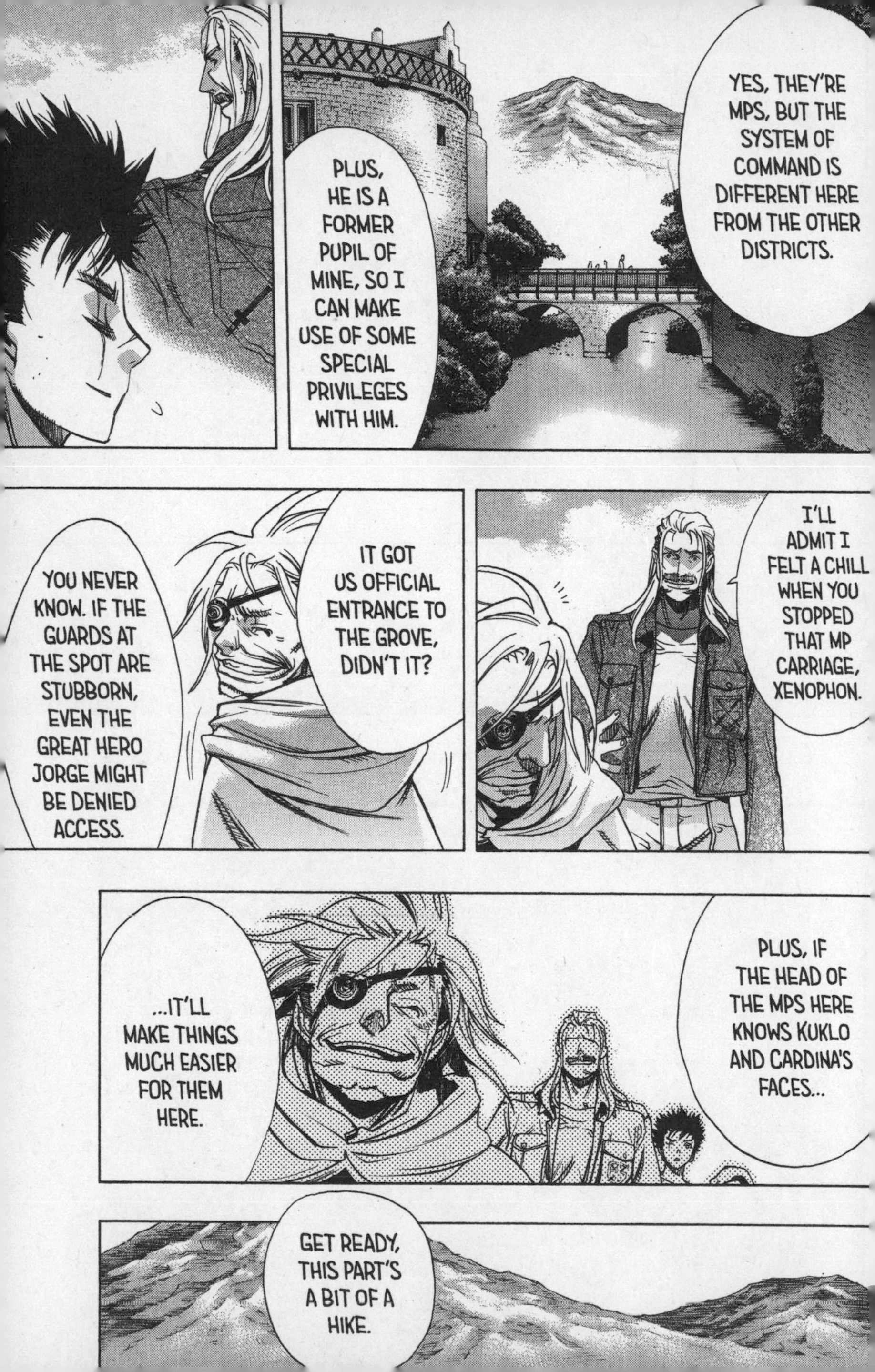
YES, THEY'RE MPS, BUT THE SYSTEM OF COMMAND IS DIFFERENT HERE FROM THE OTHER DISTRICTS.
PLUS, HE IS A FORMER PUPIL OF MINE, SO I CAN MAKE USE OF SOME SPECIAL PRIVILEGES WITH HIM.
I'LL ADMIT I FELT A CHILL WHEN YOU STOPPED THAT MP CARRIAGE, XENOPHON.
IT GOT US OFFICIAL ENTRANCE TO THE GROVE, DIDN'T IT?
YOU NEVER KNOW. IF THE GUARDS AT THE SPOT ARE STUBBORN, EVEN THE GREAT HERO JORGE MIGHT BE DENIED ACCESS.
PLUS, IF THE HEAD OF THE MPS HERE KNOWS KUKLO AND CARDINA'S FACES...
...IT'LL MAKE THINGS MUCH EASIER FOR THEM HERE.
GET READY, THIS PART'S A BIT OF A HIKE.

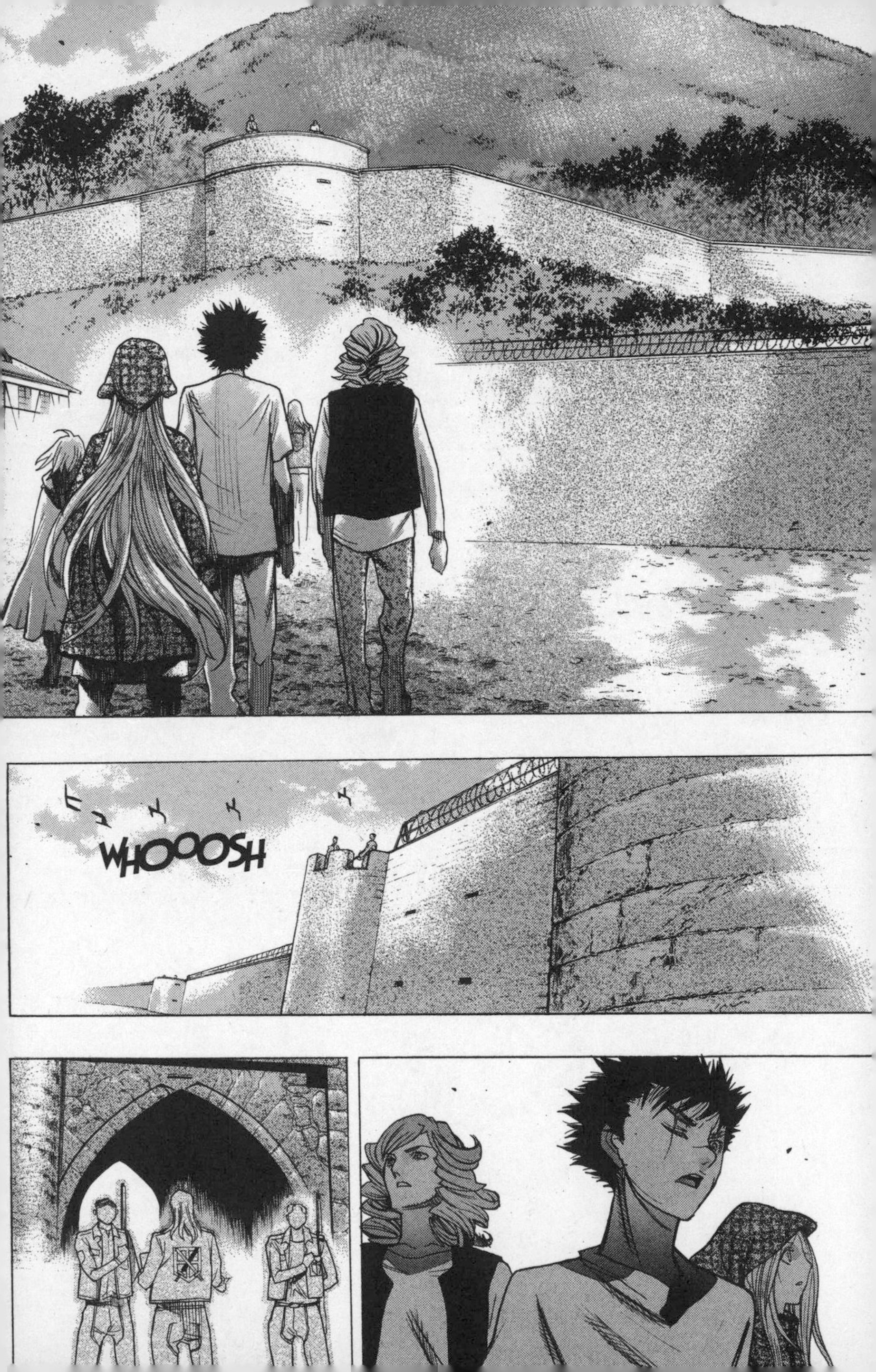
WHOOOSH

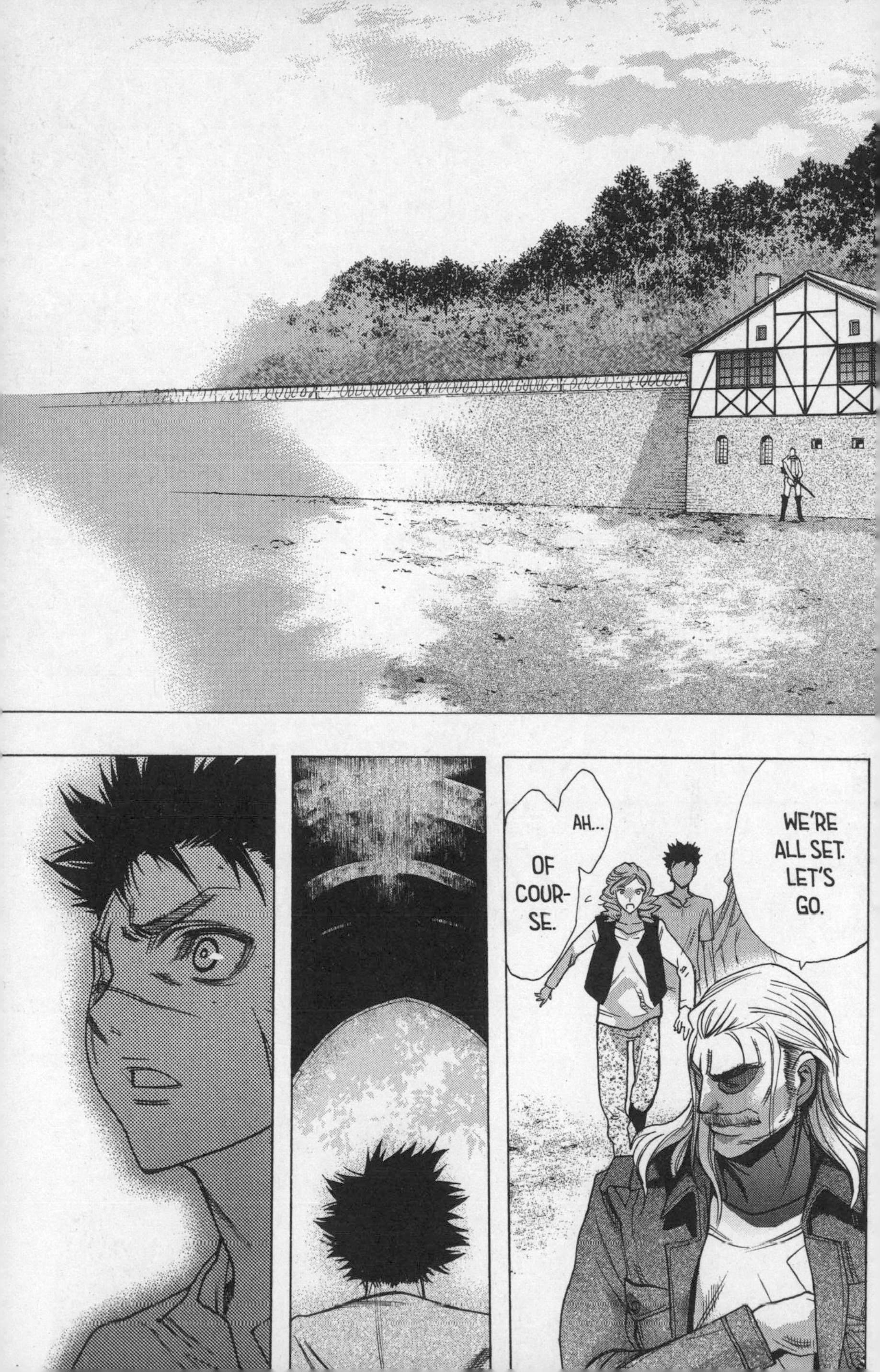
WE'RE ALL SET. LET'S GO.
AH... OF COUR-SE.

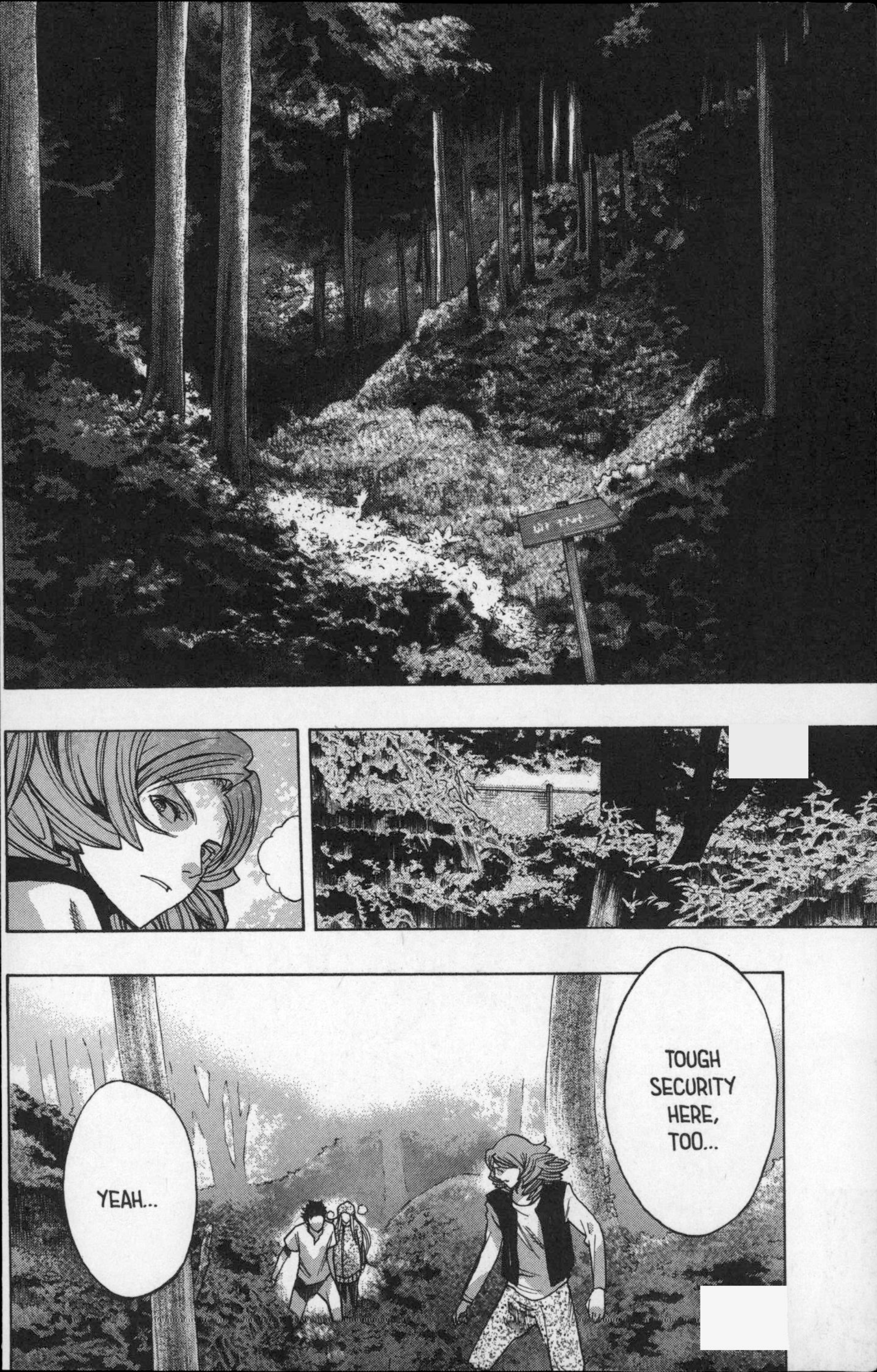
TOUGH SECURITY HERE, TOO...
YEAH...

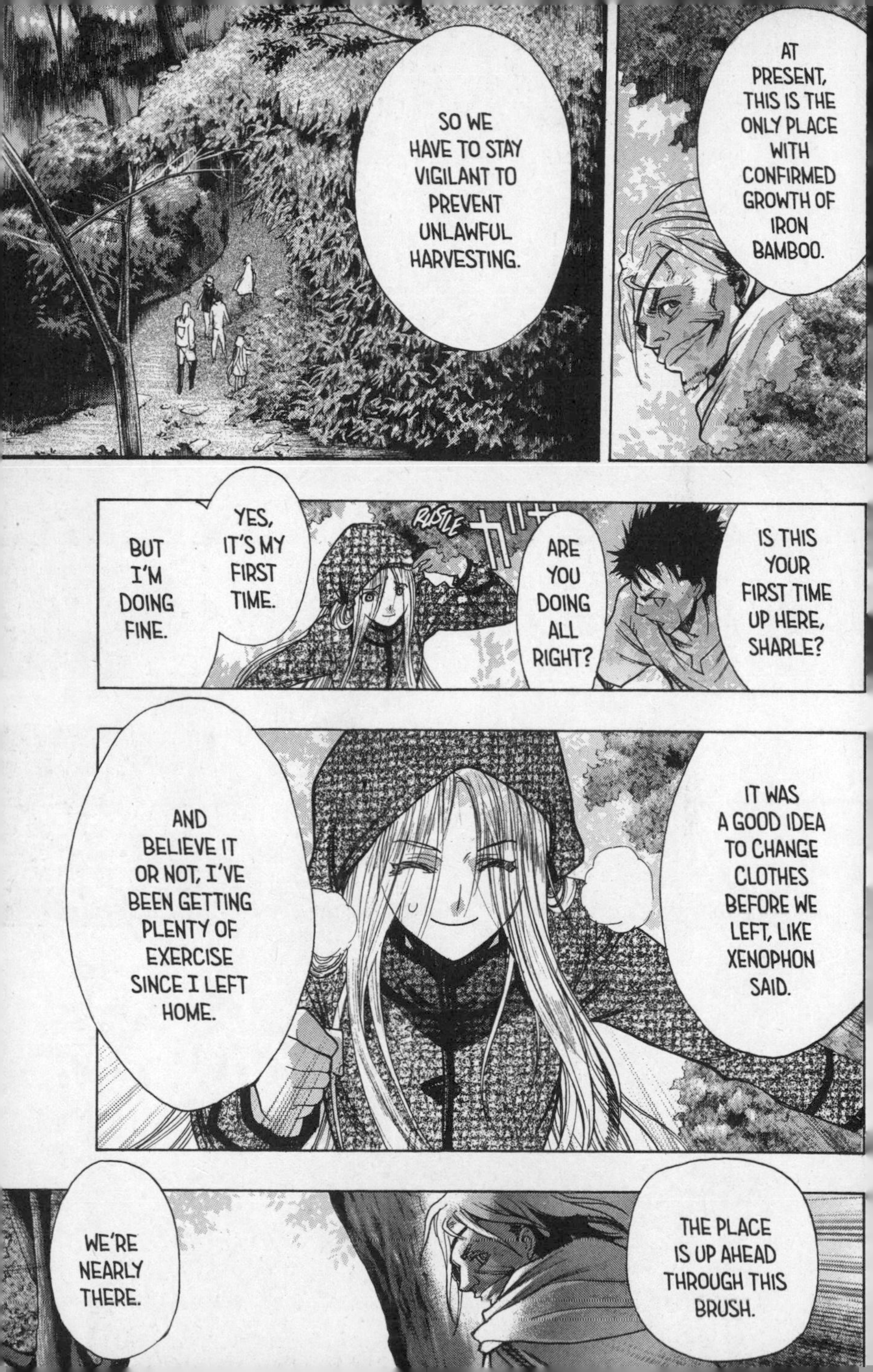
AT PRESENT, THIS IS THE ONLY PLACE WITH CONFIRMED GROWTH OF IRON BAMBOO.
SO WE HAVE TO STAY VIGILANT TO PREVENT UNLAWFUL HARVESTING.
IS THIS YOUR FIRST TIME UP HERE, SHARLE?
ARE YOU DOING ALL RIGHT?
RUSTLE
YES, IT'S MY FIRST TIME.
BUT I'M DOING FINE.
IT WAS A GOOD IDEA TO CHANGE CLOTHES BEFORE WE LEFT, LIKE XENOPHON SAID.
AND BELIEVE IT OR NOT, I'VE BEEN GETTING PLENTY OF EXERCISE SINCE I LEFT HOME.
THE PLACE IS UP AHEAD THROUGH THIS BRUSH.
WE'RE NEARLY THERE.

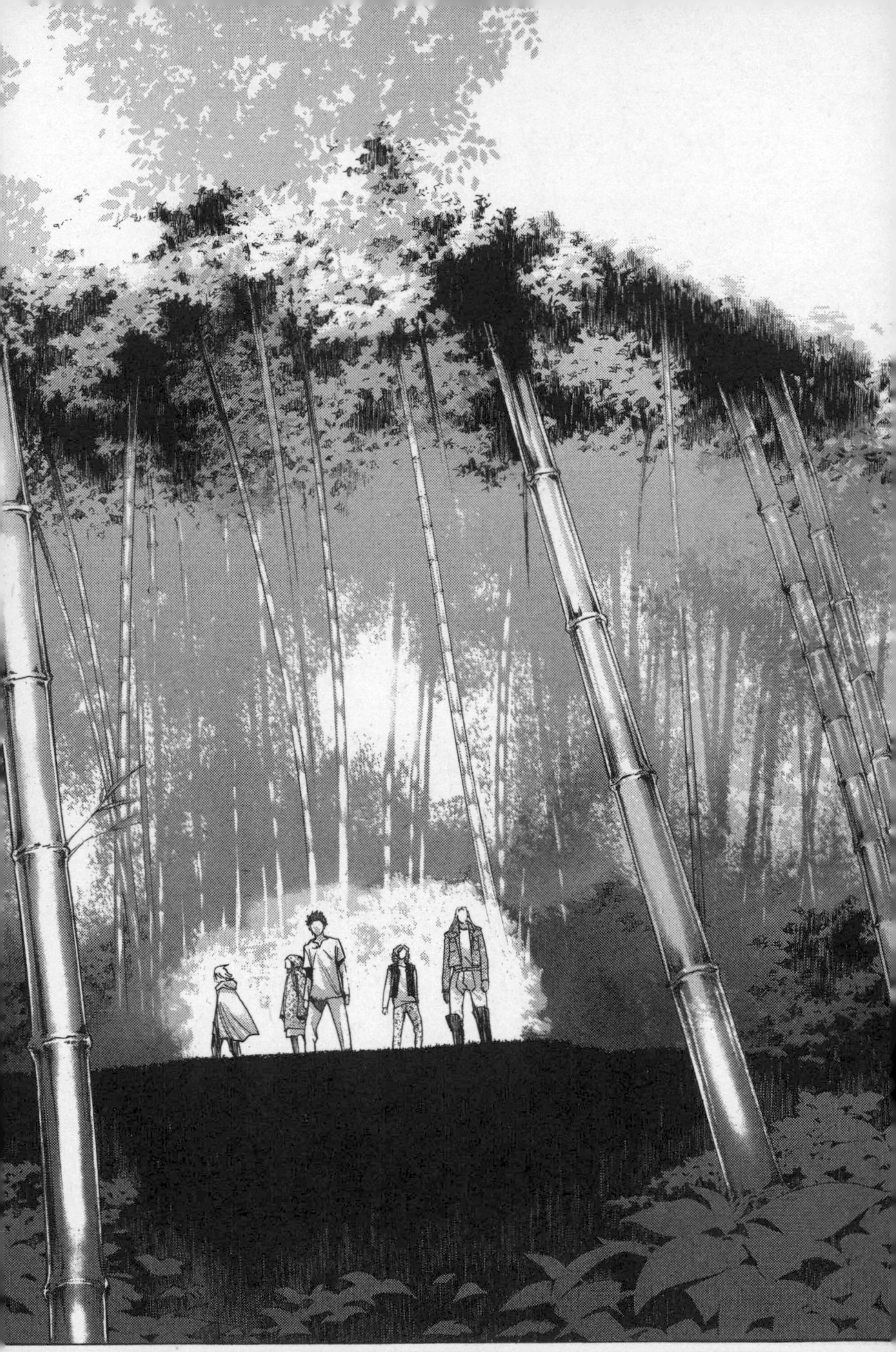

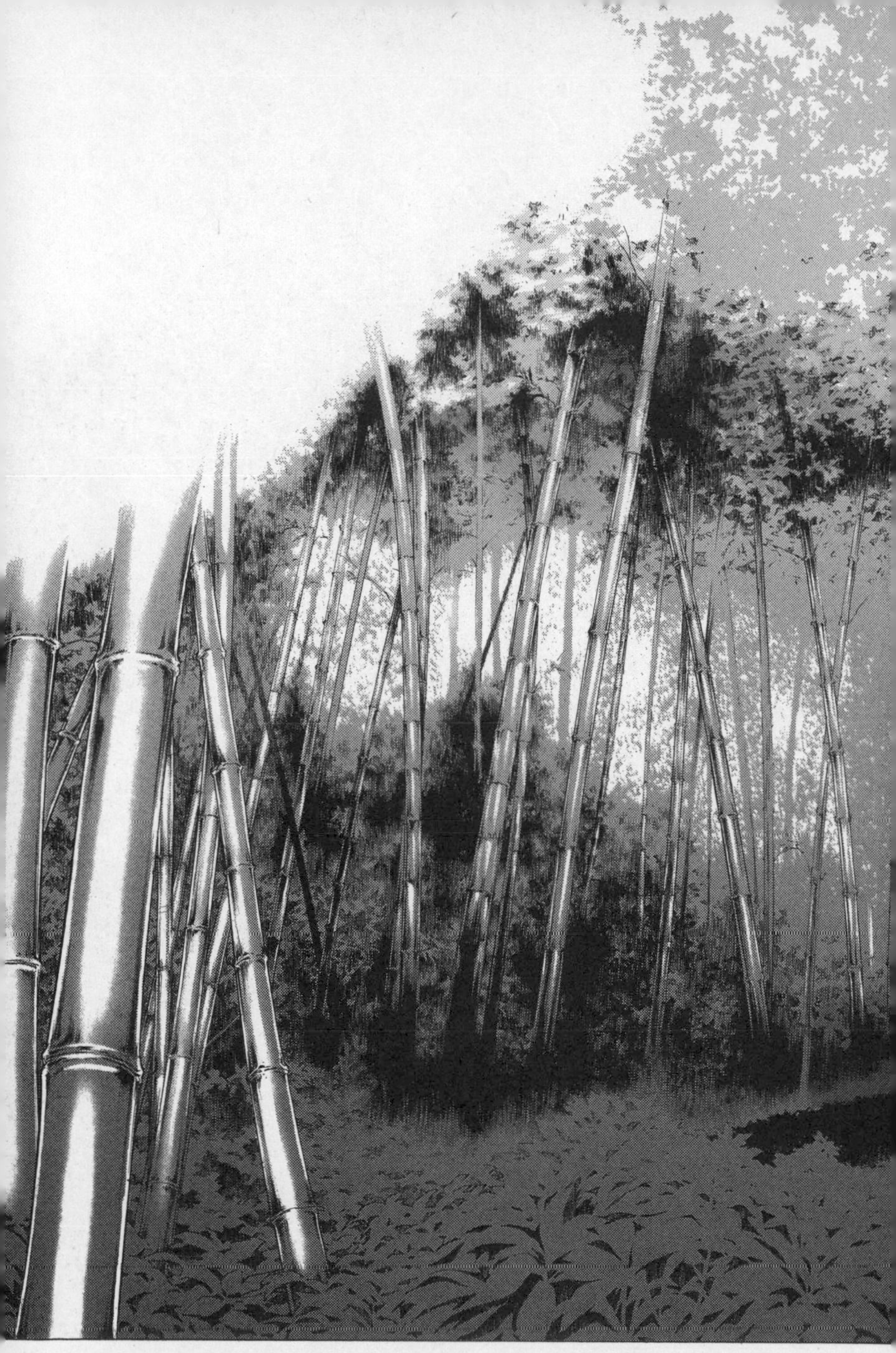

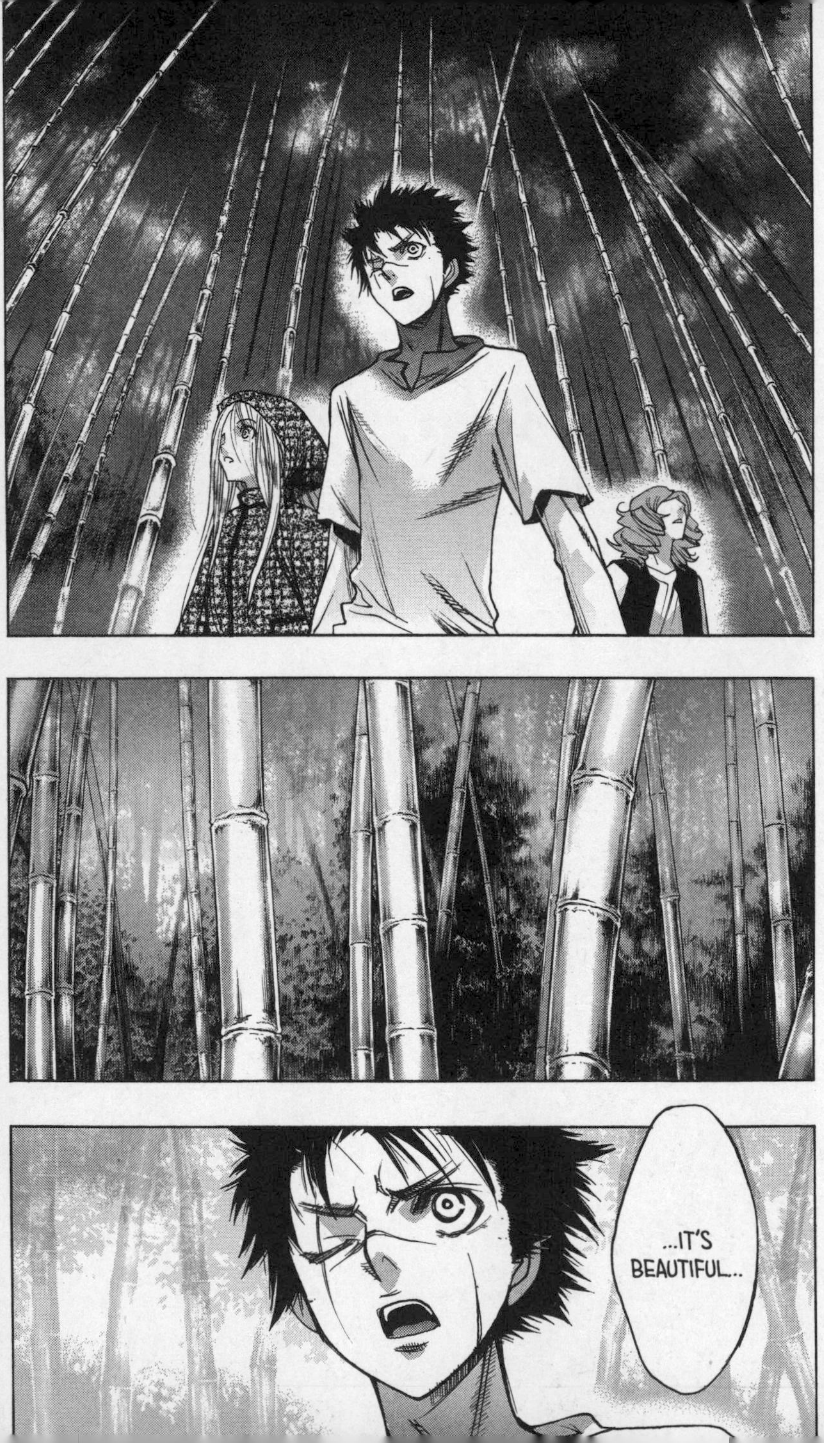
...IT'S
BEAUTIFUL...

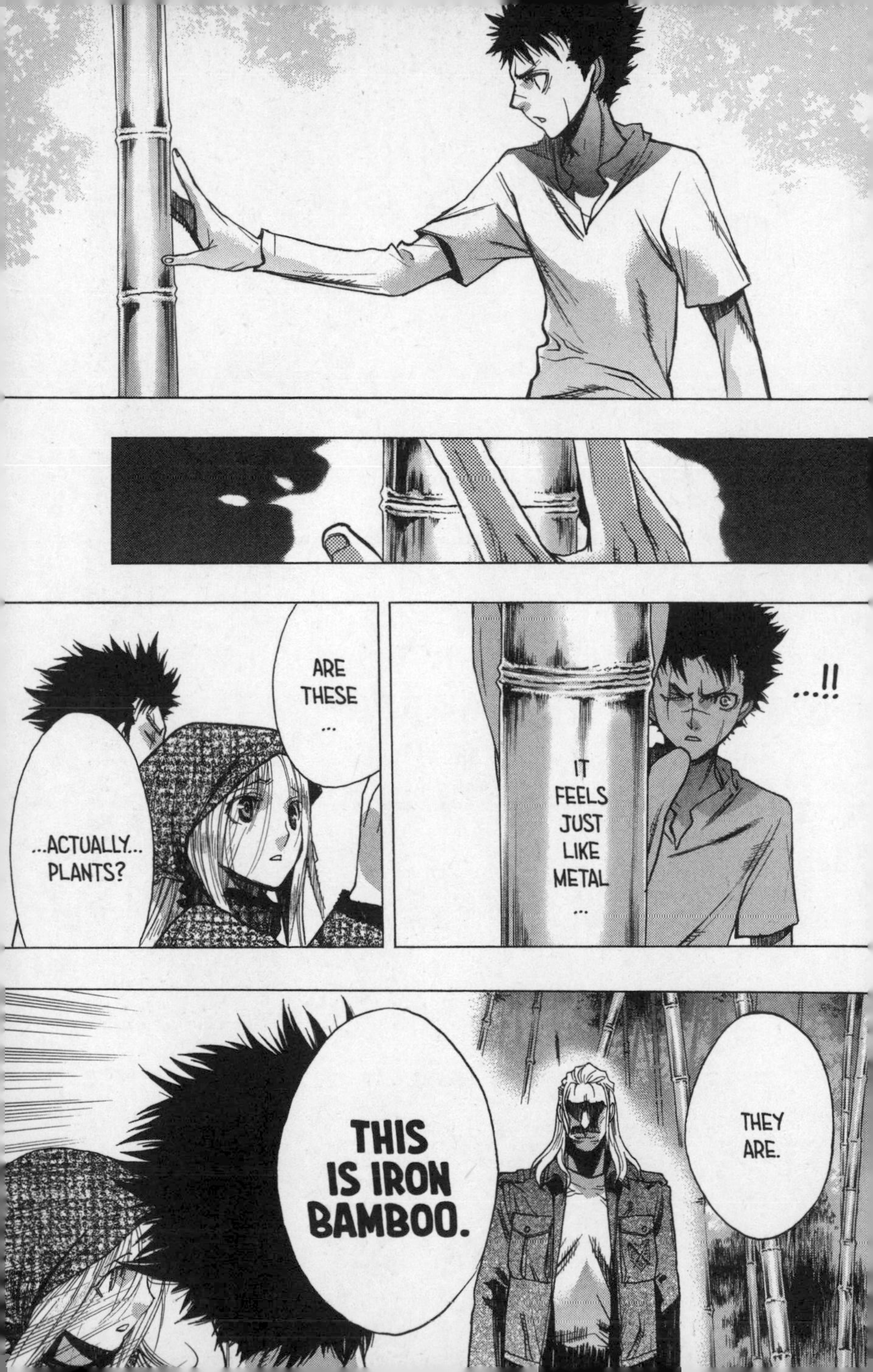
...!!
IT FEELS JUST LIKE METAL ...
ARE THESE ...
...ACTUALLY... PLANTS?
THEY ARE.
THIS IS IRON BAMBOO.

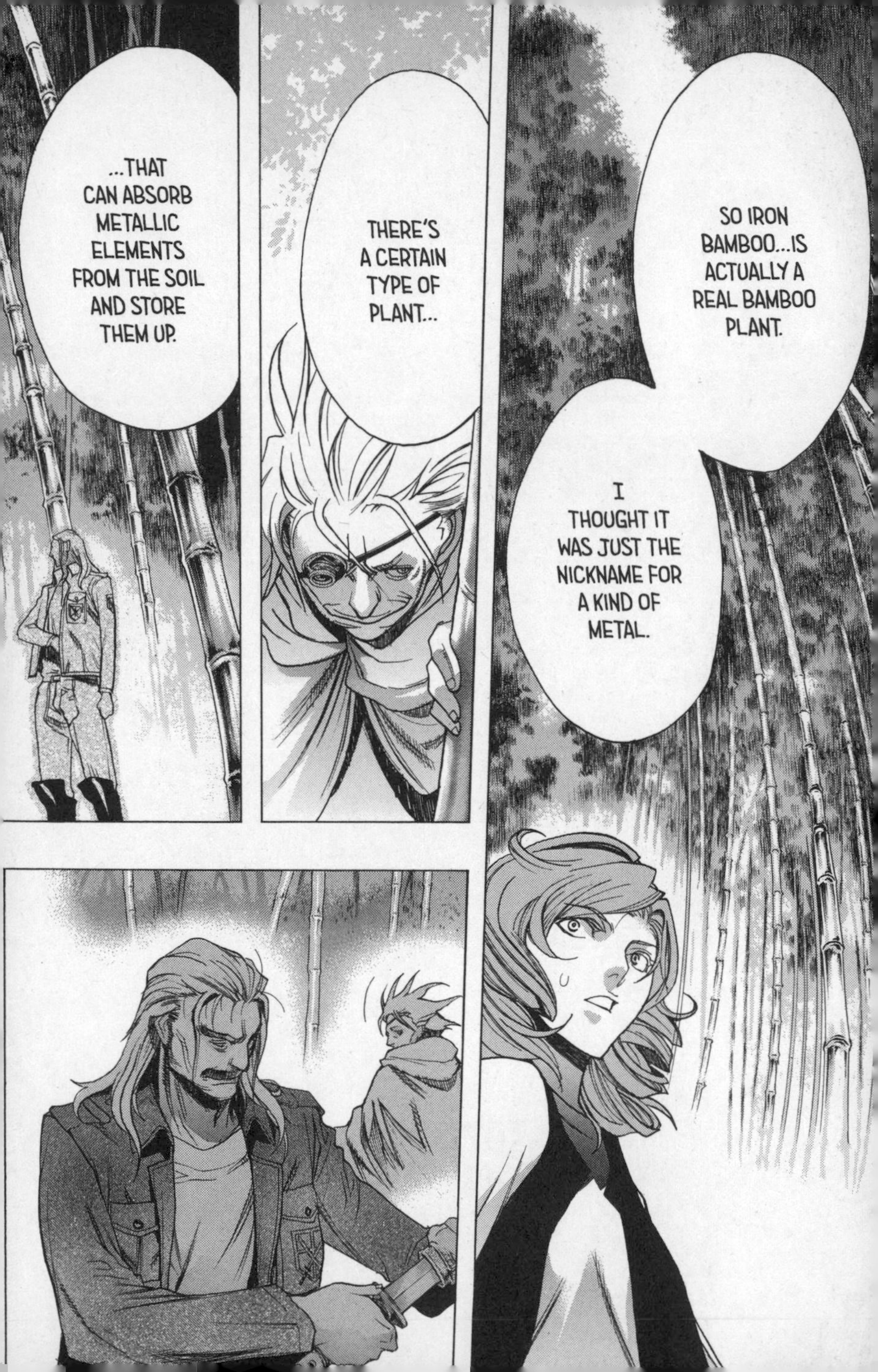
SO IRON BAMBOO...IS ACTUALLY A REAL BAMBOO PLANT.
I THOUGHT IT WAS JUST THE NICKNAME FOR A KIND OF METAL.
THERE'S A CERTAIN TYPE OF PLANT...
...THAT CAN ABSORB METALLIC ELEMENTS FROM THE SOIL AND STORE THEM UP.

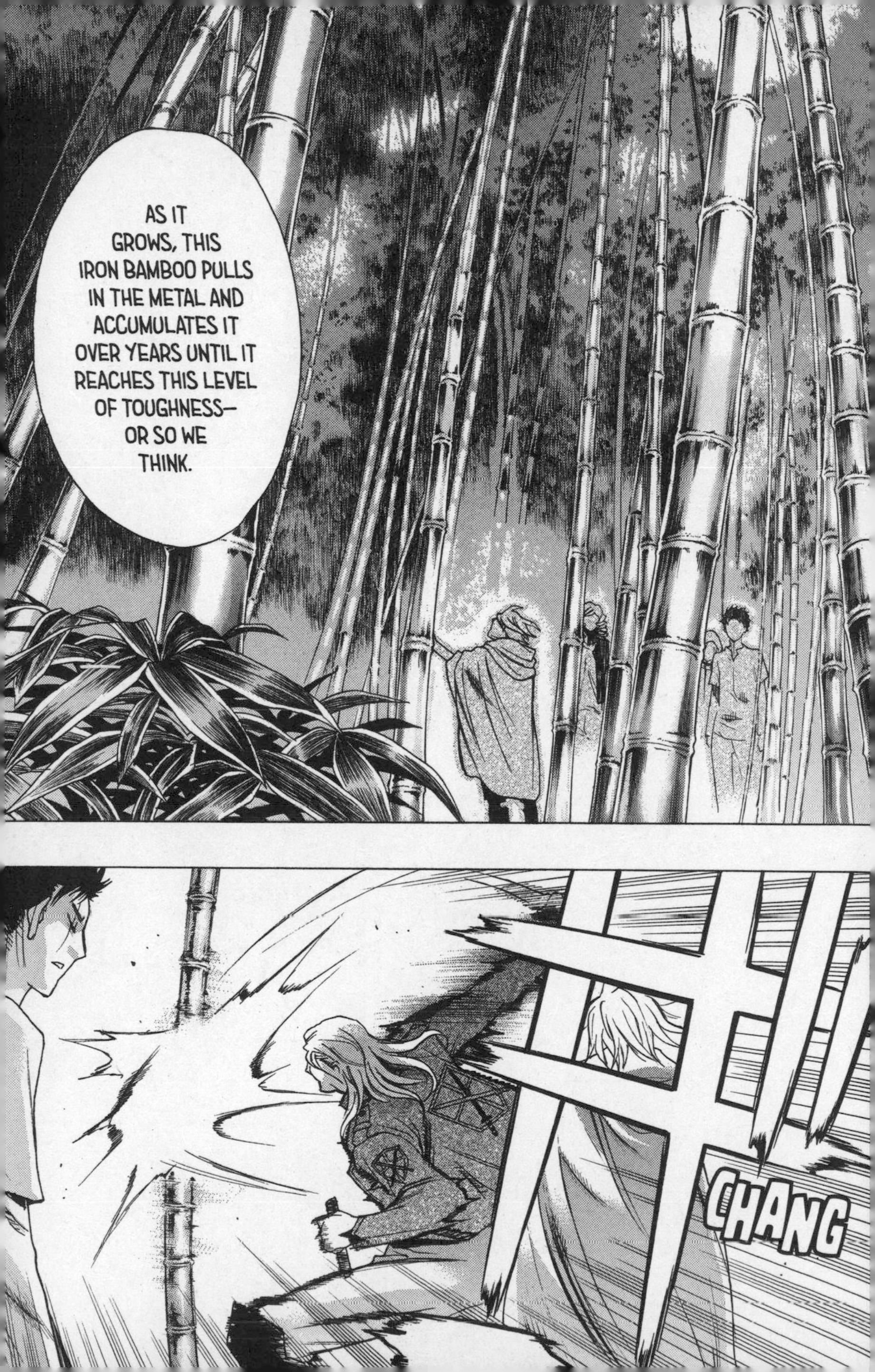
AS IT GROWS, THIS IRON BAMBOO PULLS IN THE METAL AND ACCUMULATES IT OVER YEARS UNTIL IT REACHES THIS LEVEL OF TOUGHNESS— OR SO WE THINK.
CHANG

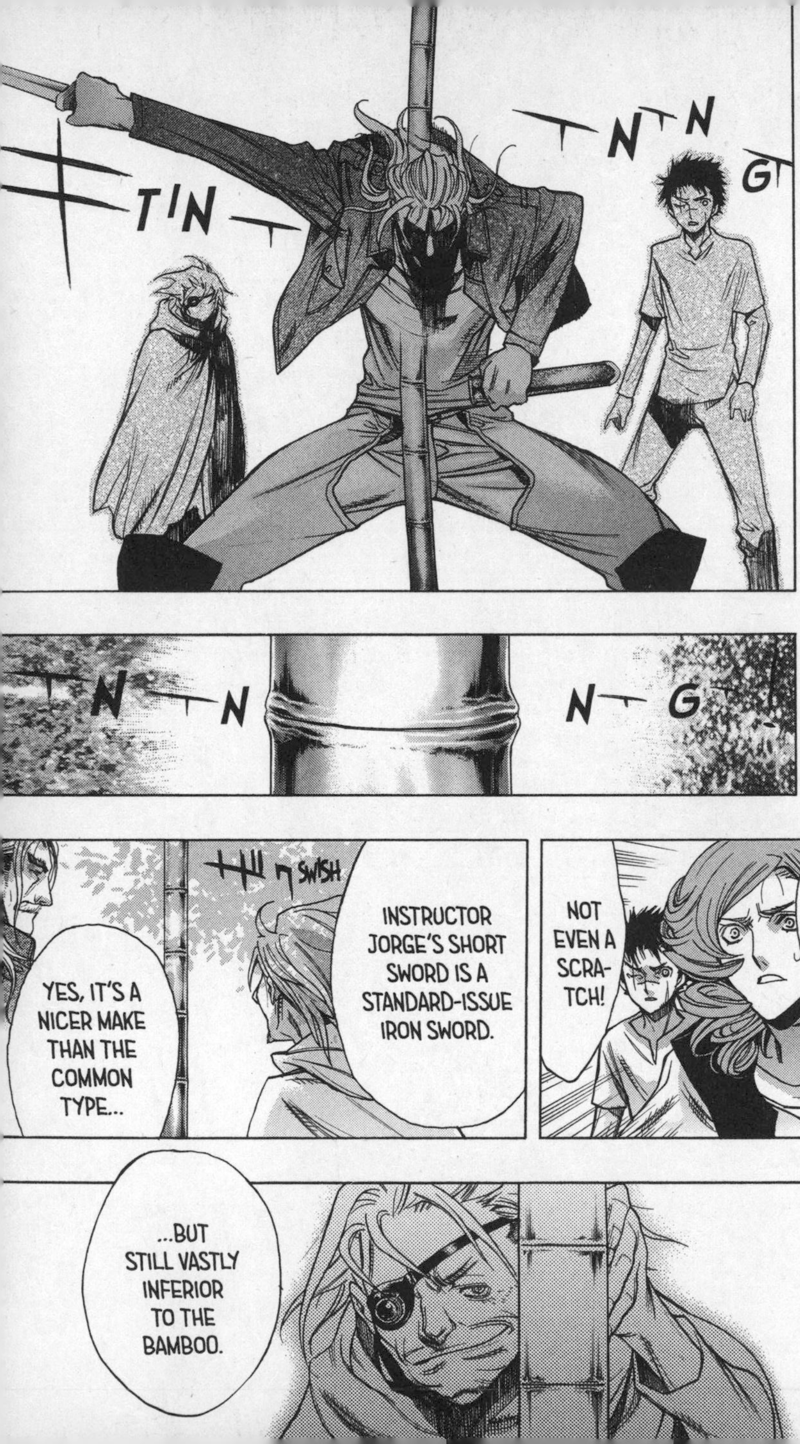
TNTNG
TIN
AMAZING!
NOT EVEN A SCRA-TCH!
SWISH
INSTRUCTOR JORGE'S SHORT SWORD IS A STANDARD-ISSUE IRON SWORD.
YES, IT'S A NICER MAKE THAN THE COMMON TYPE...
...BUT STILL VASTLY INFERIOR TO THE BAMBOO.

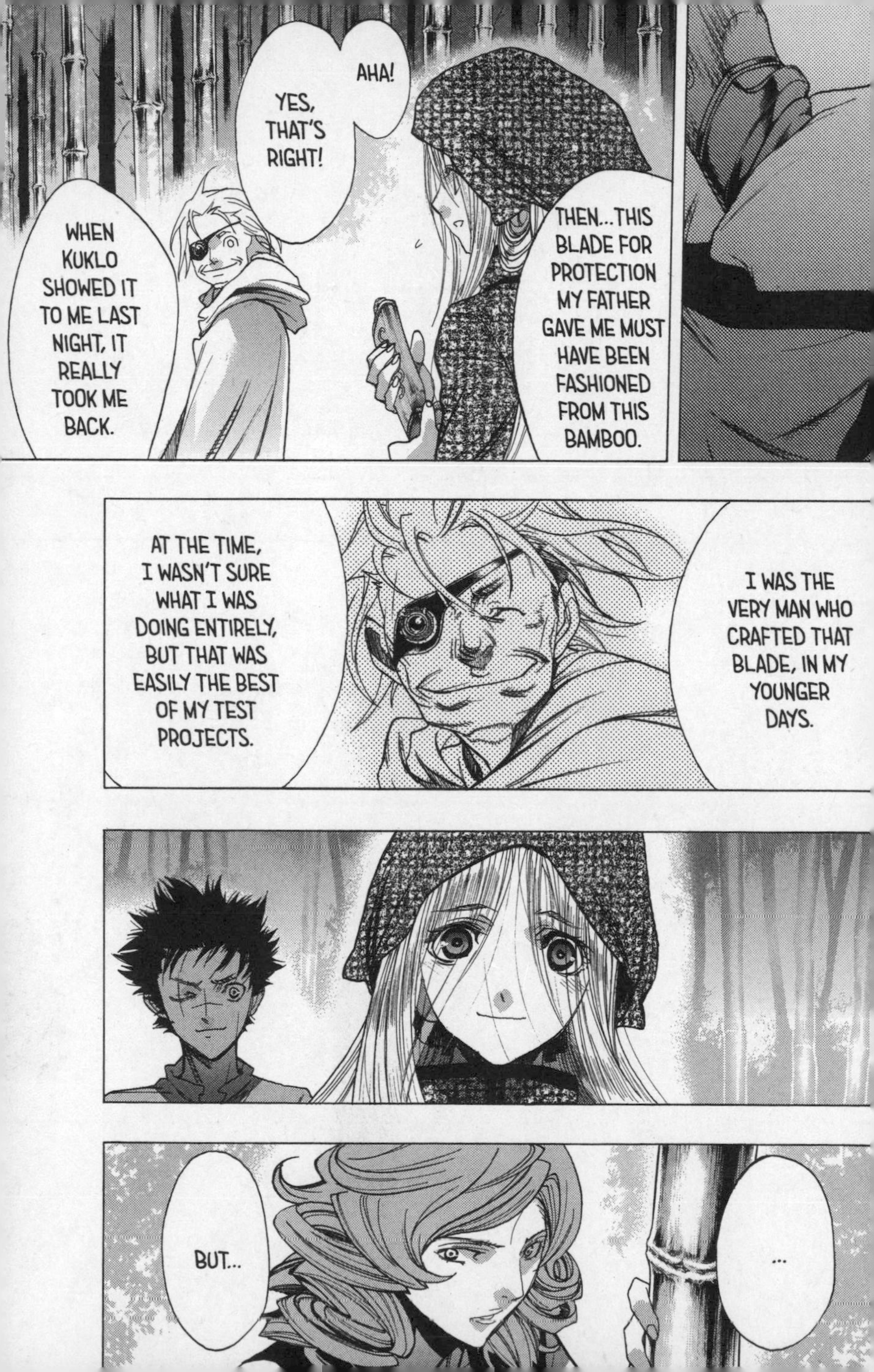
THEN...THIS BLADE FOR PROTECTION MY FATHER GAVE ME MUST HAVE BEEN FASHIONED FROM THIS BAMBOO.
AHA!
YES, THAT'S RIGHT!
WHEN KUKLO SHOWED IT TO ME LAST NIGHT, IT REALLY TOOK ME BACK.
I WAS THE VERY MAN WHO CRAFTED THAT BLADE, IN MY YOUNGER DAYS.
AT THE TIME, I WASN'T SURE WHAT I WAS DOING ENTIRELY, BUT THAT WAS EASILY THE BEST OF MY TEST PROJECTS.
...
BUT...

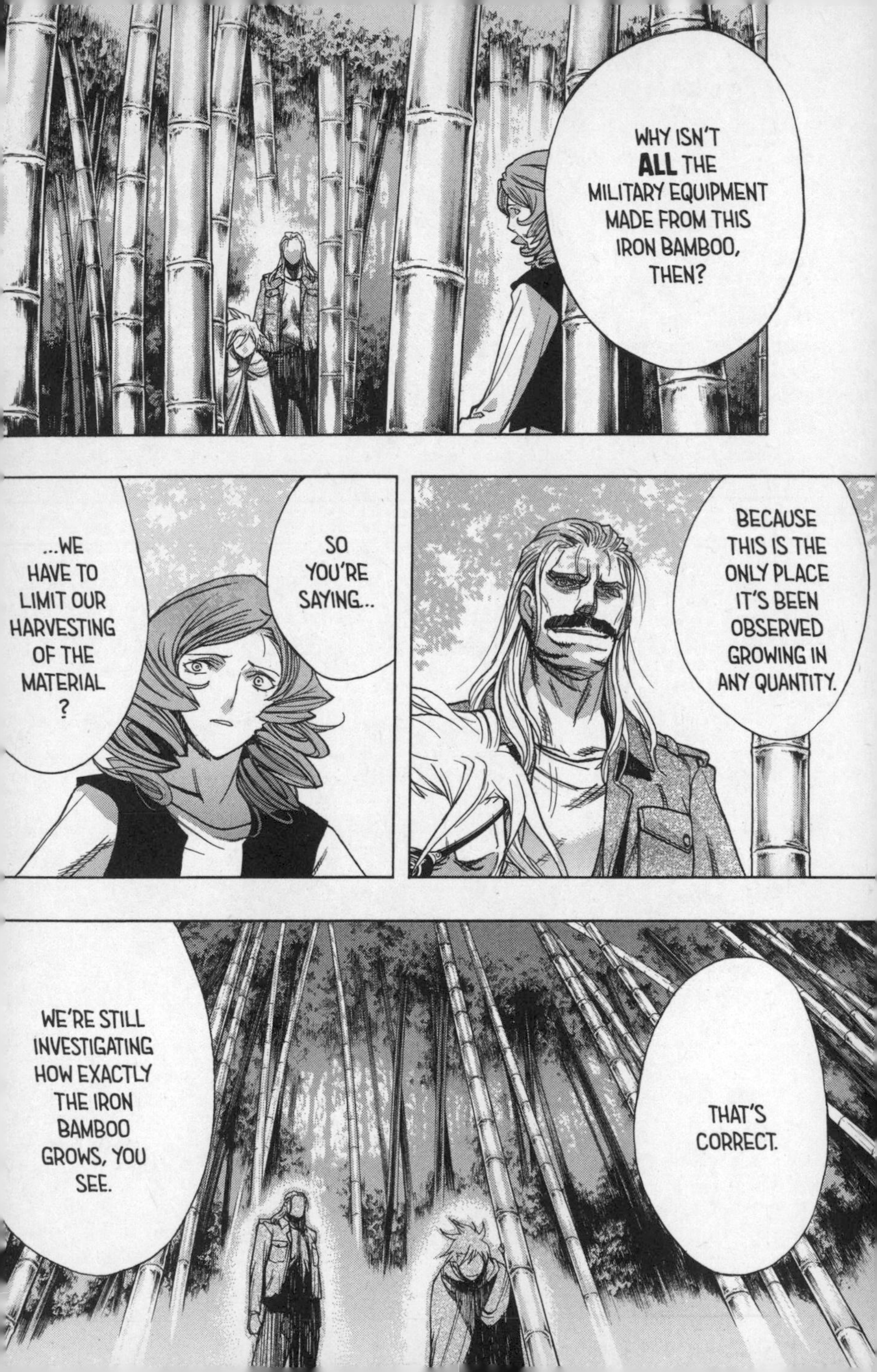
WHY ISN'T **ALL** THE MILITARY EQUIPMENT MADE FROM THIS IRON BAMBOO, THEN?
BECAUSE THIS IS THE ONLY PLACE IT'S BEEN OBSERVED GROWING IN ANY QUANTITY.
SO YOU'RE SAYING...
...WE HAVE TO LIMIT OUR HARVESTING OF THE MATERIAL?
THAT'S CORRECT.
WE'RE STILL INVESTIGATING HOW EXACTLY THE IRON BAMBOO GROWS, YOU SEE.

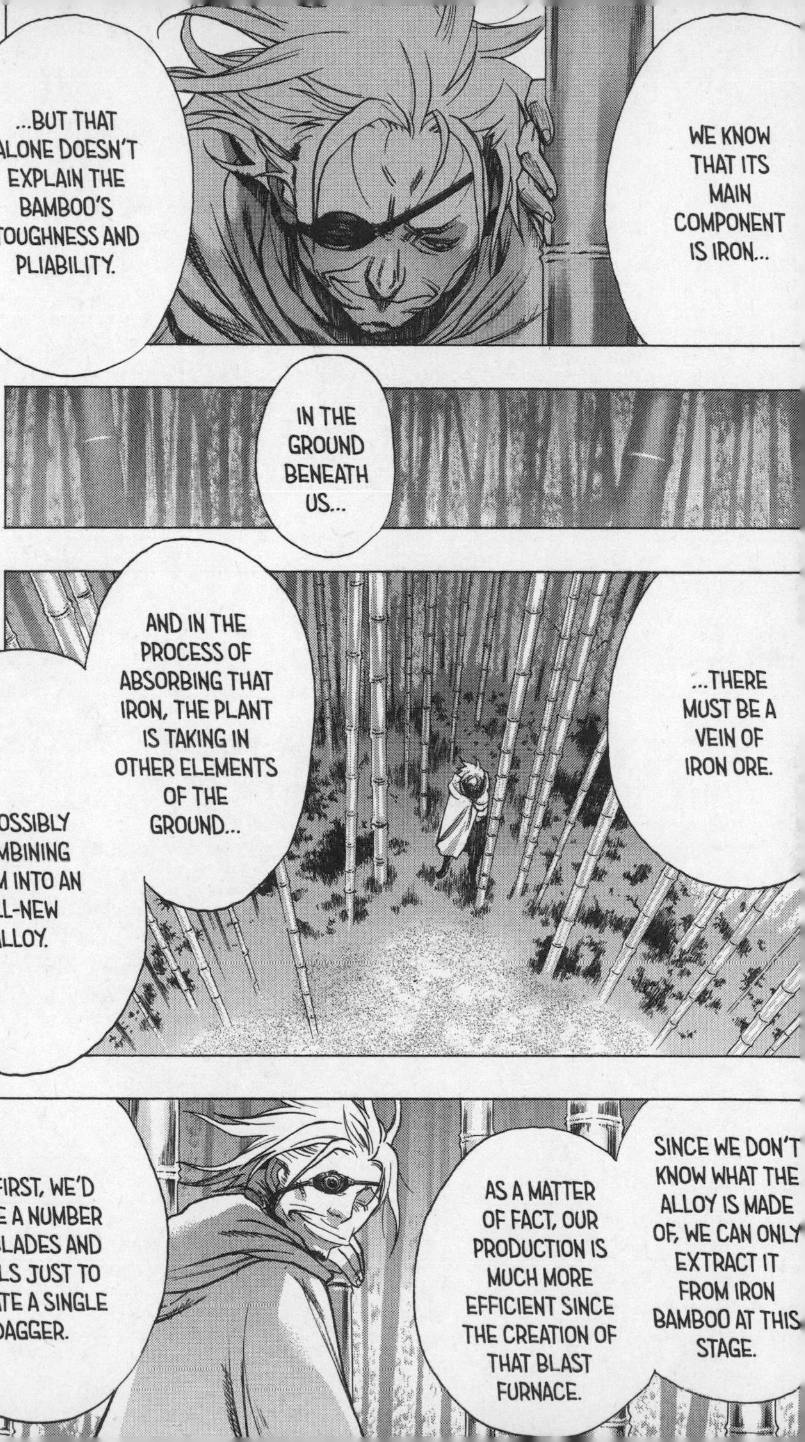
WE KNOW THAT ITS MAIN COMPONENT IS IRON...
...BUT THAT ALONE DOESN'T EXPLAIN THE BAMBOO'S TOUGHNESS AND PLIABILITY.
IN THE GROUND BENEATH US...
...THERE MUST BE A VEIN OF IRON ORE.
AND IN THE PROCESS OF ABSORBING THAT IRON, THE PLANT IS TAKING IN OTHER ELEMENTS OF THE GROUND...
...POSSIBLY COMBINING THEM INTO AN ALL-NEW ALLOY.
SINCE WE DON'T KNOW WHAT THE ALLOY IS MADE OF, WE CAN ONLY EXTRACT IT FROM IRON BAMBOO AT THIS STAGE.
AS A MATTER OF FACT, OUR PRODUCTION IS MUCH MORE EFFICIENT SINCE THE CREATION OF THAT BLAST FURNACE.
AT FIRST, WE'D LOSE A NUMBER OF BLADES AND TOOLS JUST TO CREATE A SINGLE DAGGER.

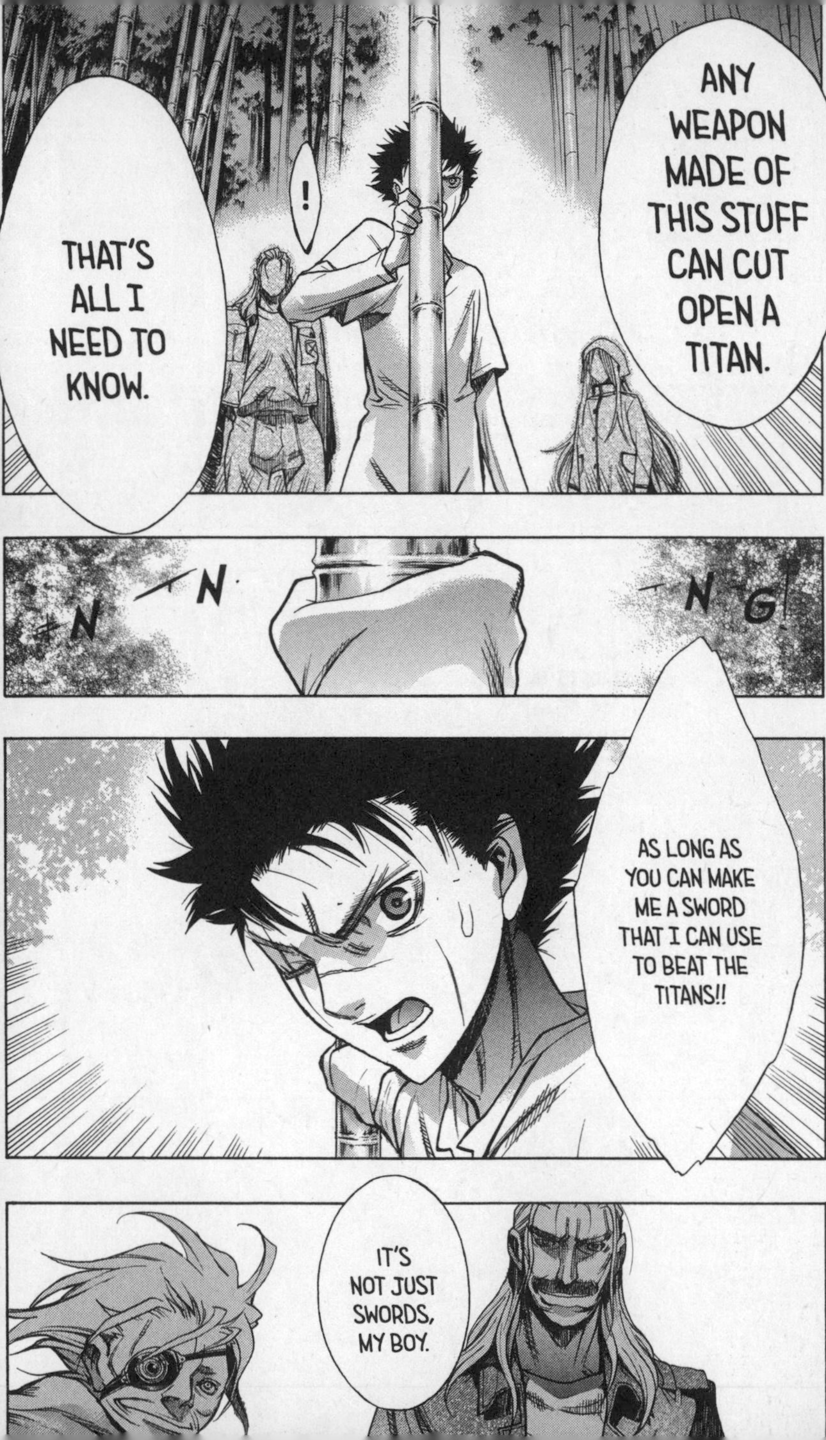
ANY WEAPON MADE OF THIS STUFF CAN CUT OPEN A TITAN.
!
THAT'S ALL I NEED TO KNOW.
NNNG!
AS LONG AS YOU CAN MAKE ME A SWORD THAT I CAN USE TO BEAT THE TITANS!!
IT'S NOT JUST SWORDS, MY BOY.

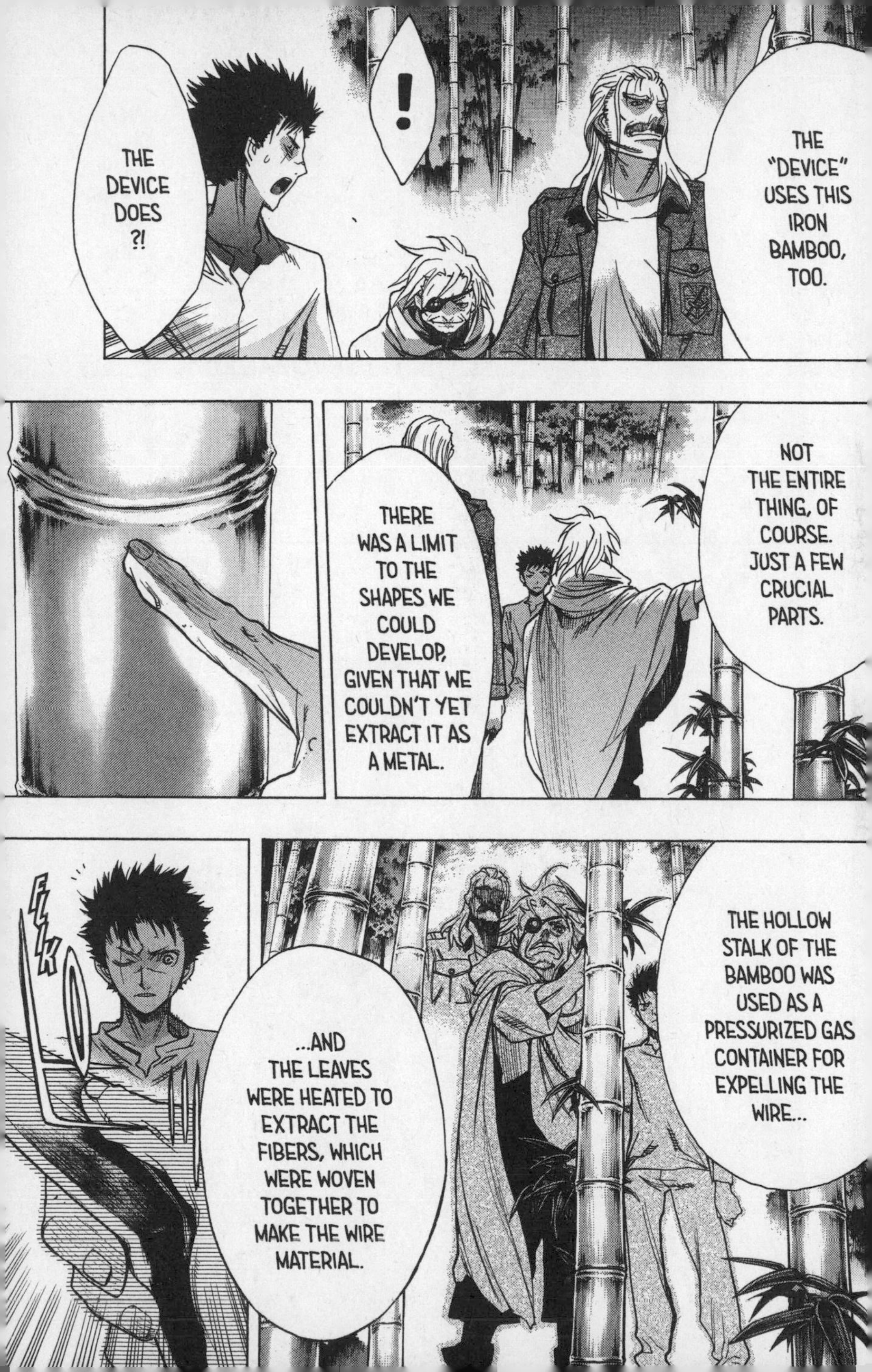
THE "DEVICE" USES THIS IRON BAMBOO, TOO.
!
THE DEVICE DOES ?!
NOT THE ENTIRE THING, OF COURSE. JUST A FEW CRUCIAL PARTS.
THERE WAS A LIMIT TO THE SHAPES WE COULD DEVELOP, GIVEN THAT WE COULDN'T YET EXTRACT IT AS A METAL.
THE HOLLOW STALK OF THE BAMBOO WAS USED AS A PRESSURIZED GAS CONTAINER FOR EXPELLING THE WIRE...
...AND THE LEAVES WERE HEATED TO EXTRACT THE FIBERS, WHICH WERE WOVEN TOGETHER TO MAKE THE WIRE MATERIAL.
FLIK

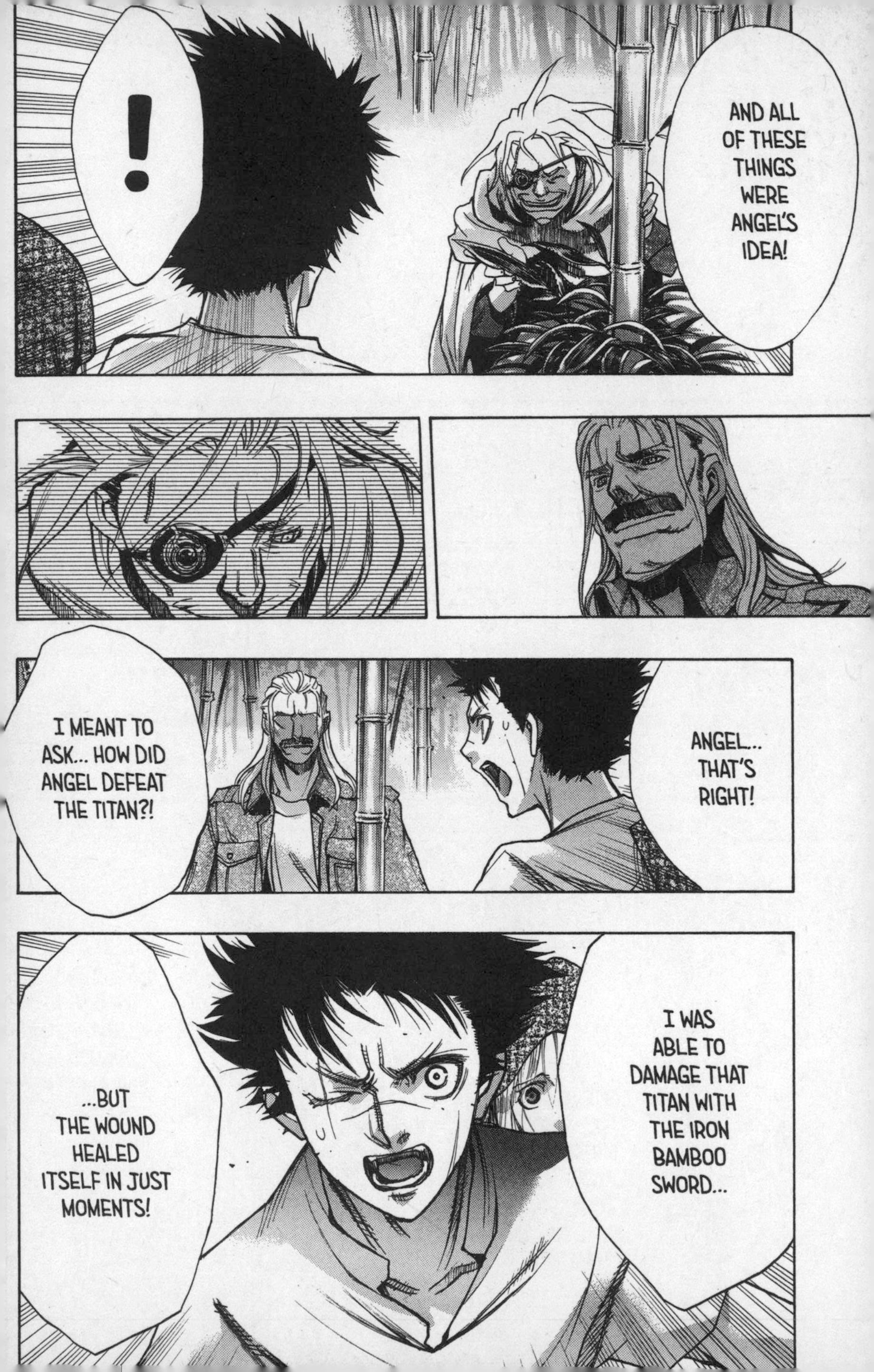
AND ALL OF THESE THINGS WERE ANGEL'S IDEA!
!
ANGEL... THAT'S RIGHT!
I MEANT TO ASK... HOW DID ANGEL DEFEAT THE TITAN?!
I WAS ABLE TO DAMAGE THAT TITAN WITH THE IRON BAMBOO SWORD...
...BUT THE WOUND HEALED ITSELF IN JUST MOMENTS!

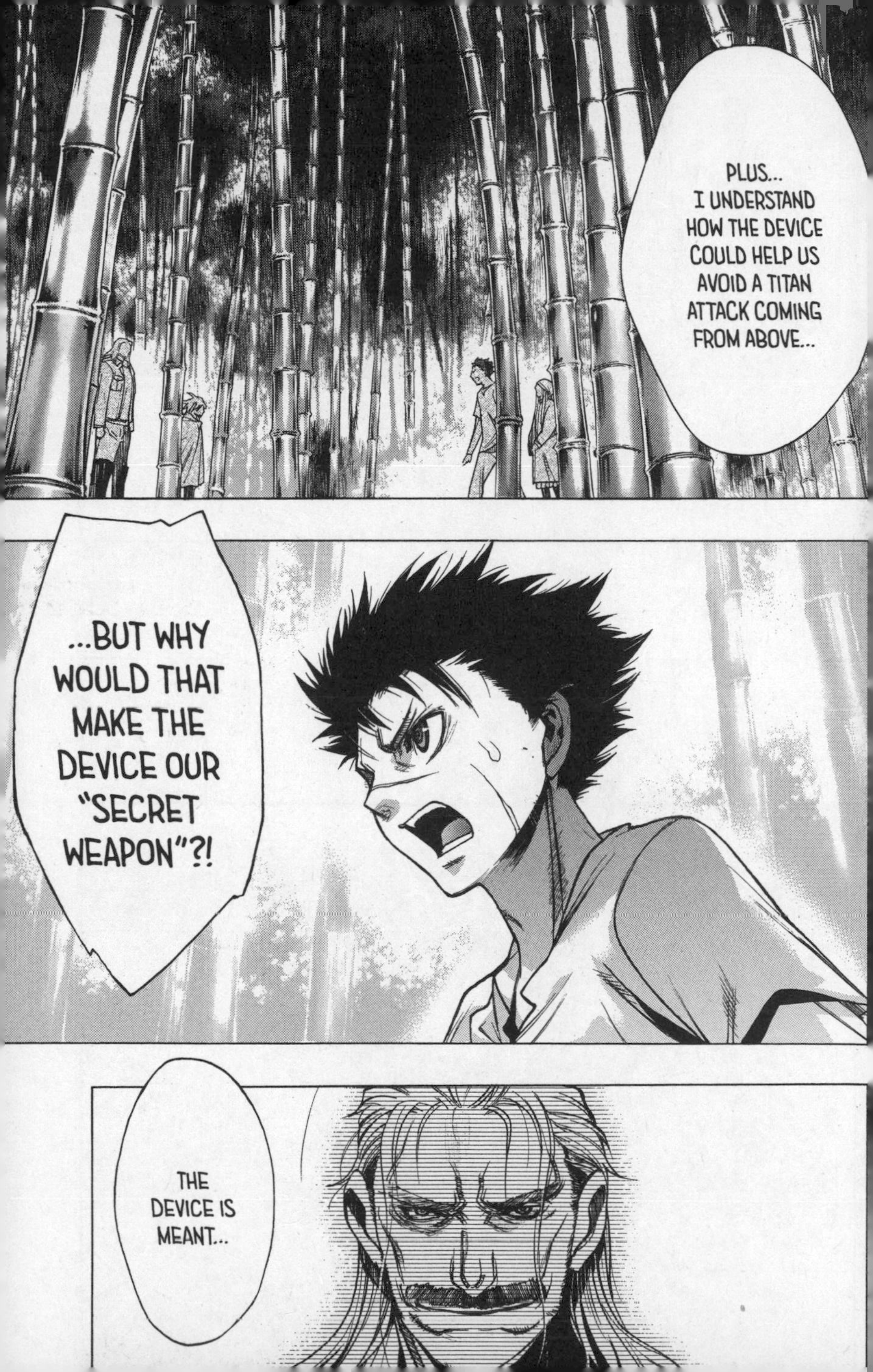
PLUS... I UNDERSTAND HOW THE DEVICE COULD HELP US AVOID A TITAN ATTACK COMING FROM ABOVE...
...BUT WHY WOULD THAT MAKE THE DEVICE OUR "SECRET WEAPON"?!
THE DEVICE IS MEANT...

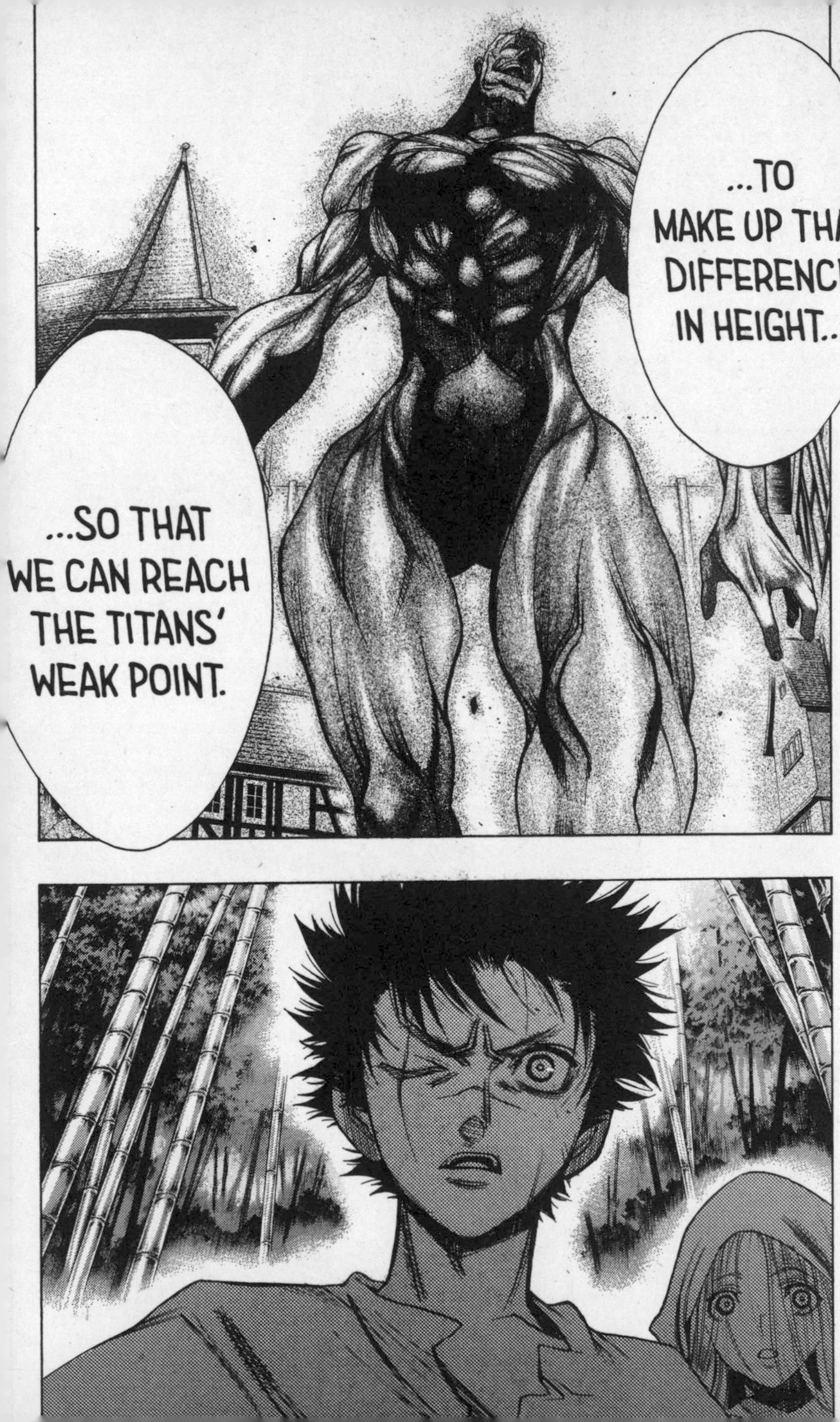
...TO MAKE UP THAT DIFFERENCE IN HEIGHT...
...SO THAT WE CAN REACH THE TITANS' WEAK POINT.

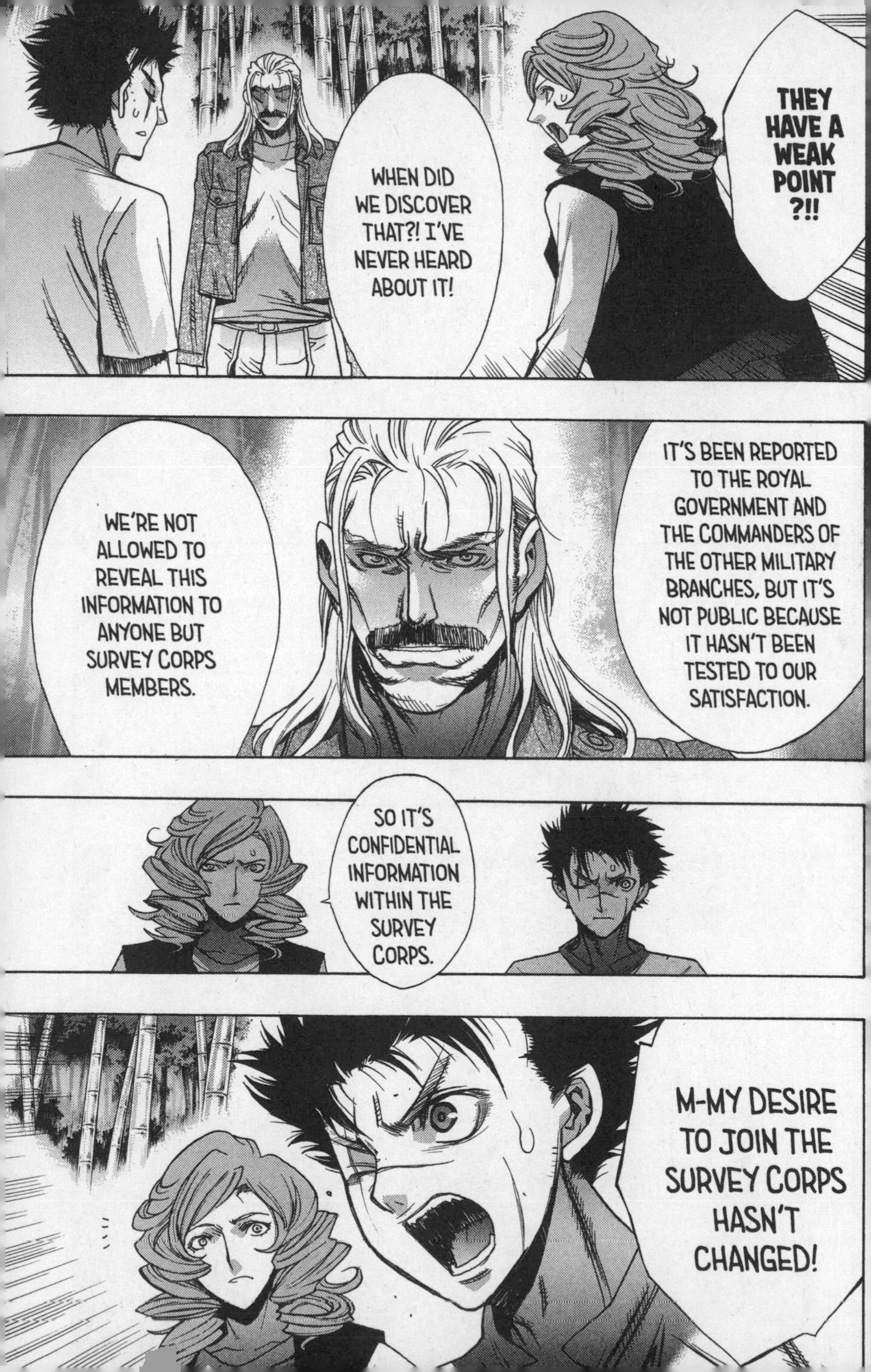
THEY HAVE A WEAK POINT?!!
WHEN DID WE DISCOVER THAT?! I'VE NEVER HEARD ABOUT IT!
IT'S BEEN REPORTED TO THE ROYAL GOVERNMENT AND THE COMMANDERS OF THE OTHER MILITARY BRANCHES, BUT IT'S NOT PUBLIC BECAUSE IT HASN'T BEEN TESTED TO OUR SATISFACTION.
WE'RE NOT ALLOWED TO REVEAL THIS INFORMATION TO ANYONE BUT SURVEY CORPS MEMBERS.
SO IT'S CONFIDENTIAL INFORMATION WITHIN THE SURVEY CORPS.
M-MY DESIRE TO JOIN THE SURVEY CORPS HASN'T CHANGED!

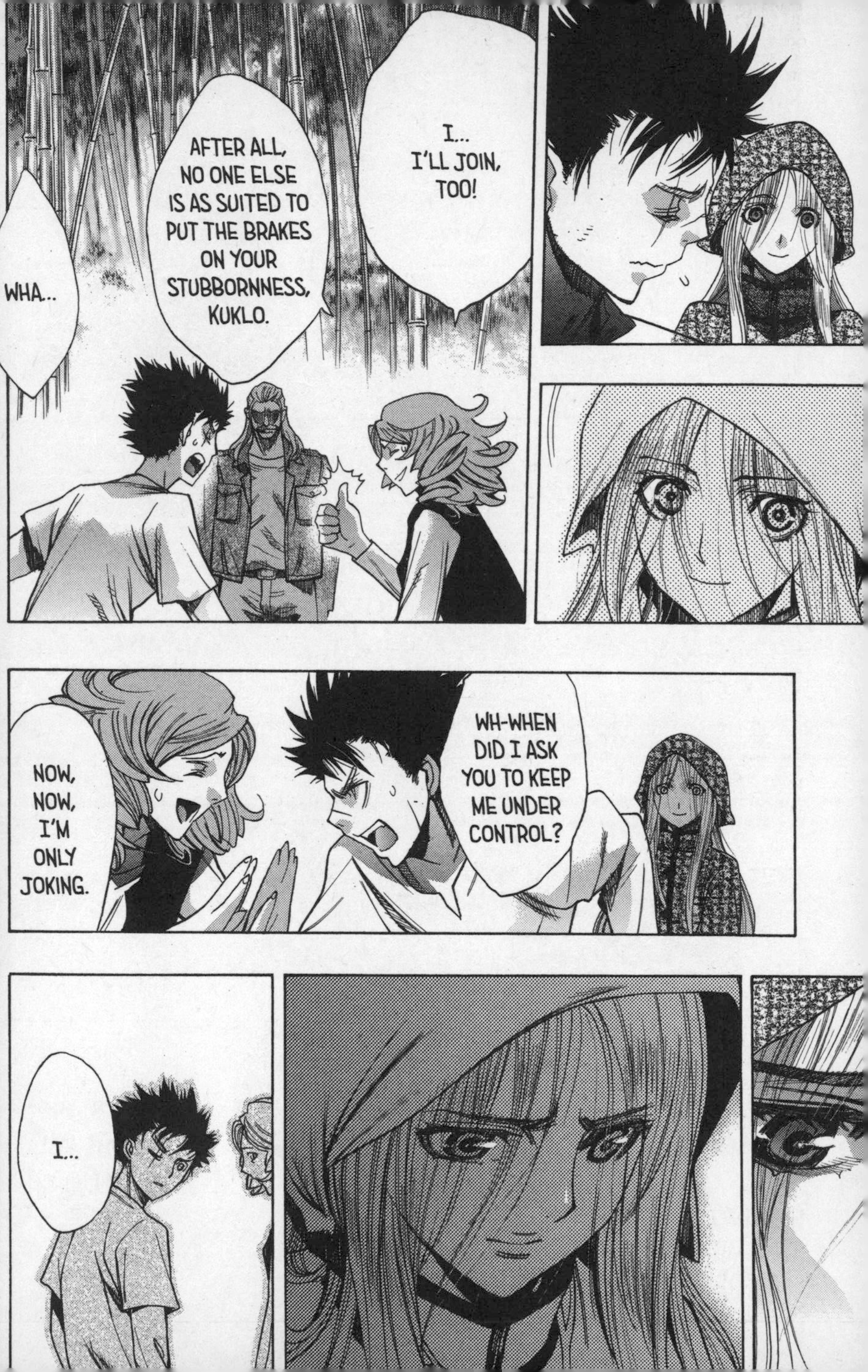
I... I'LL JOIN, TOO!
AFTER ALL, NO ONE ELSE IS AS SUITED TO PUT THE BRAKES ON YOUR STUBBORNNESS, KUKLO.
WHA...
WH-WHEN DID I ASK YOU TO KEEP ME UNDER CONTROL?
NOW, NOW, I'M ONLY JOKING.
I...

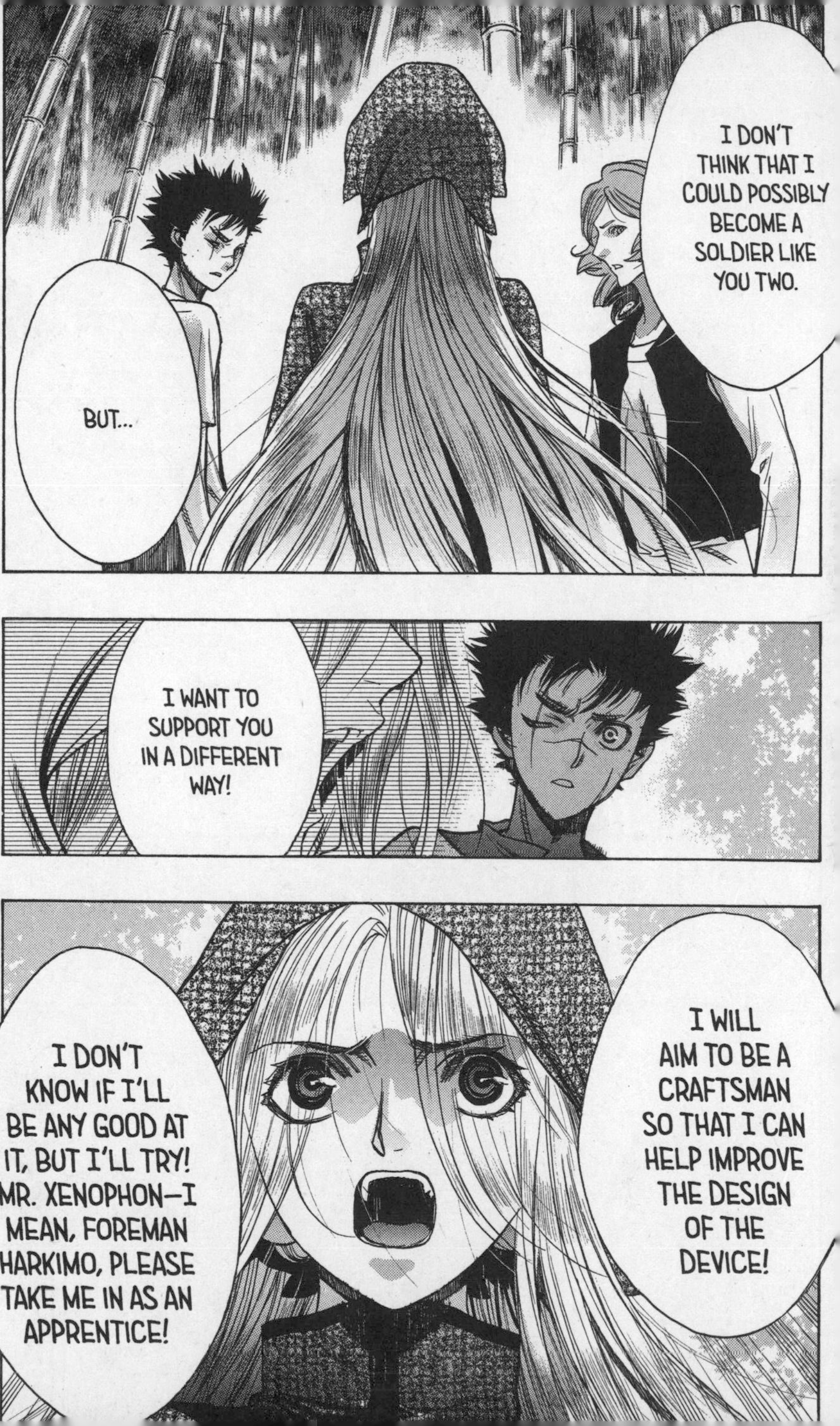
I DON'T THINK THAT I COULD POSSIBLY BECOME A SOLDIER LIKE YOU TWO.
BUT...
I WANT TO SUPPORT YOU IN A DIFFERENT WAY!
I WILL AIM TO BE A CRAFTSMAN SO THAT I CAN HELP IMPROVE THE DESIGN OF THE DEVICE!
I DON'T KNOW IF I'LL BE ANY GOOD AT IT, BUT I'LL TRY! MR. XENOPHON—I MEAN, FOREMAN HARKIMO, PLEASE TAKE ME IN AS AN APPRENTICE!

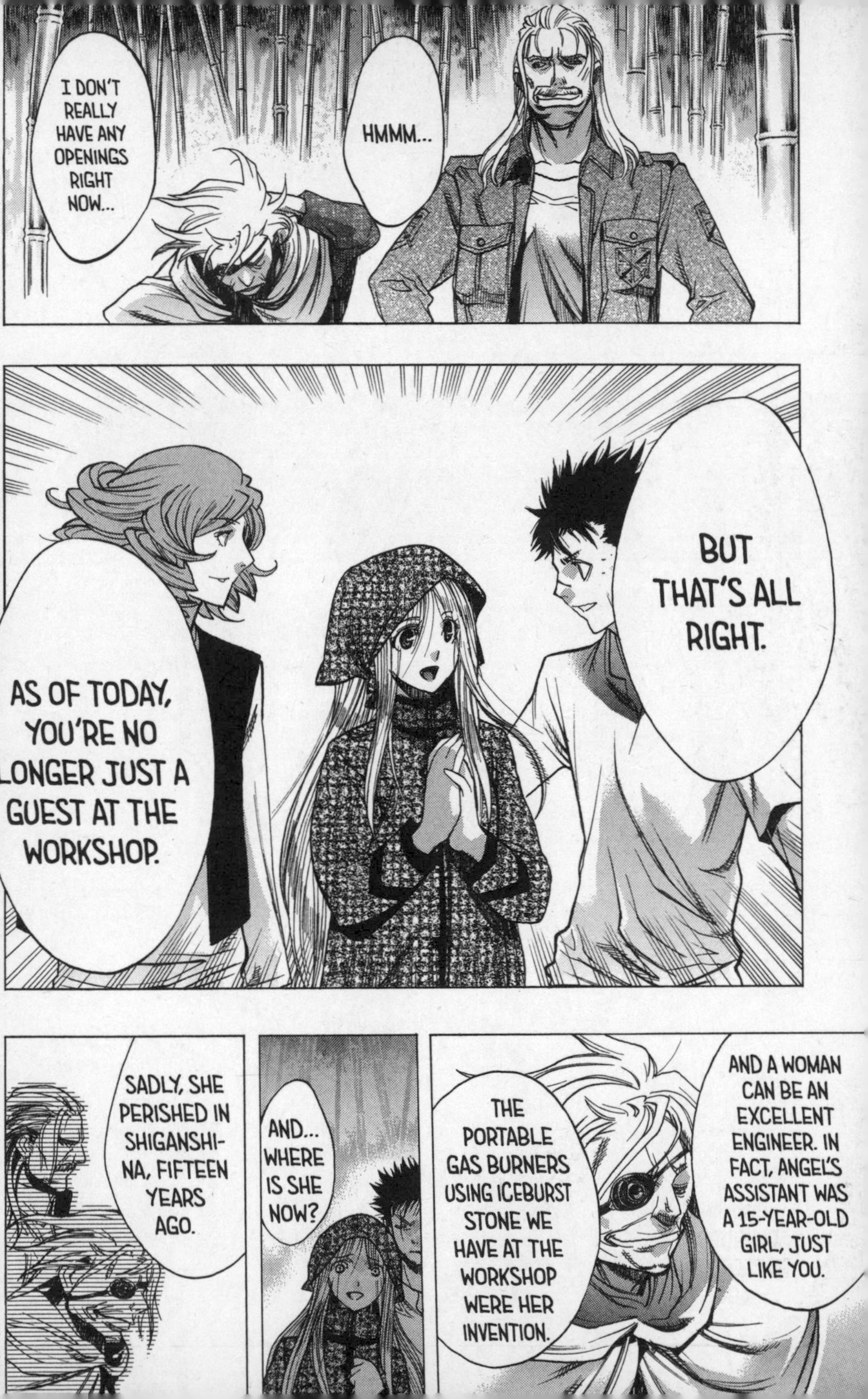
HMMM...
I DON'T REALLY HAVE ANY OPENINGS RIGHT NOW...
BUT THAT'S ALL RIGHT.
AS OF TODAY, YOU'RE NO LONGER JUST A GUEST AT THE WORKSHOP.
AND A WOMAN CAN BE AN EXCELLENT ENGINEER. IN FACT, ANGEL'S ASSISTANT WAS A 15-YEAR-OLD GIRL, JUST LIKE YOU.
THE PORTABLE GAS BURNERS USING ICEBURST STONE WE HAVE AT THE WORKSHOP WERE HER INVENTION.
AND... WHERE IS SHE NOW?
SADLY, SHE PERISHED IN SHIGANSHI-NA, FIFTEEN YEARS AGO.

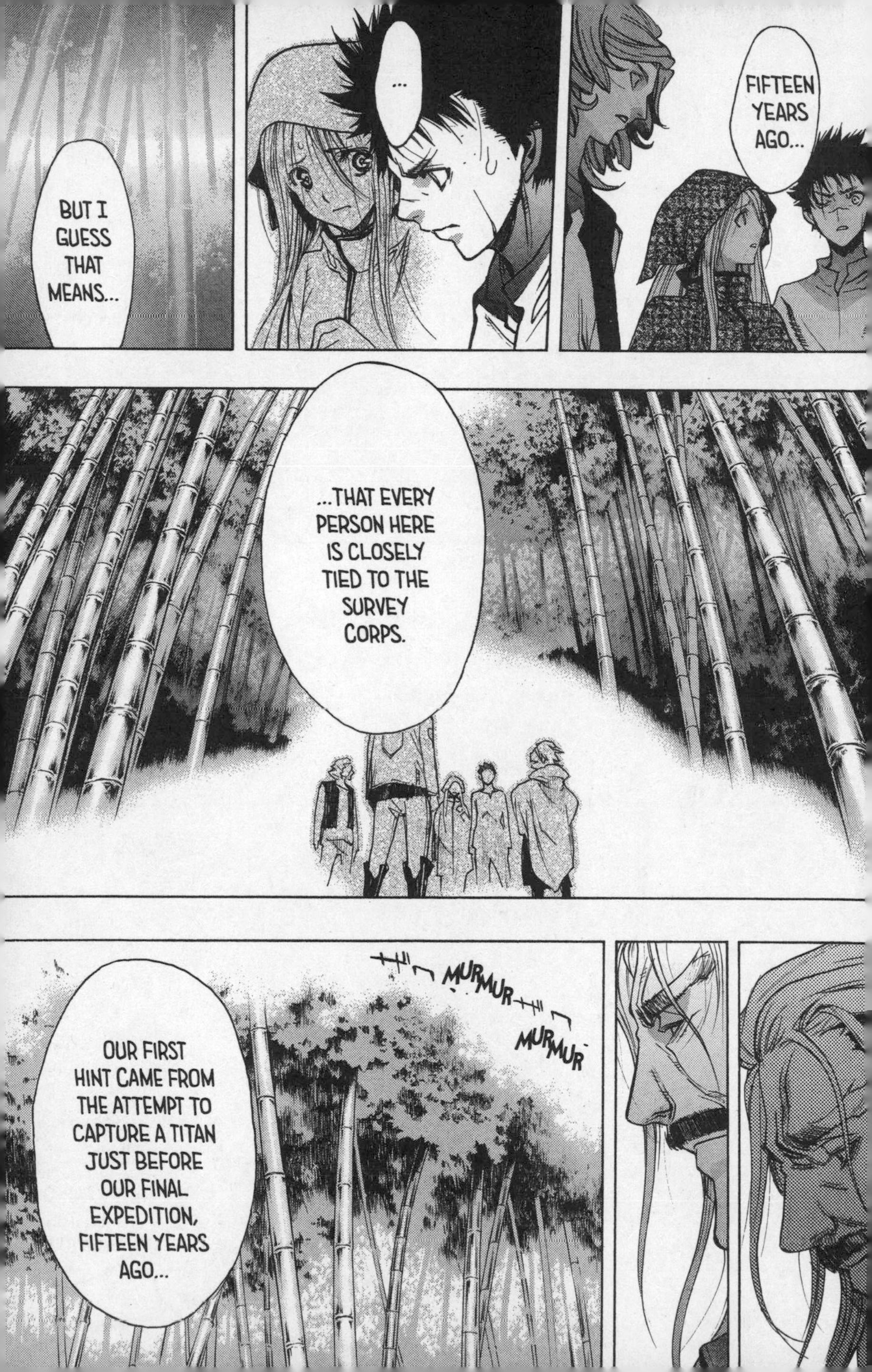
FIFTEEN YEARS AGO...
...
BUT I GUESS THAT MEANS...
...THAT EVERY PERSON HERE IS CLOSELY TIED TO THE SURVEY CORPS.
MURMUR
MURMUR
OUR FIRST HINT CAME FROM THE ATTEMPT TO CAPTURE A TITAN JUST BEFORE OUR FINAL EXPEDITION, FIFTEEN YEARS AGO...

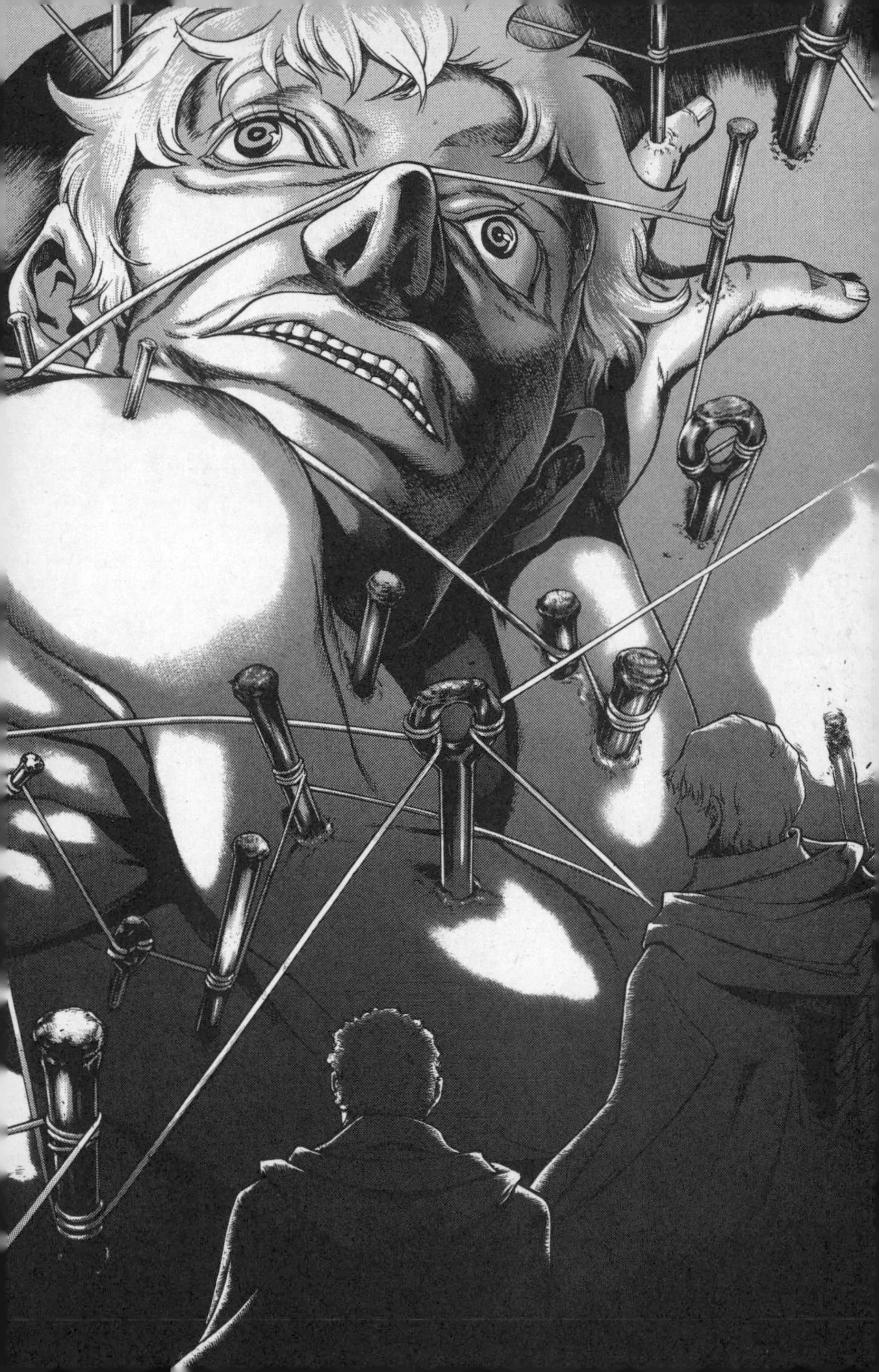

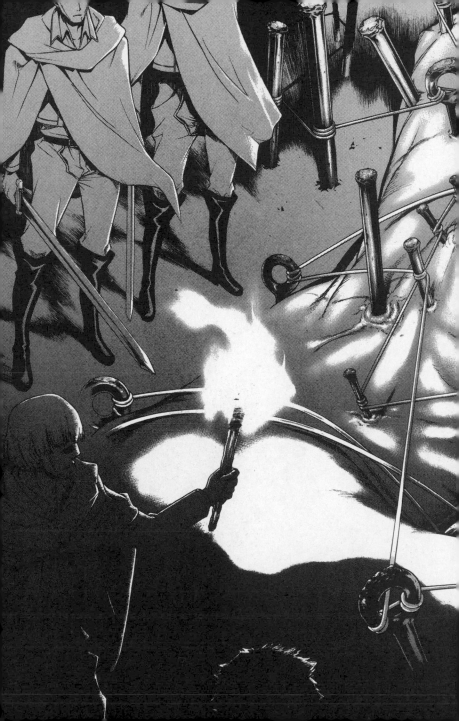

GAHH
THE PURPOSE OF THE OPERATION WAS TO FIND A WAY TO KILL A TITAN...
SO, FIND ITS WEAK POINT... AND SEE HOW MUCH PAIN WE NEEDED TO INFLICT TO KILL IT.

Chapter 16: Thicket of Iron Bamboo · End

ATTACK on TITAN

BEFORE THE FALL

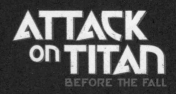

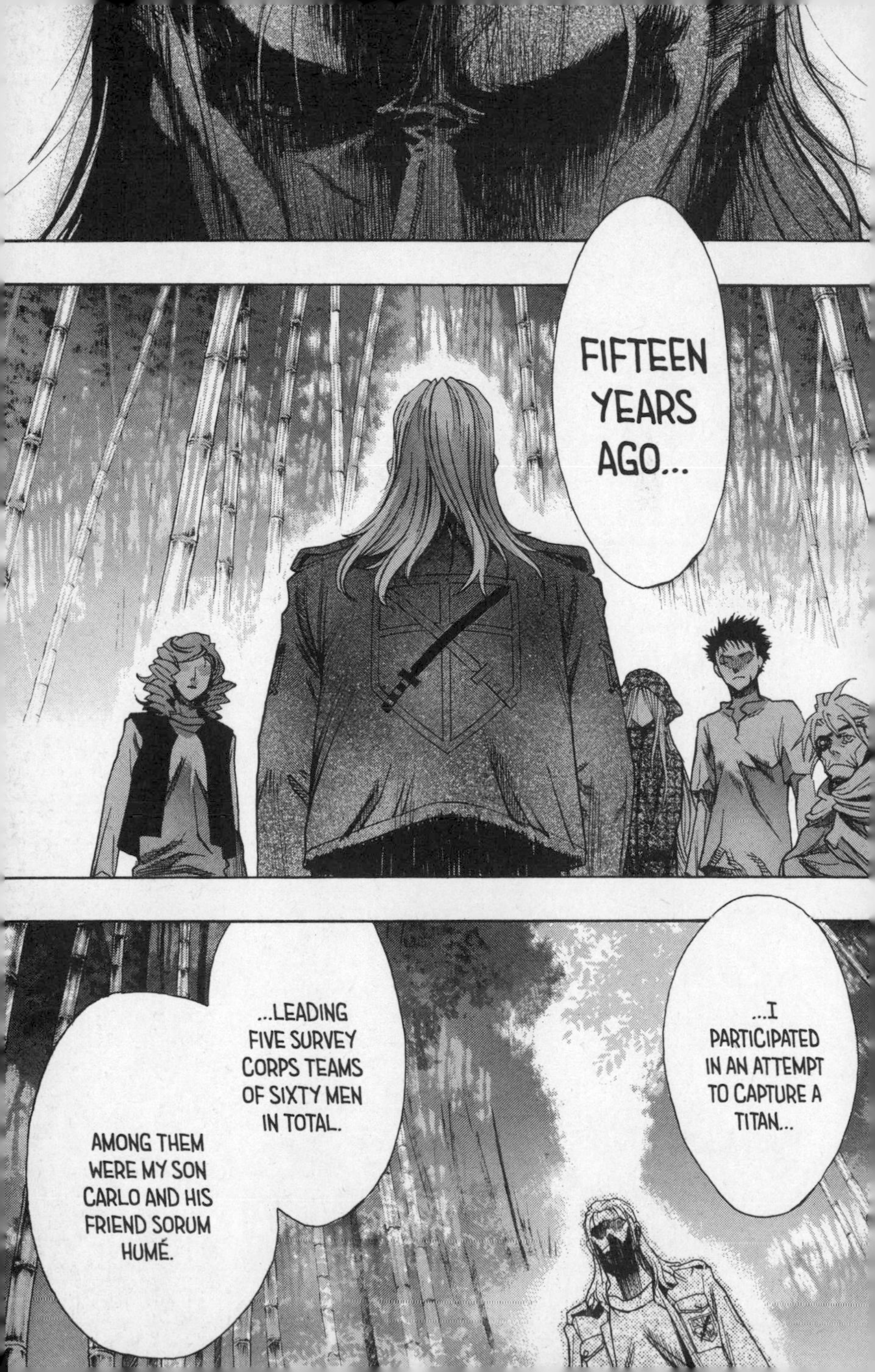
FIFTEEN YEARS AGO...
...I PARTICIPATED IN AN ATTEMPT TO CAPTURE A TITAN...
...LEADING FIVE SURVEY CORPS TEAMS OF SIXTY MEN IN TOTAL.
AMONG THEM WERE MY SON CARLO AND HIS FRIEND SORUM HUMÉ.

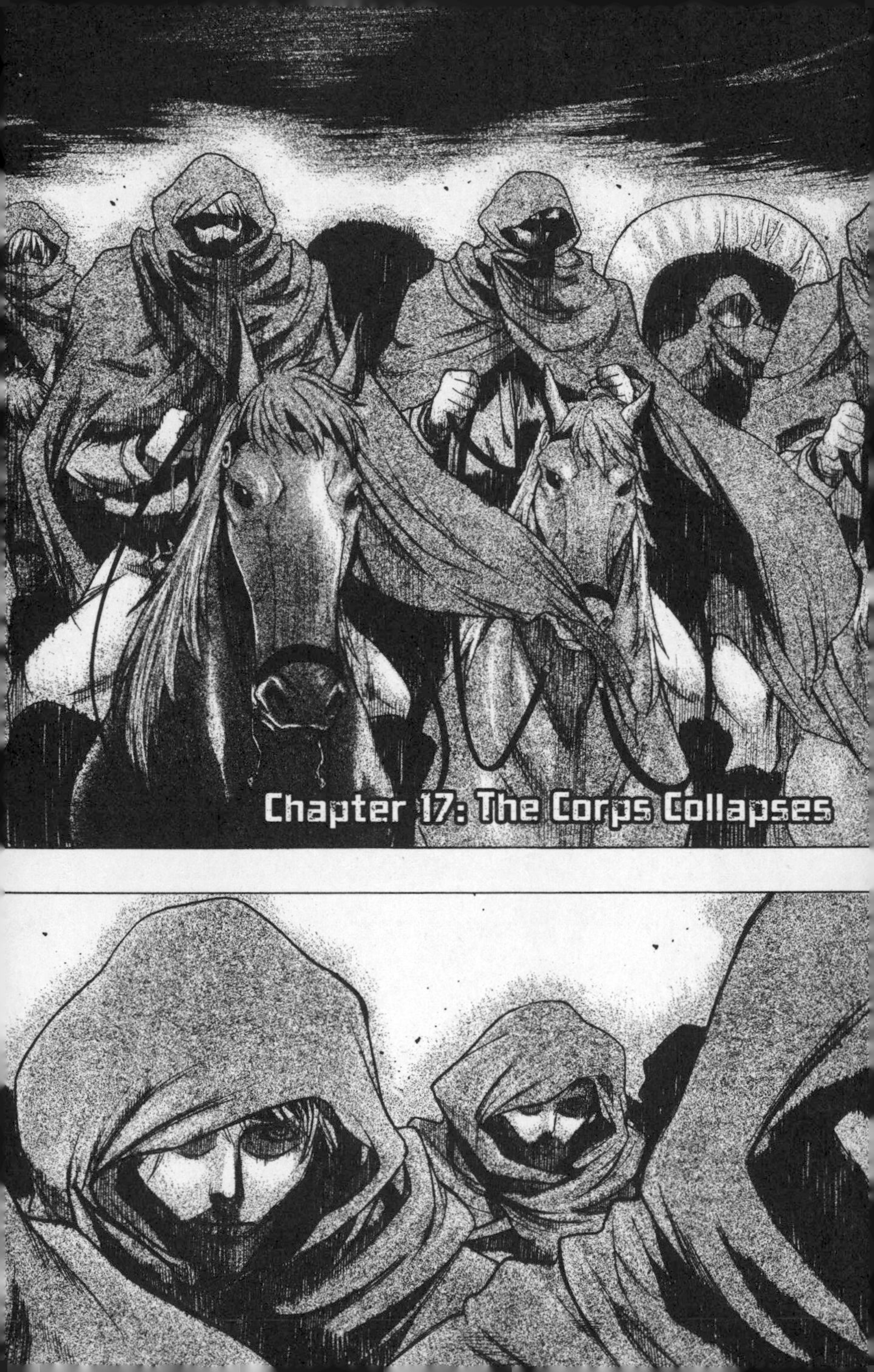
Chapter 17: The Corps Collapses

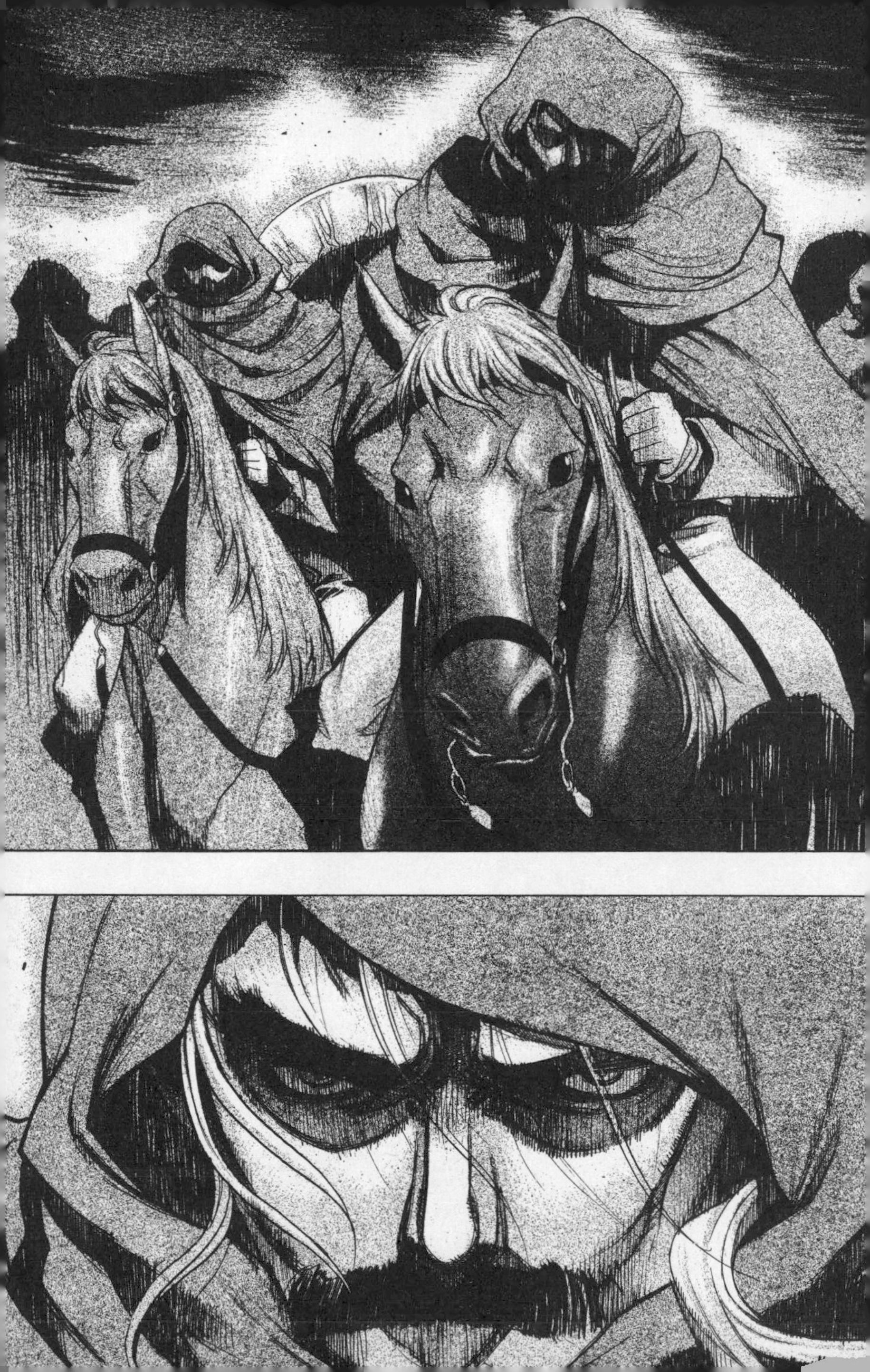

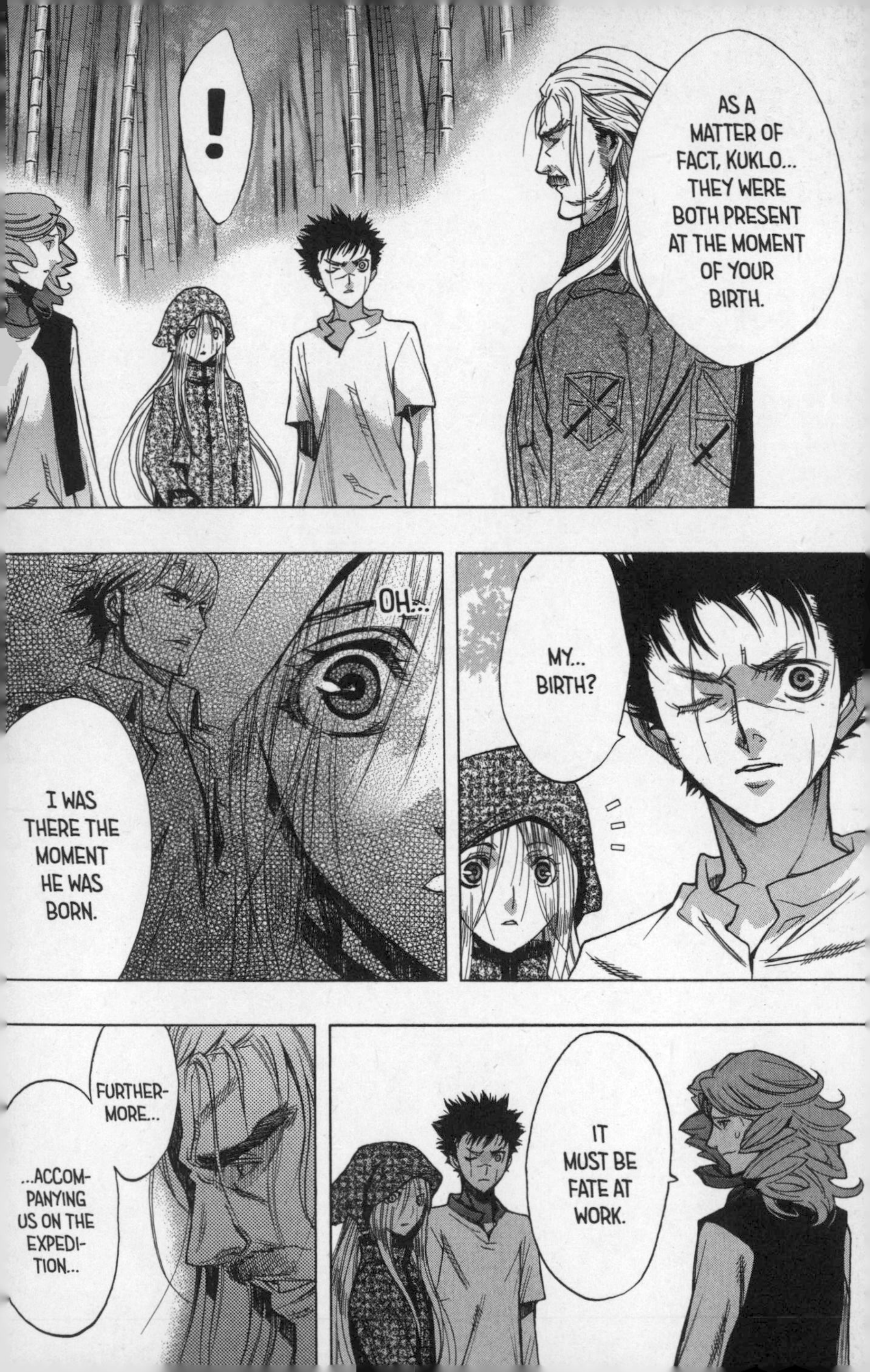
AS A MATTER OF FACT, KUKLO... THEY WERE BOTH PRESENT AT THE MOMENT OF YOUR BIRTH.
!
MY... BIRTH?
OH...
I WAS THERE THE MOMENT HE WAS BORN.
IT MUST BE FATE AT WORK.
FURTHERMORE...
...ACCOMPANYING US ON THE EXPEDITION...

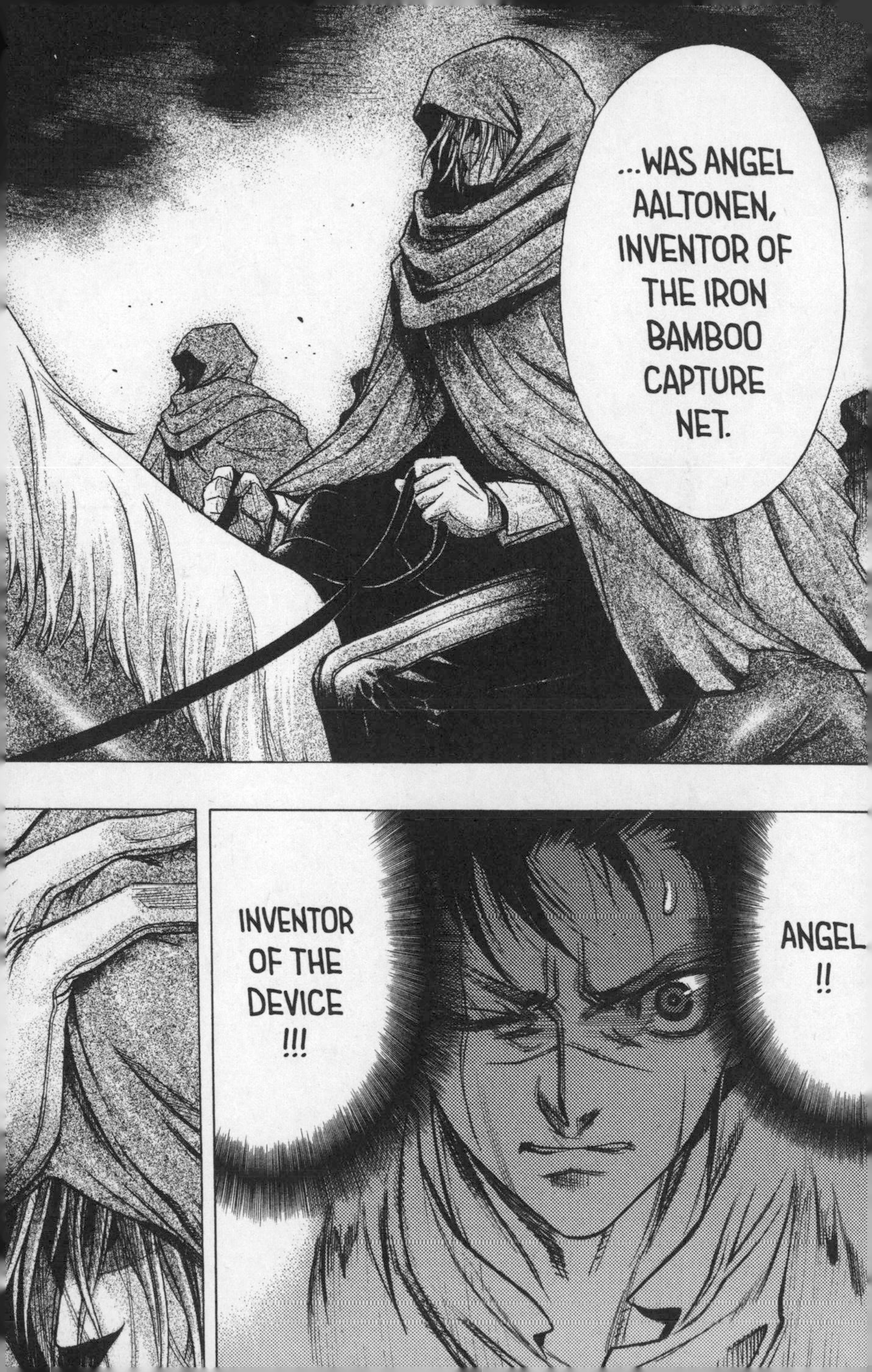
...WAS ANGEL AALTONEN, INVENTOR OF THE IRON BAMBOO CAPTURE NET.
ANGEL !!
INVENTOR OF THE DEVICE !!!

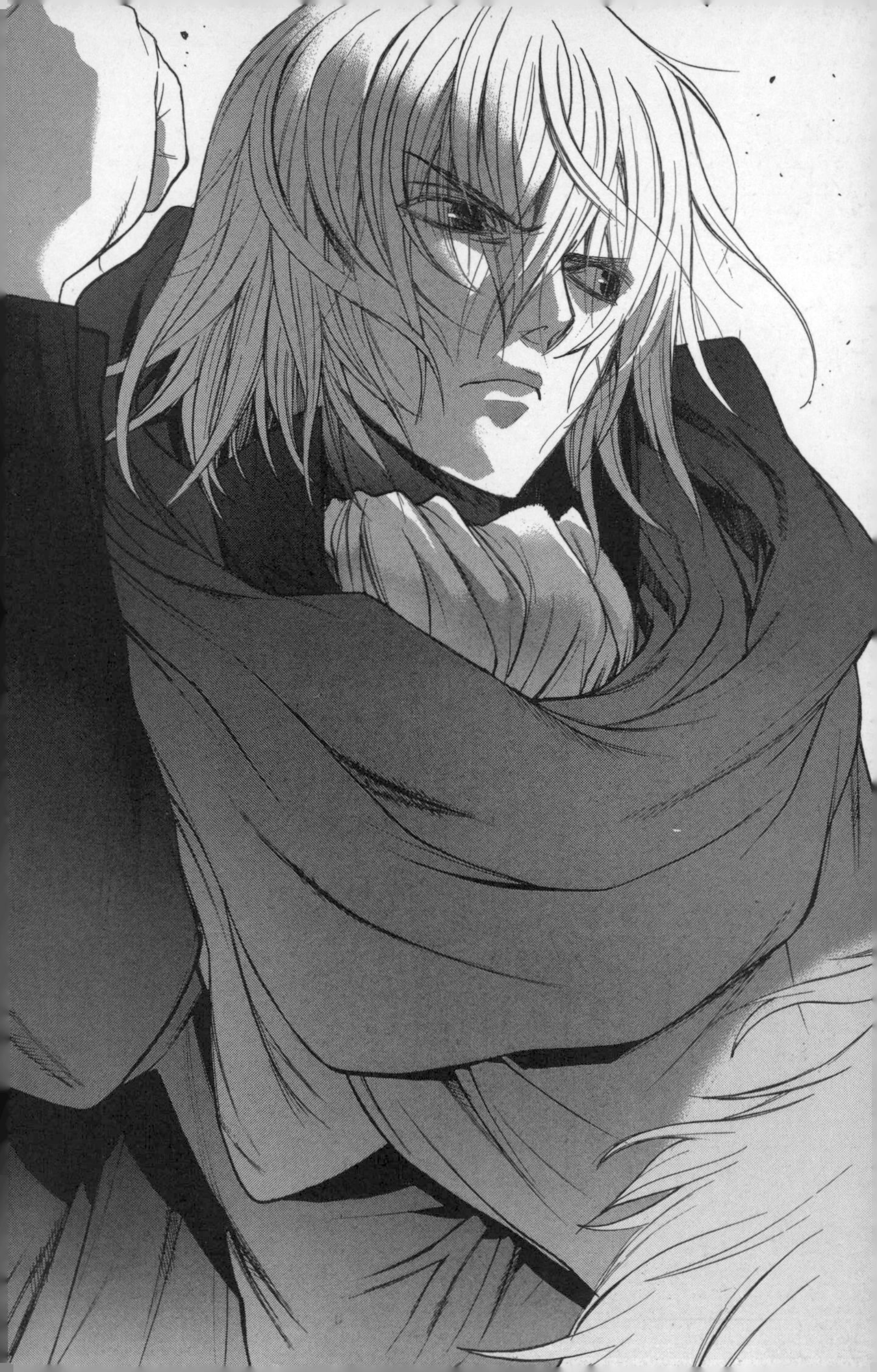

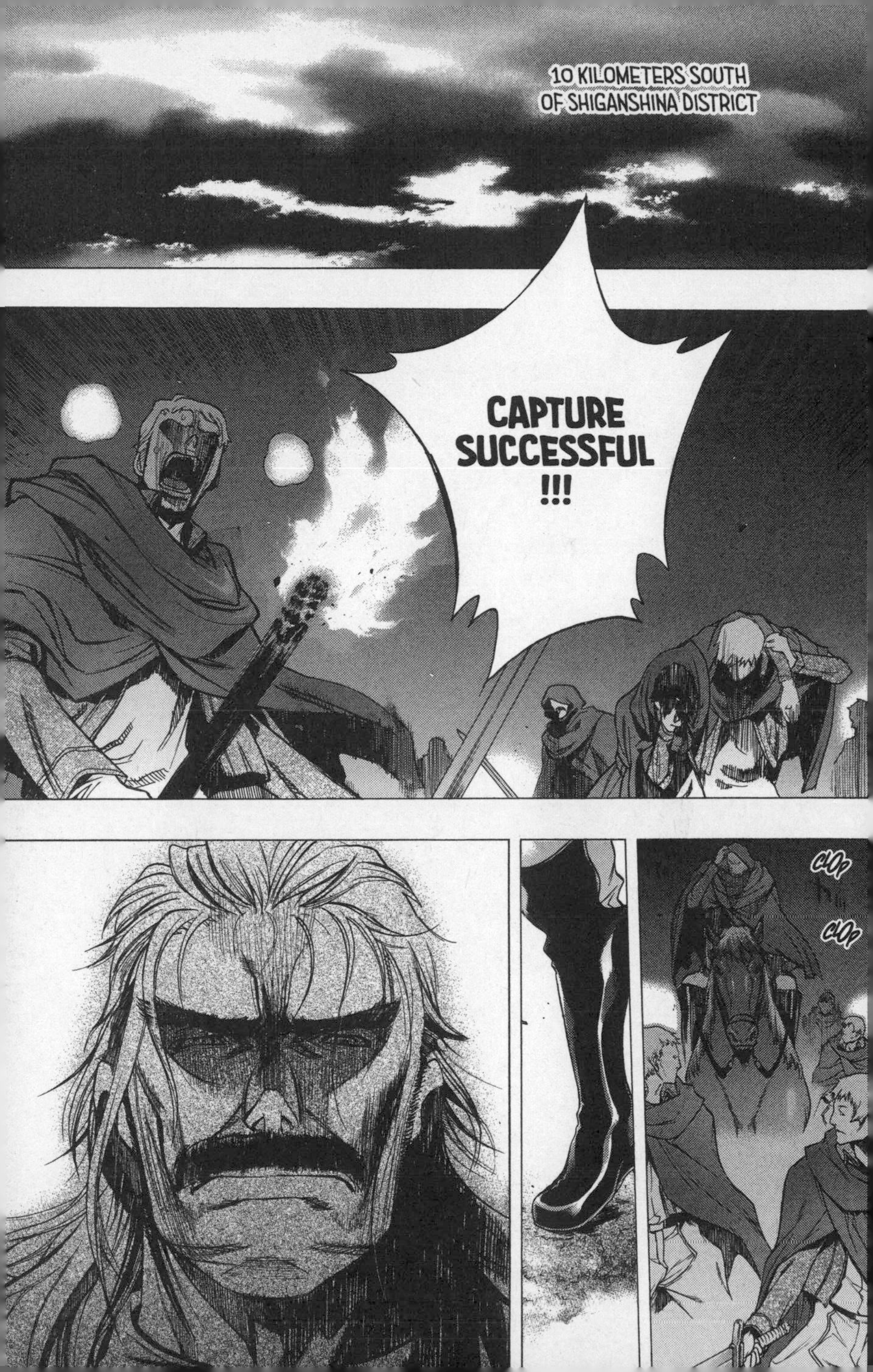
10 KILOMETERS SOUTH OF SHIGANSHINA DISTRICT
CAPTURE SUCCESSFUL !!!
CLOP
CLOP

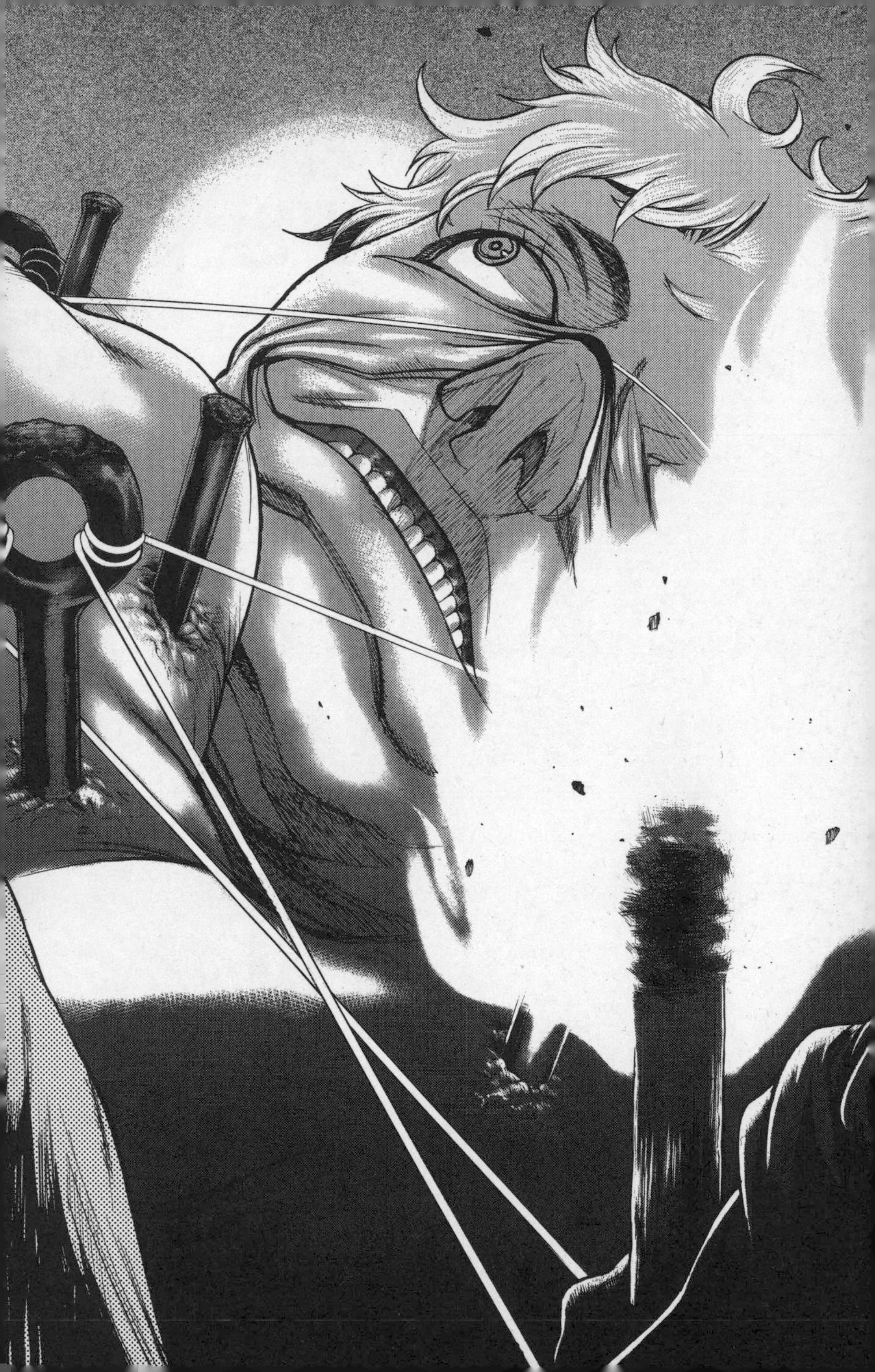

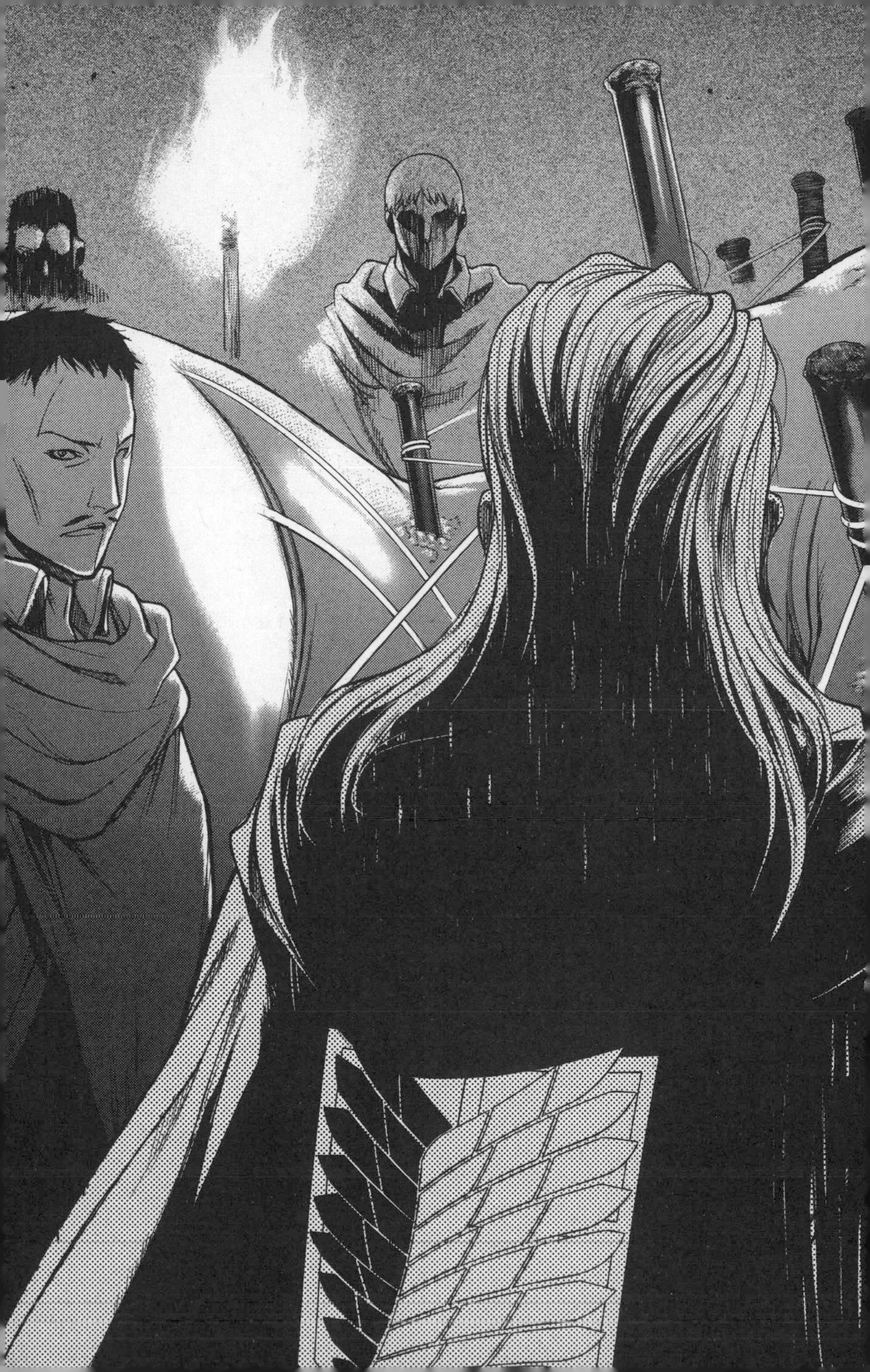

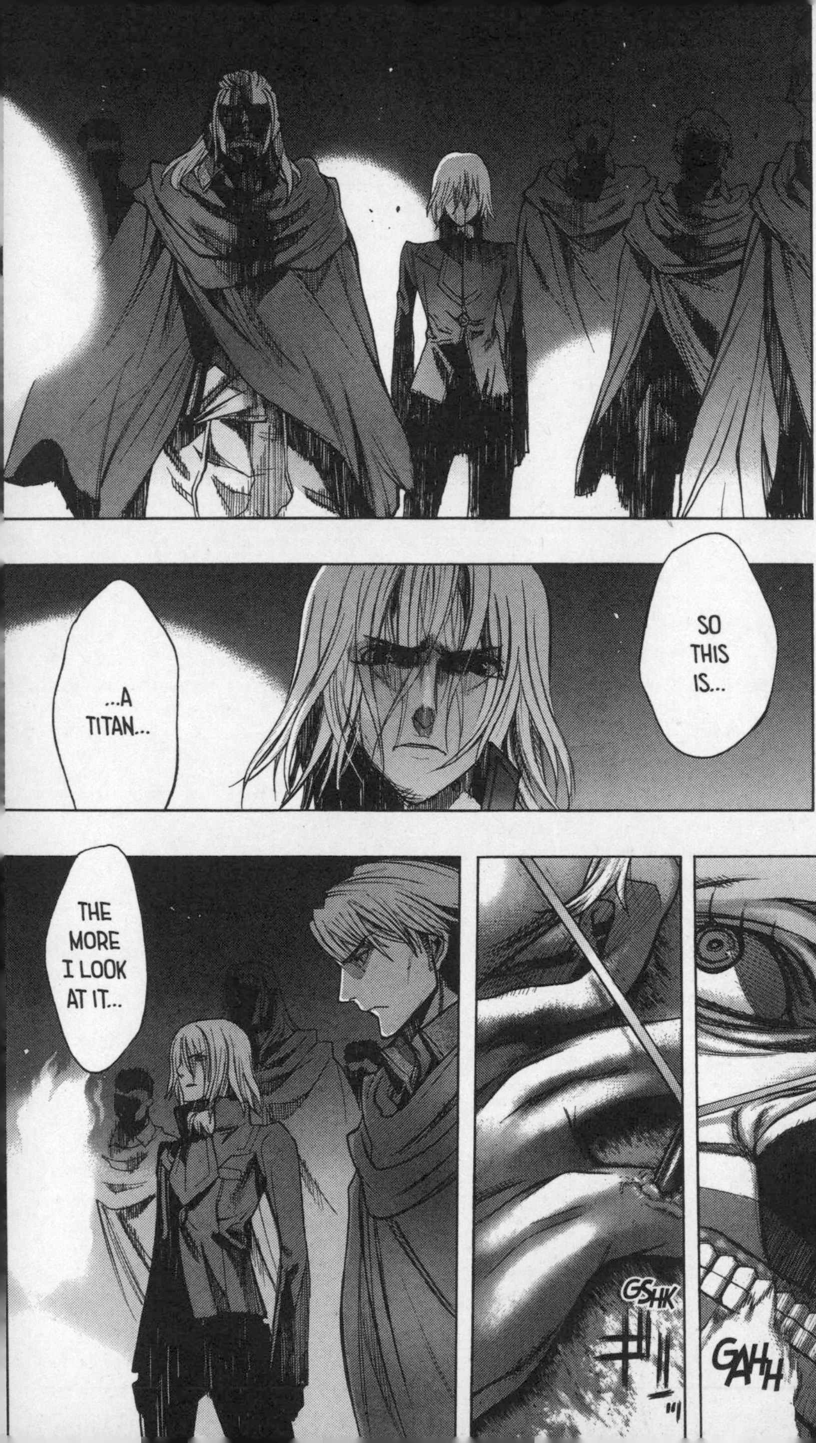
SO THIS IS...
...A TITAN...
HFF
GAHH
GSHK
THE MORE I LOOK AT IT...

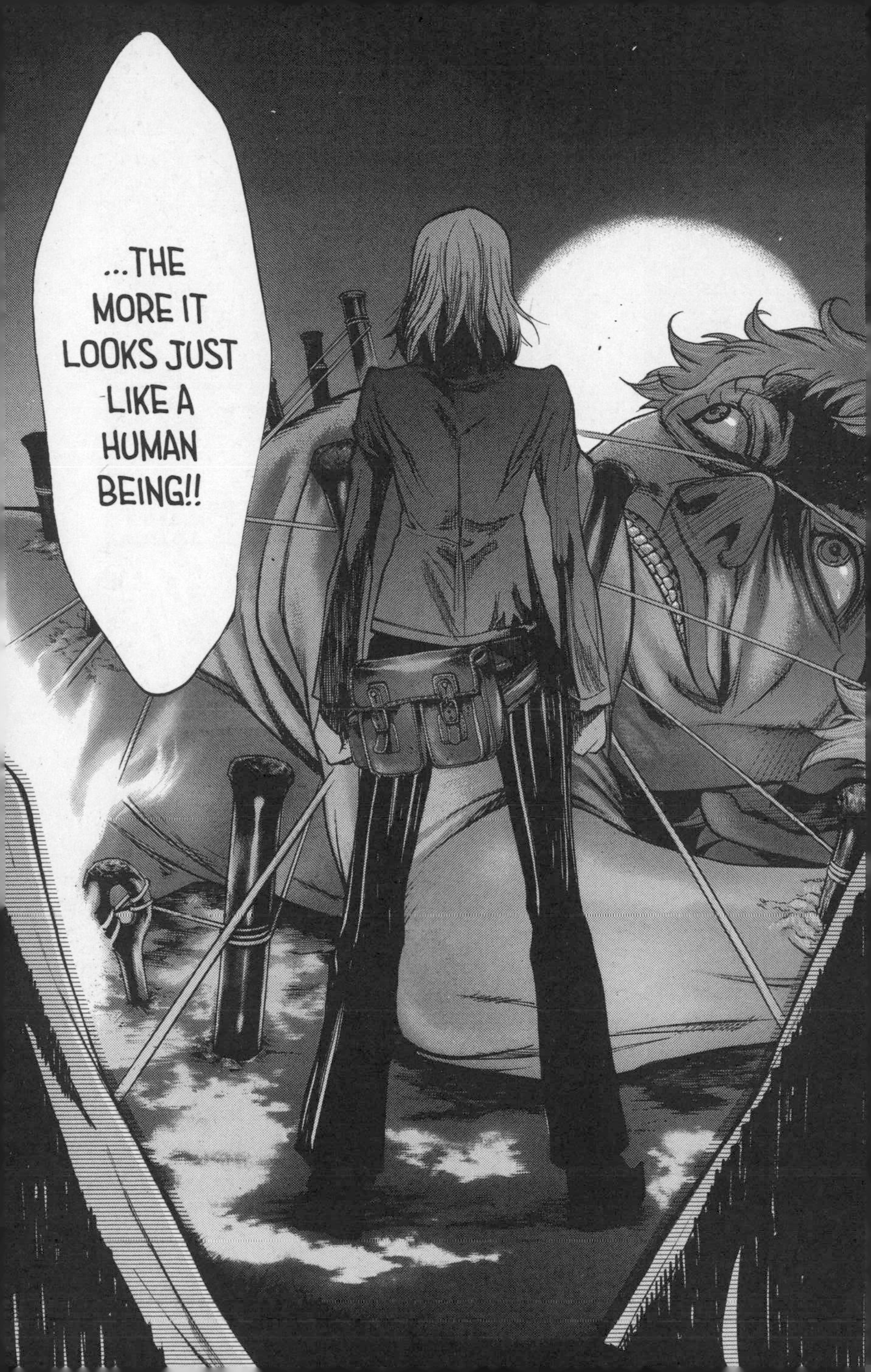
...THE MORE IT LOOKS JUST LIKE A HUMAN BEING!!

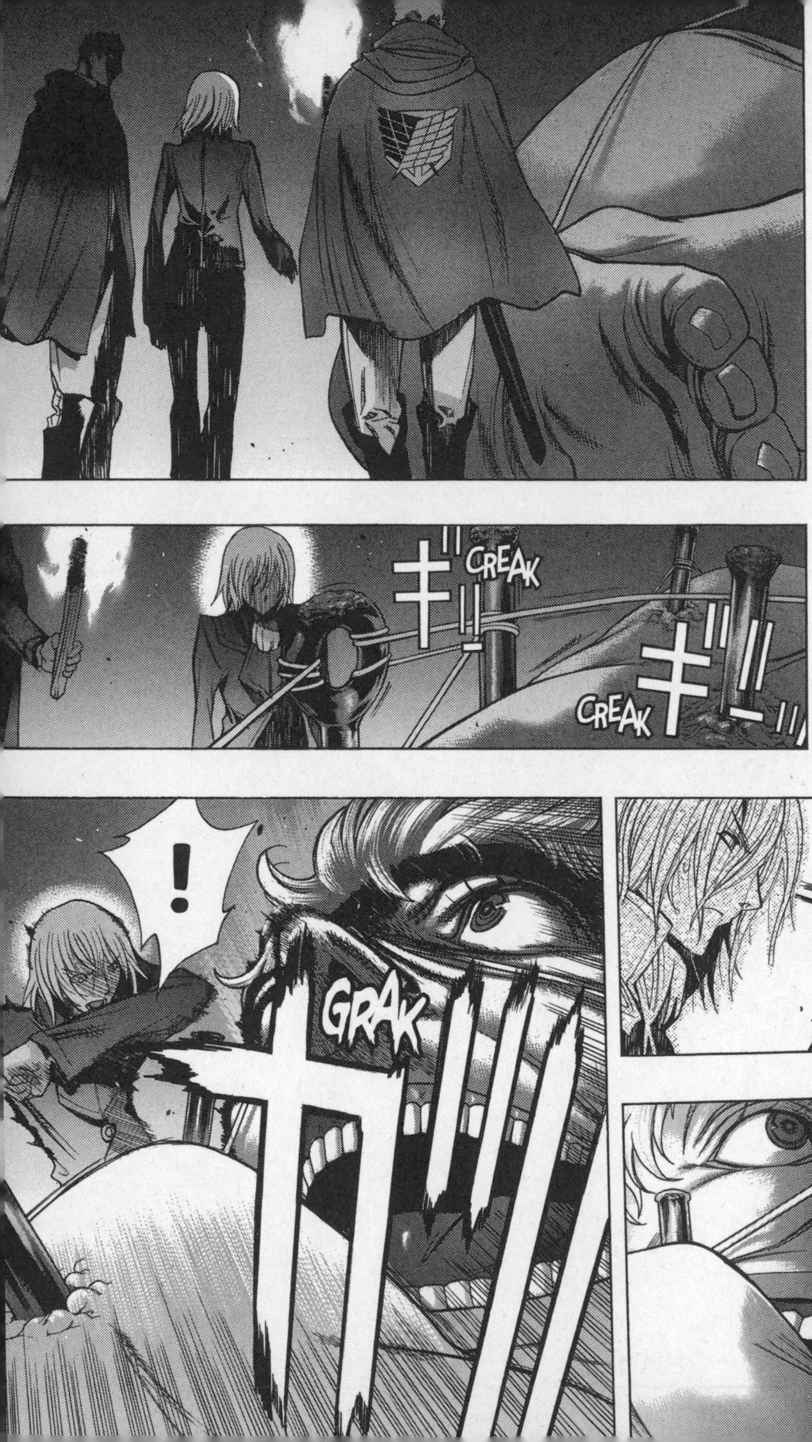
CREAK
CREAK
CREAK
!
GRAK

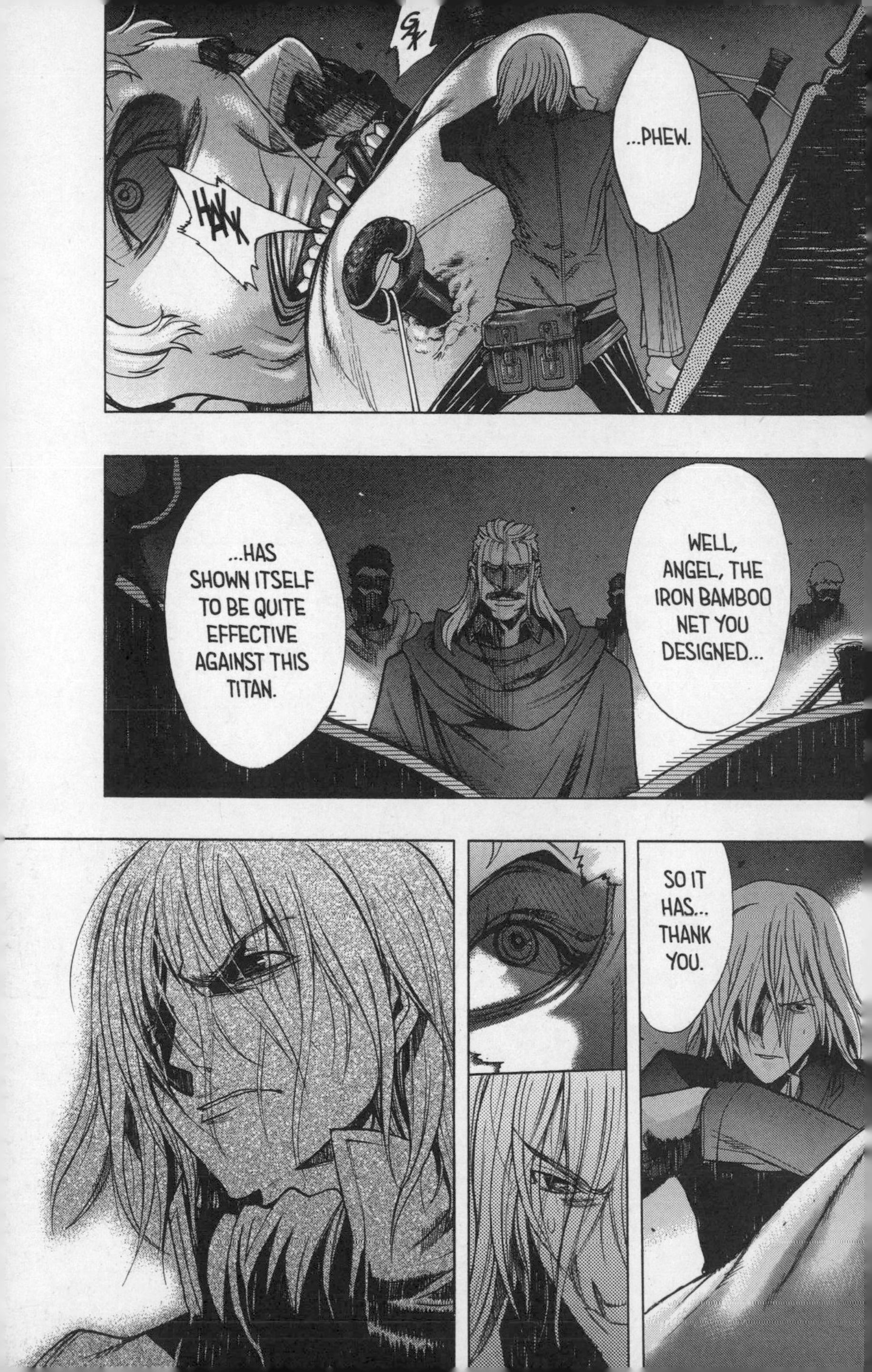
GAK
HAK AK
...PHEW.
WELL, ANGEL, THE IRON BAMBOO NET YOU DESIGNED...
...HAS SHOWN ITSELF TO BE QUITE EFFECTIVE AGAINST THIS TITAN.
SO IT HAS... THANK YOU.

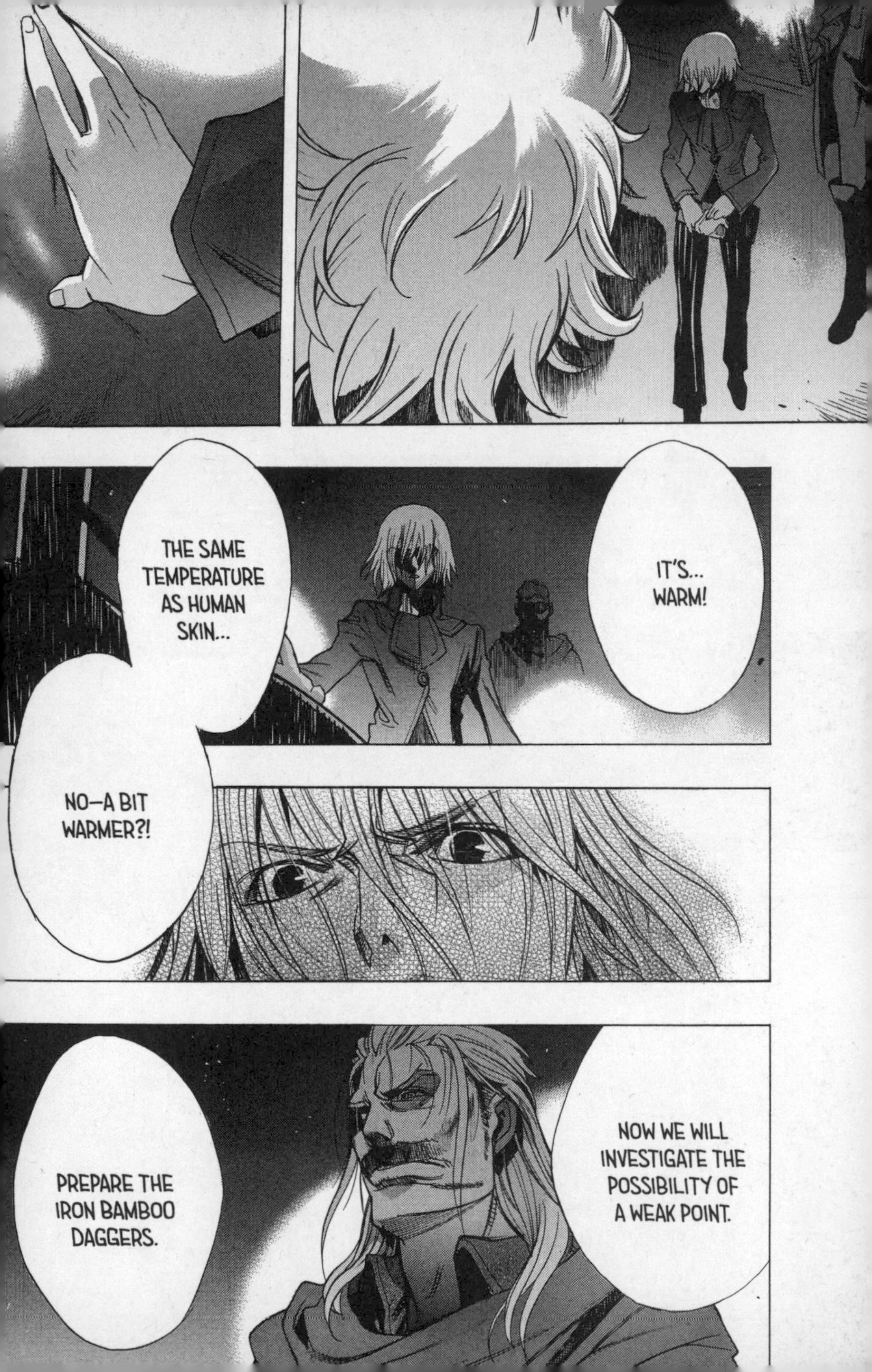
IT'S... WARM!
THE SAME TEMPERATURE AS HUMAN SKIN...
NO—A BIT WARMER?!
NOW WE WILL INVESTIGATE THE POSSIBILITY OF A WEAK POINT.
PREPARE THE IRON BAMBOO DAGGERS.

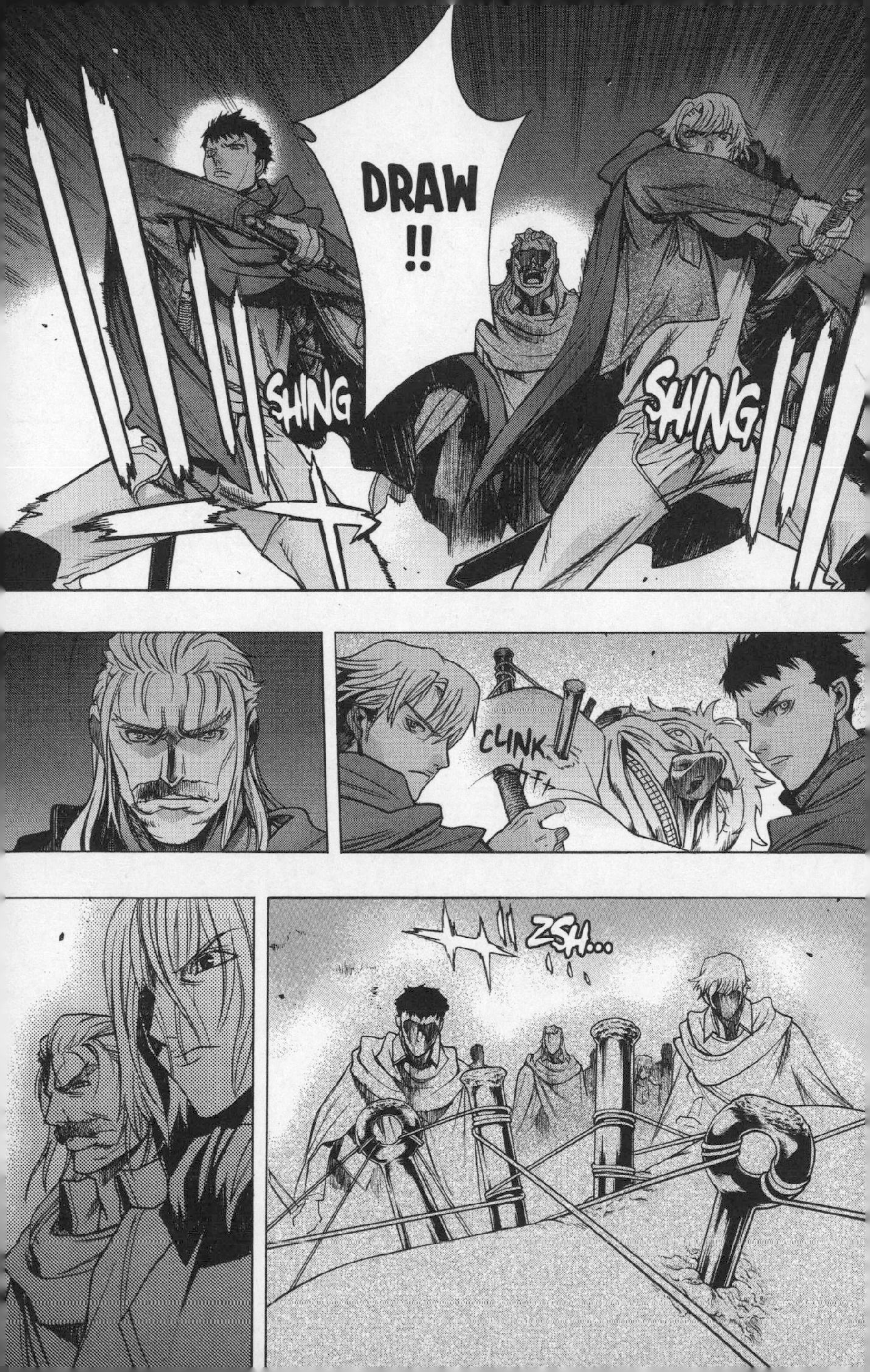
DRAW!!
SHING
SHING
CLINK
ZSH...

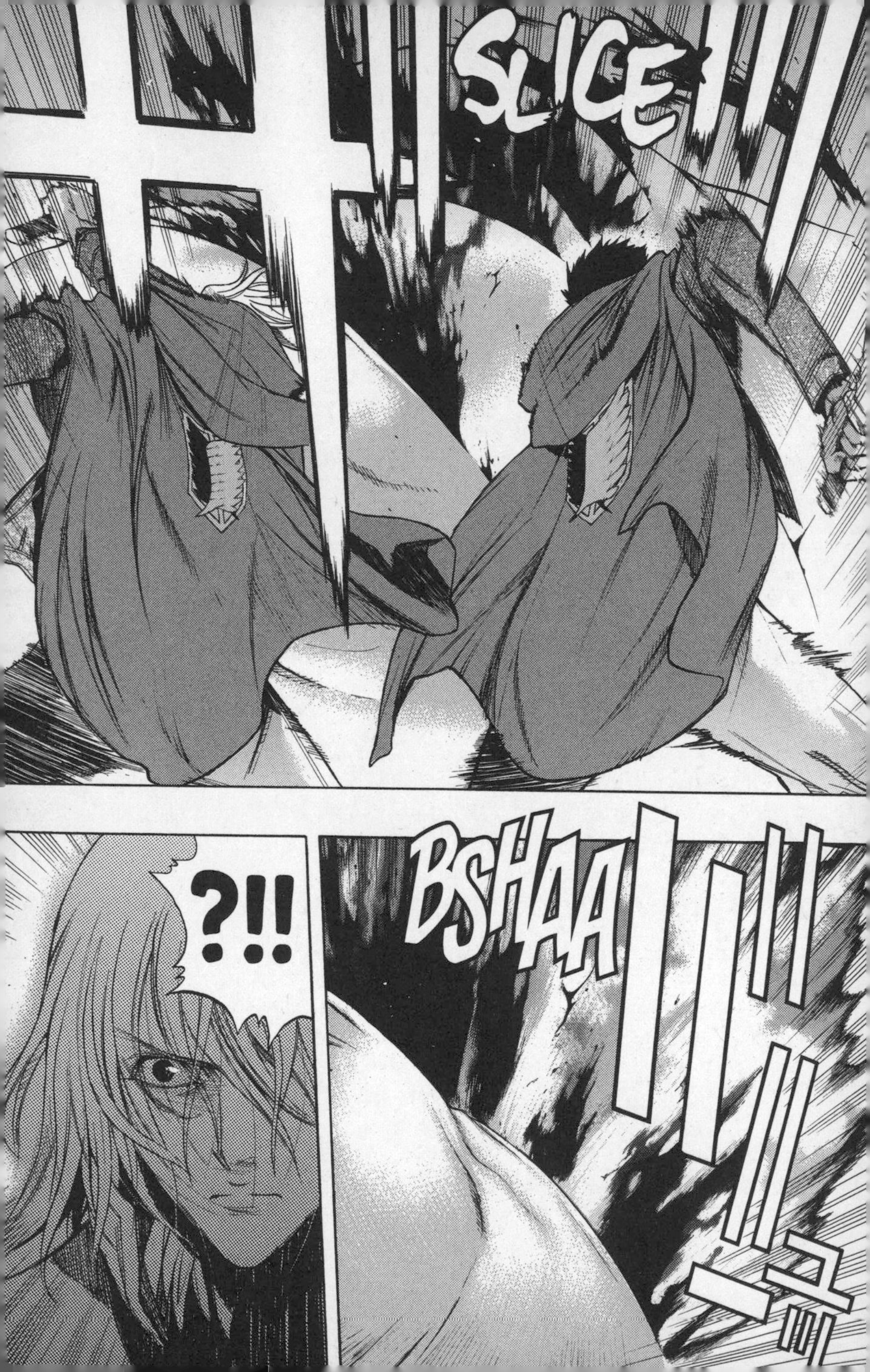
SLICE
BSHAA
?!!

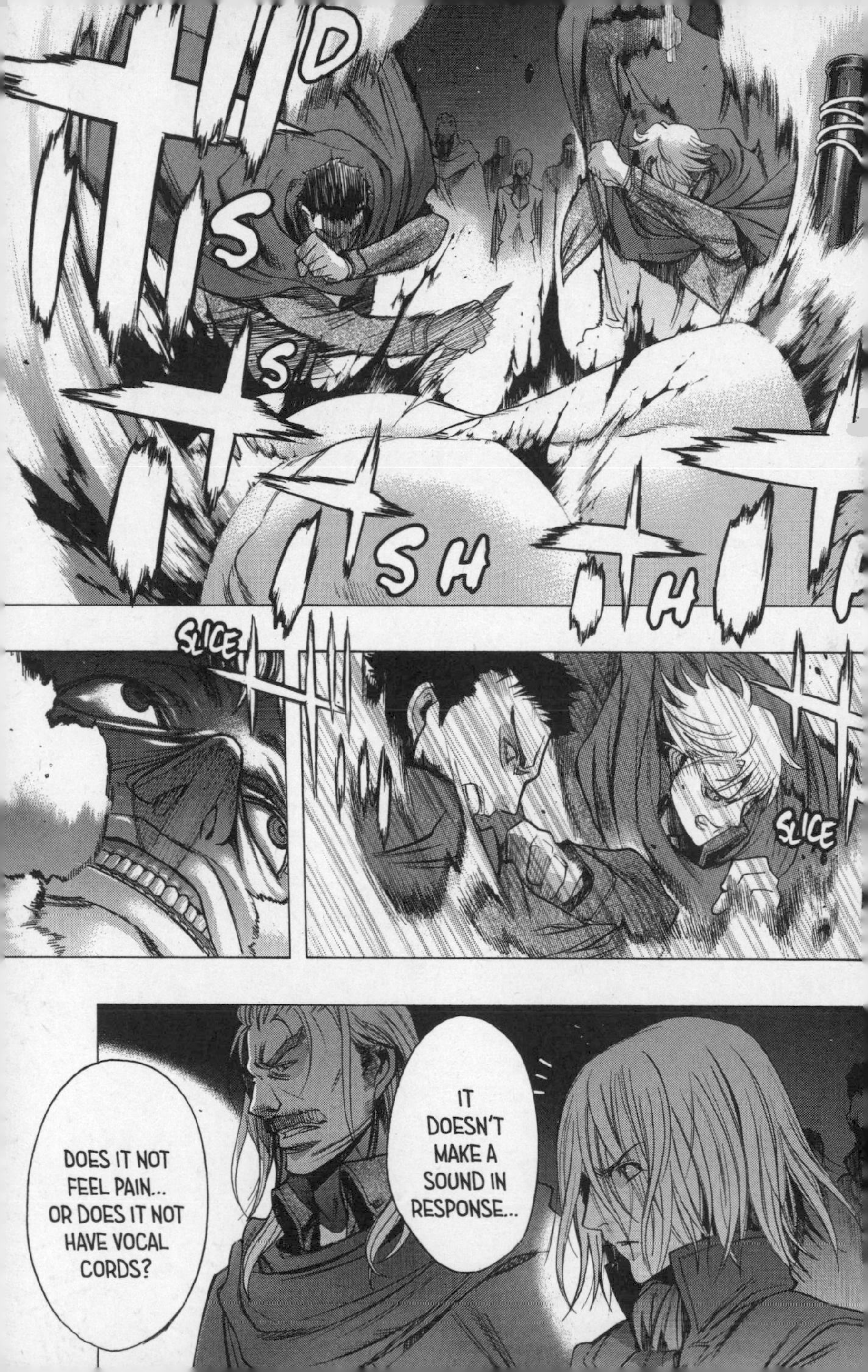
SH
SLICE
SLICE
IT DOESN'T MAKE A SOUND IN RESPONSE...
DOES IT NOT FEEL PAIN... OR DOES IT NOT HAVE VOCAL CORDS?

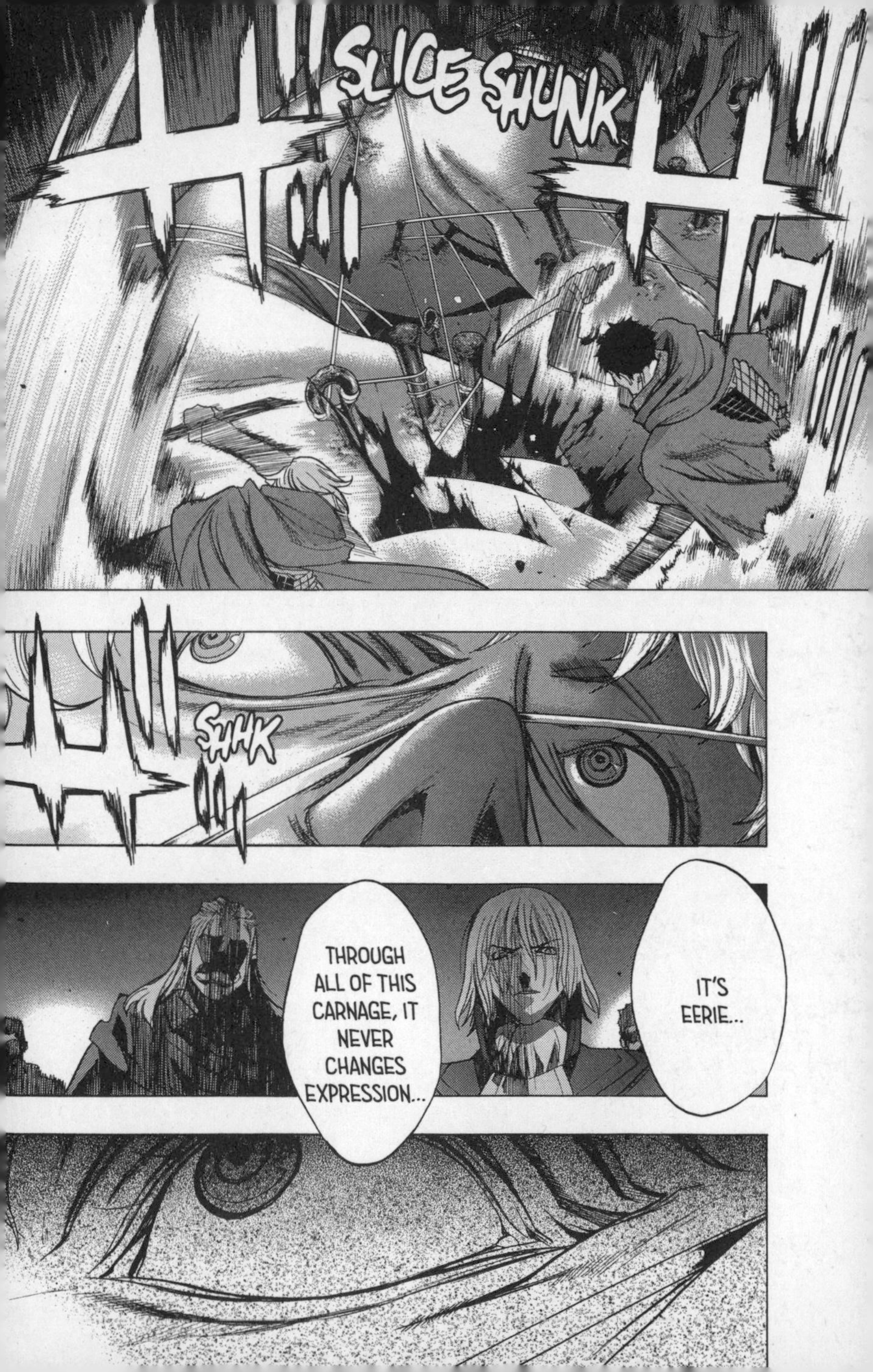
SLICE SHUNK
SHHK
IT'S EERIE...
THROUGH ALL OF THIS CARNAGE, IT NEVER CHANGES EXPRESSION...

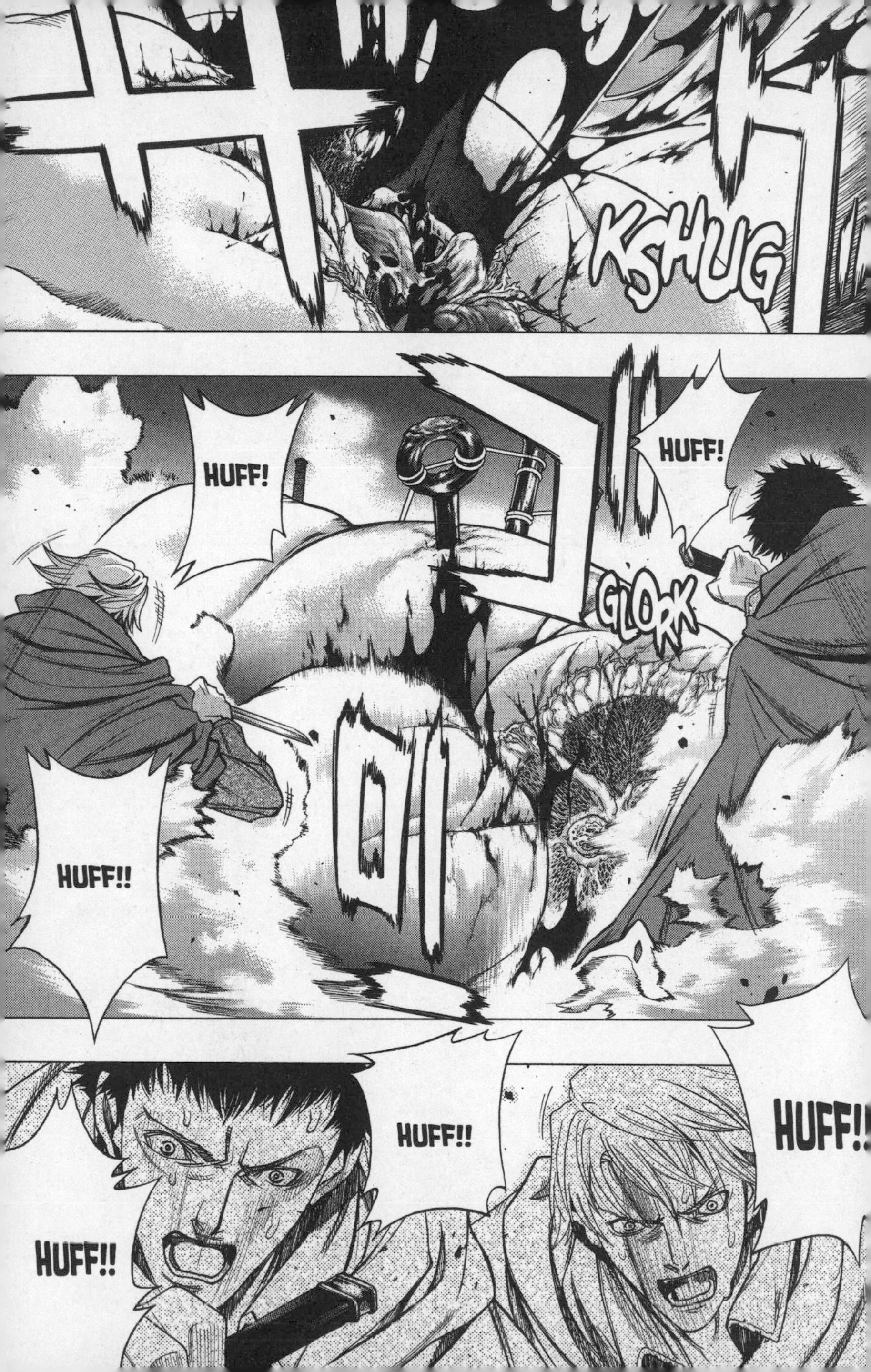
KSHUG
HUFF!
GLORK
HUFF!
HUFF!!
HUFF!!
HUFF!!
HUFF!!

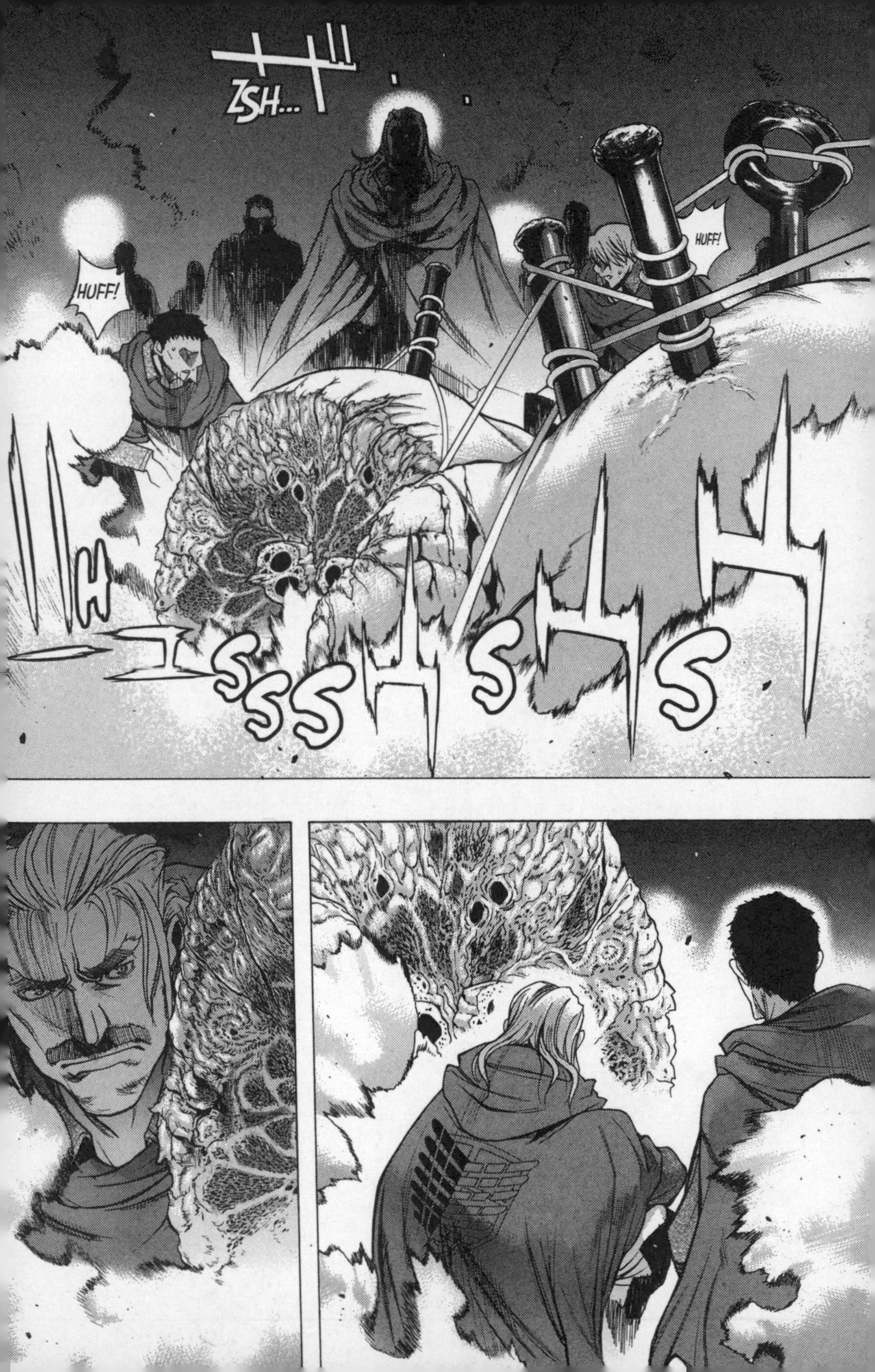
ZSH...
HUFF!
HUFF!
HISSSHSHSH

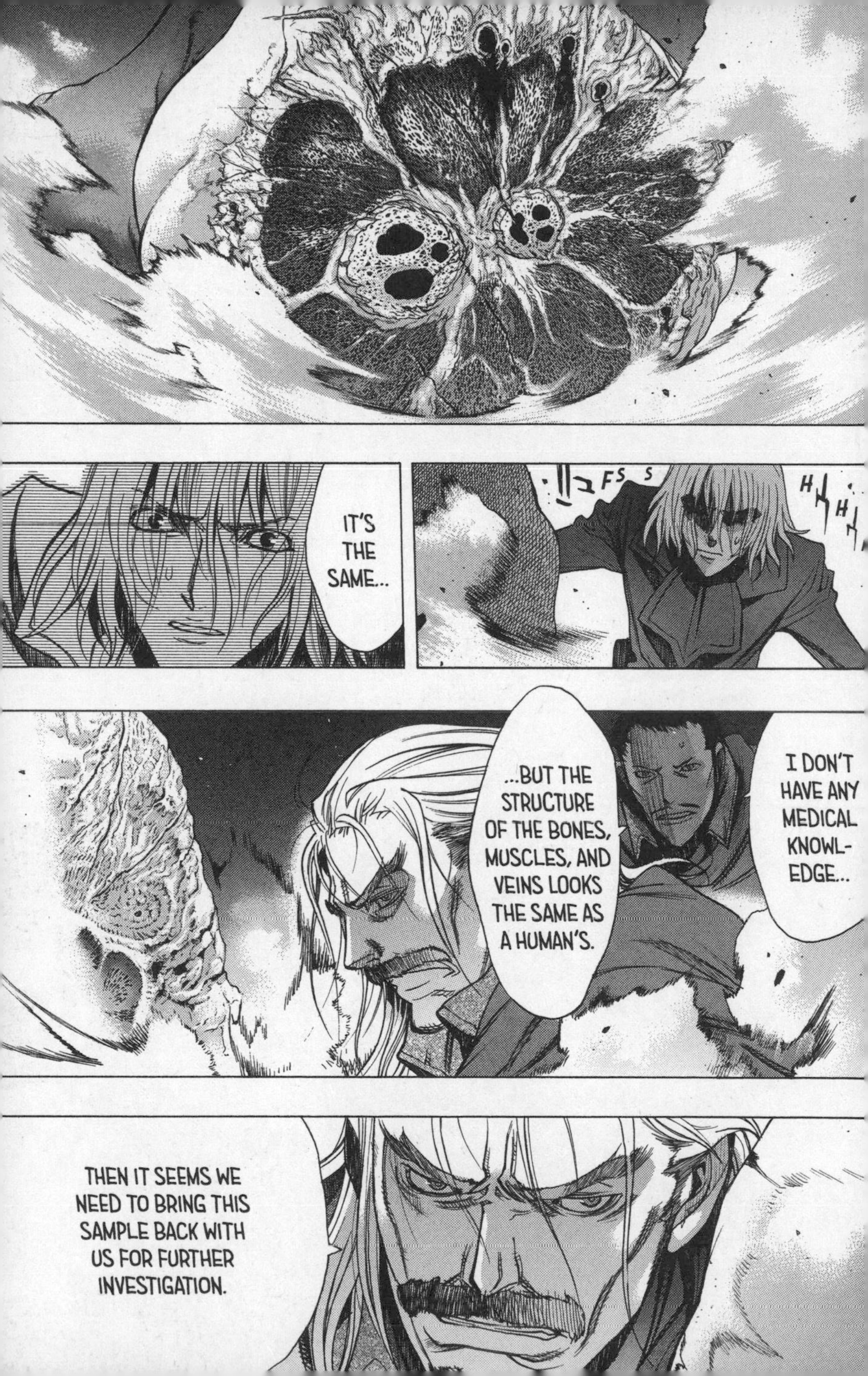
IT'S THE SAME...
I DON'T HAVE ANY MEDICAL KNOWL-EDGE...
...BUT THE STRUCTURE OF THE BONES, MUSCLES, AND VEINS LOOKS THE SAME AS A HUMAN'S.
THEN IT SEEMS WE NEED TO BRING THIS SAMPLE BACK WITH US FOR FURTHER INVESTIGATION.

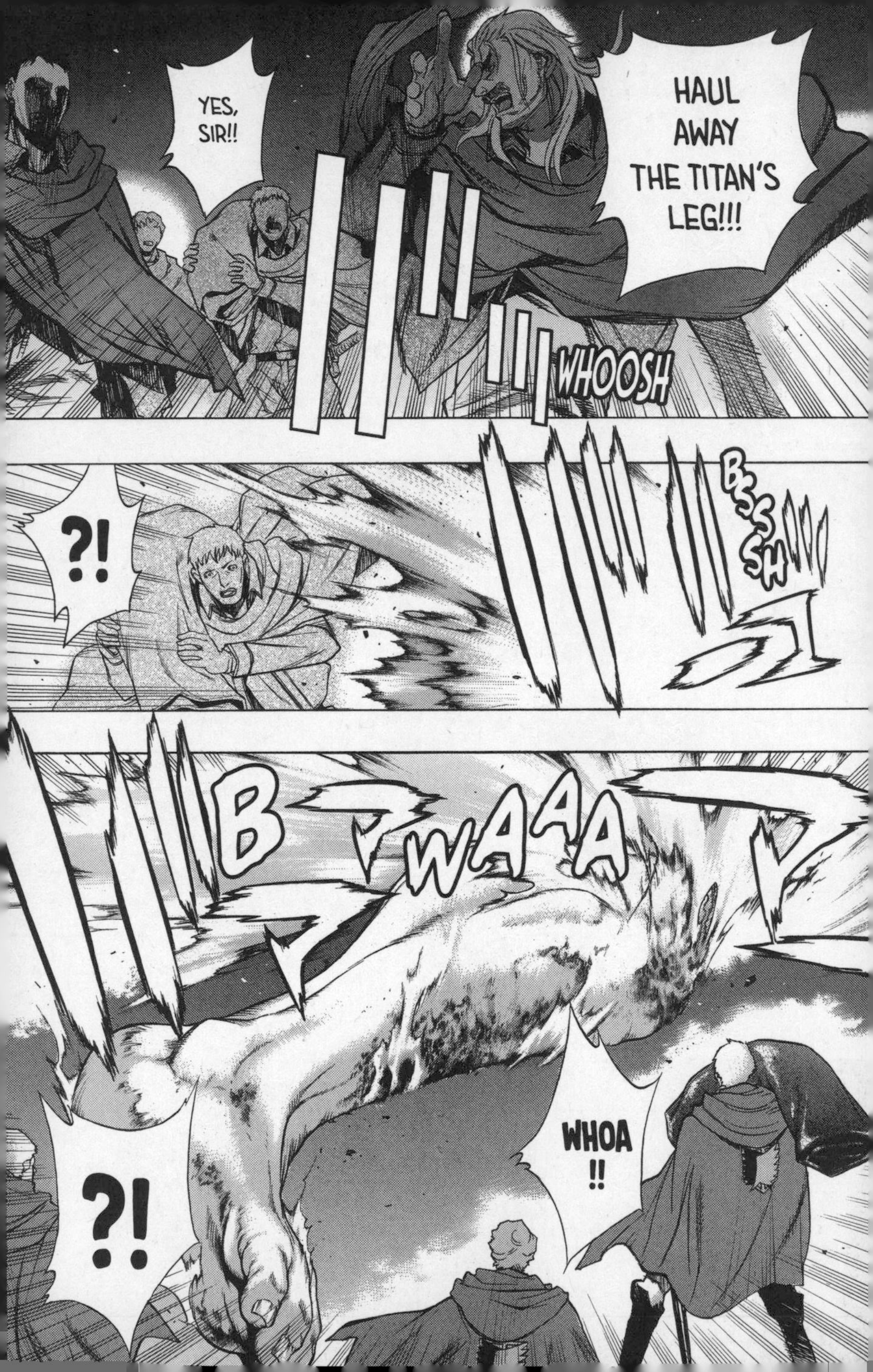
HAUL AWAY THE TITAN'S LEG!!!
YES, SIR!!
WHOOSH
BSSSH
?!
BWAAA
WHOA !!
?!

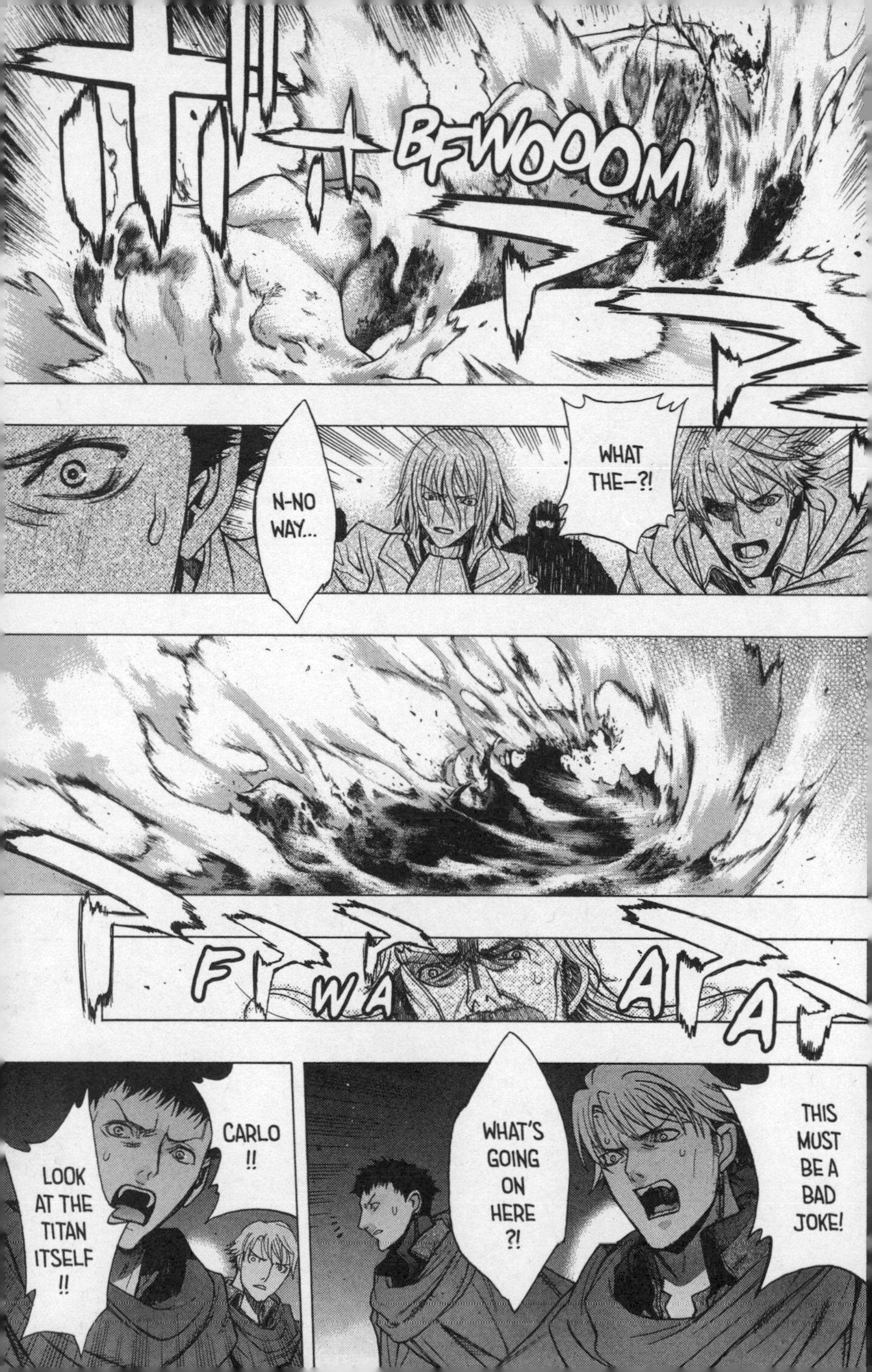
BFWOOOM
WHAT THE–?!
N-NO WAY...
FWAAA
THIS MUST BE A BAD JOKE!
WHAT'S GOING ON HERE ?!
CARLO !!
LOOK AT THE TITAN ITSELF !!

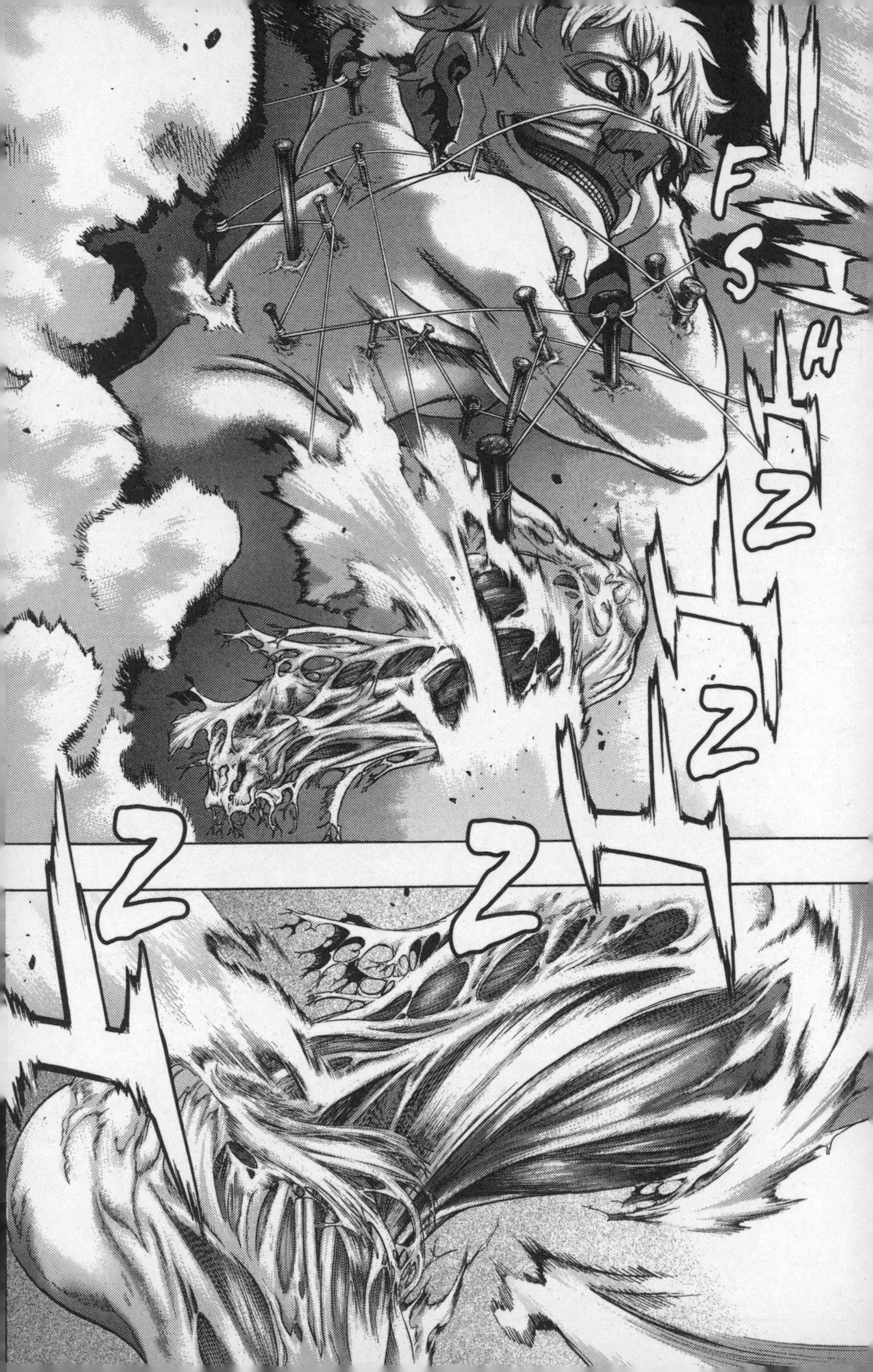
FSH
ZZZZ

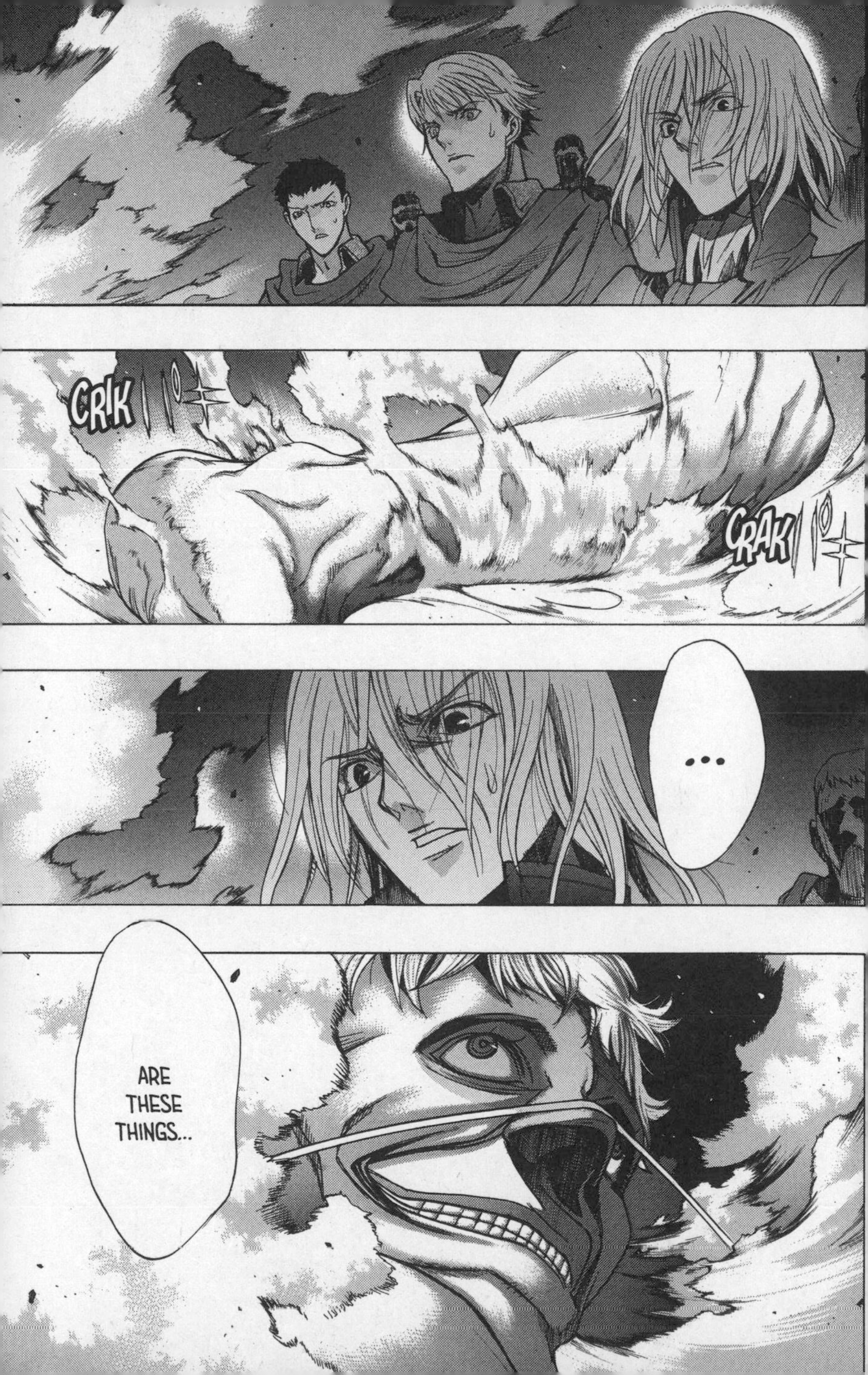
CRIK
CRAK
...
ARE THESE THINGS...

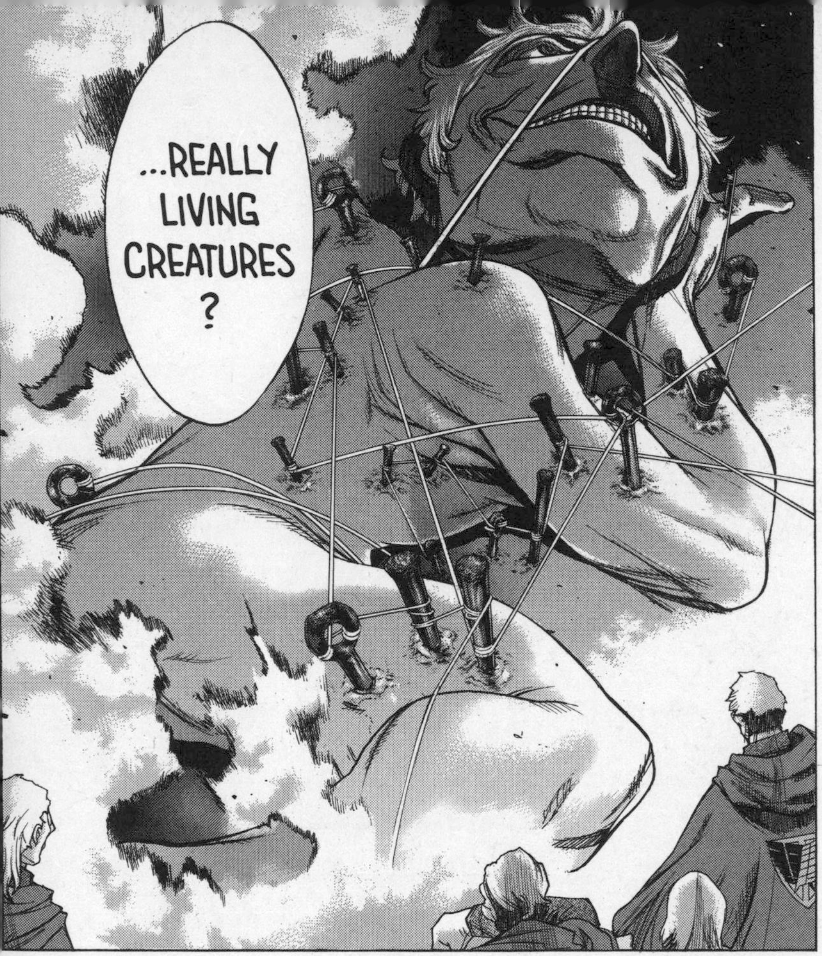
...REALLY LIVING CREATURES ?

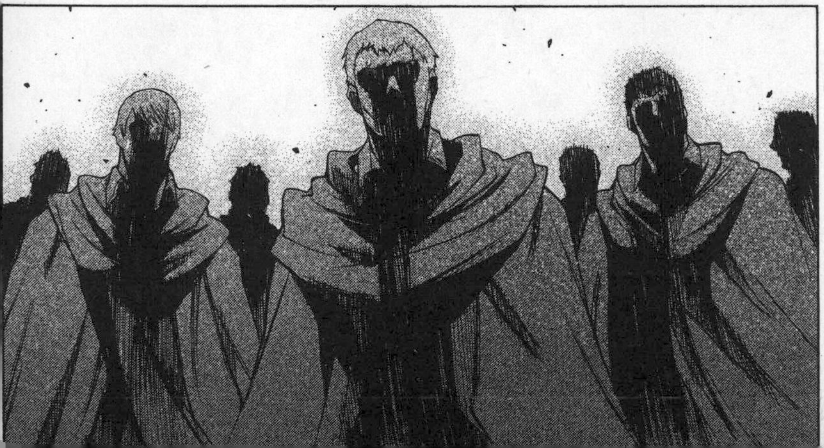

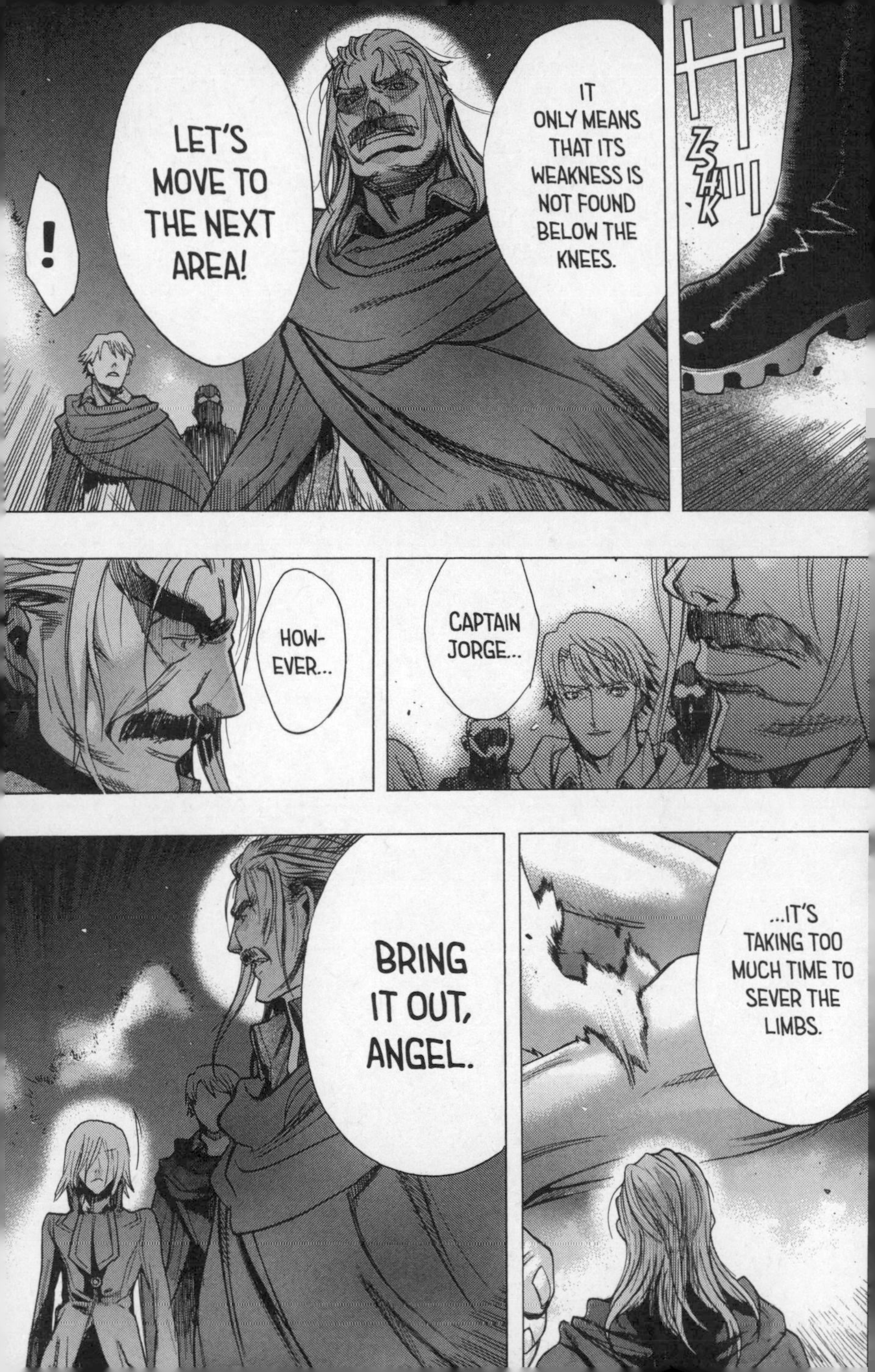
ZSHK
IT ONLY MEANS THAT ITS WEAKNESS IS NOT FOUND BELOW THE KNEES.
LET'S MOVE TO THE NEXT AREA!
!
CAPTAIN JORGE...
HOW-EVER...
...IT'S TAKING TOO MUCH TIME TO SEVER THE LIMBS.
BRING IT OUT, ANGEL.

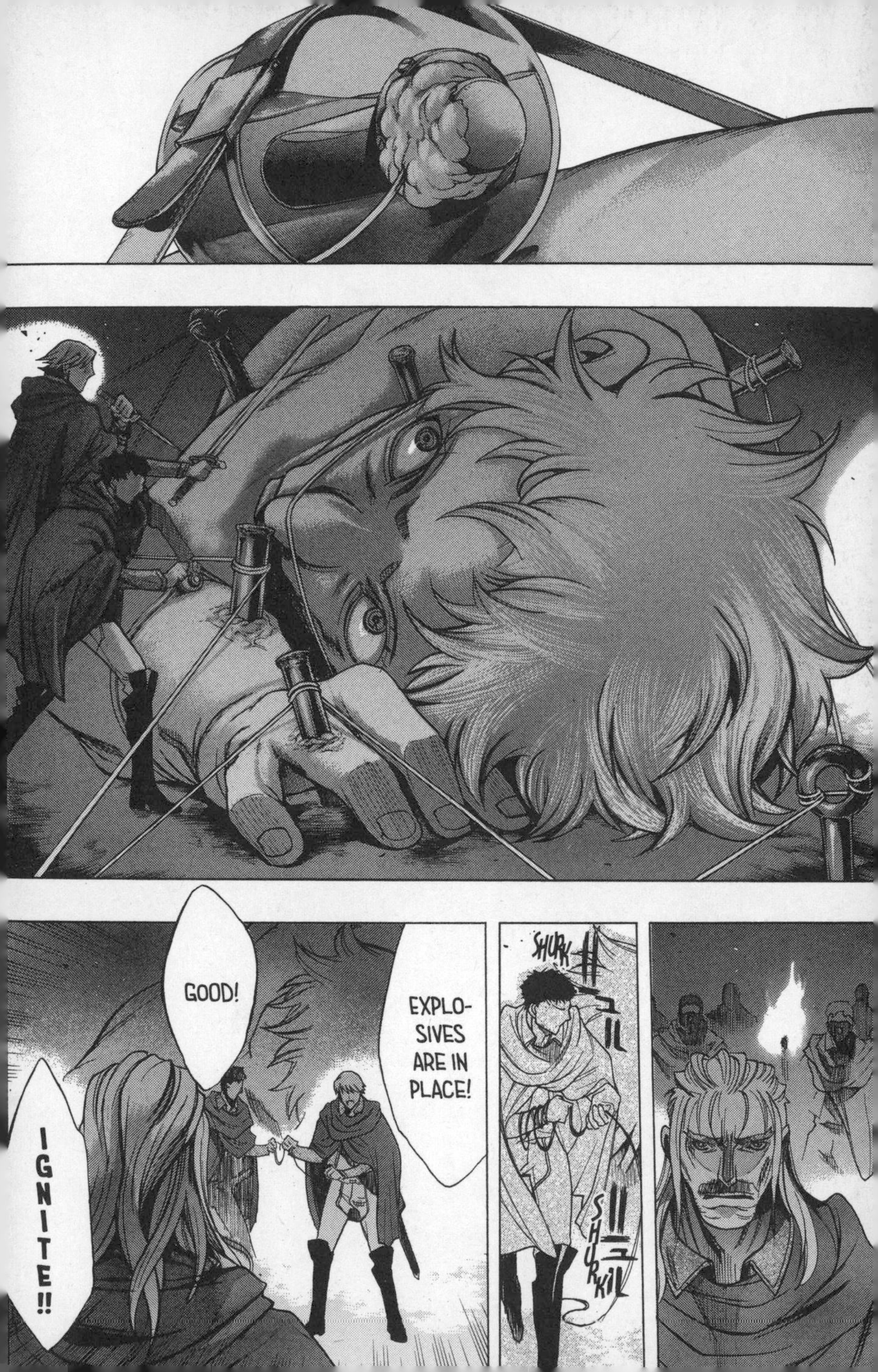
SHURK
SHURK
EXPLO-SIVES ARE IN PLACE!
GOOD!
IGNITE!!

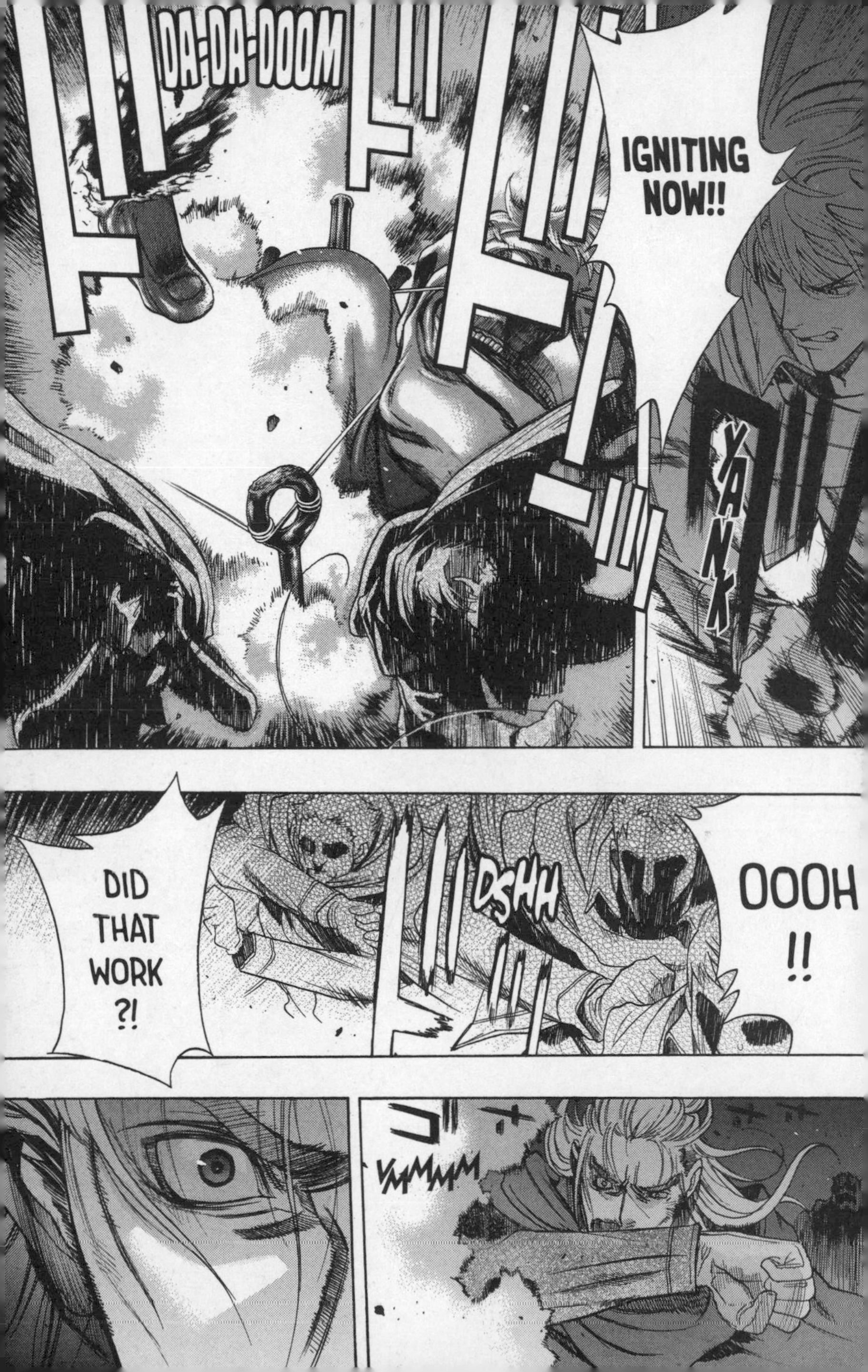
IGNITING NOW!!
YANK
DA-DA-DOOM
OOOH !!
DSHH
DID THAT WORK ?!
VMMMM

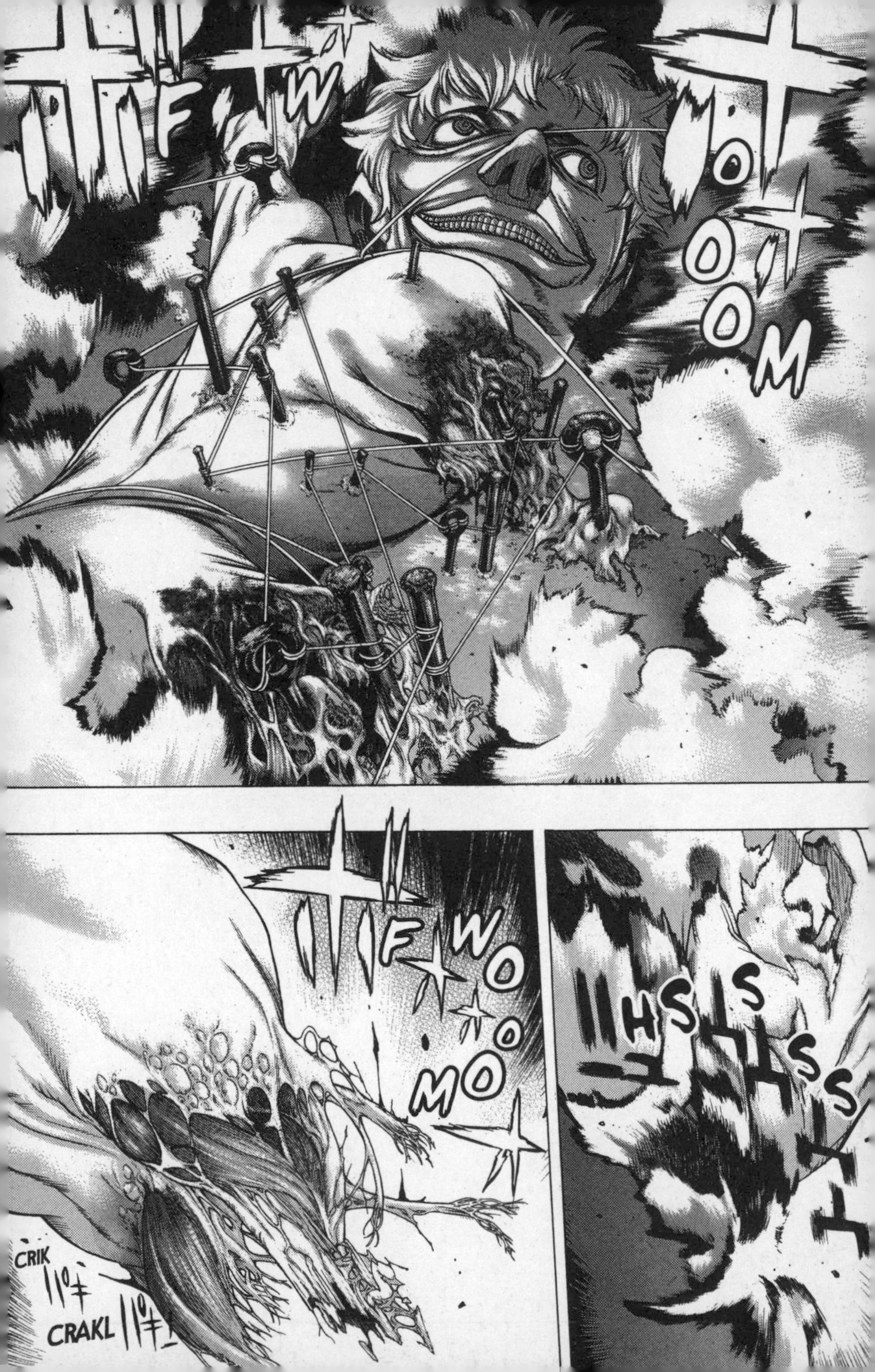
FWOOOM
HSSSS
FWOOOM
CRIK
CRAKL

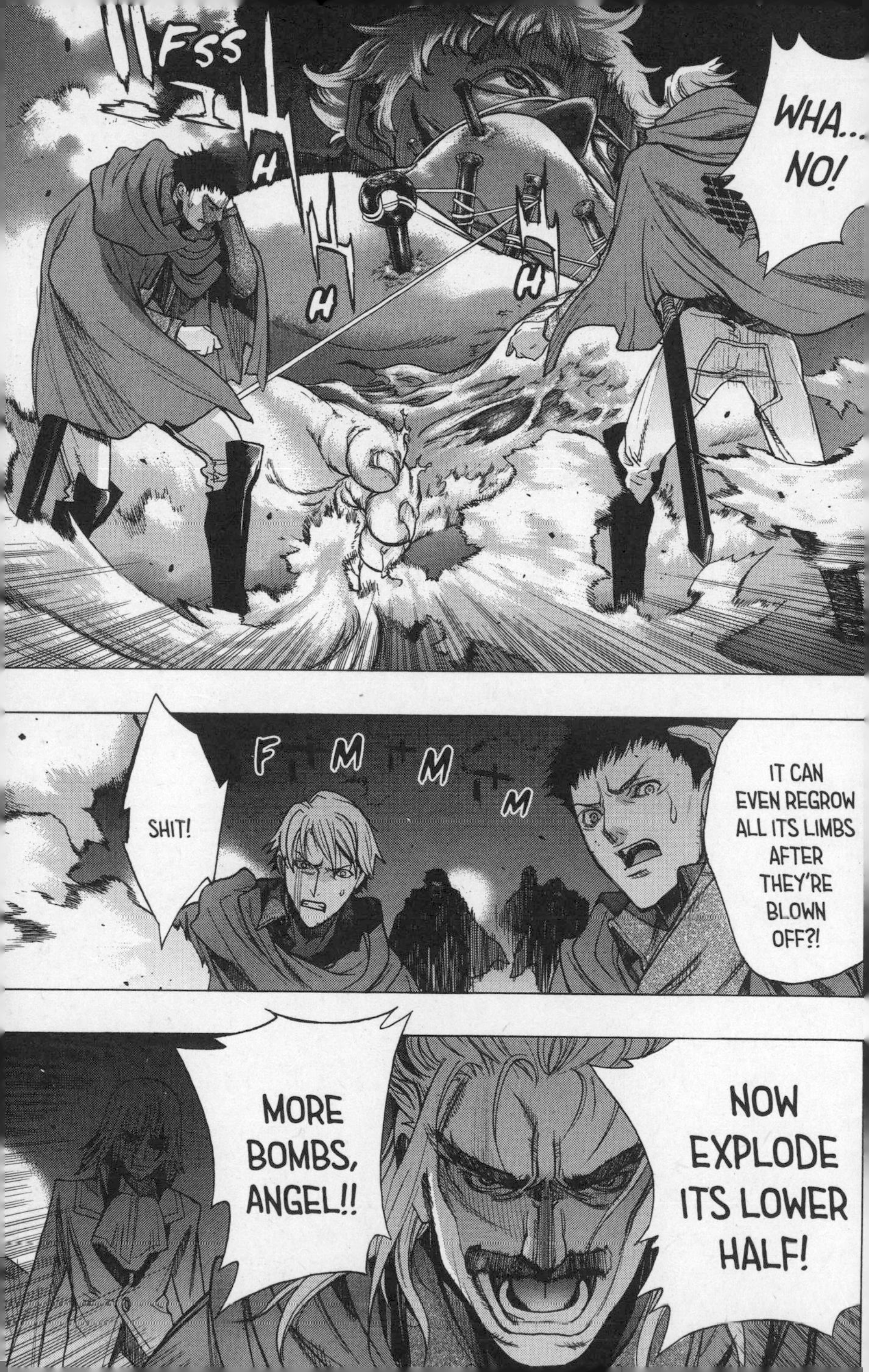
WHA... NO!
FSS
H
H
H
H
IT CAN EVEN REGROW ALL ITS LIMBS AFTER THEY'RE BLOWN OFF?!
FMMM
SHIT!
NOW EXPLODE ITS LOWER HALF!
MORE BOMBS, ANGEL!!

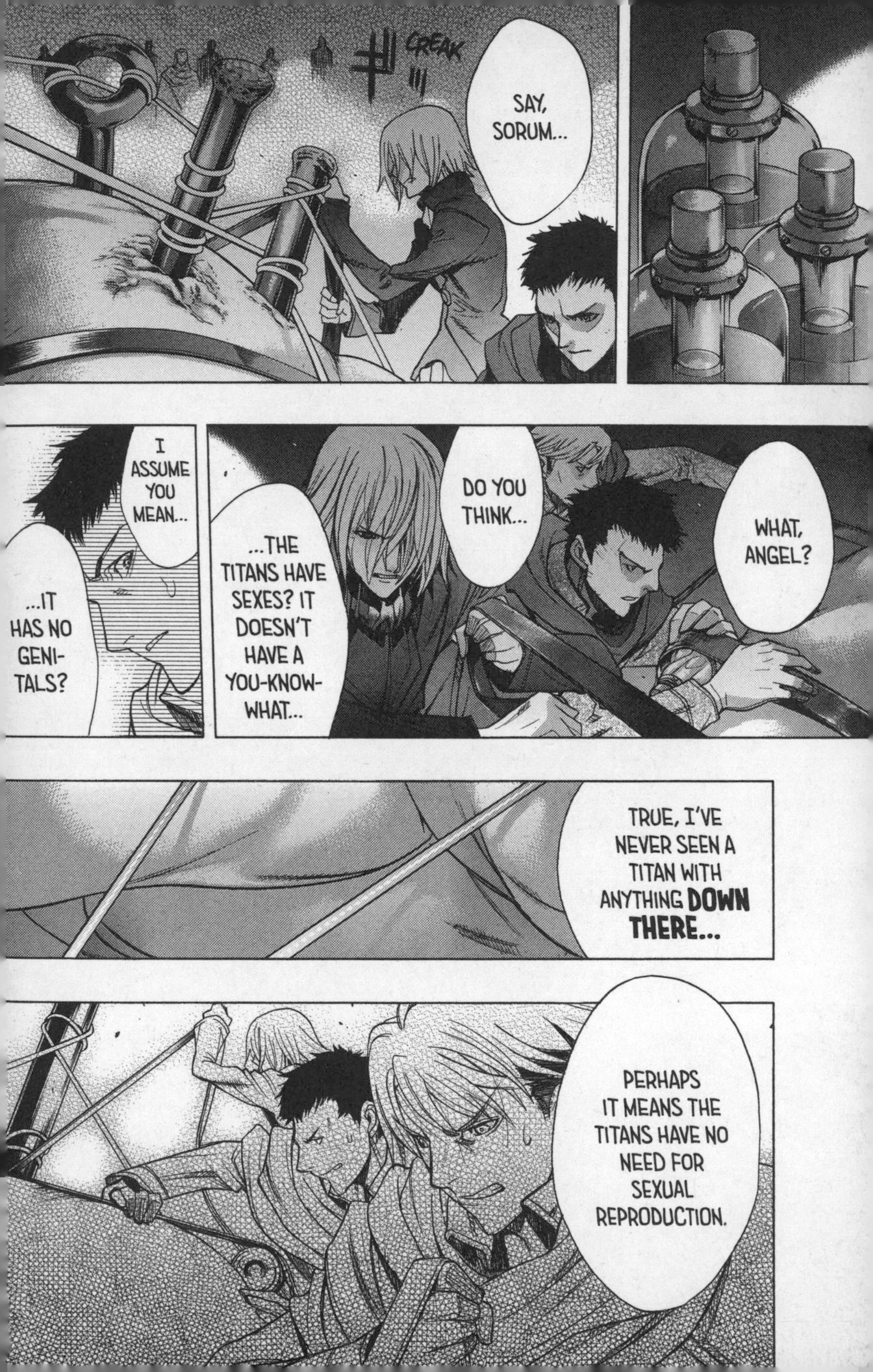
CREAK
SAY, SORUM...
WHAT, ANGEL?
DO YOU THINK...
...THE TITANS HAVE SEXES? IT DOESN'T HAVE A YOU-KNOW-WHAT...
I ASSUME YOU MEAN...
...IT HAS NO GENI-TALS?
TRUE, I'VE NEVER SEEN A TITAN WITH ANYTHING **DOWN THERE...**
PERHAPS IT MEANS THE TITANS HAVE NO NEED FOR SEXUAL REPRODUCTION.

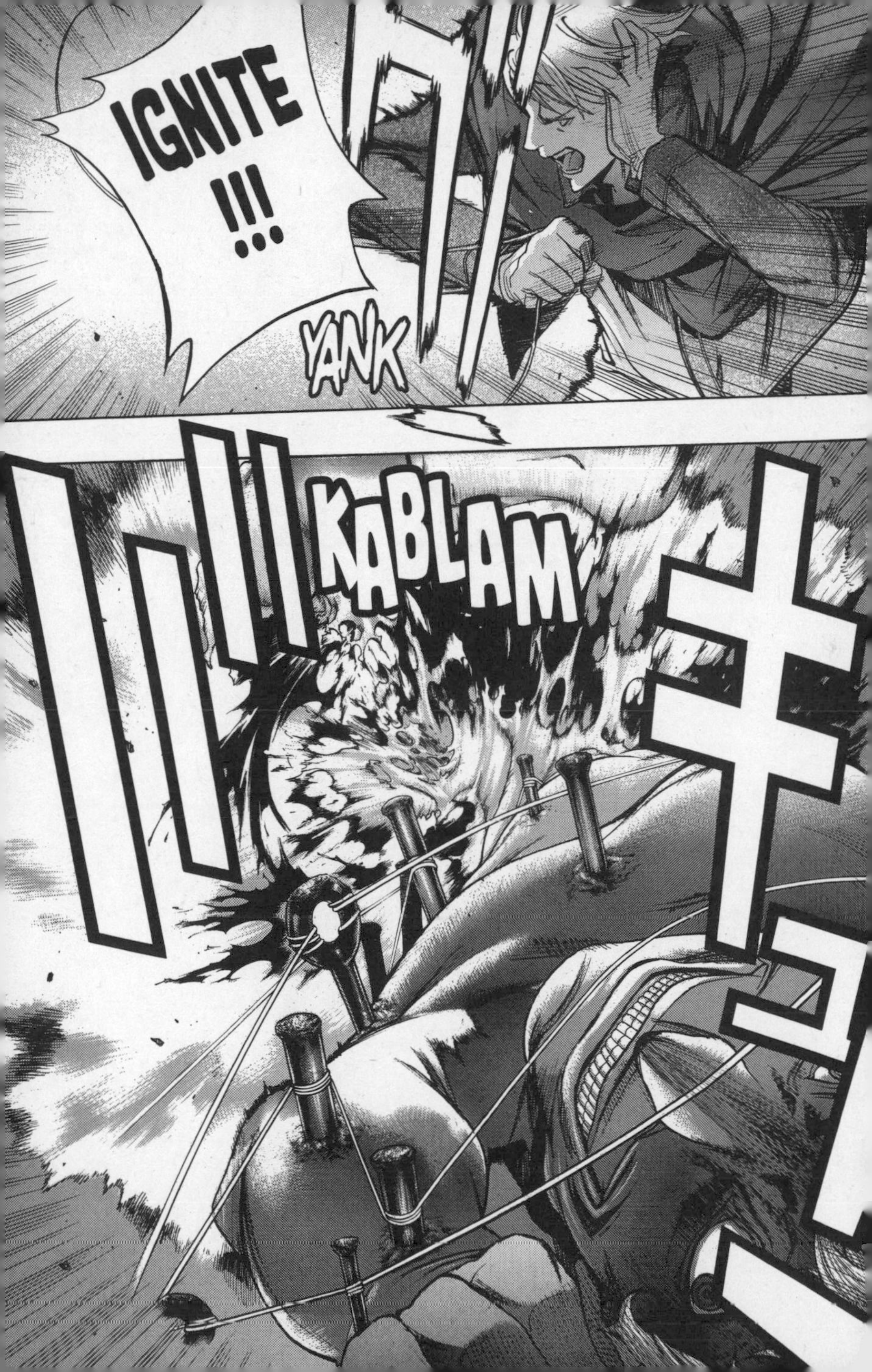
IGNITE !!!...
YANK
KABLAM

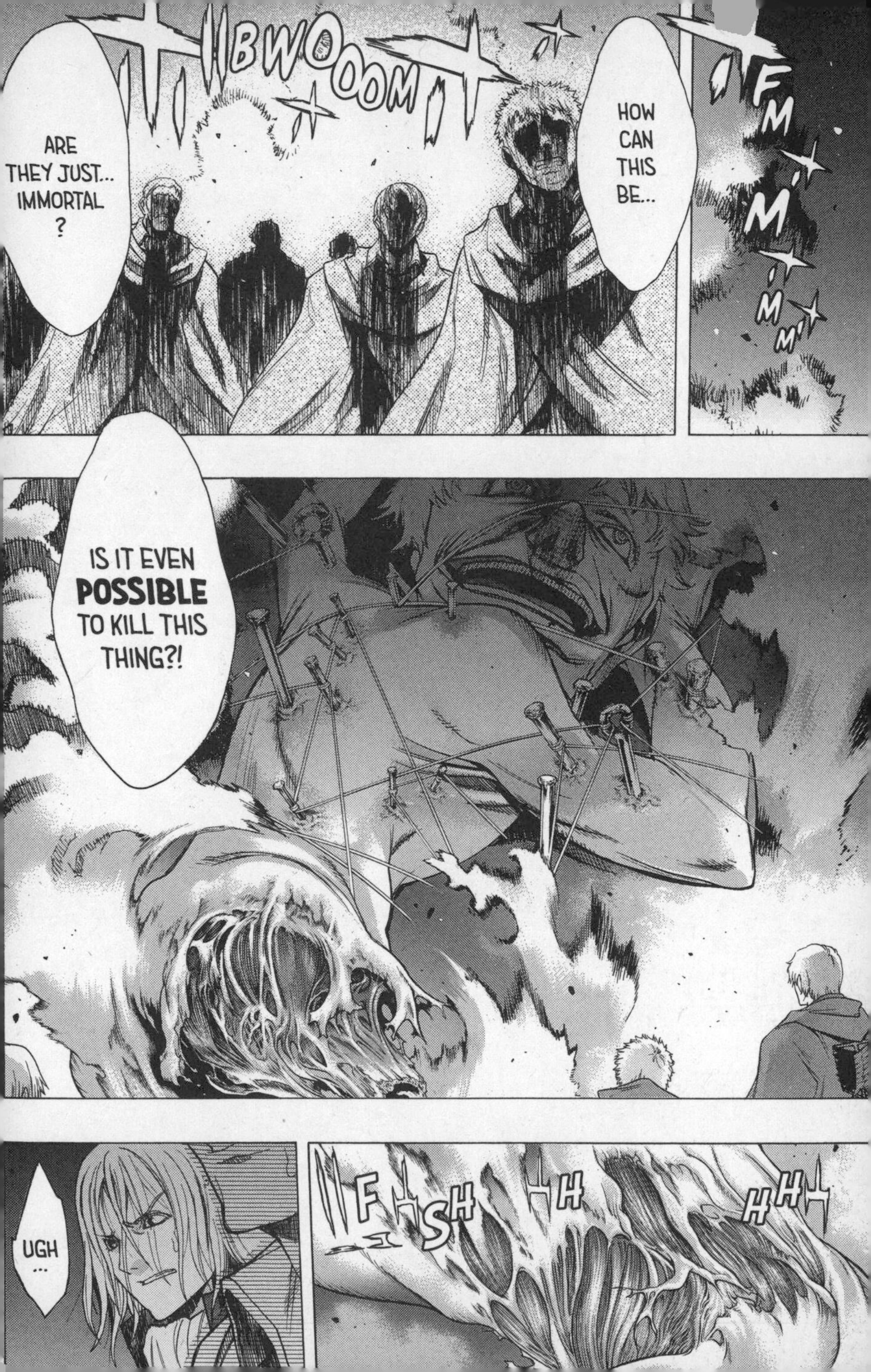
FMMMMM
BWOOOM
HOW CAN THIS BE...
ARE THEY JUST... IMMORTAL?
IS IT EVEN **POSSIBLE** TO KILL THIS THING?!
FSHHHHH
UGH...

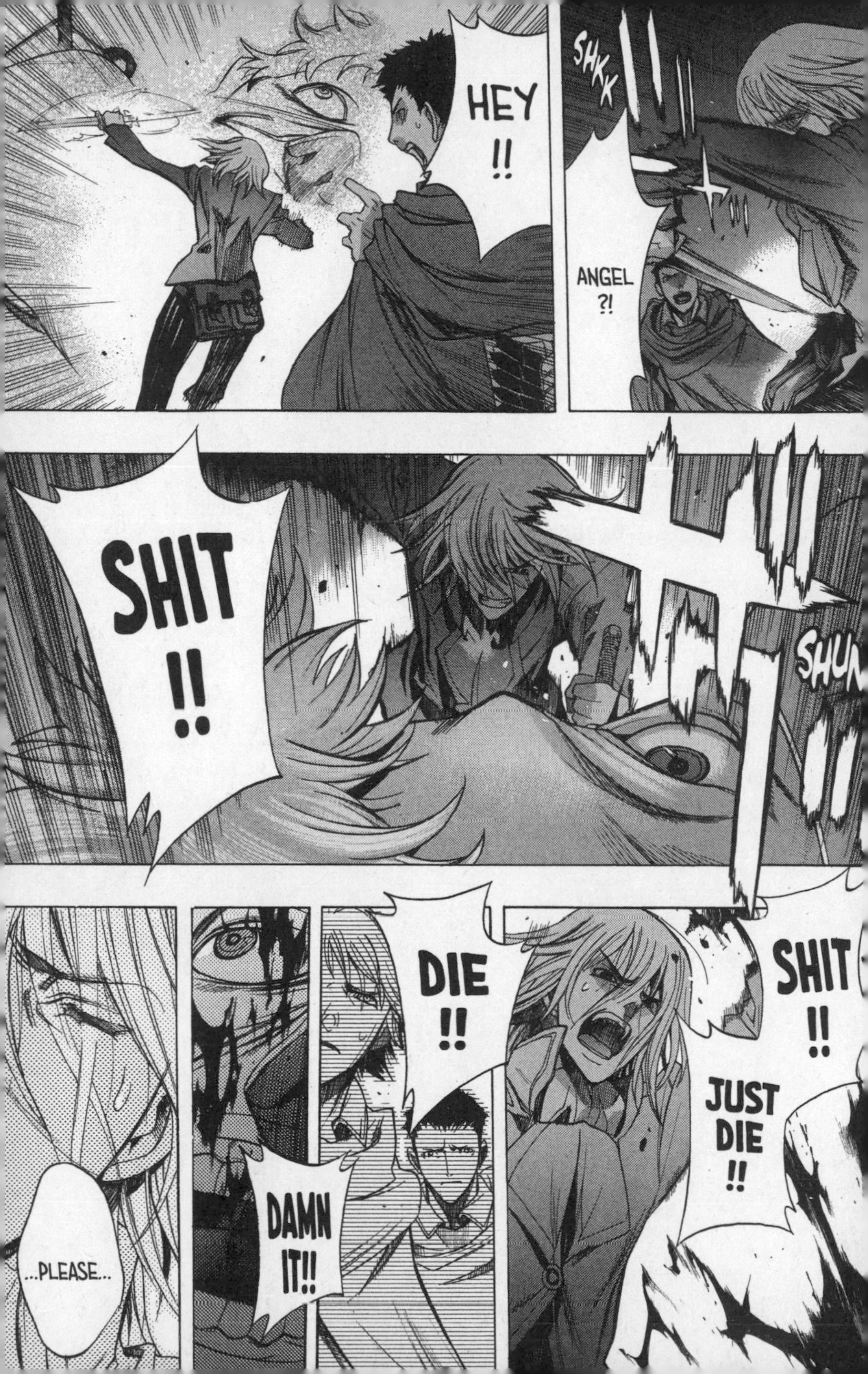
SHKK
ANGEL ?!
HEY !!
SHUN
SHIT !!
SHIT !!
JUST DIE !!
DIE !!
DAMN IT!!
...PLEASE...

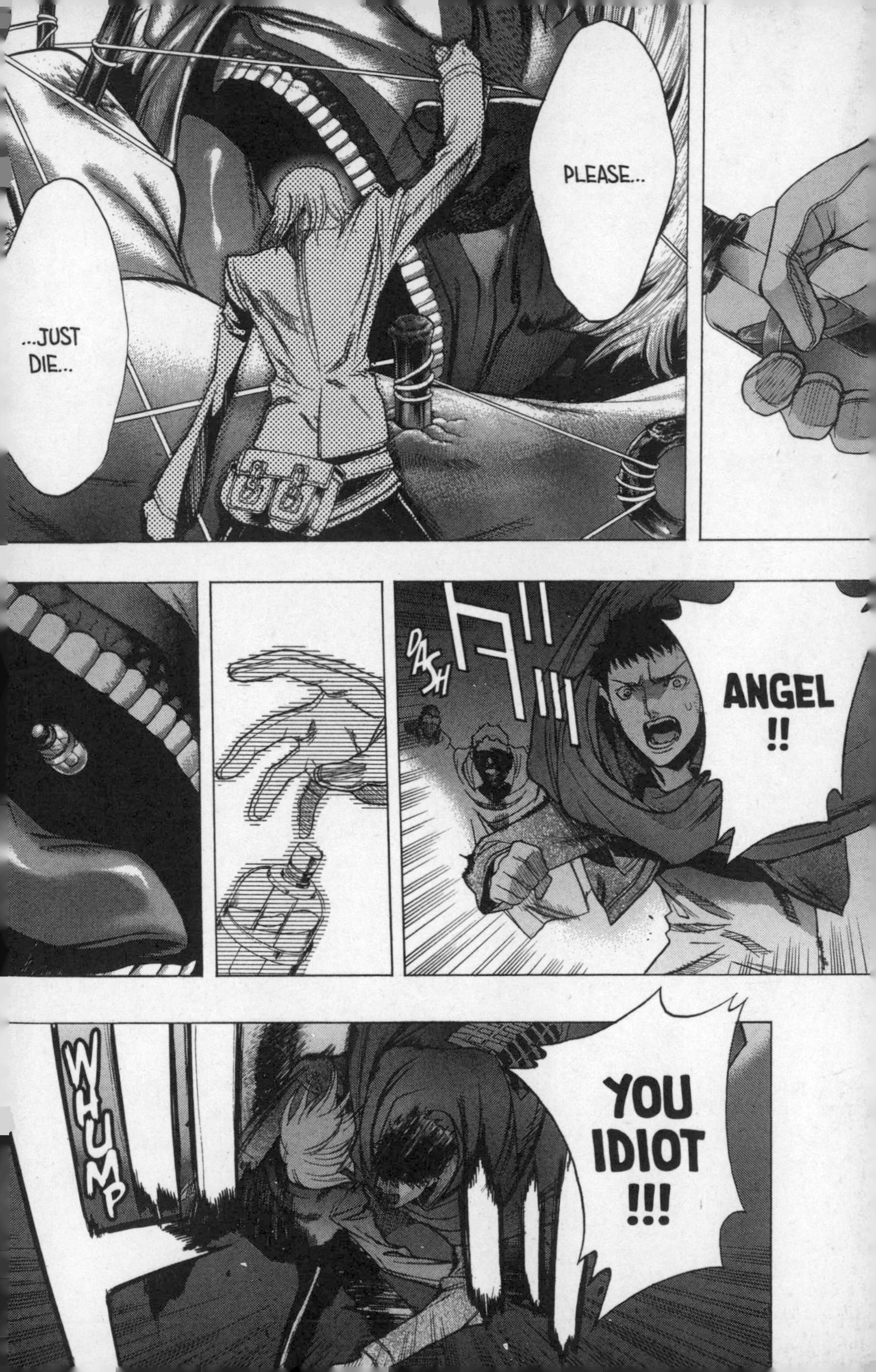
PLEASE...
...JUST DIE...
ANGEL!!
DASH
YOU IDIOT!!!
WHUMP

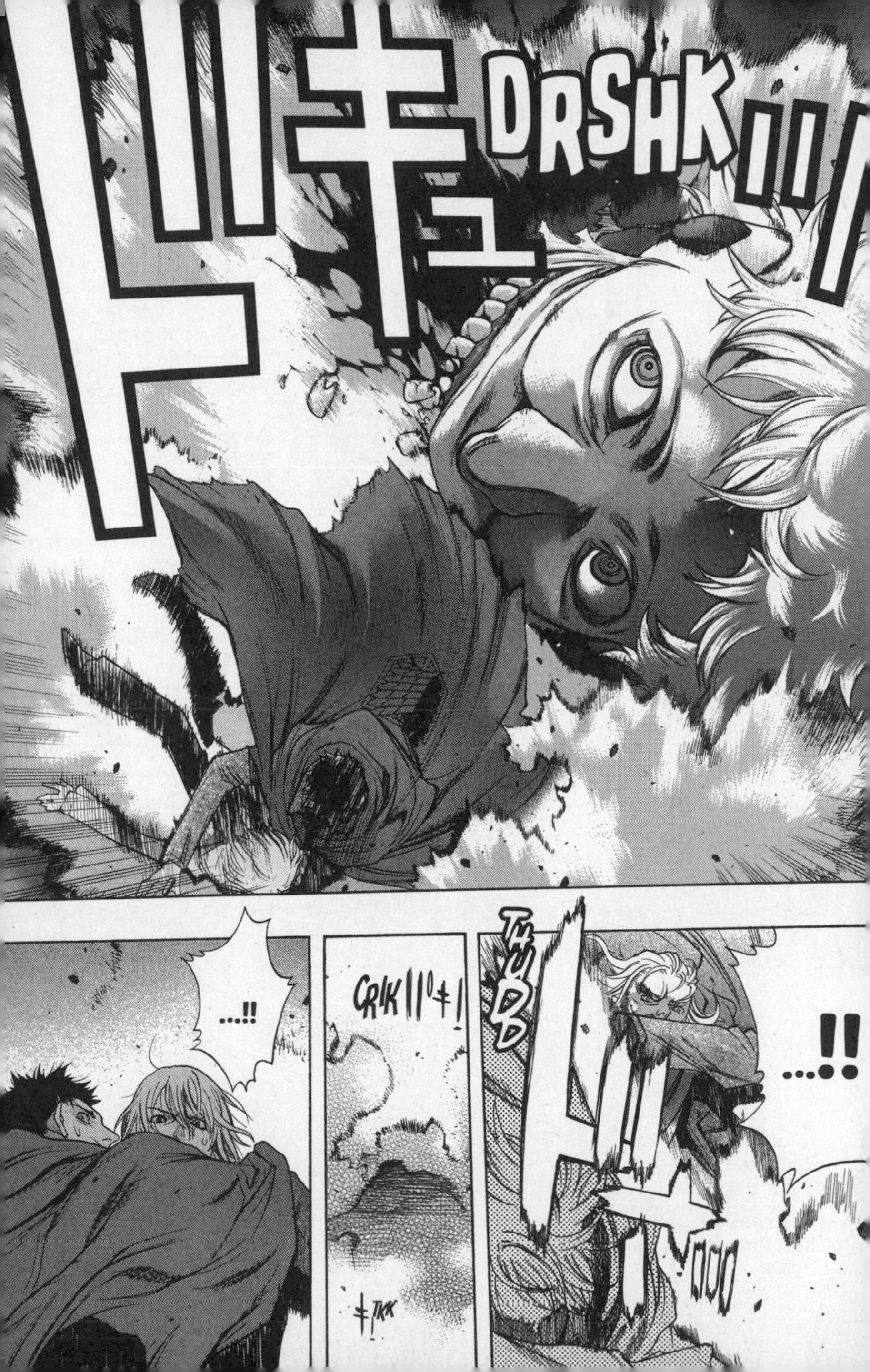
ドキュ
DRSHK!!!
THUD
...!!
CRIK
TKK
...!!

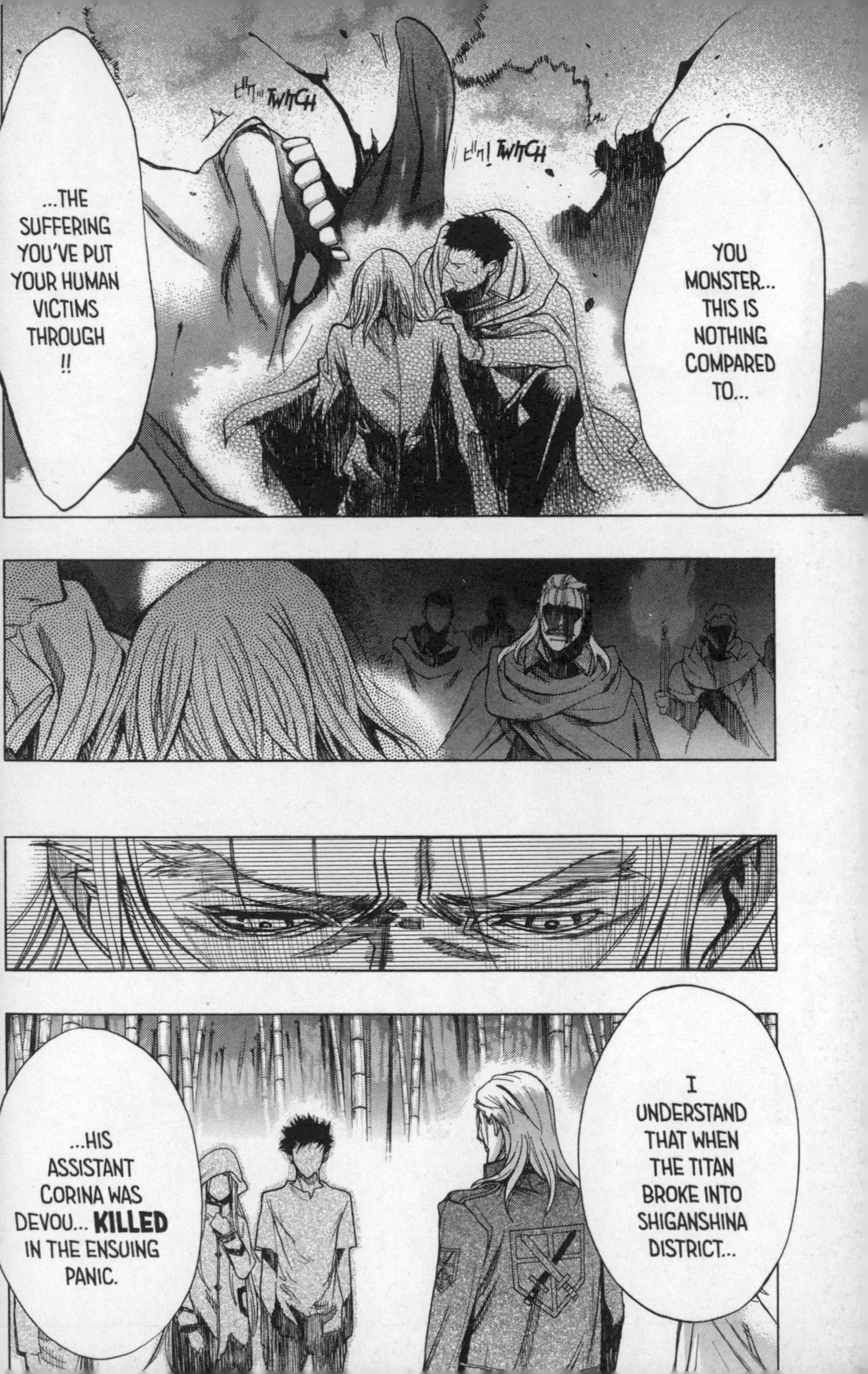
TWITCH
TWITCH
YOU MONSTER... THIS IS NOTHING COMPARED TO...
...THE SUFFERING YOU'VE PUT YOUR HUMAN VICTIMS THROUGH !!
I UNDERSTAND THAT WHEN THE TITAN BROKE INTO SHIGANSHINA DISTRICT...
...HIS ASSISTANT CORINA WAS DEVOU... **KILLED** IN THE ENSUING PANIC.

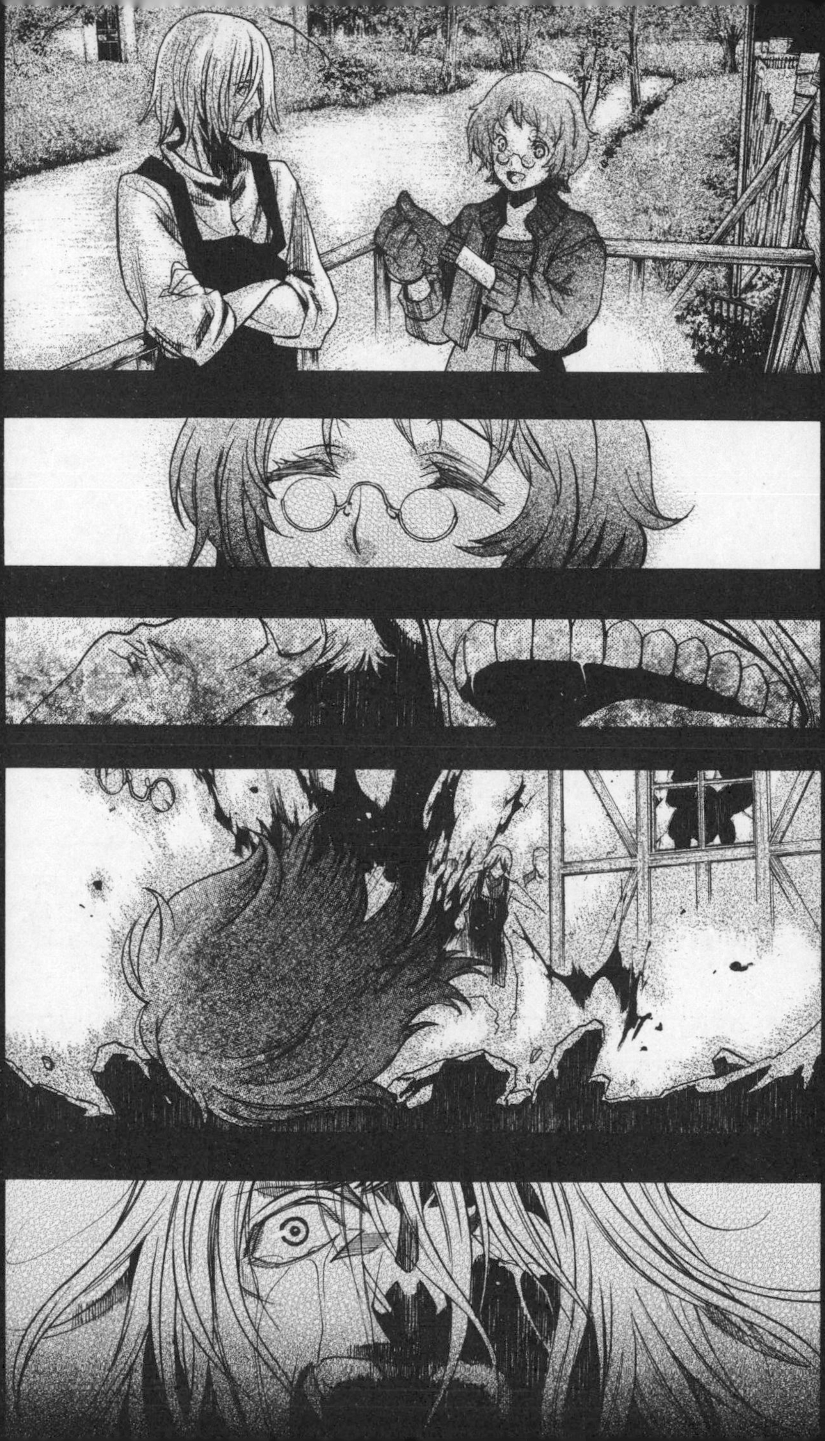

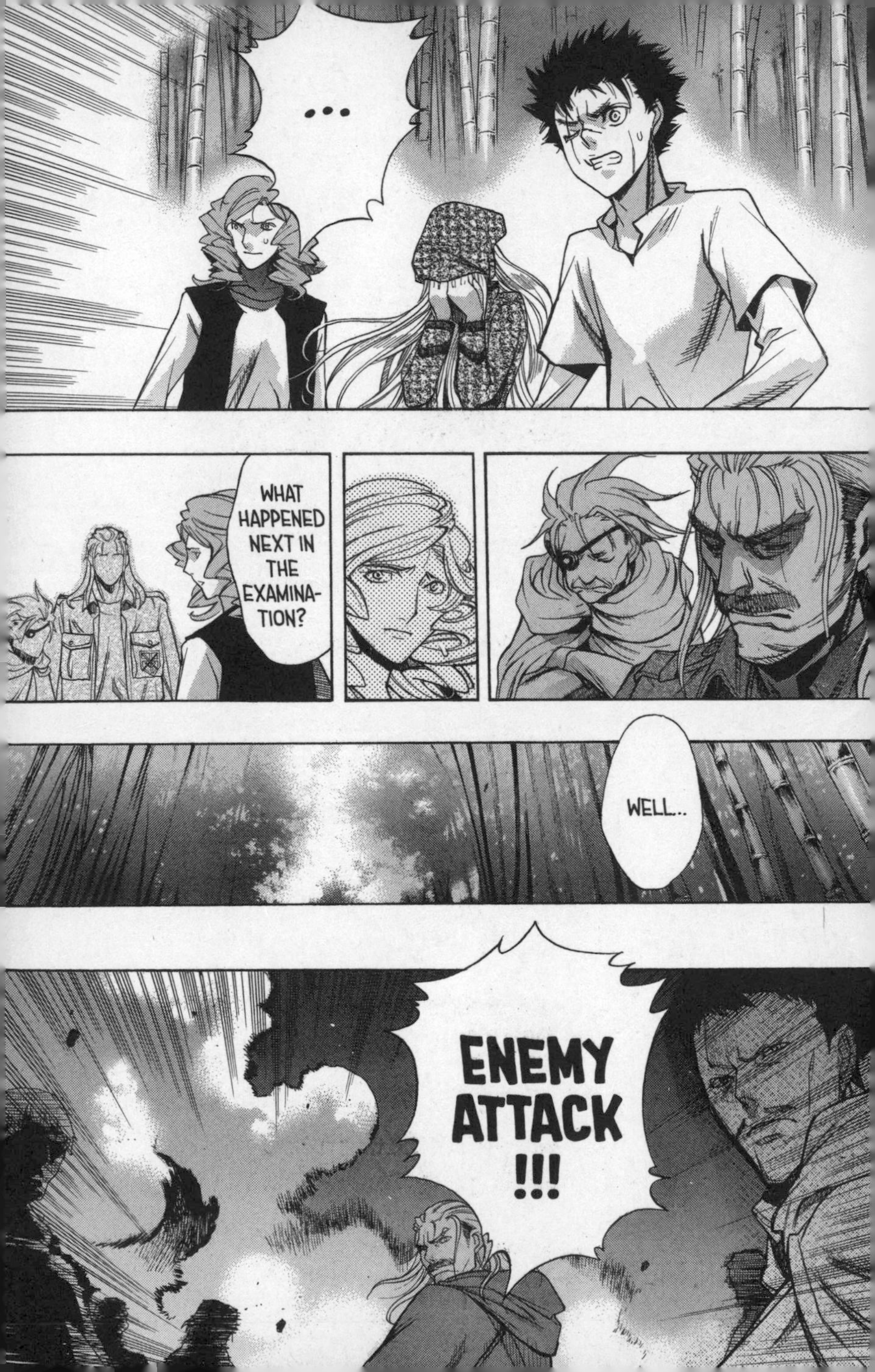
...
WHAT HAPPENED NEXT IN THE EXAMINATION?
WELL...
ENEMY ATTACK !!!

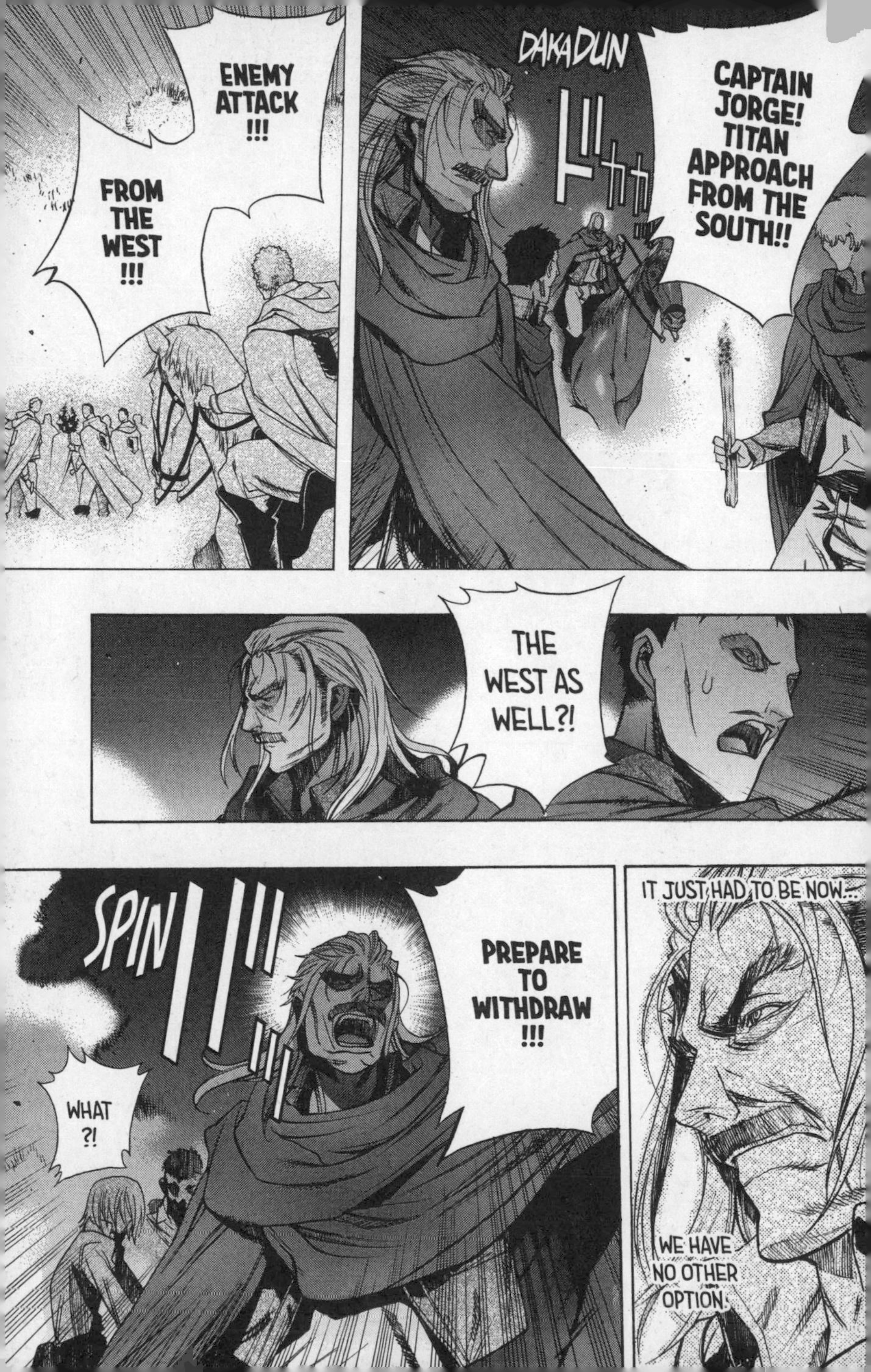
DAKA DUN
CAPTAIN JORGE! TITAN APPROACH FROM THE SOUTH!!
ENEMY ATTACK !!!
FROM THE WEST !!!
THE WEST AS WELL?!
IT JUST HAD TO BE NOW...
WE HAVE NO OTHER OPTION.
SPIN
PREPARE TO WITHDRAW !!!
WHAT ?!

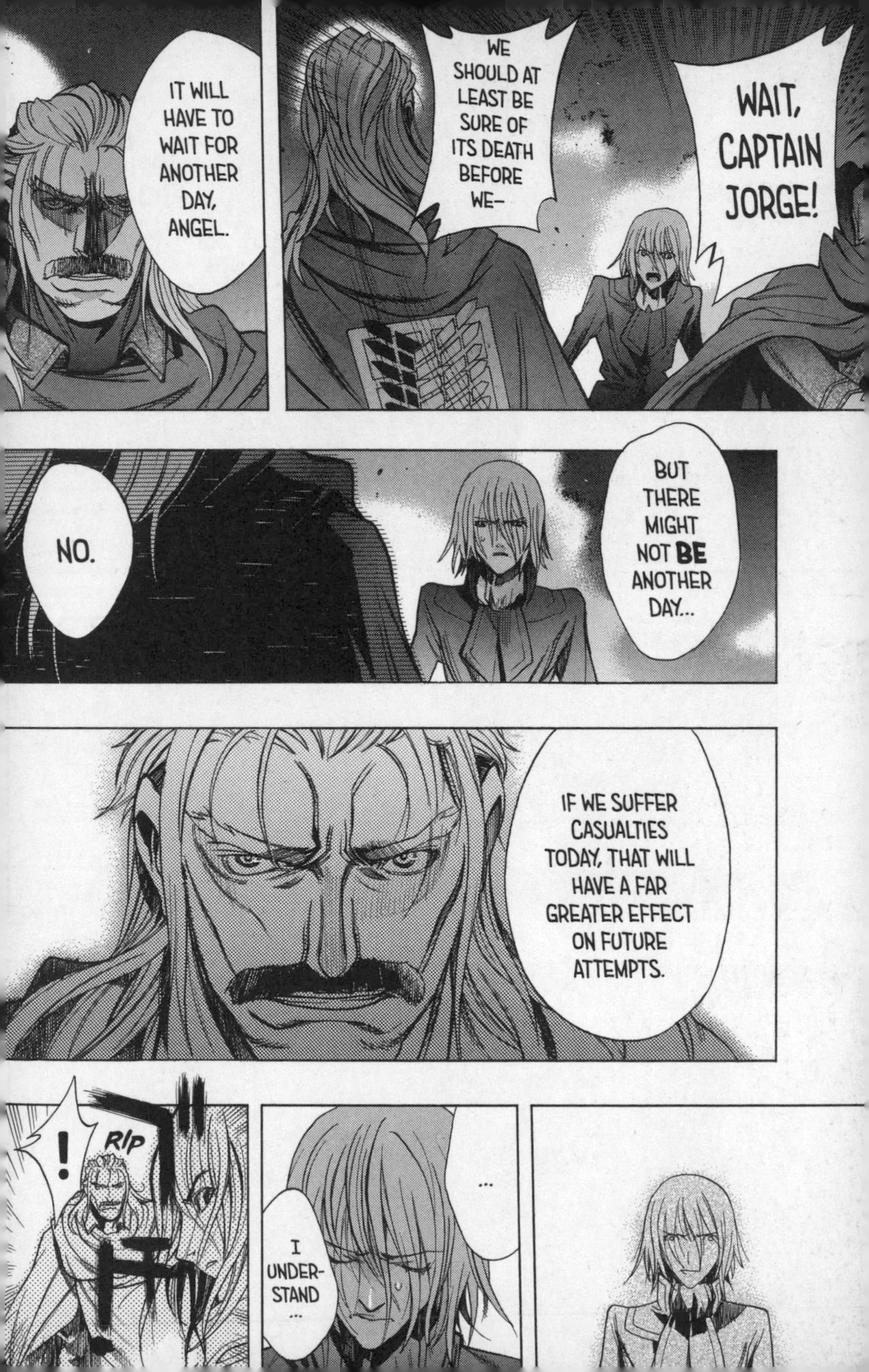
WAIT, CAPTAIN JORGE!
WE SHOULD AT LEAST BE SURE OF ITS DEATH BEFORE WE—
IT WILL HAVE TO WAIT FOR ANOTHER DAY, ANGEL.
BUT THERE MIGHT NOT **BE** ANOTHER DAY...
NO.
IF WE SUFFER CASUALTIES TODAY, THAT WILL HAVE A FAR GREATER EFFECT ON FUTURE ATTEMPTS.
...
I UNDER-STAND...
!
RIP

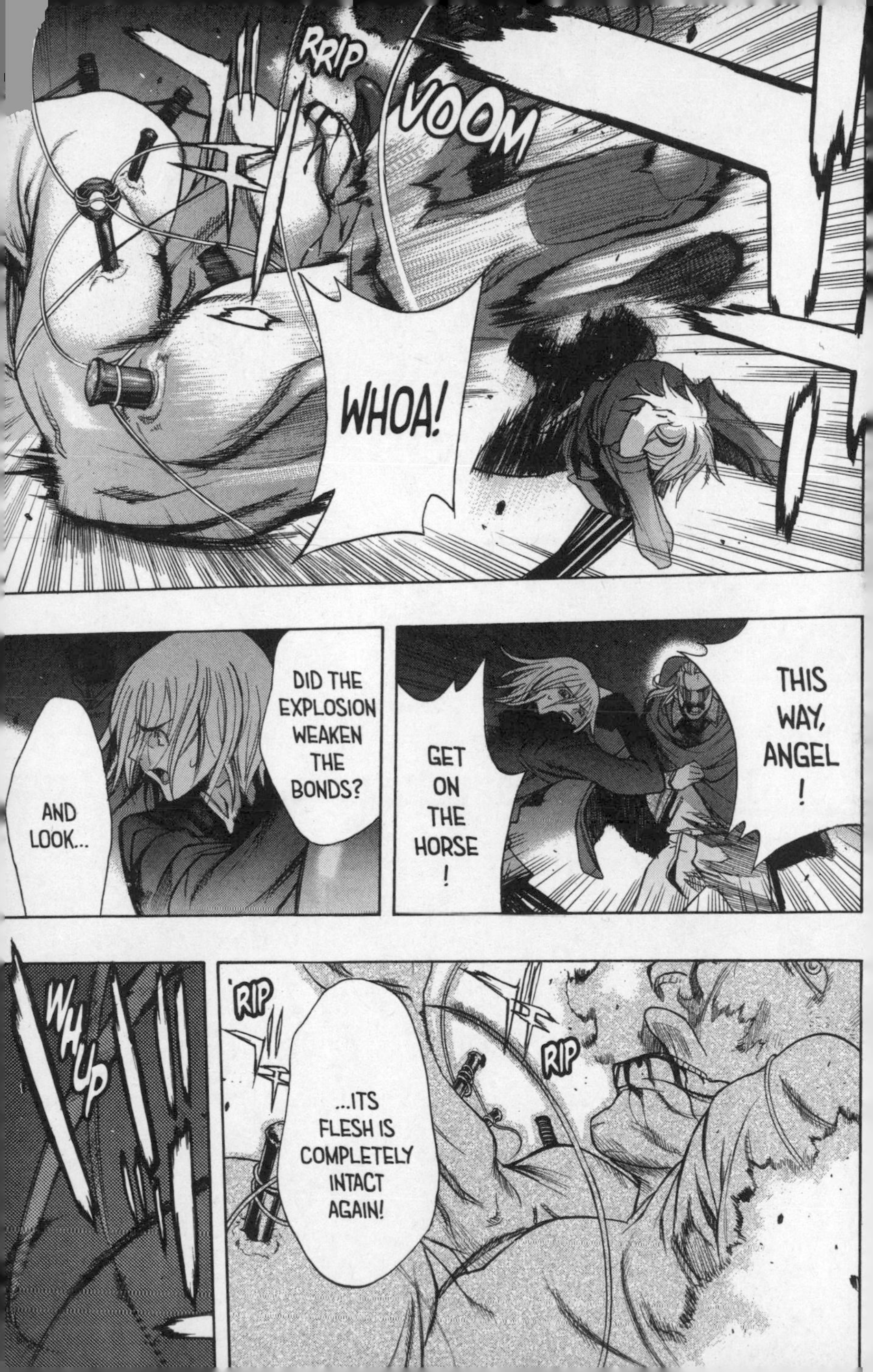
RRIP
VOOM
WHOA!
THIS WAY, ANGEL!
GET ON THE HORSE!
DID THE EXPLOSION WEAKEN THE BONDS?
AND LOOK...
RIP
RIP
...ITS FLESH IS COMPLETELY INTACT AGAIN!
WHUP

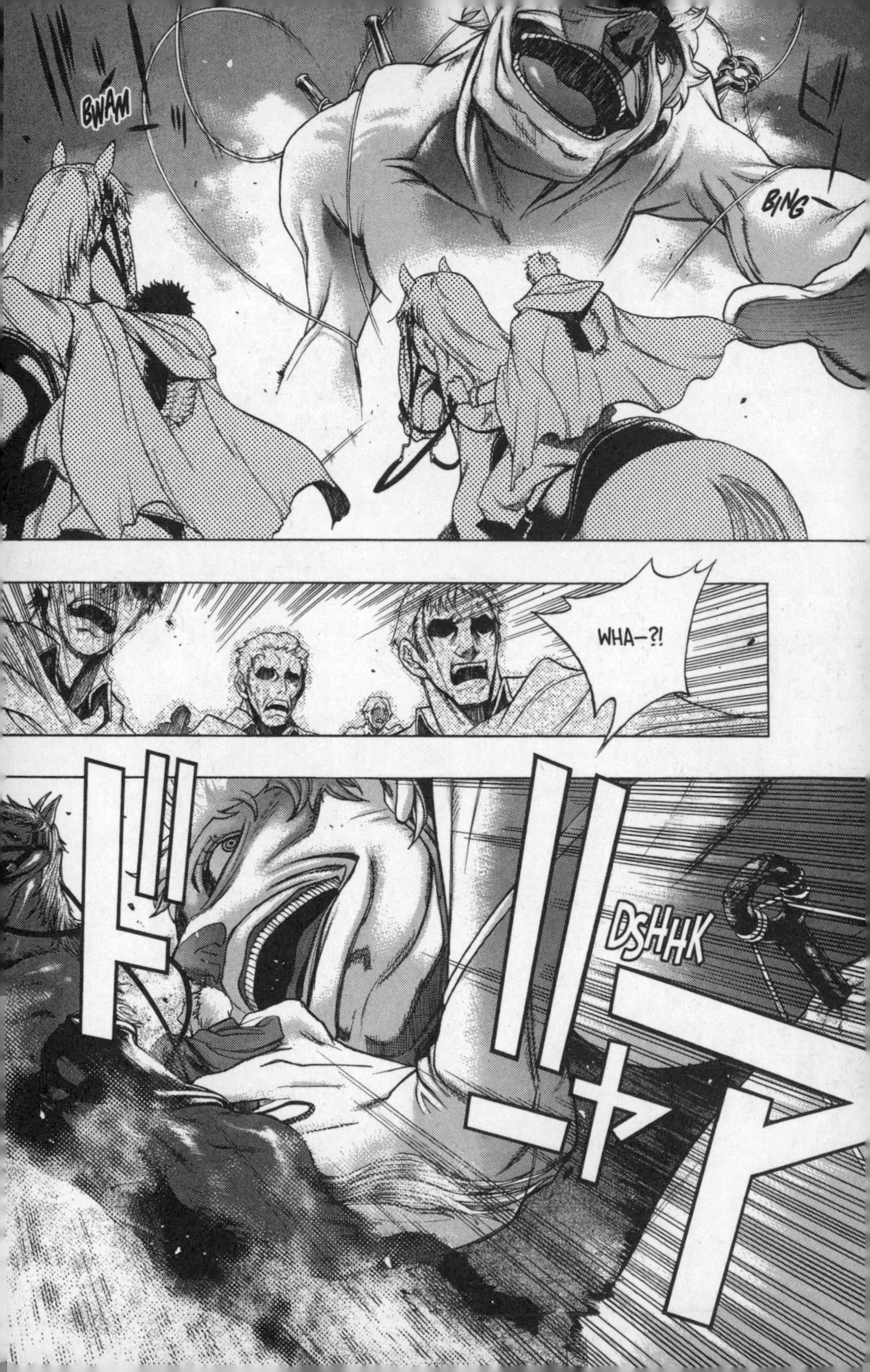
BWAM
BING
WHA-?!
DSHHK

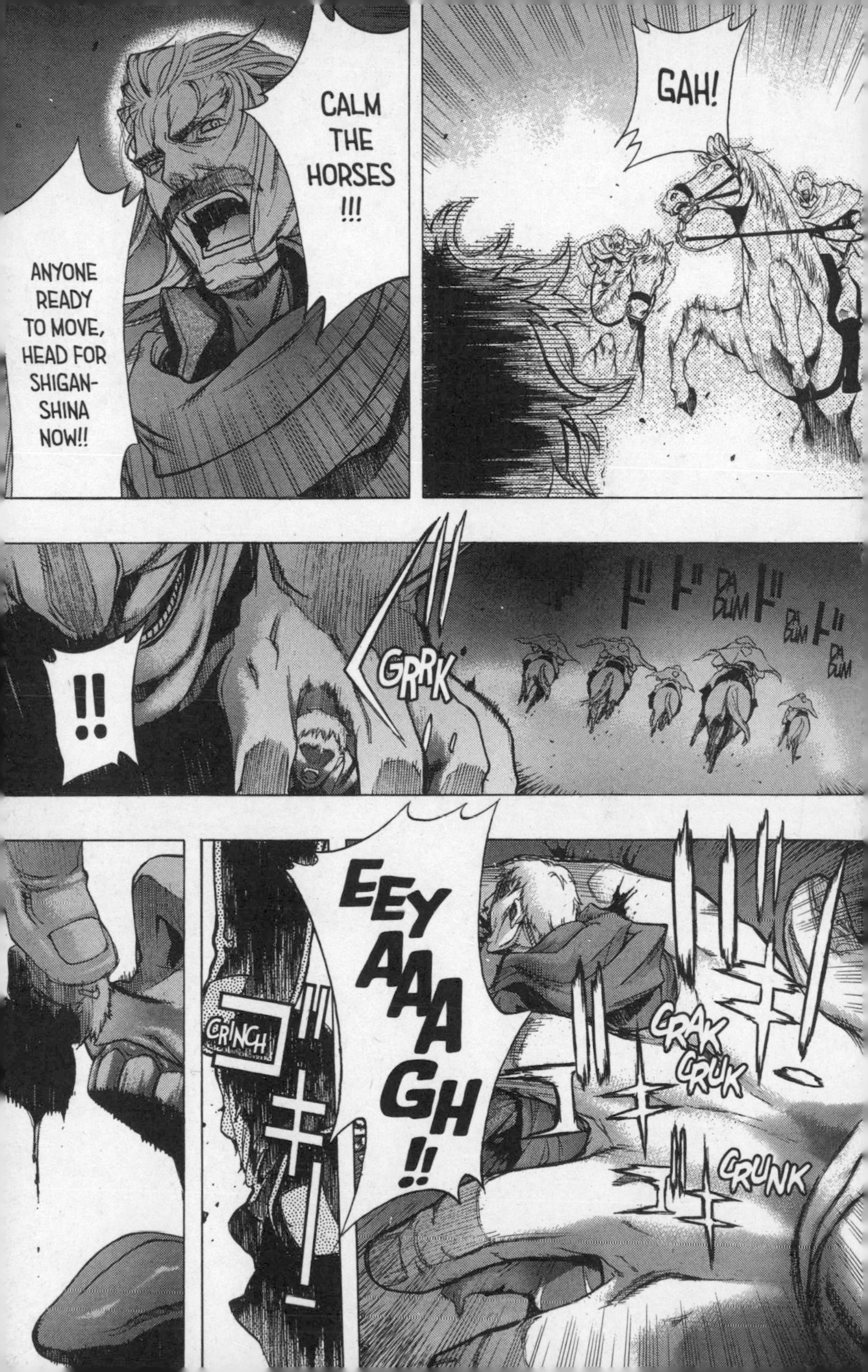
GAH!
CALM THE HORSES!!!
ANYONE READY TO MOVE, HEAD FOR SHIGAN-SHINA NOW!!
DA DUM
DA DUM
DA DUM
GRRK
!!
CRAK CRUK
CRUNK
EEYAAAAGH!!
CRINCH

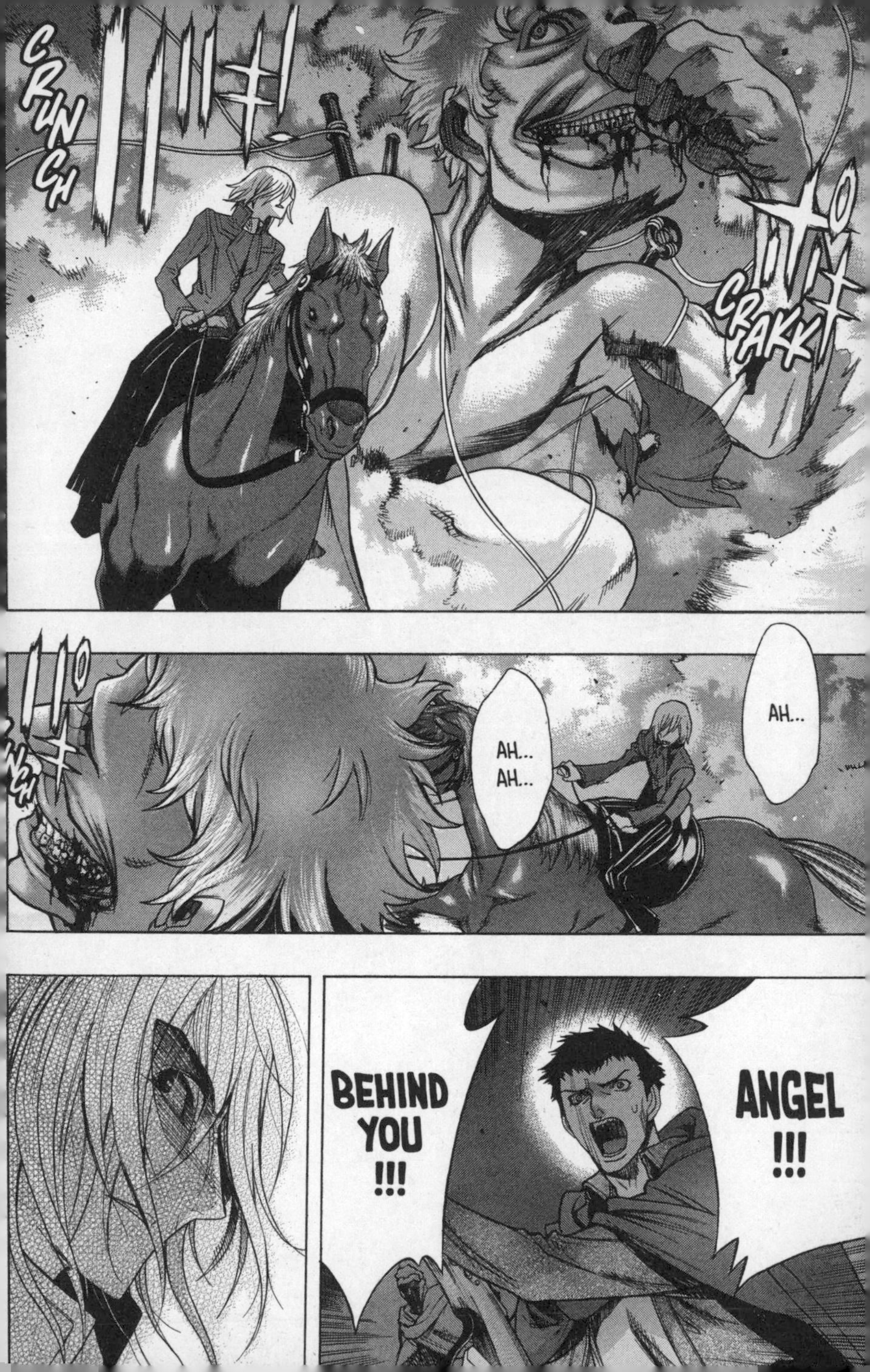
CRAKK
CRUNCH
AH...
AH... AH...
ANGEL !!!
BEHIND YOU !!!

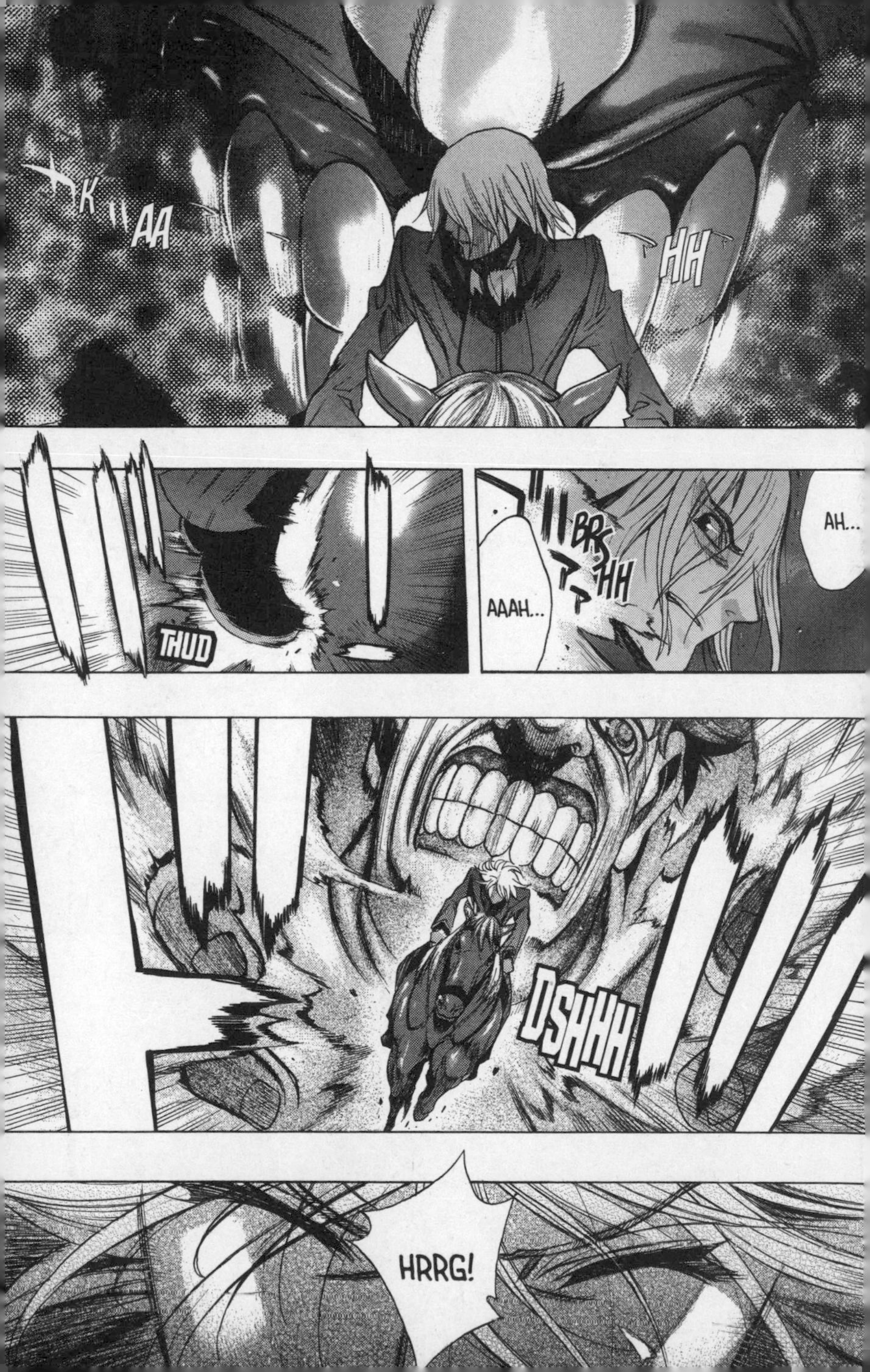
KAA
HH
AH...
BRSHH
AAAH...
THUD
DSHHH
HRRG!

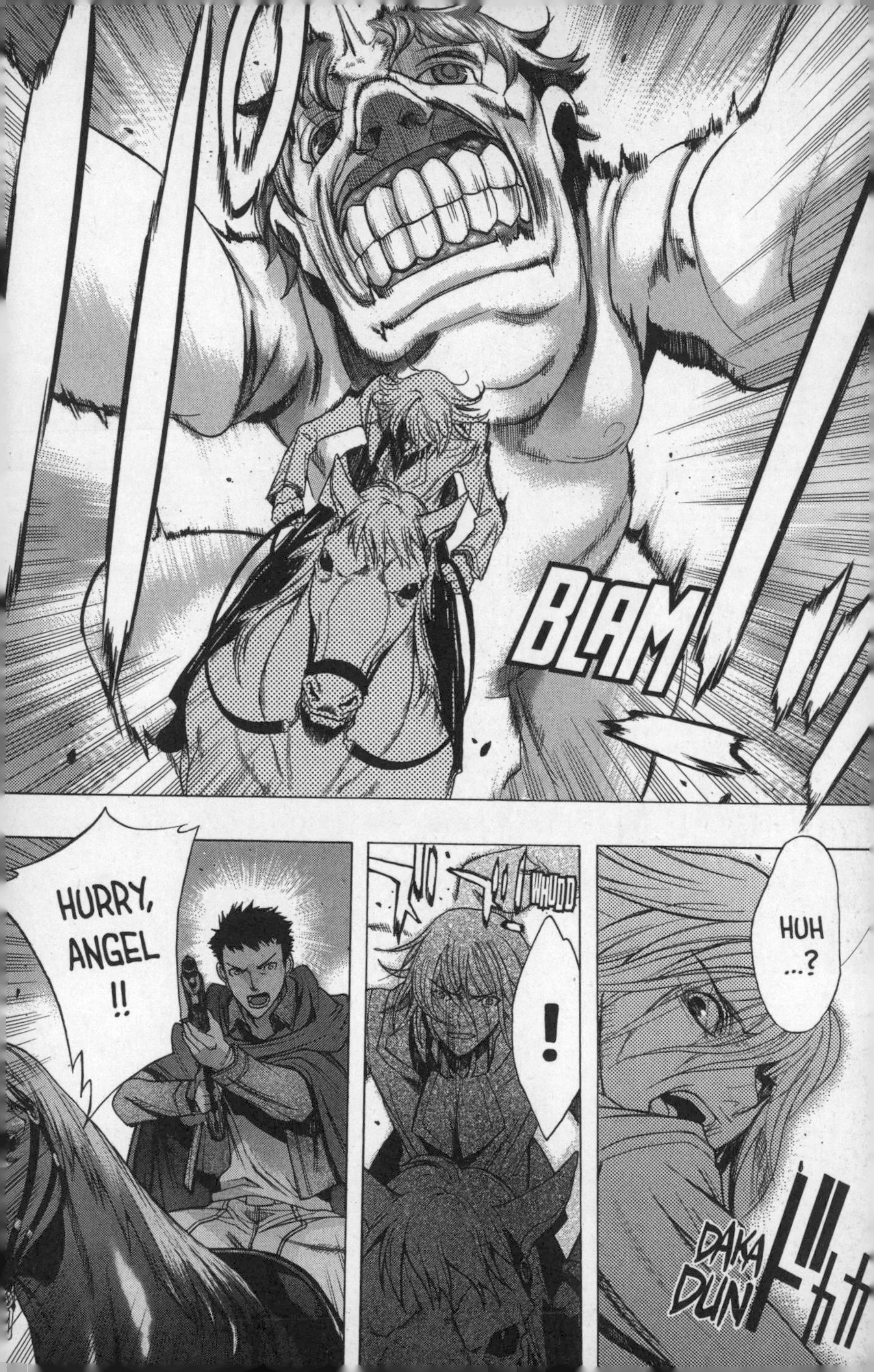
BLAM
HUH ...?
DAKA DUN
WHUOO
!
HURRY, ANGEL !!

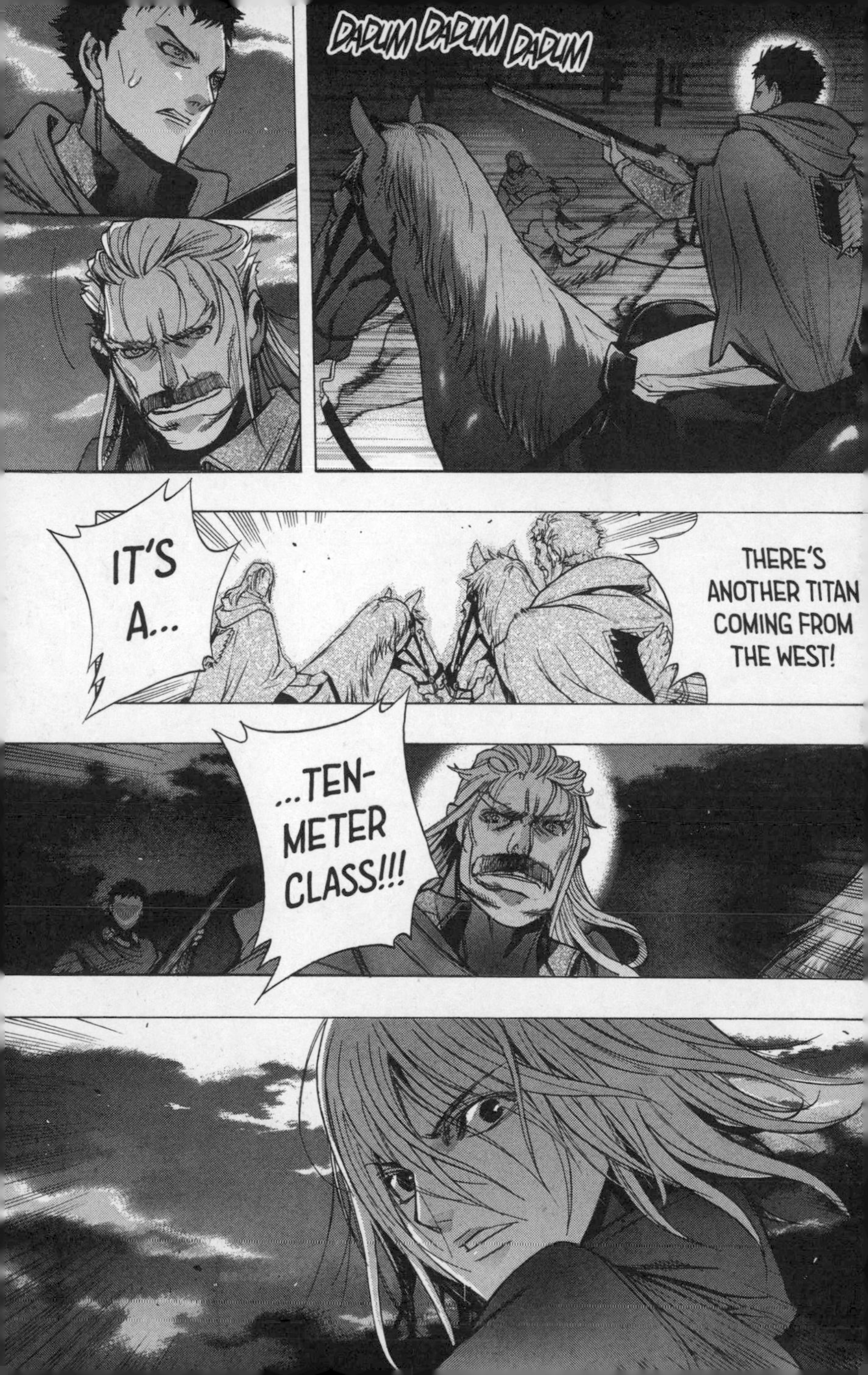
DADUM DADUM DADUM
THERE'S ANOTHER TITAN COMING FROM THE WEST!
IT'S A...
...TEN-METER CLASS!!!

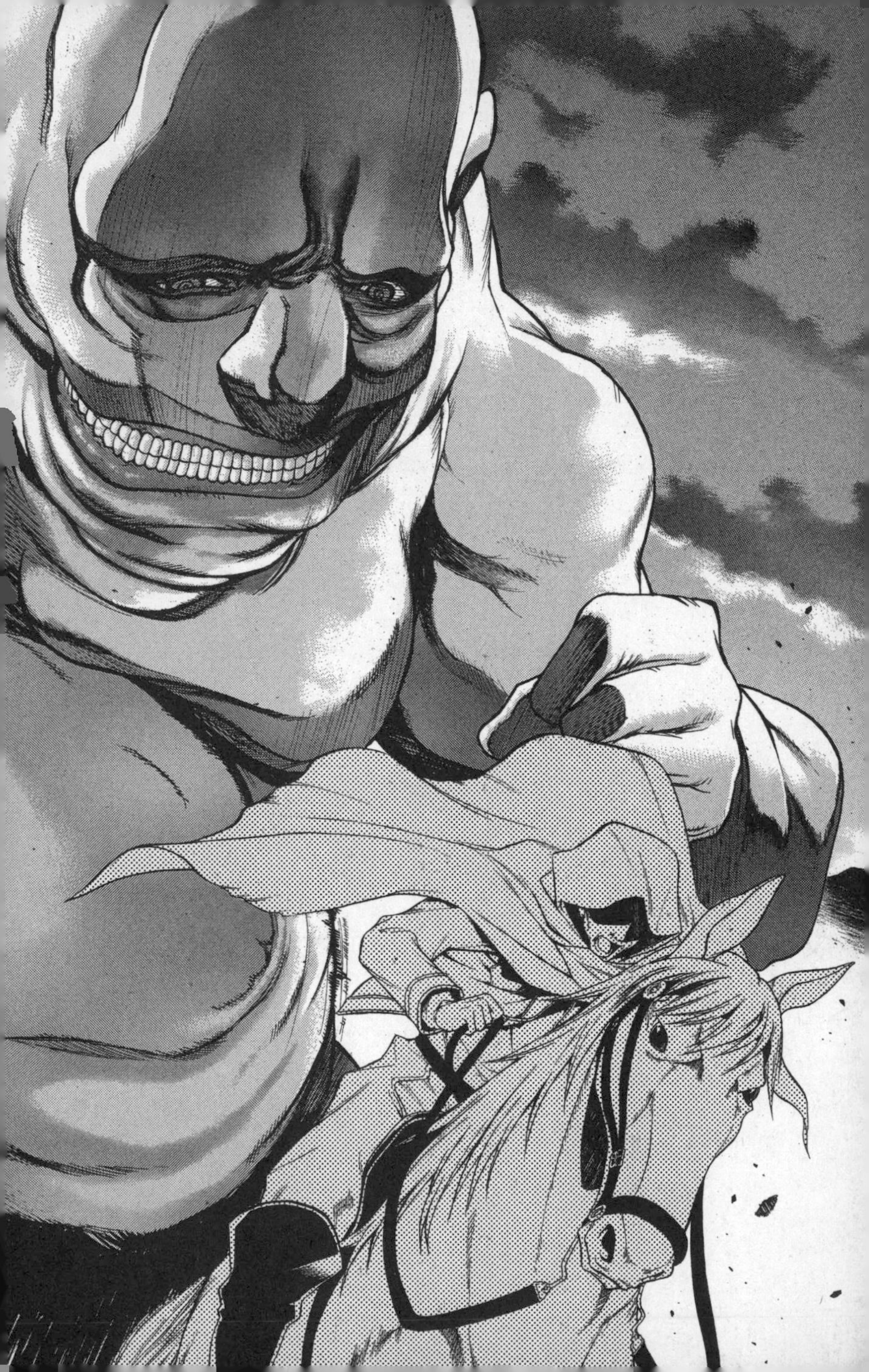

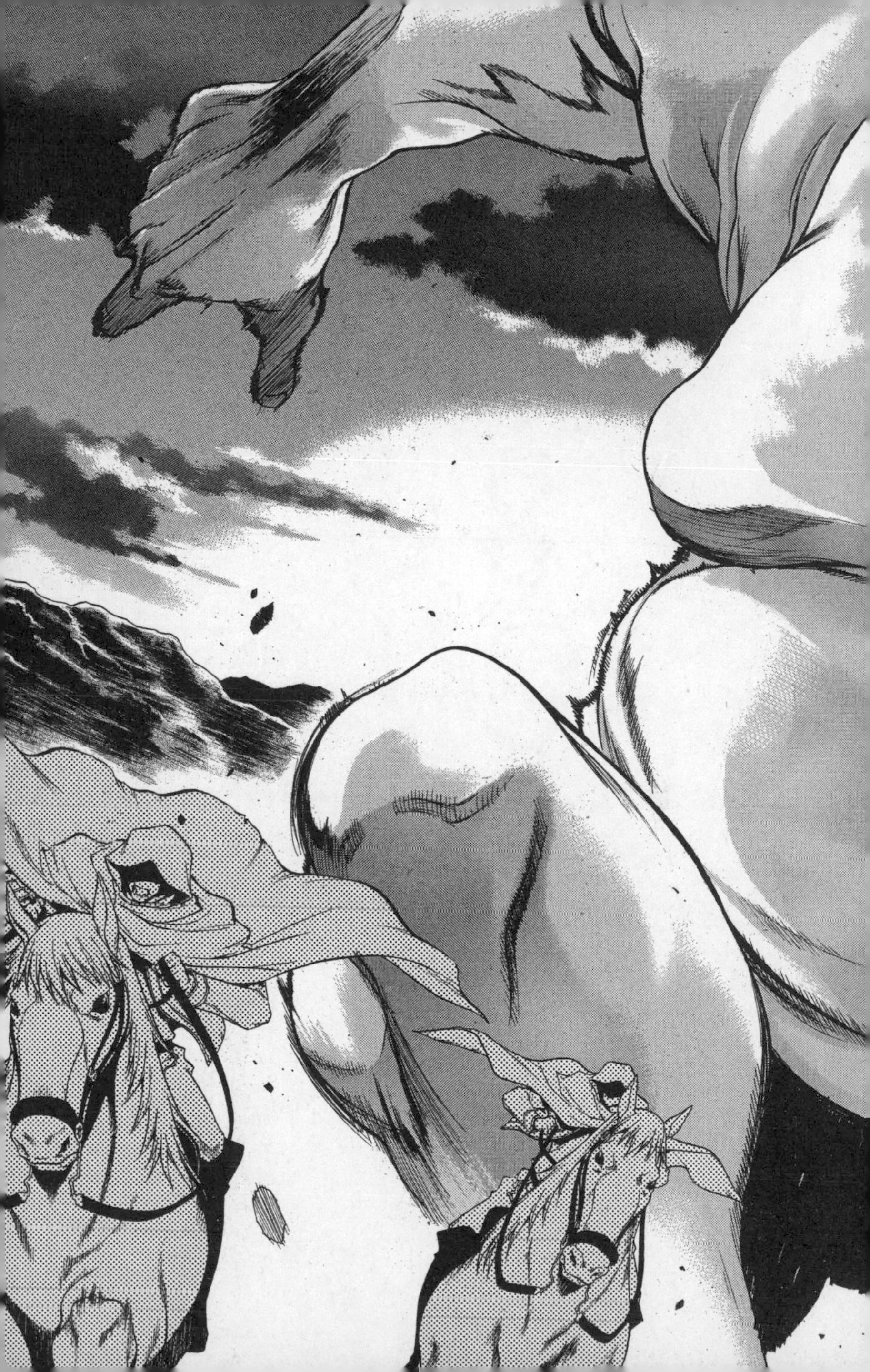

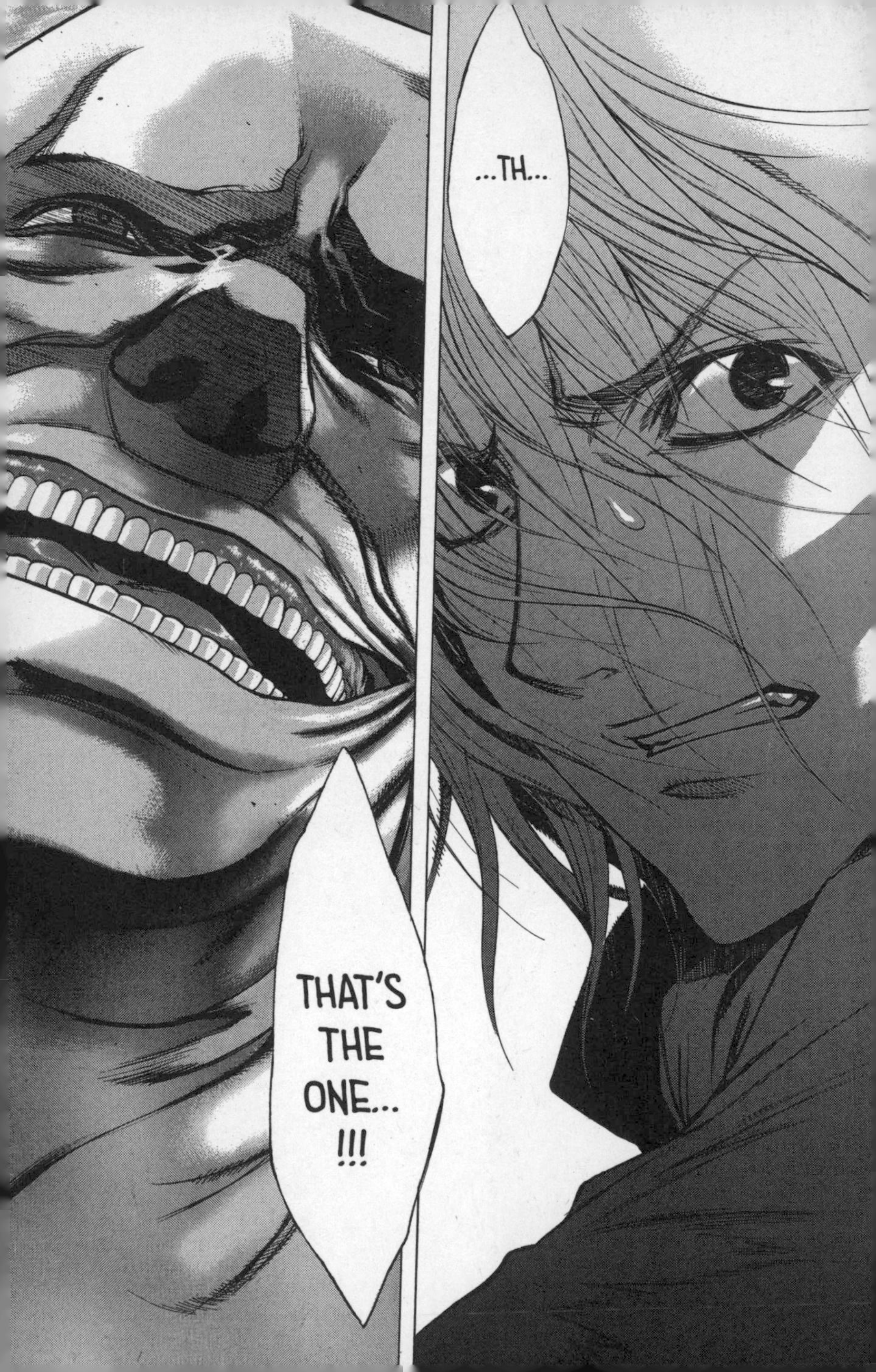
...TH...
THAT'S THE ONE... !!!

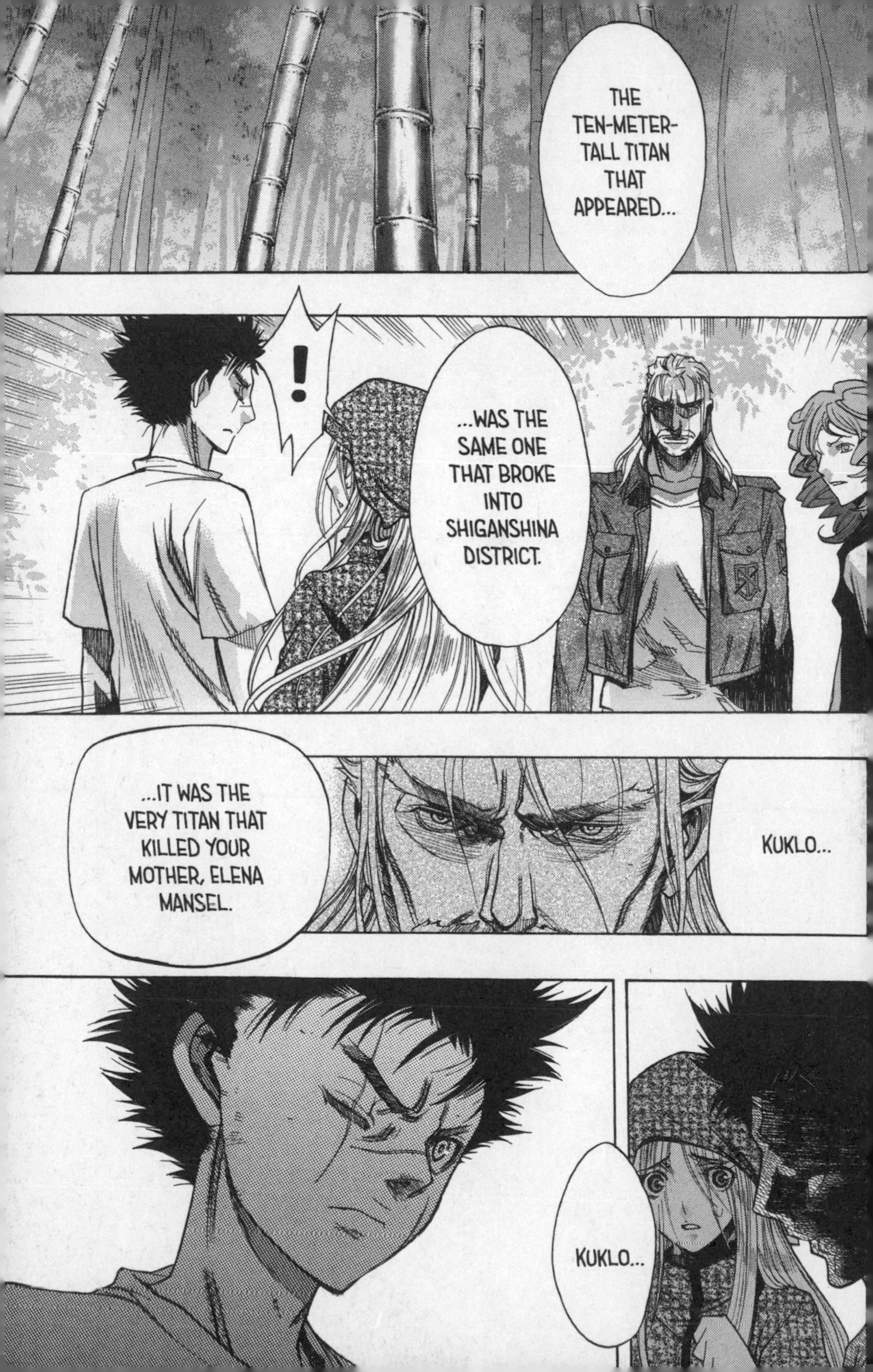
THE TEN-METER-TALL TITAN THAT APPEARED...
...WAS THE SAME ONE THAT BROKE INTO SHIGANSHINA DISTRICT.
!
KUKLO...
...IT WAS THE VERY TITAN THAT KILLED YOUR MOTHER, ELENA MANSEL.
KUKLO...

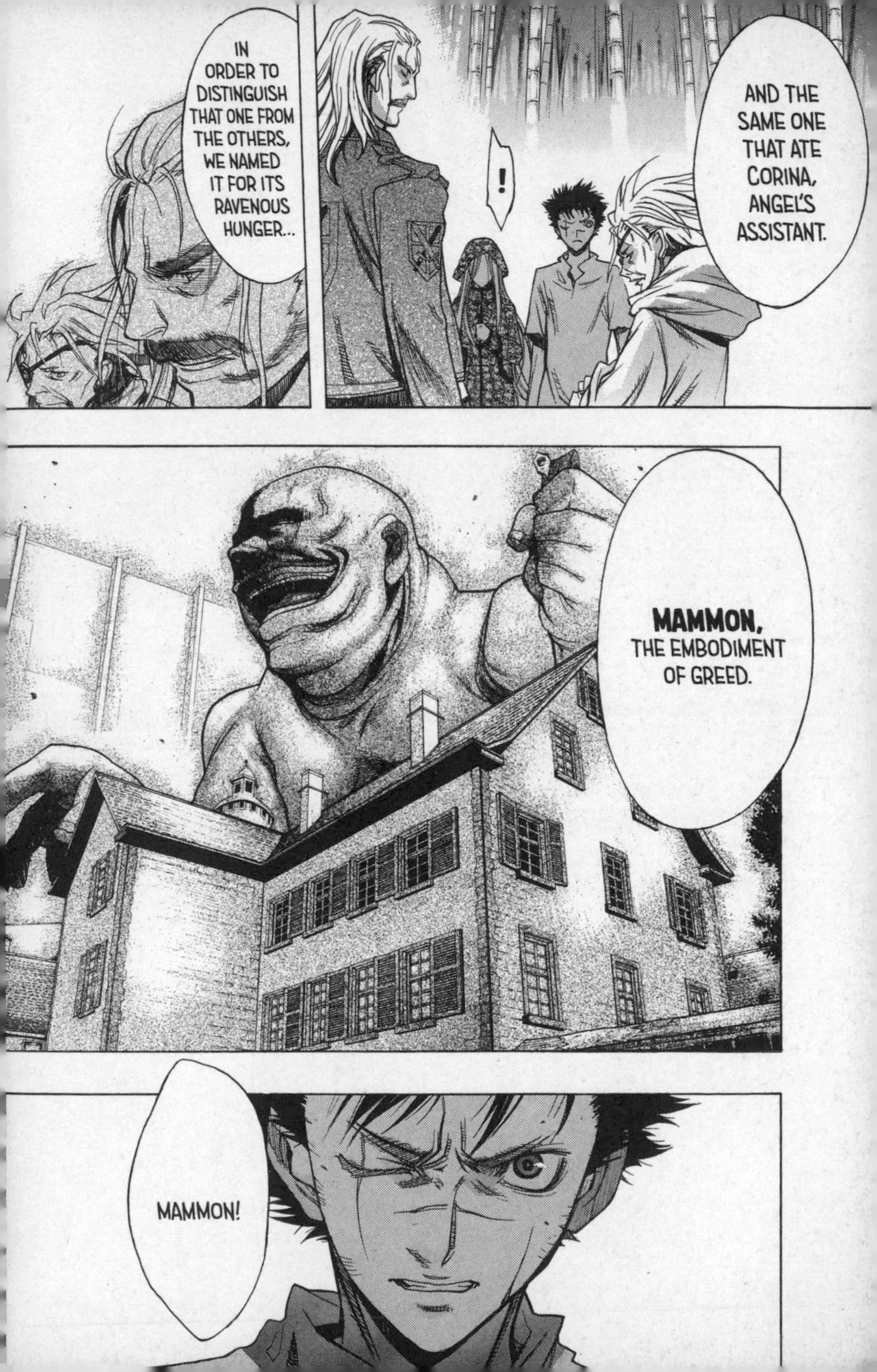
AND THE SAME ONE THAT ATE CORINA, ANGEL'S ASSISTANT.
!
IN ORDER TO DISTINGUISH THAT ONE FROM THE OTHERS, WE NAMED IT FOR ITS RAVENOUS HUNGER...
MAMMON, THE EMBODIMENT OF GREED.
MAMMON!

TO BE CONTINUED

ALITA
Battle Angel
Last Order

"Battle Angel Alita is one of the greatest (and possibly *the* greatest) of all sci-fi action manga series."

— Anime News Network

The Cyberpunk Legend is Back!

n deluxe omnibus editions of 600+ pages, ncluding ALL-NEW original stories by lita creator Yukito Kishiro!

NO.6

A PERFECT LIFE
IN A PERFECT CITY

For Shion, an elite student in the technologically sophisticated city No. 6, life is carefully choreographed. One fateful day, he takes a misstep, sheltering a fugitive his age from a typhoon. Helping this boy throws Shion's life down a path to discovering the appalling secrets behind the "perfection" of No. 6.

KC
KODANSHA
COMICS

SANKAREA
undying love

"I ONLY LIKE ZOMBIE GIRLS."

...hihiro has an unusual connection to zombie movies. He doesn't feel bad for ...e survivors – he wants to comfort the undead girls they slaughter! When ...is pet passes away, he brews a resurrection potion. He's discovered by ...cal heiress Sanka Rea, and she serves as his first test subject!

KC
KODANSHA
COMICS

Say I Love You.

My Little Monster

OPPOSITES ATTRACT...MAYBE?

Haru Yoshida is feared as an unstable and violent "monster." Mizutani Shizuku is a grade-obsessed student with no friends. ate brings these two together to form the most unlikely pair. Haru rmly believes he's in love with Mizutani and she firmly believes e's insane.

KC KODANSHA COMICS

SHERLOCK BONES

KC KODANSHA COMICS

DEDUCTIVE DOG DETECTIVE

When Takeru adopts a new pet, he's in for a surprise—the dog is none other than the reincarnation of Sherlock Holmes. With no one else able to communicate with Holmes, Takeru is roped into becoming Sherdog's assistant, John Watson. Using his sleuthing skills, Holmes uncovers clues to solve the trickiest crimes. 🐾

A Kodansha Comics Trade Paperback Original
Attack on Titan: Before the Fall volume 5 copyright © 2015 Hajime Isayama/ Ryo Suzukaze/Satoshi Shiki
English translation copyright © 2015 Hajime Isayama/Ryo Suzukaze/Satoshi Shiki

Published in the United States by Kodansha Comics, an imprint of Kodansha USA Publishing, LLC, New York.

Publication rights for this English edition arranged through Kodansha Ltd, Tokyo.

First published in Japan in 2015 by Kodansha Ltd., Tokyo as *Shingeki no kyojin Before the fall*, volume 5.

ISBN 978-1-61262-982-7

Character designs by Thores Shibamoto
Original cover design by Takashi Shimoyama (Red Rooster)

Printed in the United States of America.

www.kodanshacomics.com

9 8 7 6 5 4 3 2 1
Translation: Stephen Paul
Lettering: Steve Wands
Editing: Ben Applegate
Kodansha Comics edition cover design by Phil Balsman

STOP!

You are going the *wrong way!*

Manga is a *completely* different type of reading experience.

To start at the *BEGINNING,* go to the *END!*

That's right! Authentic manga is read the traditional Japanese way--from right to left, exactly the opposite of how American books are read. It's easy to follow: just go to the other end of the book, and read each page--and each panel--from the right side to the left side, starting at the top right. Now you're experiencing manga as it was meant to be.